300 best potato recipes

A Complete Cook's Guide

Kathleen Sloan-McIntosh

Robert
ROSE

For complete cataloguing information, see page 437.

Disclaimer
The recipes in this book have been carefully tested by our kitchen and our tasters. To the best of
our knowledge, they are safe and nutritious for ordinary use and users. For those people with food
or other allergies, or who have special food requirements or health issues, please read the suggested
contents of each recipe carefully and determine whether or not they may create a problem for you.
All recipes are used at the risk of the consumer.

We cannot be responsible for any hazards, loss or damage that may occur as a result of any
recipe use.

For those with special needs, allergies, requirements or health problems, in the event of any
doubt, please contact your medical adviser prior to the use of any recipe.

Design and production: Kevin Cockburn/PageWave Graphics Inc.
Editor: Judith Finlayson
Copyeditor and indexer: Gillian Watts
Recipe editor: Jo Calvert
Photographer: Colin Erricson
Associate photographer: Matt Johannsson
Food styling: Kathryn Robertson
Prop styling: Charlene Erricson

Cover image: Frites à la Kingsmill (see page 65)

We acknowledge the financial support of the Government of Canada through the Book Publishing
Industry Development Program (BPIDP) for our publishing activities.

Published by Robert Rose Inc.
120 Eglinton Avenue East, Suite 800, Toronto, Ontario, Canada M4P 1E2
Tel: (416) 322-6552 Fax: (416) 322-6936
www.robertrose.ca

Printed and bound in Canada

1 2 3 4 5 6 7 8 9 FP 19 18 17 16 15 14 13 12 11

Contents

This book is dedicated with love
to my beautiful little grandson
and the newest member of our
potato-loving family.
Name: Davis Tiger Kennedy
Origin: Bayfield, Ontario,
Canada, 2010
Availability: Toronto, Regina,
Bayfield
Description: Fair skin,
dark hair, deep blue eyes,
constant smile
Uses: best for loving

Pray for peace and grace and spiritual food,
For wisdom and guidance,
For all these are good,
But don't forget the potatoes.

— *John Tyler Petee*

Acknowledgments

Many thanks to Bob Dees for asking.

Grateful thanks to the best "all-purpose" editor extraordinaire Judith Finlayson, and copy editor/indexer Gillian Watts.

Also to designer Kevin Cockburn and the team at PageWave, as well as photographer Colin Erricson, associate photographer Matt Johannsson, food stylist Kathryn Robertson, and prop stylist Charlene Erricson.

Appreciative thanks to my daughter, Jenna King, for her diligent work on the glossary.

To my husband Ted and our hard-working kitchen and front-of-house staff at the Black Dog Village Pub & Bistro, deep-felt thanks for all you have done and continue to do.

Lastly, to the late Garnet Johnston, the man who developed, among many other potato cultivars, the Yukon Gold potato — thank you for the potato that inspired this book and many memorable dishes.

Introduction

In 1793 a certain Frenchwoman, Mme Meridiot, set about writing the first cookbook designed for common folk. It was entitled *La cuisine républicaine* and was devoted in its entirety to the potato. Strangely enough, try as I might, I haven't been able to get my hands on a copy, so I thought, "Well, it's about time another woman wrote a cookbook lauding the world's favorite vegetable" — and here it is.

You could say this book is a logical outgrowth of my ongoing love affair with the potato. It is the most natural of passions, as both my parents considered the potato to be a serious meal-maker. My mum, who was born in Nottingham, England, started each and every dinner by ritualistically peeling the spuds — it simply wasn't dinner without potatoes. In our house, rice was for soups or puddings and pasta was an unknown entity. One of my earliest memories is of earnestly trying to peel the supper potatoes as deftly as Mum. I would marvel at how she used her paring knife to remove just the thinnest layer of peel. No matter how hard I tried, I always took off far too much. "All the goodness is just beneath the skin," she would say. These would have been older potatoes, as she called them, good for boiling, mashing or baking. When new potatoes were available, peeling usually wasn't necessary.

As for my dad, well, he came from Belfast, in Northern Ireland, and it was he who taught me, through his fine example, how to really eat potatoes — at any time of the day or night. Leftover boiled spuds were fried in the breakfast pan with bacon or sausages or, on Monday, combined with leftover Sunday dinner and mashed turnip to enjoy for lunch or as an after-school snack (this mixture of potatoes and turnip is what the Scots call clapshot, the traditional accompaniment to haggis). Dad and I even got up to stealing a couple of cold leftover spuds from the refrigerator late at night. We'd treat them to a smear of butter and a little salt ("Butter first, so the salt sticks," Dad would say) and devour them out of hand like apples.

Whenever the need for quick nourishment struck, one of Dad's favorite dishes started with a salted pot of spuds being set to boil. Once cooked, they would be coarsely broken up with a fork against the side of the pot, and a few good-sized lumps of butter and a handful of chopped green onion would be added to the mash. This was champ, a comfort dish of Irish peasant origin (see page 55). Dad often enjoyed it with an icy glass of buttermilk, just as he had done as a boy in Ireland. I actually thought champ had been named for Dad, as he'd been a featherweight boxer in Northern Ireland and still had the emerald-green satin shorts to prove it. When Mum felt he needed extra sustenance, she would nestle a halved soft-boiled egg into the mound of mash and set a shard of cold butter on top to melt, followed by a bit of salt and white pepper. It was always white pepper, because that was Mum's preference when seasoning potatoes. I remember clambering up to sit on Dad's knee and waiting for him to nudge bits of torn bread into the lovely warm yolk for me. But I was keeping my eye on the prize — the bits of floury potato licked with butter — and invariably some came my way.

My beloved Uncle Bob, my Belfast-born godfather, was married to Auntie Madge, one of my mother's five sisters. He provided me with many of my most precious potato experiences. Visiting my five cousins on a Saturday meant staying for dinner, which usually meant watching old movies too, late into the evening. Engrossed in the magical world of black-and-white film, we barely noticed Uncle Bob heading for the kitchen to make — oh, glory of potato glories — potato bread. Not bread in the strict sense of the word, the potato bread he made has an endless list of aliases: boxty, fadge, potato griddle cakes, potato scones, tatties, parleys and any number of other names. Many years later, in a Scottish castle the day after my wedding, I was thrilled to see a variation on the theme of Uncle Bob's potato bread on my breakfast plate, along with wonderful local pork sausages, bacon, smoked trout and scrambled eggs. Our host called them tatty scones, and they were every bit as delicious as the Irish version I had always enjoyed as a child.

When Uncle Bob made bread, he combined leftover mashed potatoes with judicious amounts of butter and flour to make a dough. He handled it deftly, adding just the right quantity of butter and flour before roughly rolling it out — not too thin, not too thick — and cutting it into odd squarish shapes, which he fried in butter until speckled brown on each side. My uncle would pile the pieces on a plate and anoint them with a little more butter and a shake of salt before offering them to our eagerly waiting hands. (When Uncle Bob died, my mum and aunt picked up the making of potato bread, and the tradition lives on in Mum's Potato Breads, page 161.) How wonderful that potato bread smelled! And how it tasted — sublime! Every time I prepare it now, for my husband, my grown children and my grandsons, the memory is rekindled.

Though I hardly knew it then, this simple preparation became my benchmark for every potato dish to follow, containing as it did everything about the potato I love. Earthy and comforting as only good potato dishes can be, potato bread holds the very essence of potato flavor. When it is gone, I long for more.

That remains my fondest potato memory, but I have many more. Mum always cooked new potatoes whole, plunging a bunch of fresh mint into the boiling water along with a good bit of salt. The mint lent a very subtle influence to the potatoes, and as it bubbled in the pot, the fragrance filled the air — something good was coming. My mum also made unfailingly perfect mashed potatoes, always from scratch. They were lump-free and in her deft and capable hands had those seemingly paradoxical qualities inherent in great mashed potatoes: they were simultaneously fluffy and creamy.

Sometimes we just had boiled spuds, which Mum would drain, then crush slightly with the back of a fork against the sides of the pot. These were served with a bit of butter and maybe a little chopped fresh parsley. Baked potatoes were truly baked. Never wrapped in foil, they were scrubbed and placed on the oven rack (always alongside meatloaf). Mum baked them until the exterior was crisp and crackly; I used to steal the empty skins from everyone else's plate. On most Sundays it was roast potatoes with roast beef and Yorkshire pudding. These emerged from the oven as crusted, sticky, slightly caramelized nubs that needed nothing, not even gravy, to make them better. And scalloped potatoes with a big pink ham was the reason I skipped home with haste from Sunday school at Easter.

Then there were the chips — not French fries, mind you, but the chunkier chips for which England is renowned. At least once a week potatoes were "chipped" and tumbled into the waiting reservoir of hot drippings that Mum collected throughout the week. No chips, fries or frites I have eaten anywhere since have ever come close. We might have them on a Saturday to accompany a quick-fry steak, and I would valiantly try to reserve a few to use as filling for pieces of white bread and butter. Voilà — the chip butty! (Butty is northern English slang for a sandwich.)

One weekend evening, to combat a bout of teen ennui, my dear mum emerged from the kitchen with a bowl of homemade potato chips — saratogas, she rightly called them — just for me. Warm potato chips, shatteringly crisp, with chewy golden edges. Everyone should have that experience at least once in a lifetime.

For variety, Mum's first choice was the King Edward potato (see page 39), which at that time was grown in Ontario and Prince Edward Island, Canada, as well as in the United Kingdom. These were big spuds with creamy white flesh that she felt were without equal, originating as they did in the U.K. They remained her reliable favorite — her go-to spud. Many years later, those yellow-fleshed Canadian tubers called Yukon Golds became the darlings of chefs and home cooks from one end of the country to the other and around the world. Mum, however, being suspicious of anything new in the agricultural world, still maintained the superiority of a "good King Edward."

But no matter the variety, as with so many of the good things in life, it all boils down to taste. And a good fresh potato of any variety is nothing if not full of flavor. This fact was brought home to me the first time my husband and I carried out our own little potato harvest. Unearthing dozens of flawless Yukon Gold potatoes from the black soil was the closest I have come to uncovering buried treasure. What a thrill to lift them from the earth, wipe them clean and plunge them into boiling water with some salt, and just a few moments later to eat them tossed with butter and a sprinkling of sea salt.

For the past five years, my husband, Ted, and I have owned and operated the Black Dog Village Pub & Bistro in the village of Bayfield, a unique community perched on the shores of magnificent Lake Huron. Living and working in this heavily farmed bit of Ontario has fueled my love of potatoes even further. Ever since we opened, I have insisted that the chips that accompany our menu items be the real deal, that is, derived from fresh local potatoes and hand-cut by ourselves. We cut them and blanch them briefly in trans-fat-free oil. Once the customers have placed their orders, we drop the chips into the hot oil again and deep-fry them until they are cooked through and golden brown. Taken from the fryer, they are immediately tossed into a big stainless steel bowl, dusted with a bit of sea salt, piled into our special chip bowls and served forth. Yum. They are unfailingly great, and even better when served with one of our house-made aïolis. After five years, as our kitchen staff will attest, I still find them completely irresistible.

Of course, perfect hand-cut chips are not the only potato dish to emanate from our bustling kitchen. The world's greatest mashed potatoes, luscious potato and cheese gratins, garlic and rosemary roast potatoes, warm potato salads and our chef Andrew's crowning potato glory — our own Black Dog potato crisps (chips) — are all made on a regular basis throughout the year. I have lost count of the number of kitchen monkeys — er, staff — I have taught to make my favorite appetizer, our own version of Uncle Bob's potato bread. While it takes center stage in our lunch special, Ulster Fry (a big egg, bacon, sausage, mushroom and tomato fry-up), for special events such as wedding receptions and other private functions we dress up the sumptuous little brown squares with smoked salmon, a bit of crème fraîche and chives — real two-bite deliciousness.

Is your mouth watering yet? I do hope my passion for potatoes and this collection of more than 300 recipes will do just that. So head for your local farmers' market and start exploring the ever-expanding world of potatoes. Perhaps you may even be inspired to grow a few of your own one day. I believe there are few things you can do for yourself and those you love that will provide as much earthly pleasure.

Fada beo na prátai! Long live the potato!

— *Kathleen Sloan-McIntosh*

The Spud from All Angles

"Happiness increased"
    — *John Foster, an early advocate of potato growing*
    in England, describing potatoes in 1664.

History, Legend and Lore

No other vegetable — and few foods in general — incites passion as strongly as the potato. Since the Spaniards first brought the tasty tuber home from Peru in 1570 (thereby initiating its migration to the rest of the world), it has been feared, reviled, beloved, revered and heavily relied upon. No other vegetable has played such a significant role in history. From its original home high in the Andes it has traveled the globe, providing almost sole sustenance for millions and fueling entire armies. It was presented at court in Europe and it inexorably changed an entire country when it was beset by disease. How it came to end up next to your homemade meatloaf or chunks of golden fried haddock at your favorite pub is a long and winding story.

> ### Go Forth and Multiply
>
> While it has long been maintained that Sir Walter Raleigh brought the potato to Ireland in the 1590s, there is no actual evidence to support this theory. According to the commonly accepted story, he gave handfuls of the tubers to his gardeners at the property he owned in Cork, who planted them without comprehending exactly what they were.

The Incas understood the power of potatoes thousands of years ago. Those who dwelled in the Andes discovered wild potatoes growing some 8,000 feet (2,438 meters) above sea level. As early as 750 BCE the Incas were fervently cultivating this new food source, and they ingeniously developed a way to preserve their crop. After harvesting they allowed the potatoes to freeze overnight. The next day they trampled on the blackened tubers to extract the water, creating a freeze-dried potato preparation called *chuño*. A very early precursor to frozen French fries, *chuño* was a valuable foodstuff. When stored properly, it could be kept almost indefinitely, making it a great ally in the fight against famine. Although the Incas wouldn't have been aware of nutritional data, one acre's worth of potatoes can fulfill the protein and energy requirements of ten people for a year. This feature cannot be attributed to any cereal crop such as rice, wheat, corn or soybeans.

> ### Potato Migration
>
> A Scottish immigrant from the Isle of Skye, Lord Selkirk, settled in an area known as Orwell Point on Prince Edward Island. He brought potatoes with him from Scotland, and for many years the new Canadian community in which he lived thrived on them along with locally caught cod.

Spanish explorers can be credited with giving the potato its name. They discovered the vegetable while searching for gold in the Andes. It is the Spanish pronunciation *batata* — from *papa* or *patata*, the word the Incas used for the sweet potato — that provided the English derivation. The sweet potato carries that name too, even though it is botanically unrelated to the potato (see page 28 for more on the sweet potato).

After a Long Trip, a Lukewarm Welcome

How the potato made its way to Europe is a matter of some dispute, but it seems most likely that potatoes made the journey on Spanish ships, stuffed into the sailors' pockets as an interesting curiosity. When they arrived, the new vegetable was not happily received in Spain, even though, many years earlier, the population had embraced another new root vegetable — the sweet potato. A vine belonging to the morning glory family, the sweet potato was discovered in Haiti by Columbus, who introduced the vegetable to his adopted country. It was well received; in fact, King Ferdinand and Queen Isabella had them planted in the gardens of the royal palace.

While the Spanish — and Europeans in general — thought the potato a lovely ornamental addition to their gardens, they were more than a little suspicious of the tuber itself. Most people were not enthusiastic about consuming "edible stones," as they dubbed potatoes, especially once it was discovered they belonged to the same family as poisonous deadly nightshade, or belladonna. Incidentally, tobacco, tomatoes, sweet peppers and eggplant also belong to the same family, Solanaceae.

> ### Royal Oranges
>
> In 1793 Louis XVI and Marie Antoinette had potatoes grown as an experiment on 50 acres of fallow land. In what must have been one of the world's most successful — and earliest — marketing ploys, the king commanded armed troops to guard the growing plants. This drew so much attention that curious citizens crept into the grounds at night, when the guards were being lax, and unearthed and stole the potatoes. If the vegetables were good enough to be guarded, it seemed, they were most definitely good enough to eat. The king's strategy worked, and for a long time potatoes in France were called *oranges royales* — royal oranges.

Thirty years after its arrival in Europe, the potato could be found in eleven countries of the Old World — Spain, Austria, Holland, Germany, Belgium, Switzerland, England, France, Italy, Portugal and Ireland. It was still thought of as a humble, somewhat whimsical garden plant, a bit of a curiosity, and certainly not fit for serious cultivation alongside well-respected grains such as rice, wheat and corn. Had it not been shared, cultivated and grown by the botanists of the day (often under the auspices and in the gardens of well-to-do patrons), the potato would have taken even longer to gain acceptance.

Wretched Yet Magical

In the late 1500s the average person was accustomed to plants that reproduced through seeds. What were they to make of an edible plant with thick stems that grew two or three feet tall, with abundant foliage and intricate, strongly perfumed blossoms, and sprouted a mysterious network of underground fibers that eventually developed into oddly shaped tubers? Even more suspect in the eyes of the common people was the fact that if these tubers were replanted they would sprout again, which endowed the plant with an aura of black magic. (After all, before monks became brewers, women who made beer in their homes could be burned at the stake on suspicion of witchcraft!).

Some time around 1586 it is thought that Sir Francis Drake brought more potatoes to England. Sir Walter Raleigh is supposed to have presented them to Queen Elizabeth I and also to have introduced them in Ireland. We do know for certain that potatoes made an appearance as a field crop in Ireland in the mid-1600s, in County Wicklow, where the inhabitants were less suspicious of the new plant than their European neighbors. "Only the wretched eat this root" was the saying in Europe, where populations still relied heavily on oats as the mainstay of their diet.

As the English dallied with the tuber, trying to decide just what to make of it, and the Irish began growing it on a relatively small scale, French pharmacist and agriculturist Antoine-Augustin Parmentier wrote a thesis singing the praises and virtues of the potato. He had spent time in a Westphalian prisoner-of-war camp, and the vegetable had kept him alive during his imprisonment. The Germans had decided that the *kartoffel*, as they called it, was a suspicious vegetable fit only for pigs and prisoners. In fact, they believed that a person could catch leprosy from eating potatoes.

Parmentier was living testimony to the contrary. He worked relentlessly for 40 years to turn on his countrymen to the wonders of the potato, especially as a food source for the poor. During that time he attracted the notice of Louis XV, who funded his research and efforts to popularize the potato. In one of his publicity ventures, Parmentier hosted an evening for a select group of guests (including Benjamin Franklin) who enjoyed a 20-course dinner, each course consisting of a potato dish. Many of those dishes — which even now bear his name — are still enjoyed today, such as *potage parmentier*, a puréed leek and potato soup, and *hachis parmentier*, the French version of cottage or shepherd's pie. According to some French historians, any dish that features potatoes may include the term *parmentier*. Such was Parmentier's influence, the Paris government named a Métro station after him; it contains a statue depicting Parmentier with a basket of potatoes, offering one to a hungry peasant.

A Language Lesson

Two common words in the English lexicon came to us by way of the Irish and the potato. It was the Irish who first referred to potatoes as spuds, after the type of spade used in their cultivation. In Ireland the pot used to cook potatoes was usually lifted off the fire when they were done and set on the cottage's dirt floor, enabling the cook to mash the potatoes without getting burned by the flames. Over time and after repeated mashings, the hot pot would form a depression in the floor — a pothole.

An Added Benefit

In France, around the time when the potato was just beginning to be accepted, medical opinion was still divided as to its benefits. One doctor maintained that there was "somewhat windy" but "very substantial, good and restorative" nourishment to be had by eating them. Another doctor proclaimed that, "boiled, baked or roasted . . . eaten with good butter, salt, juice of oranges or lemons and double refined sugar . . . they increase seed and provoke lust, causing fruitfulness in both sexes."

Home At Last

As Parmentier worked to extol the virtue of the potato, the Irish were discovering how well suited it was to their country's climate and soil. The potato is unfussy; it doesn't require wonderful soil conditions or special tools, it grows relatively quickly and it thrives on rain, of which Ireland has plenty. Most important, the potato is nourishing. An average five-ounce (142 g) potato can supply half your total daily requirement of vitamin C, moderate amounts of vitamin B_6, and considerable amounts of niacin, pantothenic acid, riboflavin and thiamin. It also contains essential minerals, including copper, zinc, magnesium, potassium, phosphorus and zinc, a trace of sodium, good complex carbohydrates and even protein. So it is perhaps not surprising that the Irish embraced the potato, cultivating it extensively, as the Incas had done before them, as a field crop and staple. Praties, as the Irish called potatoes, were mainly a food of the poor in that country. Eventually the tubers at least partially replaced oats (on which the people had previously relied heavily) as a staple, especially when the oat harvest was poor.

During the early 1800s, when English garden designer and seed specialist Stephen Switzer was decrying the potato as "that which was heretofore reckon'd a food fit only for Irishmen and clowns," households across Ireland consumed on average about five pounds (2.3 kg) of potatoes per person per day. At the time it constituted 80 percent of their diet. Irish historian Austin Bourke estimates that more than three million people, or almost 40 percent of the population, were living solely on potatoes. As an Irish proverb goes, "Potatoes in the morning, potatoes at noon, and if I got up at midnight, it would still be potatoes."

Murphy's Potatoes

By the end of the 18th century the potato was an important crop in Europe, particularly in England, Germany and, of course, Ireland. At that time poor Irish families ate a daily average of ten potatoes per person. The tuber constituted 80 percent of their diet, which made the potato blight that struck in the 1840s all the more disastrous. The Irish are credited with popularizing the potato in North America, to which they moved in great numbers because of the famine in Ireland. Consequently the white potato became known in North America as the Irish or Murphy's potato.

The Famine

Crop failures usually occurred every several years in Ireland, as they did in the rest of Europe, but nothing came close to the devastation wrought by the blight of *Phytophthora infestans*, which probably arrived in 1844. So began the years of the "great hunger," as the era came to be called, some of the darkest days in Ireland's history (1845–49). Although this deadly fungus struck all of Europe, it devastated potato-dependent Ireland with particular ferocity from one end of the country to the other. It was Ireland, after all, that had embraced the growing of the potato so wholeheartedly, out of desperate poverty and need.

During this time Ireland was home to about 65,000 small farms (only an acre or less), where the modest spade was the only tool and potatoes the only crop. Other famines related to field crops had caused hardship in Ireland before, but this particular famine was unprecedented. It is no exaggeration to say that the potato represented everything to the Irish. Food, most certainly, but it was also used in lieu of cash, giving poor tenants the ability

Modest Praise

In the legendary cookbook *Mrs. Beeton's Every-Day Cookery*, published in the early 1900s, the British doyenne of the kitchen wrote about the humble spud. She began the section "Potato as Food" with these words: "No doubt much of its popularity is due to its cheapness, its good keeping power, and its unobtrusive flavor."

to pay their rent when times were hard. When the potato failed, the Irish were left with nothing. They fished the rivers and lakes empty, caught seabirds, frogs and small animals; in desperation they ate dandelion roots, nettles, wild mustard, seaweed, ferns and even tree bark. The famine was most brutal in areas where other crops had not been cultivated.

This particular potato blight ruined the entire plant, from root to tuber to leaf. One reason the famine was so widespread is that many people grew the same cultivar of potato. Farmers and home gardeners shared seed potatoes and plants with each other. Such was the absolute potency of the blight that it affected every species of potato in Ireland. Even seed potatoes and tubers in storage fell victim to the disease.

Before the famine, the population of Ireland was more than eight million. Almost a million and a half men, women and children died from starvation and related diseases during the famine. At least another million people left Ireland for North America, Australia and England. By the early 1900s, Ireland's population had fallen to little more than four million. So much and so many had been affected by this humble yet so potentially powerful plant.

Better Drunk Than Stoned?

Nineteenth-century philosopher Friedrich Nietzsche maintained, "A diet that consists predominantly of rice leads to the use of opium, just as a diet that consists predominantly of potatoes leads to the use of liquor."

Ingenious Uses

Infamous American criminal John Dillinger once carved a pistol out of a potato, stained it black with iodine (which turns black in contact with starch) and used it to escape from jail.

The World's Favorite Vegetable

Today the potato is an important crop in more than a hundred countries, with an annual production of just under 300 million tons. Until 1990 Europe and North America were the largest potato producers. Since then, China — the land of rice — has become the world's largest producer of potatoes, with Russia and India following close behind. Today these three countries grow more than 40 percent of the world's potatoes.

The Chinese government is investing heavily in potato research and production in an effort to lessen poverty and shield against possible famine. In China, as in the rest of the world, arable land is at a premium. As its already huge population increases, the challenge will be to provide nutrition-rich food for China's massive numbers of people. Enter the potato, which needs less water to grow than rice or wheat. In northern China, where much of the land is arid and infertile, potatoes are among the few crops that will grow at all, let alone flourish.

Potatoes Italian-Style

Initially, people in Italy were quite suspicious of potatoes, and while today it is not one of that country's favored vegetables (as it is in France), the potato is showcased in a number of Italian dishes. One of these is from the Abruzzi region, where in the tiny town of San Pio di Fontecchio, *patate sotto il coppo* is made. This potato presentation can be made only during the winter months in a house where a fire burns constantly. The hearth is cleaned meticulously, then spread with sliced potatoes. A heavy iron lid, or *coppo*, is placed on top and heaped with burning coals. The potatoes are left to cook beneath the searing-hot lid, their fragrance soon filling the air. Before serving, they are dressed with olive oil and vinegar.

Yet in spite of the vast quantities of potatoes in the world, farmers, especially in North America, continue to rely for the most part on just half a dozen standard cultivars. If a blight such as the one that occurred in the 19th century happened again, the impact would be far-reaching. That's why research and development of disease-resistant, nutrition-rich potato cultivars is so prevalent. Most recently, India has pioneered a protein-rich potato through genetic modification. Scientists at that country's Central Potato Research Institute have developed a "transgenic" version that inserts a gene from amaranth seeds into the potato. The result is a potato with 60 percent more protein and increased amino acid levels over what would occur naturally in your average spud.

Britain's National Dish

Winston Churchill described fish and chips — arguably Britain's national dish — as "the good companions." Not only did they seem naturally compatible, but from the late 19th century on they provided deliciously good nutrition for the hungry working class at a comparatively low cost.

These days the varieties of potatoes available to us are seemingly endless, with more being developed every year. Once fit only for peasants, pigs and prisoners, the potato now spans the globe and is grown in more than a hundred countries. It feeds millions well and remains the world's favorite vegetable, loved by farm families, urban dwellers and five-star chefs alike. Even more numerous are the increasing numbers of delicious dishes that incorporate the beloved spud, dishes that reflect both its humble beginnings and its long, rich and exotic history.

Buying and Cooking Potatoes

Potato varieties have come a long way since their initial discovery in the foothills of the Andes. Today potatoes are serious business — the world's largest food crop after rice, wheat and corn. In Scotland alone, about 700 varieties of potatoes are kept in a government reference collection, while in Peru every genetic aspect of the potato is being investigated by the Centro Internacional de la Papa. Australia has a potato research station, and in Germany a special institute is listing the some 3,000 varieties of potatoes currently in existence. Although new varieties are being created every year, not all go on to achieve stardom (for more information on potato varieties, see A World of Potatoes, pages 25 to 48). And before a new variety is introduced, there are many criteria to consider, such as resistance to disease, yield and storage capabilities, and suitability for various uses. You, the purchaser and possibly even amateur grower, should keep at least some of these in mind when buying and/or planting potatoes, whether you buy your potatoes at a bustling supermarket or a farmers' market or grow them yourself.

Potato Rituals

Not surprisingly, the Irish have a number of rituals associated with potatoes. In Cork the first potatoes were always unearthed on June 29. In Galway it was forbidden to dig potatoes until the last Sunday in July. Residents of County Mayo celebrated the end of the harvest with a feast, and in Tipperary the arrival of new potatoes on the table was met with "May we all be alive and happy this time 12 months."

Choose the Right Potato for the Task

In spite of the myriad varieties of potatoes available today, there are still only three distinct types from which to choose. Whether available from a supermarket or farm market stall or grown in your own garden, a potato will either be high-starch (floury), medium-starch (all-purpose) or low-starch (waxy). For more on potato varieties, see A World of Potatoes (pages 25 to 48).

Very Suspicious

One of the reasons for the early distrust of the potato plant was the way it reproduced. In the 1600s, both botanists and the general public were used to edible plants that reproduced from seeds, not tubers, as is the case with the potato. When the Swiss botanist Gaspard Bauhin stated that the potato belonged to the *Solanum* genus — along with deadly nightshade, tobacco, tomatoes, eggplants and sweet peppers, all of which had very negative connotations at the time — he furthered the belief that the potato was poisonous or a narcotic.

Buying Potatoes

When buying potatoes, whether they are floury, waxy or all-purpose isn't the only thing to consider. You want to make sure they are the best quality. Look for those that are firm and dry, relatively smooth, unblemished and free of sprouts or green areas. Green patches on potatoes can be caused by exposure to sunlight, which results in the formation of a toxic alkaloid called solanine. This is perfectly natural, but eaten in any quantity, green potatoes can cause stomach upset. If you were to ingest very large amounts of solanine, more serious symptoms would include cramps, diarrhea, dizziness, drowsiness and joint pain. (Incidentally, it is not only tainted potatoes that feature solanine but also other members of the nightshade family, such as peppers, ripe and green tomatoes, eggplant, paprika and gogi berries.) One or two areas of green can be cut away, but potatoes that are extensively green should be discarded.

I'd Rather Be Hungry

It took many years for certain cultures to accept the potato as a staple of their diet. Even the poorest, hungriest and most destitute, suspicious of the root, had to be forcefully convinced. In Russia in the early 1800s, the government ordered peasants to plant crops of potatoes, an edict that was met with uprisings, battles and riots in ten communities.

In addition to creating solanine, exposure to light will also cause potatoes to sprout. While many vegetable sprouts are nutritional powerhouses, potato sprouts are toxic and should not be eaten. After they have sprouted, much of the starch in potatoes is converted into sugar, making them a less suitable candidate for dishes that work best with a high-starch potato. If the potato is still firm — and often it isn't after sprouting, becoming soft, shrunken and wrinkled — you can remove the sprouts and proceed with cooking the potatoes, but I think the flavor and nutritional value are compromised.

Cooking Potatoes: Just the Basics

The Baked Potato

Few things are easier to make and more comforting and soul-satisfying to enjoy than a great big, beautiful baked potato (see page 62). I don't know whose idea it was to wrap a potato in foil before baking, but that wasteful effort results in a sort of steamed potato; it is certainly not baked. All you need for baked potato perfection is to choose big, sound potatoes of uniform size and a type that is recommended for baking, such as Idaho russets. Yukon Golds also make good baked potatoes but the flesh is slightly less fluffy than in a russet, a potato renowned for that characteristic. Classified as floury, the King Edward, Alpha, White Rose, Keswick, Norgold Russet, Norkotah, Goldrush, Idaho, Acadia Russet and Cara varieties all make great baked potatoes.

The Boiled Potato

Humble though they may be, when prepared with a little care, simple boiled potatoes tossed with butter and a bit of chopped fresh mint or parsley can be one of the nicest ways to enjoy the world's favorite vegetable. While all varieties of potatoes lend themselves to boiling, to achieve the best results, each of the three types requires a different method.

Boiling Floury or All-Purpose Potatoes

When boiling floury potatoes such as Russet or King Edward, or all-purpose varieties such as Yukon Gold or Maris Piper (see A World of Potatoes, pages 25 to 48, for more information on potato types and varieties), you can choose to simply scrub them well or peel them. An Irishwoman once told me that in her home country, potatoes are never peeled before cooking; instead they are boiled and then peeled (or not). Personally, I like a bit of skin on my potato, and, depending on its condition, I often leave the skin on even when I plan to mash the potatoes. Some maintain that the most nutritionally valuable part lies just beneath the skin, so heavy peeling will result in a potato that may not be as nutritious as it could be.

Try to choose potatoes that are similar in size. Scrub them clean or, if the skin requires it (if it is heavily marked or bruised), peel lightly. Cut the potatoes into even, medium-sized chunks — not too big, not too small. If they are too big, they will take longer to cook; too small and they will absorb too much water.

Place the prepared potatoes in a good-sized pot, one that will accommodate them comfortably. If your pot is too large, it will require too much water to cover them, and that will result in soggy, waterlogged potatoes. That is not good, because there's not much you can do to remedy the situation once they have absorbed too much water. Cover the potatoes with no more than an inch (2.5 cm) of cold water and add the salt. Place the pot on high heat, cover loosely and bring to a lively boil; then reduce the heat and cook for about 25 minutes. Using the tip of a thin knife or a skewer, check for doneness. A good rule of

Know Your Type

Confused about the best potato for your recipe? Round white potatoes are great for frying and for use in gnocchi, gratins and pancakes. The big Idaho-type potatoes are ideal for baking, frying, mashing and using in puréed soups. Choose potatoes from the round red and long white types for roasting, boiling and using in salads. Older potatoes should be peeled and brought to a boil in cold water; new potatoes can be left unpeeled and cooked in already boiling salted water.

Prevent Browning

Cutting potatoes too long before cooking them can result in discoloration. To avoid this, dip the cut potatoes in cool acidulated water (water to which you have added a few spoonfuls of lemon juice). After dipping them, drain, cover and refrigerate until ready to use. If cut potatoes have discolored, simmering them in milk will whiten them.

thumb is that if the chunk you are testing adheres to the knife or skewer, it needs additional cooking time. If it slips off, it is ready. If you can't lift it out from the water — that is, if it breaks up when touched — it is overcooked.

Boiling New or Waxy Potatoes

A simple boiling is probably the best way to enjoy the wonderfully fresh, delicate and earthy flavor of a new or waxy potato.

When boiling new or waxy potatoes such as Kipfler, Belle de Fontenay or Maris Baird (for more information on potato types and varieties, see A World of Potatoes), the best treatment is usually just to rinse them clean and leave them whole (if they are not overly large). Place the prepared potatoes in a pot large enough to handle them without crowding and cover with no more than an inch (2.5 cm) of boiling water. Add about a heaping teaspoon (7 mL) of salt (my preference is sea salt, because I think it tastes better and it's the real thing, not refined like table salt). At this point I usually taste the water, and if it tastes slightly salty, I know I have added enough. Potatoes cooked without the right amount of salt are just not that interesting flavor-wise — sad but true. Place the saucepan over high heat, cover loosely and bring to a boil. When they are boiling away merrily, reduce the heat and cook for about 20 minutes, or until the potatoes are tender when pierced with the tip of a thin knife or skewer.

Draining and Drying All Types of Boiled Potatoes

After potatoes have been boiled it is important to remove excess moisture. After they are drained (keep the cooking liquid for soup or for a sauce or gravy; it's full of good things), turn the element down to its lowest setting (if you're cooking on an electric stove, turn it off completely and just use the residual heat). Return the pot to the burner and shake once or twice to encourage the last bit of moisture to evaporate. Cover the potatoes with a clean tea towel and replace the lid. After about two or three minutes any residual moisture will have dissipated, resulting in the perfect boiled potato. (This procedure is the method to follow when cooking any potatoes and for the preparation of perfect mashed potatoes, see page 50.) At this point, add a good blob of butter and, if you like, some freshly chopped parsley or mint or a combination of both.

The Mashed Potato

Over the years I have prepared countless pots of mashed potatoes both in England and in Canada, and I've definitely found some favorite varieties for mashing. Floury varieties such as King Edward, Maris Piper, Désirée, Estima, Nadine and Red Pontiac all make excellent mashed potatoes, but I am also inordinately fond of some all-purpose potatoes such as Yukon Gold. Here's the thing, though: because of its high moisture content, you need never fear over-mixing a floury potato. Mash made from floury potatoes will be unfailingly fluffy.

While you can achieve good results with an all-purpose potato, as one chef I know puts it, "They don't take the abuse that a floury potato can." If you overwork or over-mix all-purpose potatoes, you run the danger of their losing fluffiness and becoming a little stiffer and heavier (even though they will still taste good). Waxy potatoes, on the other hand, have no hope of becoming classic mashed potatoes. Their low starch and high moisture content results in thick, lumpy, rather gluey mash.

While Classic Mash Deluxe (page 50) is the master recipe, there are numerous recipes for variations on the theme of mashed potatoes throughout this book.

Carbs to the Rescue

Chris Voigt, executive director of the Washington State Potato Commission stuck to a potato-only diet for 60 days in 2010 to help raise awareness of the healthy qualities of the world's favorite vegetable. He ate 20 potatoes a day with an average of a couple of tablespoons (30 mL) of cooking oil depending on how he cooked the potatoes. He fried, boiled, steamed, roasted, barbecued, deep-fried, baked, microwaved, mashed and even juiced them (although he doesn't recommend potato juice!). At the end of the diet he had lost 21 pounds (9.5 kg) and saw a 67-point drop in his cholesterol. Not only that, his wife stated that while he was on his potato diet, his habitual snoring ceased!

The Deep-Fried Potato

French fries, chips or frites — call them what you will — while exact preparation and cooking methods vary, these are all deep-fried potatoes. Whether you leave the skins on potatoes destined for the fryer is up to you. If they have older, thicker skin, be aware that if you make multiple batches they will eventually affect the color of the oil. For my favorite classic deep-fried potato recipes, see pages 64 and 65.

Choosing Potatoes for Deep-Frying

The best potatoes to use for deep-frying are floury or all-purpose. Because new or waxy potatoes do not contain as much starch, they won't get crisp or attain the golden brown color that is so appealing in a French fry. Any floury potato (especially with "russet" in its name) or all-purpose one (Kennebec,

The Birth of a Dish

Pommes frites, France's gift to the wonderful world of potato dishes, were long a feature at the French table. But not until the 19th century did a Parisian vendor think of serving them as a snack food in paper cones from his street cart. In no time, similar vendors all over Paris were offering hot, crispy fries to residents and tourists alike. When a British tourist took the idea home to England and teamed frites with an already popular street food, fried fish, fish and chips was born.

Yukon Gold and Yellow Finn are especially good) is a great choice for frying. In North America, fast-food chains that specialize in French fries use Idaho Russet Burbanks for their fries almost exclusively.

Choosing Fat for Deep-Frying

It is also important to carefully choose your fat for frying. The British maintain that there is nothing like beef fat, or tallow, for frying potatoes, while the French think duck and goose fat produce the finest frites. I wouldn't argue with either of these points of view. However, most home cooks will choose vegetable oil for frying. Whatever fat you choose, make sure it is clean, by which I mean that it has not been used for frying other foods.

The Roasted Potato

What a simple bit of glory is the perfectly roasted potato (see page 59)! If they are using floury or all-purpose potatoes, some cooks like to boil the chunks, partially cooking them, before adding to the roasting pan to cook alongside a roast of beef or pork. For me it is a question of time. If I have lots of time I prefer the potatoes to enter the oven raw. While floury or all-purpose potatoes will produce the classic crisp exterior and fluffy interior we associate with roasted potatoes, new or waxy potatoes have their own virtues when roasted. They benefit from a gentle boiling first, which discourages toughness. When partially cooked before roasting, new or waxy potatoes (this is especially true of fingerling potatoes) will emerge from the oven with an almost palpable sweetness. Their exteriors are sometimes a bit wrinkly, but the interiors have a slightly nutty flavor and smooth texture that are quite delish.

The Crushed Potato

I guess the crushed potato could be thought of as the lazy cook's mashed potato, but that description really takes away from this simple method, which I think results in a very satisfying dish, especially if you use unpeeled potatoes. It can be applied to waxy (see The New Crush, page 57), floury or all-purpose potatoes with great success. Follow the above methods for boiled potatoes for preparing and cooking your potatoes. Once they are cooked, use a large fork (not a carving fork) to crush the potatoes against the sides of the pot. The goal here is to crush-mash them roughly so there are still nice chunks of potato amid the slightly mashed

Nutrient-Dense

The potato is one of the highest sources of vitamin C of any vegetable in the North American diet and contains only a trace of fat and very little sodium. A medium potato contains a little over 200 calories and is also an excellent source of vitamin B_6 and niacin and a good source of potassium and fiber.

The striking pigment in purple and blue potatoes is evidence of the antioxidant anthocyanin. This flavanoid is reputed to have anti-cancer benefits, as well as being of value to a healthy heart, boosting the immune system and protecting against age-related memory loss.

Potato Royalty

The potato is the undisputed king of vegetables in Clark, South Dakota, where local farmers grow bushels of the tasty tuber. That's why, each year, the town throws a party in honor of the vegetable, including a potato wrestling contest in which contestants wrestle in elevated rings filled with mashed potato. In addition to this there are mashed potato eating contests, potato peeling contests, a mashed potato sculpting competition, a potato sack race and a series of recipe competitions.

bits. Add a bit of cold butter or heavy cream as you work, and some fresh herbs such as chopped mint, parsley, dill or chervil. These lovely crushed spuds work particularly well as a bed for braised meat dishes. Once the potatoes are crushed to your liking, you can even add a handful of cooked baby peas or sautéed shallots. This treatment is especially nice with pan-seared salmon or other firm-fleshed fish.

The Shallow-Fried Potato

Shallow frying refers to cooking food that is not fully submerged in the cooking oil, with the oil usually coming a third or halfway up the sides of whatever it is you are frying. There are a number of different opinions as to the proper way to shallow-fry potatoes. Some maintain that the potato should be slightly parcooked or even fully cooked first. Others fry potatoes from their raw state. I would choose this latter method when working with young new potatoes, as they don't take as long to cook, provided they are quite thinly sliced. However, most cooks choose to shallow-fry leftover boiled potatoes, and that is probably what you will end up doing.

Whether your potatoes are partially cooked or not, choose a heavy skillet (cast iron if you have it) and add a combination of butter and vegetable oil (I always use olive oil). Heat the fat over fairly high heat, then add the potatoes, sliced or cut into cubes. Let them get nice and golden brown on one side, then start moving them around, seasoning with a bit of salt and freshly ground pepper. If you like, when they are half done, move them to one side of the pan, add a little more butter and oil and toss in some very thinly sliced onions or leeks (white and pale green parts only). Sauté them for a bit on their side of the pan before incorporating with the potatoes and cooking for another few minutes.

> ### Kudos to George
>
> Chef George Crum is credited with the accidental invention of the potato chip. Crum worked as a chef in Saratoga Springs, New York, during the early 1850s. When an unhappy diner sent back his order of fried potatoes, complaining they were overly thick and not crisp enough, the chef sliced up a batch of potatoes as thin as possible, deep-fried them and added a sprinkling of salt. The diner was thrilled and the potato chip — the saratoga — was born . . . to the delight of us all.

The Steamed Potato

Any potato variety can be steamed with good results. Steaming is a particularly good treatment for new or waxy potatoes because it keeps every bit of their young goodness intact. Sometimes all you want is the essence of pure potato, without fat or flavorings tagging along. Klondike Rose, Red La Soda, Chieftain, Charlotte, Pink Fir Apple, Anya, Kerr's Pink and any of the fingerling varieties are among the optimum choices for steaming.

> ### Recyclable
>
> A British potato crisp (chip) manufacturer is working on an environmentally friendly naturally compostable crisp packet, made from potato peelings.

Steaming New or Waxy Potatoes

To steam new or waxy potatoes, rinse or scrub them clean and place in a steamer basket set over boiling water. Add a sprinkle of salt. Place over high heat, cover with the pot lid and steam until a thin knife blade slips in and out easily. (This may take less than 10 minutes, depending on the size of the potato).

Steaming Floury or All-Purpose Potatoes

Peel (or not, as you wish) and cut into uniform chunks. These potatoes will take somewhat longer to cook through than new or waxy varieties, about 15 to 20 minutes.

The Cultivated Potato: Growing Your Own

If you have even a little bit of garden in which to grow vegetables, you owe it to yourself to plant a few seed potatoes for the sheer thrill of it. The first time I grew potatoes, I was amazed at how ridiculously easy it was to succeed. I planted 2 pounds (1 kg) of seed potatoes, which produced 50 pounds (23 kg) of spuds!

Selecting Varieties

Make sure to choose a potato variety that is recommended for your area; chatting with growers at local farmers' markets will provide useful information. Use seed potatoes that are certified to be disease-free, which means they have been harvested from crops that are free of viruses. Or plan on retaining some potatoes from your pantry that are past their prime for eating, especially if they are certified organic — many conventional seed potatoes that you obtain from a nursery or garden center may have been dusted with substances to delay sprouting. Now you are ready to chit.

Potatoes and Presidents

U.S. president Bill Clinton loved the Yukon Gold potato so much that he instructed the White House cooks to serve it over any other potato while he was in office. Before John Adams became the second president of the United States, he mentioned potatoes in a letter written to his wife in reference to his nation's struggle for independence from Britain. "Let us eat potatoes and drink water, let us wear canvas and undressed sheepskins, rather than submit to the unrighteous and ignominious domination that is prepared for us." George Washington had the potato planted on his estate in 1767, and Thomas Jefferson wrote about potatoes in his journal in 1794. And it was Jefferson who first introduced fried potatoes to the U.S., having enjoyed them while he was in Paris.

Chitting

Chitting simply means encouraging your seed potato to sprout. You may have noticed this happening to potatoes you've forgotten at the back of the cupboard or under the kitchen sink. Whether they are small seed potatoes purchased from a nursery or from your own pantry, allowing the potato to chit, or sprout, before planting will result in strong, vigorous potato plants that in turn will produce lots of potatoes later in the year.

Generally speaking, start to chit your small seed potatoes in February or March, depending on when your growing season begins. Place them in recycled egg cartons with their blunt sides (the sides with the most "eyes") facing up; place the cartons, with lids open, in a relatively cool place. If you are using larger potatoes,

Night Plants

Potatoes love the dark. Unless you have a cool, dry root cellar or similar storage facility, buy just a few pounds of potatoes at a time rather than vast quantities. Never store potatoes in a plastic bag. Keep them in brown paper or in a vegetable bin in a cool, dark, dry place.

cut them into pieces, making sure to get the maximum number of eyes in each piece. You can also use an alternative container such as a cardboard box. A windowsill, especially one that receives a bit of indirect sun, is a good location.

If you end up with many sprouts on one potato or chunk of potato, carefully rub them off to encourage just two or three to grow especially strong. If you leave all the shoots intact before planting, while you will end up with lots of potatoes, they will all be small. What you want are short, strong greenish pink shoots, not the long, stringy white sprouts that occur when old potatoes are left completely in the dark. As they sprout, the potatoes may start to look wrinkly and decrepit, but that is just because they are losing moisture. You can plant when the sprouts are about an inch (2.5 cm) long and when all risk of frost is gone.

Planting

Potatoes are adaptable and can do well in either light or heavy soil, but they do require good drainage in a relatively open site and about 20 inches (50 cm) of rainfall or irrigation throughout their growing season. As a classic cool-season crop, potatoes grow best at 61°F to 64°F (16°C to 18°C) and require a growing season of 70 to 140 frost-free days, depending on the variety.

If space is limited you can grow potatoes in containers with good results, or consider growing "early" potato varieties, which traditionally require less room. They grow quickly but generally have a lower yield than varieties that mature more slowly.

Mound up the planting furrows to a depth of about 6 inches (15 cm). Being careful not to break off the sprouts, space the tubers about 23 inches (60 cm) apart (half this distance for early varieties). Cover lightly with soil. As soon as shoots appear, mound up the earth around each plant to keep the shoots buried. Cultivate between the rows to nip weeds in the bud, mounding the soil as you do so. Because potatoes form close to the surface, mounding the soil is especially important because it prevents them from greening (forming solanine; see above) with exposure to sunlight. When the foliage is close to 6 inches (15 cm) tall, you should start adding soil to the plants just about to the top of the leaves — this is called hilling. You should repeat this about once a week or so until your potato plant is about a foot tall and flowers start to appear.

Planting Potatoes

If you plan to grow your own potatoes, remember that the plants take up quite a bit of space, so it's a good idea to grow them in a separate patch. If you do grow them with other plants, corn, lettuce, radishes, eggplant and cabbage all make good neighbors for potatoes. Grow some catnip, coriander, horseradish or onions nearby, as they will deter the dreaded potato beetle. Potatoes won't do well next to apples, pumpkin, squash, raspberries, tomatoes, cucumbers or sunflowers. Beans are a doubly good choice to plant alongside potatoes — the plants protect each other from pests.

Recycling

One good method of storing potatoes is in discarded pantyhose! Drop a few potatoes in each leg and hang in a cool, dry, dark place. The pantyhose allow air to circulate, an all-important factor in successfully storing potatoes.

Gardening in Containers

No garden space for spuds? Grow them in a large container such as a halved wooden barrel. Put 6 inches (15 cm) of soil in the barrel and plant three seed potatoes, evenly spaced. Cover them with about 4 inches (10 cm) of topsoil. When you first spot some foliage, add more soil so that just the green tips are showing. As the potatoes grow, continue to add more soil until it comes to about 2 inches (5 cm) below the rim of the barrel. Water and fertilize the plants regularly and harvest your potatoes when the foliage starts to turn yellow and brown.

Harvesting Your Crop

Harvesting methods will depend on the variety of potato. For early varieties, start lifting the egg-sized potatoes as the flowers open. New potatoes can be dug when the lower leaves of the plant begin to turn yellow, usually about three weeks after flowering. Early potatoes will be ready from early to mid summer, second early varieties from late summer to early autumn, and main-crop potatoes from early to mid autumn. Leave healthy main-crop potatoes in the ground for as long as possible. As early autumn approaches, cut back the stems (called the haulm) of each plant to about 2 inches (5 cm) above ground level. Leave the potatoes in the ground for another two weeks (be wary of slugs!) to allow their skins to mature and harden somewhat before harvesting.

Storing Potatoes

Potatoes are most often sold in heavy paper bags with netting on one side to allow the air to circulate, but some are sold in plastic bags. If you've purchased potatoes in a plastic bag, once you get them home, transfer them to a heavy paper bag (with the top left open), a hessian (burlap) sack or a loose-lidded breathable basket for longer storage. This will help the air to circulate and keep them dry. Moisture or a humid atmosphere will encourage sprouting and also lead to the potatoes rotting.

Always store unwashed potatoes in a dry, dark, cool place, not in the refrigerator. (The exception is new potatoes, which should be kept in the refrigerator and, for best results, enjoyed within a week of purchase.) If potatoes are stored at too low a temperature, their starch will convert to sugar and they will be somewhat sweet — not necessarily a bad thing but perhaps not what you want for a specific recipe. Alternatively, if potatoes are stored at too warm a temperature, they will lose water and nutrients and dry out.

Antipathies

Never store potatoes and onions or apples together or near each other. Onions and apples give off a gas that helps speed up the rotting process in potatoes.

A World of Potatoes

One potato, two potato, three potato, four,
Five potato, six potato, seven potato, more.
Baked potato, boiled potato, 'tato mashed with cheese,
Big potato, small potato, more potato, please!

This well-known children's rhyme only scratches the surface in terms of the potato choices consumers have today. Hundreds of varieties are available and while having a wide variety of options is wonderful, it can also be confusing for consumers. Which potato to use when? With that in mind, we have provided key information on numerous varieties and grouped them according to potato type. This way you will always be able to choose the right potato for the recipe you have in mind, and that can make all the difference between a successful dish and one that you may not choose to make a second time.

Potato Types

Within the diverse world of potatoes, from a culinary perspective the differences really boil down to starch. Simply put, potatoes come in three distinct types based on their starch content: floury, waxy or all-purpose.

Floury potatoes such as Idaho Russet Burbank and King Edward, as well as a unique fingerling called La Ratte, are mealier because they are higher in starch and lower in water content. These are the potatoes to use for baking, mashing, roasting and chipping or fries. Because they tend to break up somewhat when boiled, they lend themselves well to mashing. This same characteristic makes them a poor candidate for, say, classic North American–style and German potato salads, in which we like the pieces to remain intact.

Waxy potatoes such as Kipfler and Red Pontiac, and some fingerling varieties such as Yellow Fingerling, are firmer fleshed, higher in water and lower in starch than floury potatoes. Waxy potatoes hold their shape when cooked, so they are best for salads, gratins and simple boiling, steaming or sautéing.

Naming Potatoes

In Europe it is more common for potatoes to be identified by their variety name, whereas in North America most wholesalers dub the spud with a moniker that relates to the location where the potato was grown — hence Idaho and P.E.I. potatoes. However, the Yukon Gold potato has nothing to do with the Yukon. The variety's developer, the late Garnet Johnston, chose that name in reference to the potato's gold flesh and the legendary Yukon gold rush. Other potato cultivars he developed bore the name of a river. When I interviewed him for an article I was writing many years ago, he told me that one reason he thought the Yukon Gold became so popular was that people could ask for it by name. The comment reflected Johnston's belief that specific potato varieties would make the "potato hit parade" only if they were marketed, promoted and sold by their variety name, a happy state of affairs that consumers are experiencing now as growers at farmers' markets are doing just that.

My Top 5 Floury Potatoes

① Idaho Russet Burbank: Reliable, magnificently versatile and unfailingly delicious, this variety makes the world's best baked potato. It is a great choice for making mashed potatoes too, producing a particularly fluffy result.

② King Edward: A regal spud if ever there was one. Revered as the most popular potato in Britain throughout most of the 20th century, these days it may be overshadowed by newer varieties. However, no less a food personality than England's Delia Smith pronounced it the potato to use for making gnocchi, confirming its status as a permanently shining culinary star.

③ Estima: This is my favorite choice when olive-oil crushed potatoes are on the menu. In the days when many thought that yellow-fleshed potatoes would not become popular in North America, it proved them wrong, thereby paving the way for megastars like the Yukon Gold.

④ Fabula: If you've ever had a roasted potato that was dry, it wouldn't have been a Fabula. This yellow-fleshed potato retains moisture, so even when it's roasted or baked, in a soup or a stew, it will keep its moist heart, which is especially wonderful if its exterior is sticky and crusted.

⑤ British Queen: The first time I tasted these potatoes I was in Ireland, where they are known simply as "Queens". What a potato! Afterwards I thought that until then I had never really experienced all that a potato could offer. It has the very essence of rich, earthy flavor that we crave when we think of potatoes.

All-purpose potatoes have a relatively even balance of water and starch. They were developed to be good for everything, a sort of one-size-fits-all spud. Think Désirée, Kennebec or my favorite Yukon Gold.

Specialty potatoes can be characterized as heirloom varieties — French Fingerlings or Bintje (which to confuse things even more is classified as an all-purpose potato with waxy flesh), for example — or those unusual purple, red and blue potatoes that chefs like to feature on their menus. Most of those available can be categorized as low- or medium-starch, which makes them most suitable for boiling, steaming, roasting and, in some cases (such as Roseval and Adirondack Red), for salads. Some, such as Adirondack Blue, also mash well.

The Time of Their Lives

If you have ever been confused by the terms "old" and "new" potatoes, bear in mind that these tags refer to the stages of a potato's growth. Regardless of the variety, new potatoes are harvested when they are young and a little immature. Their skins are delicate because they haven't yet fully formed, and their starch content is lower. They can be quite small, from plum-sized down to no bigger than one bite. Because of their youthfulness, new potatoes don't have the storage capacity of potatoes that were harvested later.

So-called old potatoes were left in the ground to reach full maturity, have thicker skins and, regardless of variety, contain more starch in their makeup. These are the potatoes that keep well when stored properly — up to four months or so. The longer they are stored, the more their inherent starch is converted to sugar, making them slightly sweeter than younger potatoes. This is why when older potatoes are used to make french fries or chips, the fries may appear dark brown rather than golden brown; the added sugar contributes to their color.

Other Potato Terminology

Home gardeners and commercial potato growers alike may use other terms to describe potatoes. *Early*, *second early* and *main-crop* are used to describe how long it takes for a particular variety to mature fully. Generally it takes 70 days for early varieties, 90 days for second early varieties and 120 to 140 days for main-crop potatoes. Of course, any potato can be harvested before its full maturity, but it will have different characteristics than if it were mature. If fact, the inherent characteristics of a potato may differ quite dramatically according to the variety and the season in which it is harvested. For instance, many potatoes (for example, Duke of York, page 32) are waxy when young (as new potatoes) but become starchy as they age.

> ### Truffle Potatoes
>
> The *vitelotte* is an unusual black-skinned potato with purplish blue flesh that has a waxy, firm texture and slightly nutty flavor. It is also known as the *truffe de Chine* — Chinese truffle — or truffle potato because of its resemblance to the expensive fungus. The unique flesh color doesn't fade when this potato is cooked, making it a favorite of chefs looking to provide the unusual on their menus.

No matter where you live in the world, *early* refers to new potatoes from the current crop — that is to say, they have just been harvested and have never been stored. Second early potatoes are still thought of as new potatoes but their skin is slightly more mature; growers describe it as "beginning to set." You can't scrape them before cooking as you would early potatoes, with their papery skin. Like early potatoes, these too are not stored. Finally, main-crop potatoes are available toward the end of the growing season. These will be stored throughout the winter and on hand in markets until the next season begins.

My Top 5 Waxy Potatoes

1. **Jersey Royal:** I was introduced to these potatoes in England, where they make a heralded arrival every spring, which includes being featured on restaurant menus. Along with Yukon Golds, these would be my desert-island potatoes. If I could have only these two varieties for the rest of my life, that would be just fine.

2. **Kipfler:** These buttery potatoes with a slightly nutty flavor are also known as German finger potatoes. Their lovely waxy flesh makes them perfect for the famed potato salads of Germany and Austria.

3. **Maris Baird:** The classic new potato, Maris Baird is relied on when salads grace the menu. They are also my choice for creamed new potatoes, tossed with some freshly chopped herbs. In general terms, they are great for any preparation where you want the potatoes to remain firm and intact.

4. **Pink Firr Apple:** When I lived in England, I would get very excited whenever I spotted these knobby, misshapen, pinkish-skinned potatoes at the greengrocers. They are firm and waxy, and I loved to cook them in their skins to capture all their nutty flavor.

5. **Belle de Fontenay:** This is a potato variety almost without peer. I know my dad would have loved them because they can be enjoyed hot or cold, with or without the skin. Pretty, yellow, smooth and waxy, "Belles" have great flavor that apparently improves with storage, although I have never had any around long enough to find out.

My Top 5 All-Purpose Potatoes

1. **Yukon Gold:** Canada's original mellow yellow, this potato is always great. It makes fabulous mash, terrific gratins, wonderful crushed-with-butter potatoes and delightful frites and chips.

2. **Kennebec:** This is one of the first potatoes I grew myself. Kennebec is high on the list for many home gardeners because of its reliability. It is a good solid all-rounder with distinctive flavor.

3. **Bintje:** This variety, which is particularly beautiful to look at, has been around for a long time, probably because there isn't a task it doesn't perform well. I first tasted them in Holland in a warm salad that accompanied a crispy piece of veal schnitzel.

4. **Kerr's Pink:** This potato is one of Ireland's most popular varieties. Its name comes from the lovely pale pink hue of its skin. It makes magnificent, full-flavored mashed potatoes.

5. **Maris Piper:** I think of this variety as the second of three sisters to emerge during the potato growing season in the U.K. It is preceded by Maris Baird and Maris Peer. A friend in England calls it the "undisputed king of the roasties."

Just to complicate things, in today's supermarkets not all early potatoes are waxy and not all late ones are floury. Some are picked young as well as when mature. Also, we import new potatoes when locally grown are not available.

If you are a potato neophyte, one of your best sources of information is a farmers' market, where you can talk to the people who grow them. Tell them what you plan to make and they will guide you as to the best spud for the job.

Sweet Potatoes

It must be said that I am something of a potato purist. By that I mean, as much as I love sweet potatoes, I don't really consider them to be potatoes. Botanically speaking, sweet potatoes don't belong to the same family as potatoes. The potato belongs to the Solanaceae family, which includes tomatoes, peppers, eggplant and the deadly nightshade group. The sweet potato belongs to the Convolvulaceae family, and apparently it is the only member of its clan cultivated for human consumption.

Confused about yams and sweet potatoes? Sweet potatoes come in a number of varieties, but generally your supermarket will stock either a pale or a dark type. It is the darker variety that many of us call yams. They have a thicker, orange skin and quite bright orange, sweet, moist flesh. The pale sweet potatoes have a thin, light yellow skin and similarly colored flesh that is not particularly sweet. True yams are from an entirely different family of plants and have a rather shaggy brownish exterior. Their flesh ranges in color from off-white to a rather pale yellow and their texture runs from moist to mealy. While I have included recipes in this book that use sweet potatoes, there are none for yams.

A Presidential Favorite

Thomas Jefferson had a penchant for sweet potatoes and grew them on the grounds of the White House. In a letter he wrote to an associate in Paris in 1787 he requested "…seeds of the common sweet potato" be brought back to him. The biscuits made to his recipe specifications are still served today at Philadelphia's City Tavern.

Potato Glossary

While the International Potato Center in Peru boasts a collection of more than 4,000 potato varieties, actually only about 400 to 500 varieties of potatoes are in active production around the world. Many factors must be considered before a potato variety gains real popularity: resistance to disease, storage capabilities and whether a specific variety has the cooking characteristics that may currently be in demand for that type of potato.

All-Purpose Potatoes

Potatoes classified as all-purpose have less starch than floury potatoes but more starch than those classified as waxy. The potatoes in this section fall into the general or all-purpose category and as such will perform well for most cooking purposes.

AC Chaleur

Developed in New Brunswick — the province that in terms of Canadian potato production is second only to Prince Edward Island — the AC Chaleur can be thought of as your garden-variety table potato. While a good all-purpose potato like this one can certainly be mashed, it won't have the characteristic dry fluffiness that a floury potato produces.

Origin: Canada, 1988
Availability: Canada, USA
Description: round to oval; smooth buff-colored skin; white flesh
Uses: boiling, baking

Adora

The Adora has been described by growers as a "real gourmet potato in taste, texture and appearance." With its thin skin and shallow eyes, it is very easy to peel. Home gardeners will be interested to learn that it is a fast-growing variety, while waist-watchers will be happy that it has a third of the carbohydrates and a quarter of the calories of two other very popular potatoes, the Russet Burbank and Maris Piper.

Origin: Netherlands, 1999
Availability: Canada, Netherlands, United Kingdom, USA
Description: oblong; smooth light yellow skin; pale yellow flesh
Uses: boiling, frying, baking, salads

Ambo

Ambo is a very reliable potato to grow and can be thought of as a genuine all-purpose potato — great roast potatoes, fluffy bakers, good mash, and it even works well as a salad potato.

Origin: Ireland, 1993
Availability: Ireland, New Zealand, Switzerland, United Kingdom
Description: slightly irregular oval; light skin blotched with reddish pink; very white flesh
Uses: baking, boiling, most other cooking methods

Aminca

Well-known in Europe, Aminca has a lovely creamy texture. It's a perfect choice for gnocchi or for making potato chips.

Origin: Netherlands, 1977
Availability: Denmark, Italy, United Kingdom
Description: medium to large oblong; thin light yellow skin; medium-deep eyes; dry cream or yellow flesh
Uses: boiling, baking, mashing, roasting, frying

Andover

With its remarkably good taste, Andover is a classic choice for frying — especially for fries and chips. It boasts a distinctive pedigree, as it was bred at Cornell University as part of the Cornell Foundation Seed Potato Program.

Origin: USA, 1981
Availability: Canada, USA
Description: round; rough, pale buff-colored skin; white flesh
Uses: frying, boiling, baking

Anna

A perfect choice for Potatoes Anna! (page 70)

Origin: Ireland, 1996
Availability: Ireland, United Kingdom
Description: round to slightly oval; smooth white skin; waxy yet floury flesh
Uses: baking, boiling

Arran Consul

A revered Scottish variety, this potato is another great all-rounder. It was dubbed "the potato that won the war" in the UK, as it was easy and inexpensive to grow and provided good nourishment at a time when many other foods were available only at a premium or not at all.

Origin: Scotland, 1925

Availability: Canada, United Kingdom

Description: round; white skin; creamy flesh

Uses: boiling, baking, mashing, roasting

Atlantic

With its uniform round shape and light, buff-colored skin, no wonder this is one of the preferred potatoes of the North American chip industry. Apparently it also grows well in home gardens, as long as your soil is not too sandy.

Origin: USA, 1976

Availability: Australia, Canada, New Zealand, USA

Description: oval to round; light, scaly buff-colored skin; white flesh

Uses: baking, boiling, chipping, mashing, roasting

Ausonia

Ausonia was the name given by the ancient Greeks to a region of ancient Italy. I have no idea why the Dutch used it as the name of this all-purpose potato.

Origin: Netherlands, 1981

Availability: Europe, United Kingdom

Description: oval; white skin; mealy light yellow flesh

Uses: baking, boiling, most other cooking methods

Avondale

This is an Irish variety. When fully mature, the Avondale looks like the Yukon Gold in appearance, though slightly smaller. And like the Yukon Gold, it is very versatile.

Origin: Ireland, 1982

Availability: Canary Islands, Egypt, Europe, Ireland, Israel, Morocco, Pakistan, Sri Lanka, United Kingdom

Description: round or oval; pale beige skin; moist, waxy, creamy flesh; mellow flavor

Uses: works well for most cooking methods

Barna

This red-skinned spud is apparently much sought after for its distinctive taste by people in Ireland and the United Kingdom who consider themselves potato aficionados. It is especially good for frites, fries or chips.

Origin: Ireland, 1993

Availability: Ireland, United Kingdom

Description: uniformly oval; red skin; slightly waxy flesh; warm, nutty taste

Uses: all-round variety good for most cooking methods

Batoche

While Batoche is the name of a community in Saskatchewan, this potato variety was developed in Fredericton, New Brunswick, at a Canadian government agriculture research station.

Origin: Canada, 1963

Availability: Canada, USA

Description: moderately large, uniform round to oblong; smooth bright red skin; medium-deep eyes, darker red than skin; creamy white flesh

Uses: boiling, baking, frying

Bintje

If you have spent any time in the Netherlands, you will be familiar with this delicious potato that effectively straddles the fence between waxy and floury. This variety (pronounced *BEN-jee*) was developed by a Dutch botanist/schoolmaster, Kornelis Friesland, who liked to name his hybrid potatoes after his nine children. He ran out of kids before potato varieties, so when the tenth potato emerged, he named it after his best pupil, a girl named Bintje. Today the Bintje potato is the most widely grown yellow-fleshed tuber worldwide.

Origin: Netherlands, 1910

Availability: Australia, Brazil, Canada, Denmark, Finland, France, Italy, Netherlands, New Zealand, Sweden, Thailand, United Kingdom

Description: long oval; pale yellow skin; creamy flesh

Uses: baking, boiling, frying, roasting, salads

The Bishop

We're not sure who the bishop in question was, but this long, slightly kidney-shaped potato was developed by Dr. J.H. Wilson of St. Andrew's University in Scotland.

Origin: Scotland, 1912

Availability: United Kingdom

Description: relatively long oval; pale white skin; pale yellow flesh

Uses: boiling, roasting, salads

Butte

Butte is one of the very best russet baking potatoes and has up to 20 percent more protein than other potatoes and very high vitamin C content. It's also great mashed or fried. Potato Butte is the name of a 5,292-foot (1,613 m) mountain peak in Oregon.

Origin: USA, 1963

Availability: Canada, USA

Description: long, with rounded ends; smooth light brown skin; white flesh

Uses: boiling, baking, frying

Cara White

The Cara White potato is white with pink eyes, which makes it very distinctive. Cara is known for its soft, moist and waxy characteristics and somewhat sweet, mild flavor. Great for baking, especially double-baked potatoes.

Origin: Ireland, 1976

Availability: Cyprus, Egypt, Ireland, Israel, United Kingdom

Description: round or oval; white skin with pink eyes; moist, waxy cream flesh; mild flavor

Uses: baking, boiling, frying, all other cooking methods

Caribe

A big, bluish purple–skinned potato with snow-white flesh, this is a great choice for making extra-fluffy mashed potatoes. The name is pronounced *ka-REE-bay*.

Origin: Canada, 1969

Availability: Canada, USA

Description: oblong; red-purple skin with tan patches; creamy white flesh

Uses: boiling, mashing, frying

Carlingford

This variety is typically very round and smooth, with creamy white skin and white flesh. In terms of categorization it is another one of those fence-sitters, with its flesh falling somewhere in the middle — neither completely waxy nor completely floury. It lends itself well to being grown in a tub or in patio growing bags, because it produces a large number of tubers. Excellent as a new or baby potato.

Origin: Northern Ireland, 1982

Availability: Australia, Canada, United Kingdom

Description: round or oval; white skin; shallow to medium eyes; white flesh, firm, somewhat waxy cooked texture

Uses: baking, boiling, frying, steaming

Cascade

This potato variety was specifically developed to thrive in the soil and temperature conditions of North America's Pacific Northwest region.

Origin: USA, 1969

Availability: Canada, USA

Description: oval to oblong; flaky buff-colored skin with occasional slight cracking; cream flesh

Uses: frying, baking, boiling

Catriona

Catriona is a long, oval second early potato with very distinctive and attractive purple eyes marking a smooth white skin. This an old variety, much loved by home gardeners in the UK. It has a firm, mealy texture and a pleasant flavor.

Origin: Scotland, 1920

Availability: United Kingdom

Description: large, kidney-shaped; bluish purple splashes around eyes; pale creamy flesh

Uses: boiling, baking, roasting, mashing, all other cooking methods

Chieftain

Canada's leading red potato, the Chieftain has excellent flavor. Home gardeners choose it because it is quite adaptable and easy to grow (especially in clay soil) and has fantastic yield potential.

Origin: USA, 1966

Availability: Canada, USA

Description: oblong to round; fairly smooth bright red skin; shallow eyes; white flesh

Uses: boiling, french fries

Claret

Deep red, as its name suggests, Claret is described as an "improved Désirée" (see below) type of potato. It has a typical all-round texture, midway between waxy and floury.

Origin: Scotland, 1996

Availability: Scotland

Description: round to oval; smooth red skin; firm creamy flesh

Uses: all cooking methods

Colmo

Origin: Netherlands, 1973

Availability: Netherlands, United Kingdom

Description: medium round or oval; white skin; firm light yellow flesh

Uses: all cooking methods, especially boiling and mashing

Concurrent

Origin: Netherlands, 1973

Availability: Canada, Netherlands, New Zealand, United Kingdom, USA

Description: oval; smooth light yellow skin; a few shallow eyes; light yellow flesh

Uses: boiling, baking

Désirée

As its name implies, Désirée is purported to be the world's most popular red-skinned potato. It falls midway between waxy and floury, making it very suitable for a variety of cooking methods. This potato has a lovely creamy quality when roasted.

Origin: Netherlands, 1962

Availability: Algeria, Argentina, Australia, Cameroon, Canada, Chile, Iran, Irish Republic, Malawi, Morocco, Netherlands, New Zealand, Pakistan, Portugal, Sri Lanka, Tunisia, Turkey, United Kingdom, USA

Description: oval; smooth red skin; shallow eyes; firm, creamy pale yellow flesh

Uses: boiling, baking, regular and oven-baked wedge chips, frites, roasting, mashing, salads

Dr. McIntosh

Developed by T.P. Mcintosh of Edinburgh, this heritage variety is quite popular among home gardeners, as it is considered a good general-use potato.

Origin: Scotland, 1944

Availability: New Zealand, United Kingdom

Description: long oval; smooth, pale yellow-white skin; light creamy flesh

Uses: baking, boiling, mashing, salads

Duke of York

A very popular choice for the home gardener, Duke of York was bred by William Sim in Aberdeenshire, Scotland, and is renowned for its versatility. When mature it becomes starchy, making it a good general-purpose potato. When enjoyed young, it has a waxy quality.

Origin: Scotland, 1891

Availability: France, Netherlands, United Kingdom

Description: long oval; pale whitish yellow skin; light yellow flesh; rich, sweet flavor

Uses: all cooking methods

Dunbar Standard

This potato is another heritage variety, which refers to those bred from the 19th century up to about the middle of the 20th century. Most are still grown today, albeit on a small scale.

Origin: Scotland, 1936

Availability: Ireland, United Kingdom

Description: long oval; white skin; firm white flesh; full flavor

Uses: all cooking methods

Epicure

Also known as Ayrshire, this is the traditional early potato in that part of Scotland. It can recover quickly from a bit of frost — a valuable characteristic in areas where cold weather may be a factor. The Epicure has distinctive deep-set eyes, like wide slits, and a robust flavor.

Origin: United Kingdom, 1897

Availability: Canada, United Kingdom

Description: round; white skin; firm, creamy white flesh

Uses: baking, boiling

Eramosa

Like the famed Yukon Gold potato, Eramosa was named for a river and developed by a renowned Canadian potato breeder, the late Garnet Johnston. Other varieties that he helped release are Huron, Nipigon, York, Rideau, Trent, Simcoe, Longlac, Conestoga, Saginaw Gold, Red Gold, Rose Gold, Ruby Gold, Temagami and Royal Gold — quite the legacy.

Origin: Canada, 1970

Availability: Canada, USA

Description: semi-flattened oval; smooth white skin; shallow eyes; white flesh

Uses: boiling, baking, mashing

Fianna

If you are a potato, being nematode-resistant is an important trait, and one that this cultivar can brag about (nematodes are small, usually microscopic roundworms that can do major damage to field crops such as potatoes). We're not sure what makes this particular potato anti-nematode, but we do know the variety makes excellent french fries and chips.

Origin: Netherlands, 1987

Availability: Netherlands, New Zealand, United Kingdom

Description: smooth white skin; shallow eyes; firm, floury flesh

Uses: baking, frying, mashing, roasting

Goldrush

A great storage potato with russeted skin and shallow eyes, this variety matures in mid-season with good size and yields. Developed in North Dakota, the Goldrush is versatile and delicious, with excellent flavor and very white flesh both before and after cooking.

Origin: USA, 1992

Availability: Canada, USA

Description: blocky oblong; medium-heavy golden russet skin; very white flesh

Uses: baking, boiling, roasting, mashing, fries and chips

Granola

In Germany, where this versatile variety is popular, all-purpose potatoes are called *vorwiegend festkochend*. The middle levels of starch make them a popular choice for many culinary applications.

Origin: Germany, 1975

Availability: Australia, Germany, India, Indonesia, Nepal, Netherlands, Pakistan, Switzerland, Turkey, Vietnam

Description: oval; bright yellow skin; creamy yellow flesh

Uses: baking, boiling, frying

Green Mountain

This is a popular heirloom potato that originated in Vermont; it was named in 1885 by O.H. Alexander of Charlotte, Vermont. It was designed for table use and to be grown in home gardens. Superior flavor and high yields are the reasons many seasoned gardeners continue to grow it. It makes fabulous fried spuds.

Origin: USA, 1878

Availability: Canada, USA

Description: large, short to flattened oblong, ends usually blunt; smooth buff skin, often netted; medium-deep white eyes; white flesh.

Uses: baking, boiling, frying

Hertha

Origin: Netherlands, 1968

Availability: Canada, Netherlands, USA

Description: oval; smooth yellow skin; shallow eyes; light yellow flesh

Uses: boiling, baking, frying

Home Guard

This is the perfect name for a potato that was introduced in the UK during the war years. It was a commercial success because of its consistently high yields and the fact that it could be "lifted" (harvested) early. Home gardeners loved these potatoes for their disease resistance.

Origin: Scotland, 1942

Availability: United Kingdom

Description: round to oval; white skin; floury, dry creamy white flesh

Uses: boiling, frying, roasting, most other cooking methods

Huron

Another renowned potato from Canadian breeder Garnet Johnston.

Origin: Canada, 1943

Availability: Canada, USA

Description: oblong; slightly flaked creamy buff skin; medium-deep eyes; white flesh

Uses: boiling, baking, frying

Ilam Hardie

Ilam Hardy is a very popular older variety with an oval to round shape. It is a second early potato, ready to harvest in 90 to 100 days.

Origin: unknown

Availability: New Zealand, South Africa

Description: pale yellow skin; floury white flesh

Uses: mashing, baking, boiling, frying, roasting, salads, chips, oven-baked wedges

Irish Cobbler

Irish Cobbler was the standard potato in Virginia during the 1930s and '40s and is the most widely grown crop potato throughout North Dakota and the Canadian West. This early potato is a traditional favorite for home gardeners. It has a distinctive taste and dry, creamy white flesh that boils and bakes very well. Cobblers are medium-sized round potatoes with shallow to deep eyes. As a general-purpose potato they are hard to beat.

Origin: USA, 1876

Availability: Canada, South Korea, USA

Description: medium to large, round; smooth, thin creamy white skin; dry creamy flesh; bruises easily

Uses: boiling, mashing, frying, most other cooking methods

Island Sunshine

Raymond Loo is a sixth-generation organic farmer whose father created this variety in Kensington, Prince Edward Island, in 1984. A delightful creamy, golden-fleshed potato, it grows productively, with high yields. Some say it may even surpass the Yukon Gold in popularity because of its great flavor and excellent storage properties.

Origin: Canada, 1984

Availability: Canada, USA

Description: round; rough yellow skin; dark yellow flesh

Uses: boiling, baking

Itasca

Was this potato named for Itasca County, Minnesota, where it was developed? Probably, especially since this area is also home to Potato Lake!

Origin: USA, 1994

Availability: Canada, USA

Description: oblong to round; smooth, pale skin; creamy white flesh

Uses: baking, boiling, frying, mashing, roasting

Jaerla

A Dutch variety from the late 1960s, Jaerla is classified as a first early. It has enjoyed renewed availability because a Scottish seed producer wanted a baking potato that would be available in early summer. This variety has good flavor and good all-round cooking qualities.

Origin: Netherlands, 1969

Availability: Algeria, Argentina, Greece, Netherlands, Turkey, former Yugoslavia

Description: long oval; light skin; shallow eyes; firm light yellow flesh

Uses: baking, boiling, most other cooking methods

Kennebec

The Kennebec potato has been around for more than 50 years, but lately it has found new popularity with restaurant chefs because of its uniform shape, relatively thin skin and great balanced taste, which some say has a slight nuttiness to it. As good baked as it is mashed, scalloped, roasted or fried, and a popular choice for home gardeners in North America.

Origin: USA, 1948

Availability: Argentina, Australia, Canada, Italy, New Zealand, Portugal, South Korea, Taiwan, Uruguay, USA

Description: largish, oval to round; smooth white skin; white flesh

Uses: baking, boiling, frying, mashing, roasting

Kerr's Pink

In 2002 this potato comprised 25 percent of potato production in Ireland, making it among the nation's most popular varieties. It has a distinctive pink hue and deep-set eyes and makes fantastic mashed potatoes.

Origin: Scotland, 1907

Availability: Ireland, Netherlands, United Kingdom

Description: round; pale pink skin; quite deep eyes; creamy white flesh; pleasant mealy texture when cooked

Uses: baking, boiling, frying, mashing, roasting

Lady Rosetta

The Lady Rosetta potato, a Dutch-bred variety, was recently nominated as one of the tastiest potatoes in Europe. Extensively used in manufacturing potato chips (crisps), it also makes a great baked potato. Lady Rosetta is an odd-shaped potato and has a red skin.

Origin: Netherlands, 1990

Availability: Canada, Netherlands, United Kingdom

Description: round; thin red skin; shallow yet prominent eyes; cream to yellow flesh

Uses: boiling, baking, frying

Long White

Grown primarily in California, Long Whites are available from spring through summer. With their medium level of starch, these all-purpose potatoes have a creamy yet firm texture when cooked. They are also known as California Long Whites.

Origin: USA

Availability: Canada, USA

Description: long oval; thin light tan skin; white flesh

Uses: baking, frying, most other cooking methods

Maris Piper

Like Désirée (and similar to it in starch levels), this potato is very well-known in the UK, where a friend of mine calls it "the undisputed king of the roasties." Maris Pipers are used extensively to make thick-cut English chips. Home gardeners like them because of their high yield and home cooks love them because of their great all-round versatility.

Origin: United Kingdom, 1964

Availability: Portugal, United Kingdom

Description: short oval; creamy skin; creamy white flesh; soft, dry, floury texture

Uses: boiling, baking, frying, roasting, mashing

Mona Lisa

It's not clear why this lovely old Dutch potato variety is so named, but it's a favorite in Spain, where it is often used to make one of that country's most famous dishes, potato tortilla (see page 140). With its buttery flesh and smooth skin, it is very reminiscent of the Yukon Gold potato and can be used in much the same way.

Origin: Netherlands, 1982

Availability: France, Greece, Netherlands, Portugal, Spain

Description: long oval, sometimes kidney-shaped; butter-yellow skin and flesh; shallow eyes

Uses: baking, boiling, frying, mashing, roasting

Mondial

This smooth, good-looking Dutch-bred potato is similar to the Long White. It's not great for frying.

Origin: Netherlands, 1987

Availability: Australia, Canada, Greece, Israel, Netherlands, New Zealand

Description: long oval; pale yellow skin and flesh; slightly mealy texture

Uses: boiling, baking, mashing, roasting

Norchip

This variety was developed and named by North Dakota State University in 1968. As the name suggests, it is used extensively in that region for manufacturing potato chips.

Origin: USA, 1968

Availability: Canada, USA

Description: round to oblong; smooth white skin; white flesh

Uses: baking, boiling, frying

Norland

Known for its extra-large size, this attractive red-skinned tuber from North Dakota is classified as an early to mid-season variety. While it can be used as a mashing potato, it is best to add a splash of white vinegar to the cooking water, because the Norland does discolor somewhat after cooking. A good storage potato.

Origin: USA, 1957

Availability: Canada, United Kingdom, USA

Description: medium, slightly flat oblong; medium red skin; creamy white flesh

Uses: baking, boiling, mashing, salads

Pentland Dell

While this is a reliable, tried and tested general-purpose variety, it really excels when it meets fat! If extra-long homemade chips or fries are your passion, or perfect crisp roasted potatoes, look to Pentland Dell for the job.

Origin: Scotland, 1961

Availability: New Zealand, South Africa, United Kingdom

Description: long oval; white skin and flesh

Uses: all cooking methods, especially frying and roasting

Red Rooster

Originally developed in Carlow, Ireland, this is a good all-rounder with a very distinctive red skin. Though its skin is slightly duller than that of Désirée, this is reputed to be Ireland's number-one favorite, making up 33 percent of Irish potato production in 2002.

Origin: Ireland, 1993

Availability: Ireland, United Kingdom

Description: oval; red skin; white flesh

Uses: mashing, frying, roasting, baking

Russet Lemhi

Heralded as a relatively new high-yield variety, this potato was developed by the potato-breeding program at Texas A&M University.

Origin: USA, 1981

Availability: USA

Description: large oblong; tan-brown skin; white eyes

Uses: baking, frying, most other cooking methods

Sangre

While this may look like your average red-skinned potato, this is an heirloom variety with outstanding flavor and rich, creamy texture.

Origin: USA, 1982

Availability: Canada, USA

Description: oval; smooth dark red skin; white to very pale yellow flesh

Uses: baking, boiling

Sebago

This full-flavored potato originated in 1932 in Maine. It was very popular in North America for a long time, until it began to be nudged out of the limelight by the introduction of newer varieties. It remains

the favorite potato in Australia because of its great versatility. This is a particularly excellent boiling and mashing potato.

Origin: USA, 1938

Availability: Australia, Canada, Malaysia, New Zealand, South Africa, USA

Description: round to oval; ivory white skin; white flesh

Uses: baking, boiling, frying, mashing, roasting, salads

Shannon

With a name like Shannon you would expect this pretty variety to have been bred in Ireland, and so it was. This is a very high-yield and uniformly shaped potato. Shannon is a good general-purpose, slightly waxy type, excellent for boiling. The Irish describe it as a "good eating potato" — is there any other kind?

Origin: Ireland, 1990

Availability: Ireland, United Kingdom

Description: oval; red skin; creamy flesh

Uses: boiling, most other cooking methods

Shepody

Developed in New Brunswick primarily for the french-fry industry, Shepody has the elongated shape and balanced moisture content — not too moist, not too dry — necessary to create the perfect chip. These qualities enable it to hold its shape after frying. Today it is the second most popular potato in Canada and the third most popular in the United States.

Origin: Canada, 1980

Availability: Canada, New Zealand, USA

Description: long oval; white, slightly netted skin; light creamy flesh; dry, starchy texture

Uses: frying, baking, boiling, frying, mashing

Smile

This potato has unique smile-shaped markings around the eyes and, unlike many other red-skinned varieties, retains its color after boiling. Some say the smile helps get children to eat their vegetables!

Origin: Netherlands, 1990

Availability: Europe, United Kingdom

Description: long oblong; thin bright red skin; trademark white "smile" around each eye

Uses: baking, boiling, mashing, chipping, roasting

Superior

Developed by the University of Wisconsin, the Superior is classified as an early white potato. It matures early and offers good yields. This is a very popular, reliable and versatile potato with good storage capabilities.

Origin: USA, 1962

Availability: Canada, South Korea, USA

Description: round to oblong, somewhat irregular; smooth buff skin; shallow eyes; white flesh

Uses: most cooking methods, especially baking and frying

Toolangi Delight

As this is a relatively new variety, it may be available only in its country of origin. This spud is named for the Australian Department of Agriculture's potato research station. Its purple skin easily rubs off under running water. This is a very good general-purpose variety.

Origin: Australia, 1987

Availability: Australia

Description: round; purple skin; pure white flesh

Uses: salads, boiling, mashing, baking, roasting

Yukon Gold

In North America this potato barely needs an introduction. The Yukon Gold was developed by Canadian potato breeder Garnet Johnston and quickly became the darling of restaurant chefs and home cooks alike because of its outstanding versatility and flavor — and the fact that its lovely yellow flesh looks ready-buttered. While US president Bill Clinton was in the White House, it is reputed to have been the only potato served at his table. While there are many yellow-fleshed varieties in Europe, this was the first to be successfully bred in North America.

Origin: Canada, 1980

Availability: Canada, USA

Description: large, oval to round; buff-colored skin; pink eyes; slightly mealy yellow flesh

Uses: boiling, mashing, frying, baking

Floury Potatoes

Floury potatoes contain the most starch of all the potato types. Bearing in mind that there are only two main components of a potato — water and starch — the more starch a potato has, the more floury it is. This texture lends itself perfectly to boiling, mashing, baking, gratins, frying and roasting.

AC Dubuc

Another variety developed by Agriculture Canada in Fredericton, New Brunswick, these are longer than they are round and make great baked potatoes.

Origin: Canada, 1998

Availability: Canada

Description: long, sometimes slightly curved; smooth buff skin; white flesh

Uses: boiling, frying, baking

Acadia Russet

According to the US potato industry, 65 percent of all potatoes grown for commercial production are — like this one — russets, and are often marketed as Idaho potatoes. Perfect for baking, the Acadia Russet is well adapted to the climate of the Canadian Maritimes and has been favorably compared to the Kennebec.

Origin: Canada, 1968

Availability: Canada, USA

Description: oblong, slightly flattened lengthwise; lightly netted creamy buff skin; creamy white flesh

Uses: boiling, baking

Agria

This long, oval potato is reputed to have the darkest yellow flesh of all the yellow-fleshed potatoes. Highly versatile, the Agria has excellent flavor, making it a favorite with restaurant chefs, since it doesn't discolor after cooking. A great choice for fries and chips, and particularly recommended for gnocchi because of its full flavor and good starch balance.

Origin: Germany, 1985

Availability: Canada, New Zealand, Switzerland, United Kingdom

Description: good-sized long oval; cream skin; deep yellow flesh

Uses: baking, boiling, frying, roasting

Ailsa

Origin: Scotland, 1984

Availability: United Kingdom

Description: medium round or oval; white skin; light creamy flesh; pleasant flavor

Uses: boiling, frying

Ajax

Origin: Netherlands

Availability: Netherlands, Pakistan, Vietnam

Description: oval; smooth yellow skin; firm pale yellow flesh; slightly bland flavor

Uses: boiling, frying, roasting

Alta Crown

This relatively new russet potato cultivar was developed as an alternative to the Russet Burbank.

Origin: Canada

Availability: Canada, USA

Description: Large, long oblong; russeted brown skin; shallow eyes; cream-colored flesh

Uses: boiling, baking, frying

Alta Russet

Developed in Lethbridge, Alberta, this potato is a cross between two other popular russet potatoes — Russet Nugget and Ranger Russet. It has good storage qualities.

Origin: Canada, 1987

Availability: Canada, USA

Description: oblong; russeted brown skin; shallow eyes; white flesh

Uses: frying

Arran Victory

With its vivid violet-blue skin and contrasting white flesh, this is a beautiful potato. While quite common at one time, today it is not always easy to find. Thanks to the renewed interest in heirloom varieties such as this one, it is enjoying newfound popularity.

Origin: Scotland, 1918
Availability: United Kingdom
Description: oval; deep purple skin; bright white flesh
Uses: baking, boiling, roasting, most other cooking methods

British Queen

I first enjoyed these potatoes in Ireland, where they are known simply — and not surprisingly — as Queens. This is a heritage variety, nicely dry and floury when cooked and full of deep potato flavor (cook with the skin on to retain the most flavor). Not as easy to obtain as previously; they are grown in small quantities but are on their way to becoming more popular.

Origin: Scotland, 1894
Availability: Ireland, United Kingdom
Description: kidney-shaped; smooth white skin; very white flesh
Uses: boiling, baking, roasting, salads

Centennial Russet

Centennial Russet is a medium- to late-maturing potato released by Colorado State University.

Origin: USA, 1977
Availability: USA (California, Colorado, Idaho, Oregon, Texas, Washington)
Description: oblong to oval; thick, dark, netted skin; shallow eyes; white flesh
Uses: baking, boiling, mashing

Century Russet

As any supermarket shopper will attest, the beauty of russet potatoes is that they are available year-round. The ideal potato for baking, russets such as this one make creamy mash too, and a great french fry.

Origin: USA, 1995
Availability: Canada, USA
Description: large oblong; lightly russeted tan skin; shallow to medium-shallow eyes; white flesh
Uses: boiling, baking

Coliban

Popular in Australia, this is a nice-looking potato with attractive white round to oval tubers and shallow eyes that is suitable for microwaving.

Origin: Australia, 1974
Availability: Australia, Canada
Description: round; smooth cream-colored skin; white flesh
Uses: boiling, baking, mashing, fries and chips, steaming

Cupids

Origin: Canada, 1965
Availability: Canada
Description: round to oval; white skin; shallow eyes; pale yellow flesh
Uses: boiling, frying

Dakota Pearl

As the name suggests, this potato boasts a bright white flesh. It is classified as a round white potato.

Origin: USA, 1984
Availability: Canada, USA
Description: round; smooth light yellow skin; cream-colored flesh
Uses: boiling, baking, frying

Denali

Origin: USA, 1968
Availability: Canada, USA
Description: uniform oval to oblong; smooth, tough buff-colored skin; shallow eyes; white flesh
Uses: baking, frying

Edzell Blue

A magnificently colored potato, the Edzell Blue is a vibrant violet-purple when wet and dries to a deep mauve. The flesh is bright white; while it retains its whiteness when cooked, the skin does not, turning an ordinary brown and leaving the cooking water dark green. An old variety, this potato has a mild flavor and is especially flavorful as a new (young) potato.

Origin: Scotland, 1914
Availability: Scotland
Description: round; purple-blue skin; bright white flesh
Uses: boiling, steaming, mashing

Estima

Estima potatoes could almost fit into any category with their thin pale yellow skin, light yellow flesh and versatility. Choose these when your recipe calls for a firmer cooked texture — say, for salads, soups or curries — although they can also be used for baking and mashing. This is the second most popular potato for home gardeners in the United Kingdom, and supposedly the variety that helped disprove the theory that yellow-fleshed potatoes could not be popular.

Origin: Netherlands, 1973
Availability: Algeria, Canada, northern Italy
Description: oval; light yellow skin and flesh; shallow eyes; firm, moist texture
Uses: baking, boiling, frying, roasting

Exploits

This potato was bred expressly for Newfoundland and Labrador and its relatively harsh growing conditions and climate. It was named for Newfoundland's longest river.

Origin: Canada, 1983
Availability: Canada
Description: round; smooth light yellow skin; cream-colored flesh
Uses: boiling, baking

Fabula

Another lovely yellow-fleshed potato, Fabula is giving the Yukon Gold a run for its money in terms of popularity, especially when organically grown. Home cooks maintain that Fabulas are preferable when the dish in question needs to remain moist — think stews and roasted spuds.

Origin: Netherlands, 1999
Availability: Canada, Netherlands, USA
Description: oval; smooth light yellow skin; light yellow flesh
Uses: boiling, baking, mashing

Fambo

A good friend who lives in the UK grows this variety every year, and this is what she says: "This is a big, beautiful main-crop potato, good for just about everything, but it makes the most supreme mash in the world!" Apparently Fambo potatoes rival Estima in popularity in some European countries.

Origin: Netherlands, 1986
Availability: Canada, Netherlands, United Kingdom
Description: oval to oblong; smooth to rough light yellow skin; shallow eyes; light yellow flesh
Uses: boiling, baking, frying

Fjord

Origin: Canada, 2006
Availability: Canada, USA
Description: oblong; flaky brown skin; white flesh
Uses: boiling, baking, frying

Frontier Russet

Like Russet Burbank and Russet Norkotah, Frontier Russet is a go-to potato for baking, mashing, roasting or frying.

Origin: USA, 1990
Availability: Canada, USA
Description: oblong to long cylinder with blocky ends; tan-brown skin; white flesh
Uses: baking, frying

GemStar Russet

This is a newer variety of russet.

Origin: USA, 1990
Availability: Canada, USA
Description: oblong; russeted brown skin; white flesh
Uses: baking, frying

Golden Wonder

Anyone who has spent time in the UK will be familiar with the crisp (potato chip) brand known as Golden Wonder. Well, this is the potato that gave its name to the brand. Originating in Arbroath, Scotland, this russet-skinned potato is ideal for many applications. On the potato Richter scale of waxy to floury, this one buries the needle for floury.

Origin: Scotland, 1906
Availability: United Kingdom
Description: large oval; brown skin; light yellow flesh
Uses: boiling, frying, roasting

HiLite Russet

Origin: USA, 1987
Availability: Canada, USA
Description: oblong; russeted brown skin, with reddish pink to deep purple coloration under stress conditions; shallow eyes; white flesh

Uses: baking, frying

Impact

Origin: Canada, 1990
Availability: Canada
Description: oblong to long; netted buff skin; shallow eyes; white flesh
Uses: boiling, baking

Innovator

This is a rather new russet-style variety with a difference, in that it features yellow flesh.

Origin: Netherlands, 1998
Availability: Canada, Netherlands, USA
Description: large to very large long oblong; tan skin; shallow eyes; pale yellow to yellowish white flesh
Uses: baking, mashing, frying, roasting

Jemseg

Origin: Canada, 1967
Availability: Canada
Description: large and uniform; smooth dark tan skin; shallow light buff eyes; white flesh
Uses: boiling, baking, frying

Karlena

In 1995 an Irish supermarket chain put out a call for an Irish potato that looked good, was easy to peel and tasted wonderful, and it had to be versatile. After six years and trials and tests on 60 different potato varieties — all of which were grown in County Dublin — they settled on what they considered the perfect potato: Karlena. Then they promptly decided it needed a new name, so they called it Oilean — Irish Gaelic for "island" — because, like Ireland, the potato stands on its own.

Origin: Germany, 1993

Availability: Egypt, France, Germany, Hungary, Ireland, Israel, Scandinavia, United Kingdom

Description: medium-sized round; yellow skin; golden yellow flesh

Uses: baking, frying, mashing, roasting

Keswick

This potato was developed in Fredericton, New Brunswick.

Origin: Canada, 1943

Availability: Canada, USA

Description: oblong; smooth, dark creamy buff skin; medium-deep eyes; white flesh

Uses: baking, frying, boiling

King Edward

One of my — and the world's — top floury potatoes, the King Edward has been around for a very long time; it was one of the first potatoes to be known by its name. In England and North America it became best-known variety because of its floury quality and versatility. It is derived from a breeding-stock potato called Rough Purple Chili, which was used almost exclusively after the devastation of the Irish potato famine. Developed by John Butler of Lincolnshire, the variety is thought to have been so named because its introduction coincided with the coronation of King Edward VII in 1902. Further testament to its grandness and the fact that it is virtually synonymous with *potato* is the English commercial baking oven called the King Edward — specifically designed to bake potatoes!

Origin: United Kingdom, 1902

Availability: Australia, Canada, Canary Islands, New Zealand, Portugal, Spain, United Kingdom

Description: oval to kidney-shaped; skin in gradations of white and pink; pale yellow flesh

Uses: baking, frying, mashing,

roasting, most other cooking methods

Krantz

This is another russet variety of potato.

Origin: USA, 1985

Availability: Canada, USA

Description: oblong; brown russeted skin; white flesh

Uses: baking, boiling, frying

La Rouge

A smooth, very attractive velvety red potato with deep eyes, this is a good boiling potato.

Origin: USA, 1962

Availability: Canada, USA

Description: medium-size irregular flattened round or oval; smooth red skin; deep eyes; white flesh

Uses: boiling, roasting

Latona

Origin: Netherlands, 1981

Availability: Canada, Netherlands

Description: large, uniform, round to oval; smooth to medium-rough yellow skin; shallow eyes; light yellow flesh

Uses: baking, boiling

Lili

Origin: Sweden, 1971

Availability: Canada, Sweden, United Kingdom, USA

Description: oval to oblong; flaky yellow skin; shallow eyes; yellow flesh

Uses: boiling, baking, frying

Majestic

Brought to us by Archibald Findlay, this potato was a very popular variety in the United Kingdom in the 20th century and the variety most grown in UK home gardens. Tried and true, it

consistently produces a good crop in virtually all soil types.

Origin: Scotland, 1911

Availability: Italy, United Kingdom

Description: large oval; white skin; soft white flesh; mild flavor

Uses: baking, boiling, mashing

Matilda

Origin: Sweden, 1970

Availability: Canada, New Zealand, Sweden, United Kingdom

Description: round to oval; netted yellow skin; shallow eyes; creamy yellow flesh

Uses: boiling, baking

Morning Gold

Origin: Netherlands, 1965

Availability: Canada, Netherlands, USA

Description: oval; smooth yellow skin; shallow eyes; light yellow flesh

Uses: boiling, baking

Mouraska

Origin: Canada, 1965

Availability: Canada, USA

Description: round to oval; smooth buff skin; shallow to medium-deep eyes; white flesh

Uses: baking, frying

Nooksack

A North American West Coast potato, the Nooksack has many fans, especially among the grow-your-own set. It was developed to do well in the heavier clay soils of western Washington State. It has delicious, almost butter-flavored flesh and is great for baking.

Origin: USA, 1973

Availability: Canada, New Zealand, USA

Description: slightly flat oblong; heavily russeted skin; very white flesh

Uses: baking, boiling, frying

Onaway

This reliable old-time favorite is a round white potato with tender skin and moist flesh. It's great for gratins.
Origin: USA, 1956
Availability: Canada, USA
Description: short and round; smooth creamy white skin and flesh
Uses: baking, boiling

Ranger Russet

This is a genetically modified potato bred to resist some of the problems that beset other russet varieties. According to the researchers, this potato has an "enhanced french-fry" aroma.
Origin: United States, 1991
Availability: Canada, United States
Description: long and slightly flattened; brown skin; white flesh
Uses: baking, frying

Red La Soda

Described as an improved Pontiac, this variety matures a little later in the season and makes a terrific baked potato. However, it does not store well.
Origin: USA, 1953
Availability: Algeria, Australia, Canada, Uruguay, USA, Venezuela
Description: round to oval; smooth deep red skin; quite deep eyes; creamy white flesh
Uses: baking, boiling, roasting

Red Pontiac

Also called Dakota Chief, this red-skinned early main-crop potato was originally bred in the United States. It is suitable for microwaving.
Origin: USA, 1983
Availability: Algeria, Australia, Canada, Philippines, Uruguay, USA, Venezuela
Description: round to oval; dark red skin; deep eyes; waxy white flesh

Uses: baking, boiling, mashing, roasting, salads

Red Rascal

A relatively new variety, this full-flavored potato (with a great moniker) features dark red skin and is quite versatile. It is especially good when simply boiled or steamed and tossed with a homemade mayonnaise or a bit of sour cream, some good mustard and chopped chives.
Origin: New Zealand, 1993
Availability: Canada, New Zealand, USA
Description: round to flat; red skin; white flesh
Uses: baking, roasting, frying, mashing

Red Ruby

Origin: USA, 1994
Availability: Canada, USA
Description: oblong; dark red skin with russet patches; bright white flesh
Uses: baking, boiling

Romano

This main-crop potato falls right in the middle of the chart in terms of starch content, which makes it a good candidate for a number of uses. Cooked with its skin on, the color changes from a solid red hue to an attractive shade of rust.
Origin: Netherlands, 1978
Availability: Balearic Islands, Cameroon, Hungary, Netherlands, Portugal, Spain, United Kingdom
Description: round; red skin; cream-colored flesh
Uses: boiling, mashing, roasting, baking

Russet Burbank (Idaho)

This is the original "Idaho" potato, reputed to have made that state

renowned for potato growing. It is ubiquitous throughout North America and invariably finds itself at home beside a hefty steak or as a burger's best companion — french fries. It is the most commonly grown potato in Canada's premier potato-growing regions, Prince Edward Island and New Brunswick.
Origin: USA, 1875
Availability: Australia, Canada, New Zealand, United Kingdom, USA
Description: oval to long; brownish skin; pale yellow to white flesh
Uses: baking, frying, mashing, roasting

Russet Frontier

Origin: USA, 1990
Availability: Canada, USA
Description: long oval; light, slightly russeted skin; creamy white flesh
Uses: baking, boiling, frying

Russet Norking

Origin: USA, 1977
Availability: Canada, USA
Description: oblong; medium-heavy russet skin; creamy white flesh
Uses: baking, boiling, frying

Russet Norkotah

This variety was developed in North Dakota, hence its name.
Origin: USA, 1987
Availability: Canada, USA
Description: long oval; darkly russeted skin; white flesh
Uses: baking, frying

Russet Nugget

Here's another russet variety, this one bred in Colorado.
Origin: USA, 1989
Availability: Canada, USA

Description: slightly flat oblong; evenly russeted skin; creamy white flesh

Uses: baking, boiling, frying, roasting

Samba

A French cultivar, this potato is described as having a "good culinary quality." Certainly, at least one restaurant in France thinks so. At L'Amour de pomme de terre in Brest, the westernmost part of Brittany, all the main-course dishes are based on the Samba potato.

Origin: France, 1989

Availability: France, Portugal, Spain

Description: regular oval; white skin; yellow flesh

Uses: baking, boiling, mashing

Santé

Often sold young, as new potatoes, the Santé has the distinction of being the most successful organic potato, due in part to its high yield and resistance to specific diseases.

Origin: Netherlands, 1983

Availability: Bulgaria, Canada, Netherlands, United Kingdom

Description: oval or round; white or light yellow skin and flesh; dry, firm texture

Uses: baking, boiling, frying, roasting

White Rose

The flesh of the White Rose has a medium starch level that is firm and creamy when cooked. Grown primarily in the U.S., White Rose potatoes are also known as California Long White, American Giant and Wisconsin Pride.

Origin: USA, 1893

Availability: Canada, USA

Description: large, very long and flat; smooth white skin; deep eyes; bright white flesh

Uses: baking, boiling, frying, very well suited for mashing

Waxy Potatoes

The term waxy *really doesn't do justice to the delicious, velvety quality of the flesh of these potatoes. Waxy potatoes are the go-to potatoes for the world's best potato salads. They are equally good in rich, creamy gratins or for simple boiling, steaming or sautéing.*

Abeille

A full-flavored potato, Abeille (its name means "honeybee") was bred and released by the Quebec Ministry of Agriculture, Fisheries and Food. Excellent for boiling and baking, it is the product of a cross between Saginaw Gold and a breeding potato called Tata.

Origin: Canada, 2002

Availability: Canada, USA

Description: round; yellow skin and flesh; shallow eyes

Uses: boiling, baking

AC Belmont

Origin: Canada, 1967

Availability: Canada

Description: round to oval; smooth white skin; shallow eyes; white flesh

Uses: boiling, baking

AC Brador

A late-maturing yellow-fleshed potato, this variety is ideal for simple boiling or steaming.

Origin: Canada, 1966

Availability: Canada, USA

Description: oblong; smooth yellow skin; shallow eyes; light yellow flesh

Uses: boiling, baking, frying

AC Domino

This interesting variety is high yielding. Developed in Canada, it is reputed to be well adapted to

the unique growing conditions in Newfoundland. It stores well.

Origin: Canada, 1977

Availability: Canada, USA

Description: round; smooth blue-purple skin; medium to deep eyes; white flesh

Uses: boiling

Accent

This is pretty much a five-star-rated potato. Even though this variety is reputed to be best enjoyed when just boiled, it makes excellent fries and chips. Some home gardeners say they actually prefer it over the very highly rated Jersey Royal.

Origin: Netherlands, 1994

Availability: Canada, Netherlands, United Kingdom

Description: medium-size oval or round; smooth light yellow skin; waxy pale yellow flesh that holds its shape; mild taste

Uses: boiling, baking

Agata

Like other waxy potatoes, the Agata is an early-season potato, usually harvested during the months of June or July. This medium-sized potato is quite moist after cooking. While it may be available later in the year, the later-season varieties are noticeably starchier and, therefore, may be used for mashing.

Origin: Netherlands, 1976

Availability: Netherlands, Switzerland, United Kingdom

Description: oval to oblong; smooth light yellow skin; shallow eyes; yellow flesh

Uses: baking, boiling, salads

Alcmaria

With its slightly sweet flesh and satiny texture, this is a favored potato for boiling, sautéing or steaming.

Origin: Netherlands, 1970

Availability: United Kingdom

Description: long oval; yellow skin; shallow eyes; firm flesh

Uses: baking, boiling, most other cooking methods

Alex

A classic new potato with all the attributes of that variety, the Alex originated in Denmark. Its colorful skin ranges from pale yellow-beige to light brown with splashes of red. Its distinctive elongated shape is reminiscent of other salad potatoes such as French fingerlings. This one will not fall apart after cooking, making it perfect for salads and roasting.

Origin: Denmark, 1995

Availability: Europe, United Kingdom

Description: long, thick finger; pale yellow skin with bluish red hue; creamy flesh

Uses: salads, roasting

Ampera

A second early variety, this potato has a firm texture.

Origin: Germany, 1989

Availability: Canada, Germany, United Kingdom, USA

Description: round; smooth yellow skin; shallow eyes; medium to dark yellow flesh

Uses: boiling, frying, salads

Aquilon

Home gardeners may be interested to learn that this variety is currently under study to discover its potential resistance to the dreaded golden nematode.

Origin: Canada, 1986

Availability: Canada, USA

Description: oval; smooth white skin; white flesh

Uses: boiling, frying

Arran Banner

This medium-size potato was originally bred by Donald McKelvie and first marketed around 1927. Arran Banner produces a moderate yield of round, white-skinned tubers with white flesh.

Origin: Scotland, 1927

Availability: Cyprus, New Zealand, Portugal, United Kingdom

Description: round; white skin; quite deep eyes; firm, creamy flesh

Uses: boiling

Arran Comet

This variety is an excellent early-season new potato.

Origin: Scotland, 1957

Availability: United Kingdom

Description: round to oval; white skin; creamy flesh

Uses: boiling, frying

Belle de Fontenay

One of my favorites, this potato has an excellent buttery flavor that improves with storage. In French cuisine it is widely used in salads. It may be enjoyed with or without the skin, in hot, warm or even chilled preparations.

Origin: France, 1885

Availability: Australia, France

Description: long and slightly bent; pale yellow skin; firm, yellow flesh

Uses: boiling, mashing, salads

BF15

A descendant of Belle de Fontenay that is larger than its parent, this is an excellent salad potato.

Origin: France, 1947

Availability: France

Description: long and slightly curved; smooth yellow skin

Uses: boiling, salads

CalWhite

CalWhite is a mid- to late-season maturing potato. This very high-yielding variety grows well in hot climates. Absolutely the best white baking potato, it also produces great french fries.

Origin: USA, 1997

Availability: Canada, USA (California, Idaho)

Description: oblong; smooth buff-white skin; white flesh

Uses: baking, frying

Carlton

A variety that matures early, Carltons are excellent boiled whole in their skins. They are also good for baking.

Origin: Canada, 1982

Availability: Canada, USA

Description: oval; buff skin; shallow eyes; creamy white flesh

Uses: boiling, baking

Charlotte

Charlotte is most definitely a specialty salad potato but it has the distinction of being about 50 percent larger than most other salad potatoes. While it is wonderful in this capacity, it can also be sautéed or roasted in its skin, which makes for a lovely firm roasted potato. It boasts a full-bodied flavor that tastes almost buttery and sweet.

Origin: France, 1981

Availability: France, Germany, Italy, Switzerland

Description: long pear shape or oval; pale yellow skin; firm, yellow flesh; mild chestnut flavor

Uses: baking, boiling, salads

Cherokee

Bred in Maine, Cherokee potatoes are a high-yielding, adaptable variety. They will even grow in mineral and "muck" soils.

Origin: USA, 1940

Availability: Canada, USA

Description: round; slightly flaky ivory-yellow skin; shallow eyes; white flesh

Uses: boiling, baking, frying

Cherry Red

Cherry Red is a medium-early maturing potato. It is great for salads, hash browns, soups and stews.

Origin: USA, 1999

Availability: Canada, USA

Description: oval; smooth red skin; shallow eyes; white flesh

Uses: baking, boiling

Cleopatra

Origin: Netherlands, 1980

Availability: Algeria, Hungary

Description: oval; pink and red blemished skin; dense pale yellow flesh

Uses: boiling

Coastal Russet

A progeny of Russet Burbank, Coastal Russet is a mid-season russet-skinned potato.

Origin: USA, 1994

Availability: Canada, USA

Description: oblong to long; medium russeted tan skin; shallow eyes; white flesh

Uses: boiling, baking

Conestoga

There's a good chance this early, white-skinned potato was named for the Conestoga River in central Ontario, Canada. It has great table manners — it's good for boiling, baking and making fries and chips.

Origin: Canada, 1971

Availability: Canada

Description: blocky and slightly flattened; very slightly flaked white skin; shallow eyes, usually same color as the skin; white flesh

Uses: boiling, baking, frying

Diamant

An early main-crop potato, Diamant has a distinctive nutty flavor, with what wine tasters describe as a long finish.

Origin: Netherlands, 1982

Availability: Cameroon, Canada, Egypt, New Zealand, Pakistan

Description: long oval; rough white skin; firm, light yellow flesh; sharp, nutty aftertaste

Uses: baking, boiling, salads

Ditta

A progeny of Bintje, Ditta's claim to fame is its super-buttery flavor and texture.

Origin: Austria, 1950

Availability: Austria, Netherlands, United Kingdom

Description: long oval; rough brownish skin; firm, pale yellow flesh; buttery, almost melt-in-the-mouth flavor

Uses: boiling, roasting, sautéing, salads

Divina

Home gardeners love this high-yielding variety that boasts good storage potential. Good choice for simple boiling or steaming in preparation for salads.

Origin: Netherlands, 1983

Availability: Canada, Netherlands, New Zealand

Description: oval; smooth creamy yellow skin; shallow to medium-deep eyes; cream-yellow flesh

Uses: boiling, baking

Draga

Another popular choice for home gardeners, this potato is best enjoyed while young.

Origin: Netherlands, 1970

Availability: Iran, New Zealand

Description: round; pale yellow skin; creamy yellow flesh; full-flavored

Uses: boiling, mashing, salads, casseroles, soups

Duke of York Red

This variety is one of the parents of the Smile potato and is considered to be a heritage first early potato. It was first discovered in a Dutch crop of Duke of York potatoes and is a particularly vigorous cultivar, with spectacular foliage and bright red skin. It has great flavor and is the perfect choice for roasting, especially for Hasselback potatoes (page 61), which will be vibrantly colored if you prepare them unpeeled.

Origin: Netherlands, 1842

Availability: Netherlands, United Kingdom

Description: large, long oval; very red skin (loses color when cooked); tasty light yellow flesh

Uses: boiling, salads

Dundrod

I had some of the best mashed potatoes ever in a little pub in Donaghadee, Northern Ireland. When I enquired as to why they were so good, I was told the variety name — Dundrod — and never forgot it. Northern Ireland has a long history of successful potato breeding. John Clarke, OBE, bred varieties such as Dundrod and Dunluce as well as the famous Ulster varieties, Ulster Sceptre and Ulster Prince.

Origin: Northern Ireland, 1987

Availability: Canada, Netherlands, Northern Ireland, Sweden, United Kingdom

Description: oval to round; light yellow skin; creamy white flesh

Uses: boiling, frying, mashing

Elvira

Origin: Germany, 1974

Availability: Canada, Italy, Morocco, Netherlands, USA

Description: medium-sized oval; yellow skin; shallow eyes; creamy yellow flesh

Uses: boiling, frying

Envol

A good boiling potato with excellent culinary qualities.

Origin: Canada, 1983

Availability: Canada

Description: round to oval; smooth white skin; white flesh

Uses: boiling, salads

Eva

This attractive tuber was developed at Cornell University and named for the mother of the potato breeder who developed it. It is reputed to be a versatile variety with good flavor.

Origin: USA, 1986

Availability: Canada, USA

Description: round to slightly oval; smooth bright white skin; shallow eyes; white flesh

Uses: boiling, baking, frying

Franceline

Comparable to another French variety, Roseval, this is a good, reliable variety of waxy potato.

Origin: France, 1993

Availability: France, Germany, United Kingdom

Description: red skin; soft, white or cream flesh

Uses: boiling, salads, steaming, gratins

Frisia

A nice moist-fleshed potato that holds its shape well.

Origin: Netherlands

Availability: Bulgaria, Canada, Europe, New Zealand

Description: oval; creamy yellow skin; moist, slightly waxy white flesh

Uses: baking, boiling, roasting, salads

Fundy

A smooth potato developed in the National Potato Breeding Program of Canada. It is a progeny of a floury potato, Keswick.

Origin: Canada, 1950

Availability: Canada

Description: medium-sized round; smooth buff skin; white flesh

Uses: boiling, baking

Gigant

A terrific choice for baking.

Origin: Netherlands

Availability: Canada, Netherlands, New Zealand, United Kingdom, USA

Description: large, round or oval; light yellow skin and flesh

Uses: baking, boiling

Glenwood Red

This variety is well adapted to the growing conditions in Newfoundland, for which it was selected.

Origin: Canada, 1991

Availability: Canada, USA

Description: round; smooth light red to red skin; shallow eyes; white to cream-colored flesh

Uses: baking, boiling

Hunter

This is a white-skinned, white-fleshed potato released by New Brunswick in the early 1950s. It is derived from a wild Mexican species and Katahdin, crossed with Irish Cobbler.

Origin: Canada, 1952

Availability: Canada

Description: round; smooth, dark creamy buff skin; shallow eyes; white flesh

Uses: boiling, baking

International Kidney

This is the variety commonly known and marketed as Jersey Royals (see below) when not grown on Jersey. It has a delicious buttery flavor and is a little smaller than the famous Jersey Royal.

Origin: England, 1879

Availability: Australia, Canada, Europe, United Kingdom, USA

Description: long oval; smooth white/yellow skin; creamy white flesh

Uses: boiling, salads

Jersey Royal

Around 1879, a Jersey farmer named Hugh de la Haye discovered a potato that he initially named Jersey Royal

Fluke. It developed into today's renowned Jersey Royal. Grown by just 55 island farmers, it accounts for two-thirds of the tiny island's agricultural output and is the only U.K. vegetable with an E.U. designation of origin. Like the Yukon Gold potato, its name is trademarked. Only Jersey Royals that have been bred on Jersey, in the Channel Islands, can be given this moniker. Grown in the very special soil of Jersey, rich in nutrients owing to *vraic*, a local seaweed, they have a distinctive flavor and textural quality. Much of the Jersey Royal crop is grown in steep fields and must be harvested by hand. Ninety-nine percent of the crop is exported to the United Kingdom. The rest is enjoyed — albeit briefly, because of the short-lived season — by the inhabitants of Jersey. Lucky them. (The British potato season begins in April with waxy Jersey Royals, which continue into June.)

Origin: Jersey (Channel Islands) 1879

Availability: Jersey, United Kingdom

Description: long oval smooth white/yellow skin, creamy white flesh

Uses: boiling, salads

Katahdin

An old standard variety, this is a high-yielding potato cultivar adaptable to many growing conditions. It has excellent storage capabilities and, after Green Mountain, is one of the best-known Maine potato varieties. It makes lovely moist baked potatoes and is terrific in soups.

Origin: USA, 1932

Availability: Canada, New Zealand, USA

Description: round to oblong; smooth buff skin; white flesh

Uses: baking, boiling, salads, soups

Kipfler

Kipfler (a.k.a. the German Finger Potato) is a waxy potato with a thick, elongated finger shape and attractive creamy-colored flesh. It is great boiled, steamed and in potato salads and makes a very pretty plate presentation.

Origin: Germany, 1955

Availability: Australia, Austria, Germany

Description: small to medium elongated; yellow flesh and skin

Uses: baking, boiling, roasting, salads

Lady Christl

Lady Christl was judged to have the best taste out of a number of Dutch potato varieties tested by a panel including a master chef and representatives from the industry in Holland. It was also given an Award of Garden Merit (AGM) by Britain's Royal Horticultural Society.

Origin: Netherlands, 1985

Availability: Canada, Netherlands, USA

Description: oblong; smooth pale yellow skin; light yellow flesh

Uses: boiling, salads

Marfona

Marfona has a distinctive buttery flavor and a smooth, waxy texture, making it a very popular variety for baking in a conventional oven or microwave.

Origin: Netherlands, 1975

Availability: Cyprus, Greece, Israel, Netherlands, Portugal, Turkey, United Kingdom

Description: large oval; light beige to yellow skin and flesh

Uses: baking, boiling, frying

Maris Baird

An early potato, Maris Bard is described as having a traditionally new potato taste, earthy and flavorful. It is a good reliable potato with great culinary characteristics. Its resistance to garden pests makes it a favorite with home gardeners.

Origin: England, 1972

Availability: Canada, United Kingdom

Description: slightly irregular round to oval; smooth light skin; white to cream flesh

Uses: boiling

Maris Peer

Maris Peer is described as a salad potato because of its small, uniform, egg shape and waxy, firm flesh. It can be peeled effortlessly after boiling. Its cooked aroma has notes of sweet butter. A simply delightful potato.

Origin: United Kingdom, 1962

Availability: United Kingdom

Description: round to oval; cream skin and flesh; shallow to medium eyes

Uses: boiling, frying, salads

Minerva

This early variety grows quite large.

Origin: Netherlands, 1988

Availability: Netherlands

Description: oval; white skin; creamy yellow flesh

Uses: boiling, frying

NorDonna

Another potato variety developed in North Dakota. Ancestors for this potato cultivar include Norchief and Chieftain. It is a full-flavored potato with good storage capabilities.

Origin: USA, 1995

Availability: Canada, USA

Description: oval to round; dark red skin; white flesh

Uses: baking, boiling, roasting, salads, soups, microwaving

Pink Fir Apple

A lovely long, knobby, sort of cigar-shaped spud with wonderful flavor. While they originated in France in 1850, apparently they were kept almost exclusively by British potato lovers for many years. Because of their good storage ability they have always been a favorite with home gardeners. They may be the classic waxy potato with an unbeatable nutty flavor.

Origin: France, 1850

Availability: Australia, France, United Kingdom

Description: long, narrow, knobbly shape; often with side growths; pink/white skin; yellow flesh

Uses: Boiling, baking, microwaving, the perfect salad potato

Premiere

Some waxy or new potatoes are great for frying — like this one. As it is an early potato, its flesh is dry, with less starch built up, hence it's a paler color when fried.

Origin: Netherlands, 1979

Availability: Bulgaria, Canada, Netherlands, United Kingdom

Description: large, round to oval; light yellow skin; firm yellow flesh

Uses: baking, boiling, frying, roasting

Red Delcora

This potato is very popular in New Zealand. It isn't the waxiest of waxy potatoes, making it a good candidate for crushed potatoes.

Origin: Netherlands, 1988

Availability: Netherlands, New Zealand

Description: long oval; pink/red skin; light yellow flesh

Uses: boiling, frying, mashing

Red Pontiac

Also known as Dakota Chief, this potato has a very good yield for the home gardener and is a good choice for storage.

Origin: United States, 1983

Availability: Algeria, Australia, Canada, Philippines, Uruguay, USA, Venezuela

Description: thin, bright red skin; full-flavored white flesh

Uses: baking, boiling, roasting, microwaving; good for salads but not for frying

Viking

Viking potatoes have an almost meaty, moist flesh and a slightly sweet, buttery flavor. Maturing in mid-season, they have good storage qualities and make an excellent baked potato.

Origin: USA, 1963

Availability: Canada, USA

Description: large, oblong to round; smooth pale red skin; very white flesh

Uses: boiling, roasting, salads

Specialty Potatoes

Years ago, in a four-star restaurant, sliced purple potatoes were served to me with my main course and I thought, How odd, but interesting. *Although I'm a classic potatophile, my tuber experience up to then had been relegated to lovely white and beautiful gold-fleshed potatoes. These days colorful potatoes ranging from red to blue to violet-purple often take center stage. Oddly shaped potatoes are also becoming common. Although vividly colored potatoes may seem strange to us, the purple-fleshed potatoes native to the Andes were held in very high regard by the ancient Incas, who used their pigmented flesh as a dye source and in religious ceremonies.*

Most of the potatoes we categorize as "specialty" can be categorized as low or medium-starch. This makes them most suitable for boiling, steaming or roasting. Some, such as Roseval and Adirondack Red, are good for salads and others, such as Adirondack Blue, mash well. Interestingly, purple/blue potatoes take a little less time to cook than traditional white and yellow potatoes.

AC Blue Pride

Developed by Newfoundlander Kenneth Proudfoot (a native of Belfast, Northern Ireland, and a member of the Atlantic Agricultural Hall of Fame), AC Blue Pride is heralded by growers as a wart-resistant variety that stores well. It is a great boiling potato.

Origin: Canada, 1994

Availability: Canada

Description: oval to long; smooth blue-purple skin; shallow eyes; white flesh

Uses: boiling

AC Domino

Another variety from Mr. Proudfoot of Newfoundland, AC Domino is very similar to AC Blue Pride, with a rounder shape.

Origin: Canada, 1977

Availability: Canada

Description: round; smooth blue-purple skin; medium-deep eyes; white flesh

Uses: boiling

Adirondack Blue

Unlike many colored potatoes, the Adirondack Blue retains its lovely color — a deep-purplish blue with the odd thread of white — after cooking. Like the Adirondack Red this is a comparatively new hybrid, developed by Cornell University potato breeder Walter De Jong, to be specifically appealing to food lovers. Researchers at Cornell are working with students at the Culinary Institute of America and chefs to develop similar varieties, in the future.

Origin: USA, 2003
Availability: Canada, USA
Description: large, slightly flattened, round to oblong; purple skin and flesh
Uses: baking, boiling, steaming, mashing, salads

Adirondack Red

See Adirondack Blue, above.
Origin: USA, 2004
Availability: Canada, USA
Description: Oblong to long, slightly flattened; purplish red skin; shallow eyes; pink to red flesh
Uses: boiling, mashing, pan-frying, salads

Anya

Developed from a cross between the revered Désirée and Pink Fir Apple, this popular potato was bred at the Scottish Crop Research Institute. It is grown exclusively for the UK supermarket chain, Sainsbury's, by breeder Albert Bartlett, and was in fact named for Lady Sainsbury. This fingerling-type potato is great hot or cold and is a favorite of British food maven Delia Smith.

Origin: Scotland, 1996
Availability: United Kingdom
Description: long, knobbly oval; pale pink-beige skin; waxy white flesh; pleasant nutty flavor
Uses: boiling, salads

Baby Boomer

Origin: Netherlands, 1982
Availability: Canada, Netherlands, USA
Description: oval; flaky buff skin; moderately deep eyes; yellow flesh
Uses: boiling, baking

Banana

Also known as the Russian Banana potato, this is a favorite with chefs and is renowned for its use in salads. This is probably the most popular yellow-fleshed fingerling-type potato.

Origin: Baltic region
Availability: Canada, USA
Description: banana shape; smooth light yellow skin; shallow eyes; uniform pale yellow flesh
Uses: boiling, baking, frying, salads

Blue Lady

Origin: Netherlands, 1994
Availability: Canada, Netherlands, United Kingdom, USA
Description: round to oval; smooth blue skin; shallow eyes; yellow flesh
Uses: baking, boiling

Blue Mac

Blue Mac is a small purple-skinned, white-fleshed potato. These tubers are resistant to potato wart.
Origin: Canada, 1969
Availability: Canada
Description: round, with stem end slightly flattened; blue-purple skin; white flesh
Uses: boiling, baking

Brigus

A good boiling potato with good storage qualities.
Origin: Canada, 1971
Availability: Canada
Description: round to oval; smooth purple skin; shallow eyes; cream to very pale yellow flesh
Uses: boiling, frying

Candyfloss

Developed by Alberta, Canada, farmer Will Bilozir, Candy Floss has a firm, buttery texture and beautifully colored flesh that becomes brilliant pink when cooked.

Origin: Canada, 1998
Availability: Canada, USA
Description: Medium-size; red skin; red flesh
Uses: Boiling, salads, sautéeing

Congo

This deeply colored purple potato with deep purple flesh retains almost all its color after cooking. The color seems to be its main claim to fame, as its flavor is not nearly as unique or exciting.

Origin: Democratic Republic of the Congo
Availability: Australia, United Kingdom
Description: small, thin and knobbly; shiny, very dark purple-black skin; dark purple flesh; mild flavor
Uses: boiling, mashing, salads

Fortyfold

This is reputed to be from the oldest known potato cultivar. It has a strong, nutty flavor.
Origin: United Kingdom, 1836
Availability: United Kingdom
Description: irregular smallish, round tubers; white or purple skin; deep eyes; creamy white flesh
Uses: all cooking methods, especially baking, boiling, roasting.

French Fingerling

The story of how the French Fingerling potato made its way to North America may be the most folkloric yet. It seems an American visited a farm in France to buy a racehorse. While there he enjoyed a meal where delicious fingerlings were served. He fell in love with the potato but was not allowed to bring any home because of importation laws. He did, however, buy the horse. When the racehorse arrived at his farm, he discovered a single French fingerling tuber in the bottom of the horse's feedbag (the common name for this spud is Nosebag). Inadvertent though its arrival may have been, this introduced the potato to North America.

A relatively late-maturing variety, this is an extremely popular specialty potato that grows well for home gardeners. It has the waxy texture characteristic of most fingerling varieties.

Origin: France

Availability: Australia, Canada, Europe, New Zealand, United Kingdom, USA

Description: curved long finger shape; red skin; ivory-yellow flesh, streaked with red

Uses: roasting, grilling, soups, salads, boiling, steaming, gratins

La Ratte

Also known as Asparges, this is a classic waxy salad potato and a favorite in France. Make sure to cook it whole to enjoy its full flavor.

Origin: France, 1872

Availability: Canada, Europe, United Kingdom, USA

Description: finger shape; yellow skin; deep yellow flesh; nutty flavor

Uses: salads, boiling, steaming

McIntyre

This potato has been grown in Canada's Prince Edward Island for over a century. In the early 1900's it represented 70 percent of all the potatoes grown on the island. It was introduced to offset the losses to other varieties caused by "late blight." Once other white-fleshed potatoes were developed that had the same resistance, its popularity fell off.

Origin: unknown

Availability: Canada, USA

Description: slightly flattened oblong; slightly russeted creamy white skin with purple shading; light cream-colored flesh

Uses: boiling, baking

Michigan Blue

This potato loses some of its deep color after boiling, but the cooked potato will still have a blueish hue.

Origin: USA

Availability: Canada, USA

Description: round; iridescent purple skin; blue-white flesh

Uses: boiling, baking, mashing

Purple Majesty

Recently developed in Colorado from a traditional purple potato. Makes lovely pale mauve mash!

Origin: USA

Availability: Canada, United Kingdom, USA

Description: oval dark purple skin and flesh

Uses: boiling, salads, french fries or chips

Purple Peruvian

The petite purple fingerling potato, also known as Purple Peruvian Fingerling, is an heirloom variety that is most often found in farmers' markets. It is richly flavorful.

Origin: Andes, Peru (at least 3,000 years ago)

Availability: Australia, Canada, South America, USA

Description: short, roughly tubular, with rounded ends; deep violet skin and flesh; creamy, waxy flesh

Optional Uses: salads, grilling, sautéing

Roseval

A favored potato in France, this is a very attractive classic deep red fingerling with yellow flesh often marked with a pink blush. Cooking quality and flavor are excellent. It has striking foliage with ruby-red stems.

Origin: France, 1950

Availability: Australia, Canada, France, Israel, New Zealand, United Kingdom

Description: long oval; dark red, almost purple skin; waxy golden yellow flesh, tinged with pink

Uses: boiling, salads

True Blue

Developed by Alberta farmer Will Bilozir, True Blue keeps its vibrant color when baked, boiled, mashed or microwaved. This potato is a favorite in California and is produced in large quantities in Ohio for the potato chip market. It keeps well and tolerates colder storage temperatures.

Origin: Canada, 1996

Availability: Canada, USA

Description: oblong; smooth dark purple skin; shallow eyes; blue-purple flesh with some white and pink

Uses: boiling, baking

Top Twenty Classics
Mashed, Roasted, Baked, Scalloped and More

There are fancy potato dishes that leave a lasting impression and then there are those everyday dishes that touch the comfort nerve in us all. As with any classic food preparation there are a few hard and fast rules to achieving perfect simplicity, and never more so than where potatoes are concerned. This section is dedicated to the straight spuds — simple potato preparations that have stood the test of time. Here you will find the definitive recipes to guide you in the art of potato mashing, roasting, baking and frying, with wonderful variations on each theme. From the simple to the sublime, the classics have never tasted better.

Classic Mash Deluxe

There are those who maintain that you can make mashed potatoes with waxy potatoes. I think that is heresy, and the surest way to end up with gluey, lumpy mash, which in this cook's opinion is nothing to be proud of. I should also point out that while many cooks swear by potato ricers, food mills, hand-held blenders and the like, I have never used anything but my old standard potato masher and a couple of steps learned at my mum's elbow, which are included in the method.

Makes 4 to 6 servings

2 lbs	floury potatoes, peeled and quartered (see Tips, left)	1 kg
1 tsp	salt	5 mL
½ tsp	freshly ground white pepper	2 mL
¼ cup	butter, softened	60 mL
¼ cup	heavy or whipping (35%) cream	60 mL
½ cup	whole milk (approx.)	125 mL

Tips

This recipe makes about 5 cups (1.25 L) of mash.

If you don't have a scale in your kitchen and are wondering just how much your potatoes weigh, a large one will usually come to about 8 oz (250 g). Weigh scales are almost always available at farmers' markets and in the produce departments of supermarkets, so the next time you see one, weigh a few potatoes of different sizes — small, medium and large — to get an idea of how much each weighs. In general terms, 1 pound (500 g) of potatoes is equal to two large, three medium or four small potatoes.

If you're wondering about floury potatoes, the most widely available are russets, which are oval-shaped and brown-skinned. They are also known as baking potatoes.

For more about potato varieties, see A World of Potatoes (pages 25 to 48).

1. Place potatoes in a large saucepan and add cold water to barely cover (if you use too much water you will end up with watery mash). Add salt (see Tips, right), cover loosely and bring to a boil over high heat. Reduce heat and cook for 20 minutes or until potatoes are tender all the way through when prodded with the tip of a paring knife. Drain (see Tips, right), leaving potatoes in the saucepan. Return to very low heat and shake the pot back and forth to remove any trace of moisture. (This is an important step: the drier the cooked potato, the lighter and fluffier your mash will be.)

2. With saucepan still over very low heat, add freshly ground pepper and butter; using a potato masher, mash in thoroughly. Gradually mash in cream and milk (you might not use all the milk; just add until you reach the desired consistency). Bang masher against side of saucepan so that any sticking mixture falls into the pot. Tilt saucepan slightly and, using a flat whisk, wooden spoon or large fork, briskly stir the mixture to incorporate air into the mash, until it is smooth, creamy and fluffy. (You may decide that it needs a little more butter, cream or milk; if so, stir it in now.) Serve immediately (see Tips, right.)

Variation

Sprinkle your mash with finely chopped parsley or chives.

Tips

After adding the salt, taste the water: it should have a slightly salty taste. If not, add a little more. Potatoes are nothing without the right amount of salt, and adding it after they have been cooked just doesn't do the trick.

If you are not serving your mashed potatoes immediately, cover the surface with a clean tea towel or napkin and replace the saucepan lid. The towel will absorb any moisture and keep the mash hot.

Reserve the potato cooking water to make soups or terrific gravy.

Variations

Lower-Fat Mash Deluxe: You can easily cut back on the fat content of this recipe by omitting all but a little butter and using buttermilk in place of the cream or whole milk. You could also choose to use Yukon Golds if you opt for the reduced-fat method; although they are an all-purpose potato, they have a buttery quality and make a great mash (as does, by the way, any good, fresh floury potato).

Classic Mash Deluxe for the Lactose Intolerant: If you have problems with lactose, although your potatoes won't be as creamy, substitute lactose-free milk or a non-dairy alternative for the milk and cream and, if necessary, margarine for the butter. Bear in mind that butter contains very little lactose and is not usually a problem for people who are lactose intolerant.

More about Mash

Some home cooks swear by potato ricers, those two-handled devices that look much like a gigantic garlic press and, in fact, work in the same way. By forcing cooked potato through tiny holes you end up with the beginning of perfectly lump-free mashed potatoes. If you're using a ricer to make this mash, complete Step 1, put the potatoes through the ricer, return them to the saucepan, then complete Step 2.

Another kitchen tool that many serious chefs use is the drum sieve, or tamis, a round, wooden-edged, very fine mesh sieve that allows you to force solids — such as mashed potatoes — through the screen with a rubber pastry scraper. The idea is that you take cooked potatoes that have already been hand-mashed and had the milk and butter added and then refine them further by forcing them through the screen, to emerge even finer than before. Oh yeah, and then you add a little more butter and milk. It may sound like a lot of bother, especially since you have already mashed the potatoes, but don't knock it until you've tried it —superbe *purée de pommes de terre*!

If you're making a recipe that calls for mashed potatoes, you can adjust the quantities in this recipe to suit your needs. You'll need about 2 tbsp (30 mL) each butter and cream and $\frac{1}{4}$ cup (60 mL) milk per pound (500 g) of potatoes. In general terms, count on 1 lb (500 g) of potatoes to produce about $2\frac{1}{2}$ cups (625 mL) mash.

Garlic & Chive Mash

You have three easy choices here for adding the unmistakable flavor of garlic to your mashed potatoes. You can add blanched or roasted garlic to the finished mash (see Variations, below), but easiest of all — and the method employed here — is to peel the garlic cloves and add them to the potatoes the minute they have come to a boil, cooking them along with the potatoes.

Makes 4 to 6 servings

Tips

There are roughly two potatoes in 1 pound (500 g), depending on their size. Russets are the most common floury potatoes.

After adding the salt, taste the water. It should have a slightly salty taste. If not, add a little more. Potatoes are nothing without the right amount of salt, and adding it after they have been cooked just doesn't do the trick.

Reserve the potato cooking water to make soups or terrific gravy.

If you are not serving your mashed potatoes immediately, cover the surface with a clean tea towel or napkin and replace the saucepan lid. The cloth will absorb any moisture and keep the mash hot.

2 lbs	floury potatoes, peeled and quartered	1 kg
1 tsp	salt	5 mL
1	head garlic, separated into cloves	1
¼ cup	butter, softened	60 mL
¼ cup	heavy or whipping (35%) cream	60 mL
½ cup	whole milk	125 mL
¼ cup	finely chopped fresh chives	60 mL

1. Follow Step 1 for Classic Mash Deluxe (page 50), adding garlic and leaving it in the saucepan after draining.

2. With saucepan still over very low heat, add butter and, using a potato masher, mash it thoroughly into potatoes and garlic. Gradually mash in cream and milk (you might not use all the milk; just add until you reach the desired consistency). Bang masher against side of saucepan so any sticking mixture falls into the pot. Tilt saucepan slightly and, using a flat whisk, wooden spoon or large fork, briskly stir the mixture to incorporate air into the mash, until it is smooth, creamy and fluffy. (You may decide that it needs a little more butter, cream or milk; if so, stir it in now.) Stir in chives. Serve immediately.

Variations

Omit the garlic when boiling the potatoes and add chopped roasted garlic to the finished mash. *To roast garlic:* Cut a thin slice from the top of the head, drizzle with a little olive oil and wrap tightly in foil. Bake in a 350°F (180°C) oven for 20 minutes, until soft. The cloves can then be squeezed out of their skins, chopped and added directly to the mash.

Blanch unpeeled garlic cloves in a little boiling water for a couple of minutes. Squeeze the cloves out of their skins into the mashed potatoes.

Cantal & Potato Purée with Parsley Garlic Butter

You know that deliciously buttery mixture that French bistros reserve for escargots? Well, here it is licking up the sides of a sumptuous mash of potatoes and Cantal, a rich, nutty Cheddar-like cheese from France. This makes a lovely foundation for seared scallops, salmon or roast chicken. It's also very good with grilled sausages.

Makes 4 to 6 servings

Tips

This purée is inspired by the classic French potato preparation *aligot*, in which potatoes and Cantal cheese are beaten together with crème fraîche to make a silky smooth mound of mashed potatoes.

Parsley Garlic Butter: In a small saucepan, melt ½ cup (125 mL) butter over low heat. Add 2 cloves crushed garlic and cook, stirring, until softened; do not brown. Stir in ¼ cup (60 mL) chopped flat-leaf parsley leaves and ¼ tsp (1 mL) Dijon mustard. Remove from heat and let cool. Whisk in 2 tbsp (30 mL) freshly squeezed lemon juice and season to taste with salt and freshly ground white pepper.

2 lbs	floury potatoes, peeled and quartered	1 kg
	Parsley Garlic Butter (see Tips, left)	
1 tsp	salt	5 mL
4	strips bacon, diced	4
¾ cup	whole milk (approx.)	175 mL
¼ cup	unsalted butter	60 mL
3 cups	shredded Cantal cheese	750 mL

1. Place potatoes in a large saucepan. Add cold water to barely cover. Add salt, cover loosely and bring to a boil over high heat. Reduce heat and cook for 20 minutes or until potatoes are tender.
2. Meanwhile, in a skillet over medium-high heat, cook bacon, stirring, for about 10 minutes or until crisp. Transfer to a plate lined with paper towels and let drain.
3. Drain potatoes thoroughly, return to saucepan over very low heat and shake the pot back and forth to remove any trace of moisture. (This is an important step; the drier the cooked potato, the lighter and fluffier your mash will be.)
4. With saucepan still over the heat, add butter and, using a potato masher, mash it in thoroughly. Gradually mash in cream and milk (you might not use all the milk; just add until you reach the desired consistency). Bang masher against rim of saucepan so that any sticking mixture falls into the pot.
5. With saucepan still over the heat, fold in bacon and gradually stir in cheese, beating well after each addition, until incorporated. Tilt saucepan slightly and, using a flat whisk, wooden spoon or large fork, briskly stir the mixture to incorporate air into the mash, until it is smooth, creamy and fluffy. (You may decide that it needs a little more butter, cream or milk; if so, stir it in now.)
6. Return Parsley Garlic Butter to low heat and gently reheat. Transfer potato purée to a serving dish, drizzle with Parsley Garlic Butter and serve.

Big Cheese Mash

A mash made in heaven! Cheese and potatoes are one of the food world's happiest unions. Which cheese to pair with your perfect mashed potatoes is up to you, and the options are many.

Makes 4 to 6 servings

Tips

This recipe makes about 5 cups (1.25 L) of mash.

Strong-flavored cheeses such as aged Cheddar, nutty Gruyère, Italian fontina or Parmesan all work well. You may also consider a combination of cheeses — think four-cheese pasta — but consider reducing the amount of each cheese accordingly. Plain cream cheese, softened, results in a silky smooth mash with a slight cheese accent. Gorgonzola or Irish Cashel blue is a nice addition, especially if you are planning to serve the potatoes alongside a hefty steak.

If you are not serving them immediately, cover the surface of the mashed potatoes with a clean tea towel or napkin and replace the saucepan lid. The cloth will absorb any moisture and keep the mash hot.

2 lbs	floury potatoes, peeled and quartered	1 kg
1 tsp	salt	5 mL
¼ cup	butter, softened	60 mL
¼ cup	heavy or whipping (35%) cream	60 mL
½ cup	whole milk (approx.)	125 mL
½ to 1 cup	grated or shredded cheese, such as Parmesan or Cheddar (see Tips, left)	125 to 250 mL

1. Place potatoes in a large saucepan. Add cold water to barely cover (if you use too much water you will end up with watery mash). Stir in salt (see Tips, page 52.) Cover loosely and bring to a boil over high heat. Place lid firmly on saucepan, reduce heat and cook for 20 minutes or until potatoes are tender all the way through when prodded with the tip of a paring knife. Drain (see Tips, page 52), leaving potatoes in the saucepan. Return to very low heat and shake the pot back and forth to remove any trace of moisture. (This is an important step; the drier the cooked potato, the lighter and fluffier your mash will be.)

2. With saucepan still over the heat, add butter and, using a potato masher, mash it in thoroughly. Gradually mash in cream and milk (you might not use all of the milk; just add until you reach the desired consistency). Bang masher against rim of saucepan so any sticking mixture falls into the pot. Tilt saucepan slightly and, using a flat whisk, wooden spoon or large fork, briskly stir the mixture to incorporate air into the mash, until it is smooth, creamy and fluffy. (You may decide that it needs a little more butter, cream or milk; if so, stir it in now.) Stir in cheese. Serve immediately.

Dad's Champion Champ

When I was growing up, champ fulfilled an important role in our household. My dad was born in Belfast and this was one of his favorite meals, especially when served with a soft-boiled egg nestled in the center, as my mum was wont to do. Comfort and joy in one easy dish! If you decide not to present this with the soft-boiled egg, make a well in the center of each portion and fill with a little melted butter, as they do in Ireland.

Makes 4 servings

Tips

I prefer to use sea salt rather than refined table salt because it has a much cleaner, crisper taste and enhanced mineral content.

If you are not serving the mash immediately, before transferring it to serving dishes, cover the surface with a clean tea towel or napkin and replace the saucepan lid. The cloth will absorb any moisture and keep the mash hot.

To soft-boil eggs, place in a small saucepan with enough water to cover and bring to a boil. Remove from heat, cover and let stand for 4 minutes.

2 lbs	floury potatoes, peeled and cut into chunks	1 kg
1 tsp	salt	5 mL
⅔ cup	whole milk (approx.)	150 mL
4	green onions, finely chopped	4
4	soft-boiled eggs (optional; see Tips, left)	4
¼ cup	butter (approx.)	60 mL
	Salt and freshly ground white pepper	

1. Place potatoes in a large saucepan. Add cold water to barely cover. Add salt, cover loosely and bring to a boil over high heat. Reduce heat and cook for 20 minutes or until potatoes are tender.

2. Meanwhile, in a small saucepan over low heat, warm milk. Stir in onions and bring to a boil. Reduce heat and simmer for 15 minutes or until tender.

3. Drain potatoes, return to saucepan over very low heat and shake the pot back and forth to remove any trace of moisture. With saucepan still over the heat, add butter and, using a potato masher, mash it in thoroughly. Gradually mash in the milk mixture (you might not use all the milk; just add until you reach the desired consistency). Bang masher against rim of saucepan so that any sticking mixture falls into the pot. Tilt saucepan slightly and, using a flat whisk, wooden spoon or large fork, briskly stir mixture to incorporate air into the mash, until it is smooth, creamy and fluffy. Season to taste with salt and white pepper.

4. Spoon mashed potatoes into four warmed individual serving bowls and make a well in the center of each portion. If adding soft-boiled eggs, carefully remove from shells, then place a warm egg in each well and carefully slice it in half lengthwise, so the yolk runs out over the mashed potatoes. Season to taste with more salt, pepper and butter.

Roots Mash

By combining potatoes with other root vegetables you can come up with endless possibilities for flavor and textural contrast. Carrots, celeriac, Jerusalem artichokes, turnips, rutabaga, parsnips, sweet potatoes and even beets can be cooked separately and then combined with standard mashed potatoes. Or, as in this recipe, carrots, sweet potato, parsnip and turnip are cooked in the same pot as the potatoes. In this instance we are not looking to make an ultra-smooth mixture (although you could if you chose to) but rather to create a colorful blend of vegetables with a few small chunks here and there.

Makes 4 to 6 servings

Tips

I prefer to use sea salt rather than refined table salt because it has a much cleaner, crisper taste and enhanced mineral content.

If you are not serving the mash immediately, cover the surface with a clean tea towel or napkin and replace the saucepan lid. The cloth will absorb any moisture and keep the mash hot.

Try to make sure that all the vegetable chunks are of uniform size to ensure even cooking.

For added flavor, use half vegetable broth and half water to cook the vegetables.

2 lbs	floury potatoes, peeled and quartered	1 kg
2	carrots, peeled and cut into chunks	2
1	sweet potato, peeled and cut into chunks	1
1	parsnip, peeled and cut into chunks	1
1	small white turnip, peeled and cut into chunks	1
2 tsp	salt	10 mL
3 tbsp	butter	45 mL
¼ cup	whole milk (approx.)	60 mL
	Salt and freshly ground black pepper	

1. Place potatoes, carrots, sweet potato, parsnip and turnip in a large saucepan. Add cold water to barely cover. Cover loosely and bring to a boil over high heat. Add salt and return to a boil for about 10 minutes. Cover securely, reduce heat to medium and gently boil for about 25 minutes or until vegetables are tender.

2. Remove from heat and drain, reserving cooking liquid for use in soup or gravy, if desired. Wipe saucepan clean. Return vegetable mixture to saucepan over very low heat and shake the pot back and forth to remove any trace of moisture.

3. With saucepan still over the heat, add butter and, using a potato masher, mash it in thoroughly. Gradually mash in the milk (you might not use all the milk; just add until you reach the desired consistency). Bang masher against rim of saucepan so any sticking mixture falls into the pot. Tilt saucepan slightly and, using a flat whisk, wooden spoon or large fork, briskly stir mixture to incorporate air into the mash, until smooth, creamy and fluffy. Season to taste with salt and pepper. Serve immediately (see Tips, left).

The New Crush

My mum used to cover halved new (waxy) potatoes with boiling water, cook them till tender, drain them and then crush them slightly against the sides of the pot, usually with a little chopped parsley and butter. Since then I've eaten this same "lazy mash" in more than one contemporary restaurant, as chefs have discovered that its pleasing texture goes well beneath pieces of grilled fish or beef.

Makes 4 to 6 servings

Tip

You can vary this recipe by replacing the butter with olive oil and bits of finely chopped green onion or other fresh herbs. For instance, tarragon is a nice choice if you are planning on teaming the potatoes with salmon or tuna.

2½ lbs	small waxy potatoes, scrubbed and halved	1.25 kg
1 tsp	salt	5 mL
⅓ cup	chopped fresh mint leaves	75 mL
¼ cup	chopped fresh chives	60 mL
¼ cup	butter	60 mL
	Salt and freshly ground black pepper	

1. Place potatoes in a saucepan. Add boiling water to barely cover and bring to a boil over high heat. Add salt and return to a boil for 2 minutes. Reduce heat to medium, cover and cook until tender all the way through when tested with the tip of a knife, about 15 to 20 minutes. Do not overcook.

2. Drain potatoes. Wipe pot clean and return potatoes to saucepan over very low heat. With saucepan still over the heat and using a large fork, coarsely crush potatoes against sides of pot. Mash in mint, chives and butter until potatoes are crushed into uniform pieces. Season to taste with salt and freshly ground pepper.

Irish Buttermilk Mash

The Irish have a long legacy of producing fine dairy products: milk, cream, butter, cheese and, logically, buttermilk — the liquid left over after churning butter from cream. My Belfast-born dad loved buttermilk; he enjoyed a tall, cold glass of it with a sandwich and just before going to bed. Buttermilk always sounds so rich and enticing, so it's a bit of a plus that it is also low in fat.

Makes 4 to 6 servings

Tip

If you are not serving the mashed potatoes immediately, cover the surface with a clean tea towel or napkin and replace the saucepan lid. The cloth will absorb any moisture and keep the mash hot.

2 lbs	floury potatoes, peeled and quartered	1 kg
1 tsp	salt	5 mL
¼ cup	butter (approx.), softened	60 mL
½ cup	buttermilk (approx.)	125 mL
4	green onions, finely chopped	4
1 cup	chopped smoked ham, corned beef or smoked beef	250 mL

1. Place potatoes in a large saucepan. Add cold water to barely cover. Add salt, cover loosely and bring to a boil over high heat. Reduce heat and cook for 20 minutes or until potatoes are tender. Drain well. Return potatoes to saucepan over very low heat and shake the pot back and forth to remove any trace of moisture.

2. With saucepan still over the heat and using a potato masher, mash in butter. Gradually add buttermilk, mashing well after each addition. Bang masher against rim of saucepan so any potato mixture sticking to it falls into the pot. Tilt saucepan slightly and, using a flat whisk, wooden spoon or large fork, briskly stir mixture to incorporate a little air into the mash, until mixture is smooth, creamy and fluffy. (You may decide that it needs a little more butter or buttermilk; if so, stir it in now.) Fold in green onions and ham.

Variation

If you have leftover mash, fry it up the next day in a skillet with a bit of butter and oil until crispy on the bottom. It makes a great breakfast or brunch dish as an accompaniment to poached or fried eggs.

Roasties

Now, the thing about roast potatoes — or roasties, as the British like to call them — is the whole to-parboil-or-not-to-parboil debate. Some cooks believe adamantly in the former, claiming that precooking the potatoes (but not completely) is the only way to achieve perfection. When I am feeling lazy and/or impatient, I favor the second option and just roast the raw spuds tossed with a little good olive oil. Or, if I am roasting beef or pork, I set the potatoes around the roast to crisp up with the fat from the meat. And sometimes I use a mixture of olive oil and butter. However, I must admit that precooking the potatoes for just 7 minutes or so before roasting does seem to result in a crisper roastie, especially if you drain them and allow them to sit covered for a few more minutes to steam slightly before heading to the oven.

Makes 4 to 6 servings

Tips

Peeling gives you a crustier exterior but leaving the skins intact is quicker and a little more nutritious. Try both methods and see which one you prefer. If you do parboil, follow the instructions and then rough up the edges a bit with the tines of a fork before roasting. This results in an even more superlative roastie.

If you are using smaller potatoes, you can choose to leave them whole or slice them in half crosswise or lengthwise.

- **Preheat oven to 400°F (200°C)**
- **Large roasting pan or glass baking dish large enough to accommodate potatoes in a single layer**

6	large floury or all-purpose potatoes, peeled and cut into uniform chunks (see Tips, left)	6
1 tsp	salt	5 mL
¼ cup	olive oil (see Variation, below)	60 mL
	Freshly ground black pepper	

1. *Parboiling (optional):* Place potatoes in a large saucepan. Add cold water to barely cover. Add salt, cover loosely and bring to a boil over high heat. Return to a boil, reduce heat and cook for 7 to 10 minutes. Drain potatoes, return to saucepan over very low heat and shake the pot back and forth to remove any trace of moisture. Cover and set aside for 5 minutes.

2. In roasting pan, toss potatoes with oil to coat. Arrange in a single layer. Roast in preheated oven, turning once or twice, for 40 to 45 minutes or until crisp and golden brown. Season to taste with salt and pepper.

Variation

Use whatever fat you prefer in place of the olive oil. Melted butter, chicken or duck fat and meat drippings are all good choices. Sometimes I use a combination of fats, such as olive oil with a bit of dripping for flavor.

Garlic Roasties with Rosemary

I have made these standby spuds more times than I can count. They are simple to put together and very good with roast pork, lamb, beef or chicken.

Makes 4 to 6 servings

Tips

If the potatoes you choose are older or have very thick skins, peel them if you prefer.

I prefer to use sea salt rather than refined table salt because it has a much cleaner, crisper taste and enhanced mineral content.

I don't peel the garlic because everyone has fun squishing the sweet, nutty cloves out of their skins and eating the soft garlic along with the spuds.

- **Preheat oven to 400°F (200°C)**
- **Roasting pan large enough to accommodate potatoes in a single layer**

6	large floury or all-purpose potatoes, scrubbed and cut into uniform chunks	6
12	cloves garlic, unpeeled	12
¼ cup	olive oil	60 mL
2 tsp	dried rosemary or herbes de Provence	10 mL
	Salt and freshly ground black pepper	

1. In roasting pan, toss together potatoes, garlic, oil and rosemary. Arrange in a single layer. Season to taste with salt and freshly ground pepper. Roast in preheated oven, turning once or twice, for about 1 hour or until tender.

Hasselback Roasties

Hasselbacks are a classic Swedish preparation. They are curious-looking roasted potatoes that are made by thinly slicing a whole potato crosswise part of the way through. As it cooks, the potato opens up like an edible fan to become beautifully crispy. Sometimes fresh bay leaves are inserted between the slices. I like to add a little grated Parmesan and a smidge of butter to each potato, just to gild the lily a bit.

Makes 4 to 6 servings

Tips

If you prefer, instead of slicing a bit off one side of each potato, you can cut them in half lengthwise before slicing. Place them on a cutting board, cut side down, and slice.

I prefer to use sea salt rather than refined table salt because it has a much cleaner, crisper taste and enhanced mineral content.

- **Preheat oven to 400°F (200°C)**
- **Large roasting pan or baking dish**

6	medium floury or all-purpose potatoes, scrubbed	6
3 tbsp	olive oil	45 mL
2 tbsp	butter, melted	30 mL
	Salt and freshly ground black pepper	
1/3 cup	freshly grated Parmesan cheese	75 mL

1. Working with one potato at a time and using a sharp knife, cut a thin slice from one side to make a base. Place potato, base down, on a large serving spoon (the spoon will act as a guide to keep you from cutting right through). Cut crosswise incisions through the potato about $1/8$ inch (3 mm) apart, leaving about $1/3$ inch (1 cm) uncut at the base. Transfer to a bowl of cold water. Repeat until all the potatoes are sliced. Remove potatoes from water and pat dry with paper towels. Transfer to roasting pan.

2. In a small bowl, stir together oil and butter. Pour over potatoes and toss to coat. Season to taste with salt and freshly ground pepper.

3. Roast in preheated oven for about 55 minutes or until tender, crispy and golden brown. Sprinkle with cheese, using tongs to turn potatoes to coat them all over. Return to oven and roast for about 10 minutes more or until cheese is crusty and golden brown.

Variation

Insert very thinly sliced garlic between the slices.

The Only Baked Potato

Whose idea was it originally to wrap a perfectly good potato in foil before placing it in the oven to bake? Besides being a colossal waste of time and foil, that procedure results in a steamed potato, not a baked one. A great baked potato is a gift from heaven — or your own oven. The best baked potatoes remain in your memory for years afterward, encouraging you to repeat the experience as often as possible.

Back in the 1980s, the tony Four Seasons Restaurant in New York City offered a "power lunch" made popular by one of its regular customers, Henry Kissinger. It featured a huge, perfectly baked Idaho potato, split and drenched in exquisite northern Italian extra virgin olive oil, for $9.75. Expensive at the time, but a paltry sum compared to the baked potato the restaurant currently offers during the brief white truffle season. The baked potato receives the same treatment but is additionally crowned with shavings of white truffle — all for a mere $270!

Makes 4 servings

Tips

Pat scrubbed potatoes dry with a clean tea towel or paper towels; if they still seem damp, let them air-dry for about 10 minutes. Prick a few times with a fork before baking.

Rubbing a bit of olive oil and salt all over the potato helps to create maximum crunch and crispness. Salt draws moisture out of things, and here that contributes to the ultimate crispy skin.

To create the ideal baked potato, let it stay in the oven a little beyond the time it is done. This will help to make the exterior particularly crackly and the interior fluffy to the point of being almost creamy.

- **Preheat oven to 375°F (190°C)**

4	large floury or all-purpose potatoes (each 8 to 10 oz/250 to 300 g), scrubbed and thoroughly dried (see Tips, left)	4
¼ cup	olive oil (approx.)	60 mL
	Salt	
	Butter (optional)	
	Freshly ground black pepper	

1. Using a fork, prick each potato a few times, then rub with 1 tbsp (15 mL) of the oil and a little salt.
2. Place potatoes directly on the rack and roast in preheated oven for 1½ to 2 hours or until cooked through and skin is super crisp. Transfer to a serving platter. Split each potato lengthwise down the center and drizzle with olive oil or butter. Season to taste with salt and freshly ground pepper.

Variations

To produce a baked potato like a steakhouse chef, cut a shallow X into the top of each potato before baking. When cooked, the potato will open up, budlike, to receive a few chunks of butter, blobs of sour cream or crème fraiche, crispy bacon bits, finely chopped green onion, or shredded Cheddar cheese — you get the idea.

Baked Half-Potatoes: If you're in a hurry, cut the potatoes in half lengthwise, brush each side with olive oil and bake, adjusting the time accordingly.

The Virtuous Chip

Chips, fries, frites, sautés, home fries, hash browns . . . It seems to me that potatoes and fat were made for each other, whether in the form of chunky English chips, delicate Belgian frites with mayo or breakfast hash browns. For those who eschew fat in all its wondrous forms — even occasionally — I offer this simple recipe for chips that are almost as satisfying and as good as the real, deep-fried thing.

Makes 4 to 6 servings

Tips

Use non-stick baking sheets if you have them. Lining with parchment paper will keep potatoes from sticking and also save on cleanup.

I prefer to use sea salt rather than refined table salt because it has a much cleaner, crisper taste and enhanced mineral content.

- **Preheat oven to 400°F (200°C)**
- **Baking sheets lined with parchment paper**

6	large floury or all-purpose potatoes, unpeeled or peeled	6
¼ cup	olive oil	60 mL
	Salt and freshly ground black pepper	

1. Halve potatoes lengthwise, then slice lengthwise into french fry–style chips of uniform thickness. Transfer to a bowl and toss in oil to coat. Season to taste with salt and freshly ground pepper and, if using, other seasonings (see Variations).

2. Transfer to baking sheets, lining chips up nicely so they are not touching each other. Bake in preheated oven, turning once or twice, for 30 to 40 minutes or until cooked through and golden brown.

Variations

Along with the oil, try sprinkling a little curry powder, chili powder, lemon pepper or steak seasoning over the potatoes in the bowl. If you use steak seasoning, reduce the amount of salt and pepper accordingly.

Real English Chips

These are the chips that have sustained a nation — the United Kingdom — especially late-night pub crawlers searching for something of real substance to soak up large quantities of ale. No wonder, then, that Britain holds a National Chip Week every February to further promote (as if they had to) eating more quality chips. While I can attest to the fact that there is nothing quite like standing on a damp corner eating them straight out of the chip-shop paper, these fries are also wonderful piled high on a plate, doused with malt vinegar and sprinkled with salt. The reason those chip-shop chips taste so good is because they are fried twice — the first time for about six minutes or so, then again in hotter oil for a couple of minutes more. Don't wait until February to make these authentic chips.

Makes 4 to 6 servings

- Deep fryer, large heavy pot or Dutch oven
- Candy or deep-frying thermometer, if not using a deep fryer (see Tips, left)

6	large floury or all-purpose potatoes, peeled	6
	Vegetable oil	
	Salt	

1. Slice potatoes lengthwise into sticks about 2 inches (5 cm) long and at least $1/2$ inch (1 cm) thick (it's good to know that thick-cut chips absorb less oil, by the way) and transfer to a bowl of cold water. Set aside for at least 30 minutes or up to 24 hours, sloshing them about a bit to help release the surface starch.
2. Place 4 to 6 inches (10 to 15 cm) oil in a large heavy pot (see Tips, page 65). Heat over medium-high heat until thermometer registers 375°F (190°C). (If you're using a deep fryer, follow the manufacturer's instructions.)
3. Drain chips, transfer to a clean tea towel or paper towels and pat dry thoroughly (they must be completely dry). In batches, carefully add potatoes to oil and deep-fry for about 5 to 6 minutes or until softened and just beginning to color. Using a slotted spoon, transfer to paper towels and let drain for at least 30 minutes or up to 1 hour before the second fry.
4. Increase heat until thermometer registers 400°F (200°C). In batches, carefully return chips to oil and cook for a second time, for 3 to 5 minutes or until crisp and golden. Using a slotted spoon, transfer to a baking sheet lined with paper towels and let drain briefly. Place hot chips in a big bowl and season to taste with salt. Serve immediately.

Tips

For best results, use a deep fryer and a frying basket.

If you don't have a thermometer, drop a small cube of dry bread into the heated oil; if it floats, the oil is hot enough.

To rinse or not to rinse — that is the question where frites and fries are concerned. A rinse in cold water will wash away much of the potato's surface starch, ultimately making the fries crisper after the second frying. But some cooks don't bother and still have good results. Try both methods and see if you notice a difference. If you do rinse or soak your cut potatoes, you must make sure to dry them thoroughly before frying.

Frites à la Kingsmill

Potatoes fried in fat speak to the hedonist in all of us. Speaking of hedonists, my good friend David Kingsmill, fellow food hound and the very definition of bon vivant, says in his terrific book *Home Bistro* that real frites are "caramel-colored and crisp on the outside . . . when they come to the table all salted and hot, they go crack!" Kingsmill maintains that the difference between making great chips and great frites is all a matter of movement — chips should sit still in the hot fat while great frites need to be agitated. And don't use a deep fryer, because frites need "a fluctuating oil temperature," not a constant one. Now that I have given my buddy a shameless plug, I don't think he'll mind if I use his recipe. Just as for perfect chips, frites are fried twice.

Makes 6 to 8 servings

Tips

The oil should come a little over halfway up the sides of the pot. Do not overfill; leave at least 3 inches (7.5 cm) of headspace at the top.

If you don't have a thermometer, drop a small cube of dry bread into the heated oil; if it floats, the oil is hot enough.

I prefer to use sea salt rather than refined table salt because it has a much cleaner, crisper taste and enhanced mineral content.

- **Large heavy pot or Dutch oven**
- **Candy or deep-frying thermometer (see Tips, left)**
- **Baking sheet, lined with paper towels**

8	large Yukon Gold potatoes, peeled (see Variations, below)	8
	Vegetable oil	
	Salt	

1. Place 4 to 6 inches (10 to 15 cm) oil in a large heavy pot (see Tips, left). Heat over medium-high heat until thermometer registers 375°F (190°C) (see Tips, left).
2. Cut potatoes lengthwise into 1/4-inch (0.5 cm) sticks.
3. Carefully add a third of the chips to the oil and deep-fry for 4 to 5 minutes or until softened and just beginning to color. Using a slotted spoon or wire (spider) strainer, transfer to baking sheet lined with paper towels and let drain for at least 30 minutes or up to 1 hour before the second fry. Repeat with the remaining chips.
4. Increase heat until thermometer registers 400°F (200°C). Carefully return a quarter of the chips to the oil and cook for a second time, stirring and turning occasionally, for 3 to 5 minutes or until crisp and golden. Using a slotted spoon, transfer to a baking sheet lined with paper towels and let drain briefly. Repeat with the remaining chips. Place hot chips in a big bowl and season to taste with salt. Serve immediately.

Variations

Make a batch of wonderfully easy Basil Aïoli (page 99) as a classic accompaniment to these great frites.

Substitute Yukon Gold potatoes with other yellow-fleshed all-purpose potatoes.

Roadhouse Hash Browns

Hash browns have a storied history. Some maintain that real hash browns should always be made from leftover baked potatoes that have been shredded. They are fried, sometimes with onion, in a heavy cast-iron pan until a nice crispy brown mass is formed, then flipped, browned on the other side and served. Others like their hash browns to start with raw potatoes, shredded or sliced into very thin juliennes before cooking. Most of us think of hash browns as being based on any leftover cooked potato — boiled, steamed, baked or even mashed — fried up in a bit of butter and/or oil with onions. I think any of these preparations sounds great. So here is one version to get you started on the road to hash-brown glory.

Makes 4 to 6 servings

Tip

If you are going to shred the potatoes on the coarse side of a box grater, be careful not to overcook them, because that will make them difficult to shred.

- **Large cast-iron or heavy skillet**

¼ cup	olive oil	60 mL
1 tbsp	butter	15 mL
1	large onion, finely chopped	1
6	cooled boiled large potatoes, diced or shredded	6
	Salt and freshly ground black pepper	

1. In a skillet, heat oil and butter over medium heat. Add onion and cook, stirring, for 8 minutes or until softened. Stir in potatoes. Season to taste with salt and freshly ground pepper. Using a metal spatula, spread and flatten potato mixture evenly to form a cake, and cook, pressing it down, for about 20 minutes or until bottom is golden brown (gently lift up edge to check).

2. Invert a dinner plate over the skillet, flip potato cake onto plate, then slide cake back into skillet, uncooked side down. Cook, pressing down, until golden brown and crisp. Serve immediately.

Variations

Add bits of cooked ham, bacon or crumbled corned beef along with the potatoes.

Old-Fashioned Creamed Potatoes

Not many people make these any more — or, for that matter, any vegetables in a cream sauce. But you should try this recipe at least once, when tiny new spuds are plentiful. Let the cooked potatoes cool before attempting to peel them. This dish is lovely with roast chicken or pork or as part of a buffet with cold meats, cheese and a tomato salad. You can easily double this recipe.

**Makes
4 servings**

Tips

I prefer to use sea salt rather than refined table salt because it has a much cleaner, crisper taste and enhanced mineral content.

If you are lucky enough to come across creamer potatoes — apricot-sized red or yellow potatoes that have been harvested while still young — they are the perfect candidates for this recipe. Also called C-size potatoes, they are small and tender and almost sweet.

16	small new potatoes, scrubbed	16
1 tsp	salt	5 mL
2 tbsp	butter	30 mL
2 tbsp	all-purpose flour	30 mL
1 cup	table (18%) cream (approx.)	250 mL
¼ cup	chopped fresh chives	60 mL

1. Place potatoes in a large saucepan. Add boiling water to barely cover. Add salt, cover loosely and bring to a boil over medium-high heat. Reduce heat and cook for 20 minutes or until potatoes are tender. Drain well, reserving about ¼ cup (60 mL) cooking liquid. Set liquid aside. When potatoes are cool enough to handle, peel.
2. Return potatoes to pot and gently toss in butter to coat. Gently toss in flour to coat. Cook, stirring, over low heat for about 1 minute or until flour coating is cooked (to prevent a raw starch taste).
3. Gently stir in cream and cook for about 5 minutes or until thickened, adding more cream or reserved cooking liquid if mixture becomes too thick. Transfer to a warm serving bowl and sprinkle with chives. Serve immediately.

Variation

Try adding young peas and small pearl onions to the potatoes for the last 10 minutes or so of cooking time.

Classic Scalloped Spuds

I grew up with scalloped potatoes, not — great as they are — potatoes au gratin. These days I seem to make sophisticated gratins, usually containing expensive (albeit worth it) cheese, cream and no onion, more frequently than old-fashioned scalloped potatoes. But there is something decidedly comforting about real scalloped potatoes, which are cooked at lower heat for a longer time, served perhaps with a clove-studded ham and buttered green cabbage.

Makes 4 to 6 servings

Tips

Floury potatoes will produce scalloped potatoes that blend together in a mass, whereas using waxy or all-purpose potatoes (such as Yukon Gold) will give you a more layered version. Either way, you will be happy with the comforting results.

It isn't vital, but if you have a mandoline, slicing the potatoes and onion will be a breeze. You could also use the slicing disk on your food processor.

Lining the baking sheet with parchment makes cleanup much easier in case the mixture boils over.

- Preheat oven to 325°F (160°C)
- 10-inch (25 cm) oval, round or square baking dish, lightly buttered
- Rimmed baking sheet, lined with parchment (see Tips, left)

6 tbsp	butter	90 mL
6	large potatoes, peeled and thinly sliced (see Tips, left)	6
1	large white onion, thinly sliced	1
¼ cup	all-purpose flour (approx.)	60 mL
	Salt and freshly ground black pepper	
1 cup	whole milk	250 mL
1 cup	table (18%) or heavy or whipping (35%) cream	250 mL

1. In prepared baking dish, arrange a quarter of the potatoes in a single layer, scatter evenly with a quarter of the onion, dot with a quarter of the butter and sprinkle with salt and freshly ground pepper to taste. Repeat three times. Place dish on prepared baking sheet.

2. In a bowl, combine milk and cream. Place baking sheet holding dish on center rack in preheated oven. Carefully pour milk mixture evenly over potato mixture to just cover (don't overfill). Loosely cover dish with parchment paper or buttered foil (it shouldn't touch the potatoes) and bake for 1 hour.

3. Uncover, increase oven temperature to 375°F (190°C) and bake for another 15 minutes or until potato mixture is golden brown and bubbling. Remove from heat and let stand for 15 minutes before serving.

Classic Potato & Cheese Gratin

There is almost no end of variations on this theme. Your cheese choices could also include aged Cheddar, fontina or taleggio. But my favorite combination for this recipe is real, cave-aged Gruyère with either Grana Padano or Parmesan in a supporting role.

Makes 4 to 6 servings

Tips

While good-quality cheese, such as Gruyère, is a little expensive, it is more than worth it for the fragrance and nutty quality it lends to the dish.

Floury, all-purpose or medium-starch potatoes (such as the red-skinned ones specified) may be used for this recipe.

If top is browning too quickly, loosely cover dish with parchment paper or buttered foil, but don't let it touch potato mixture.

- Preheat oven to 350°F (180°C)
- 10-inch (25 cm) oval, round or square baking dish, lightly buttered
- Rimmed baking sheet, lined with parchment

3 tbsp	butter	45 mL
6	large red-skinned potatoes, peeled and thinly sliced (see Tips, left)	6
2	cloves garlic, finely chopped	2
	Salt and freshly ground black pepper	
¾ cup	shredded Gruyère cheese	175 mL
½ cup	freshly grated Grana Padano or Parmesan cheese	125 mL
2 cups	low-sodium chicken broth	500 mL
¼ cup	chopped flat-leaf parsley leaves	60 mL

1. In prepared baking dish, arrange a third of the potatoes in a single layer, scatter evenly with a third of the garlic and sprinkle with salt and pepper. Repeat two more times. With palms, press down potato mixture. Dot with butter. Place dish on prepared baking sheet.

2. In a bowl, combine Gruyère and Grana Padano. Place baking sheet holding dish on center rack in preheated oven. Carefully pour chicken broth evenly over potato mixture to just cover (don't overfill). Sprinkle cheese mixture evenly over the top. Bake for 75 minutes or until potatoes are cooked through and cheese is golden brown and bubbling. Remove from oven and let stand for 15 minutes. Sprinkle with parsley and serve.

Variations

Finely chopped herbs such as chives, parsley, sage, thyme or green onion are also nice additions to this recipe; add them as you are layering the potatoes. Play around with this recipe as much as you like — you won't be marked on your creations!

Grande Dame Anna Potatoes

Okay, I'll say it: this is the best potato recipe in the world. I am very grateful to the chef who was inspired to create this, the most harmonious blend of potato and butter you are ever likely to encounter. Even though it has but two ingredients — potatoes and butter — *pommes de terre Anna* is the very essence of potato flavor. The real name for it is simply Pommes Anna, but I have elevated her status somewhat after learning that a French chef during Napoleon's day named this dish after one of the leading *grandes cocottes* of the day. There is even a special copper baking dish designed for this dish that bears the name *cocotte à pommes Anna*. When I first made it, I didn't own a copper pan, so I used cast iron and it worked perfectly. The quantity of butter may seem excessive, but I would happily eat like a sparrow for a whole week if I knew I would be sharing this with my man on Saturday night, along with a rare sirloin and a big, luscious Rioja!

Makes
4 servings

Tips

When I make this, I work rather quickly so the potato slices don't have a chance to discolor. If you prefer, you can transfer the potatoes to a bowl of cold water as you slice them, but make sure to dry them off really well before proceeding.

For best results, use a mandoline or the slicing blade of a food processor to cut thin, uniform slices.

If — unlike me — you are a perfectionist, you can use a small round cookie cutter to cut the potato slices into perfect circles.

- **Preheat oven to 375°F (190°C)**
- **9- or 10-inch (23 or 25 cm) cast-iron or copper-bottomed skillet**

3 to 4	large all-purpose potatoes	3 to 4
3/4 cup	butter, melted	175 mL
	Salt and freshly ground black pepper	

1. Using a sharp chef's knife, cut potatoes crosswise into slices about $1/8$ inch (3 mm) thick (see Tips, left).
2. Over medium-high heat, brush bottom and sides of skillet with a drizzle of the butter. Working from the center out, arrange a single layer of overlapping potato slices in a spiral. Drizzle with some of the butter and sprinkle with salt and pepper. With pan still on burner and using a metal spatula to press down the layers, repeat with the remaining potatoes, drizzling each layer with butter and sprinkling with salt and pepper (if you work very slowly, remove from heat after about 10 minutes, to prevent overcooking bottom layer of potatoes).
3. Cut a circle of parchment paper to fit skillet, and butter one side. Place butter-side-down over potatoes, then place a weight on top (such as another heavy skillet). Bake in preheated oven for 45 minutes or until center is tender and edges are golden brown. Remove from oven. Slide a thin spatula around the edges and give the pan a knock. Place a warmed round serving plate over the skillet and quickly invert the potato cake onto the plate (for a less formal presentation, just bring the skillet to the table). Cut into wedges and serve pan-side-up.

A Bowl of Soup
To Nourish, to Comfort, to Impress

Besides onions, perhaps no other vegetable lends itself to soups with as much versatility and reliability as the potato. Potato soups run the gamut from simple and nourishing to hearty and soul-satisfying, cool and elegant and everything in between. Potatoes can enjoy the leading role in a soup — think classic vichyssoise — or be a great supporting character, for instance, in clam chowder. They can also be part of the backdrop, as they are when potato purée is used to thicken a broth.

Almost without exception, the potatoes used when making soup are the floury or all-purpose types. But every now and then, when you are looking for a potato that doesn't fall apart under pressure — perhaps for a chunky vegetable soup or in an oyster, clam or fish chowder, where the firm texture is a nice foil for the soft fish or seafood — a firmer, waxy potato fills the bill.

Spring Vegetable Soup with New Potatoes & Gruyère Toasts

This light and pretty spring soup is inspired by the season's first tender young vegetables. Vary the vegetables to suit whatever is available and most delectable. Tiny, slim carrots would be a nice addition. If you or someone you know has a favorite foraging spot for morels, wild leeks, asparagus or fiddleheads, wouldn't they be perfect in this gently flavored potage? Be sure to make the cheese toasts first, so everything can come together quickly at the end. You don't want the tender vegetables to get overly soft.

Makes 6 servings

Tip

Gruyère Toasts: Arrange 12 thin slices of baguette on a baking sheet and toast on one side under a preheated broiler. Remove from oven. Combine 4 oz (125 g) shredded Gruyère cheese, 2 tbsp (30 mL) softened butter and a pinch of cayenne pepper in a small bowl. Use the back of a spoon to blend until smooth. Spread over untoasted side of baguette and place under preheated broiler until cheese is brown and bubbling, about 1 minute, watching carefully to ensure they don't burn. Set aside.

- **Preheat broiler**

12	Gruyère Toasts (see Tips, left)	12
¼ cup	butter	60 mL
4	slim young leeks, trimmed and thinly sliced	4
4	thin green onions, trimmed and thinly sliced	4
4 cups	chicken or vegetable broth	1 L
6	small waxy potatoes, scrubbed and diced	6
1 cup	shelled fresh peas	250 mL
2 cups	baby spinach	500 mL
	Salt and freshly ground black pepper	
3 tbsp	chopped fresh chives	45 mL

1. In a large saucepan, melt butter over medium-high heat. Reduce heat to low, add leeks and green onions, and cook, stirring occasionally, for about 10 minutes, until very soft but not brown. Add broth and potatoes. Increase heat to medium and cook for about 10 minutes or until potatoes are almost tender. Add peas and cook until vegetables are just tender (don't overcook), about 5 minutes.

2. Stack spinach leaves like a deck of cards and, using a sharp knife, slice into strips. Add to soup and cook for about 1 minute or until spinach is just wilted. Season to taste with salt and pepper. Ladle soup into warmed serving bowls. Sprinkle evenly with chives. Serve immediately with toasts on the side.

Watercress & Potato Soup

This is a lovely soup for cool spring days. It is emerald green in color, which beautifully contrasts with the snow-white crème fraîche.

Makes 4 servings

Tips

The potatoes to use for this recipe straddle the fence between all-purpose and waxy. Thin-skinned, round and of medium size, they have either white or red skins and are often referred to as boiling potatoes. These are medium-starch potatoes. They have less starch than a floury or all-purpose potato but more than a waxy potato, which means that when they are used in a recipe like this one, they give a satiny quality to the soup once it has been blended. Confused? Make this soup and you will see what I mean.

You can buy prepared crème fraîche in well-stocked supermarkets or specialty stores, or you can make your own (see Tips, page 132.)

● **Food processor or immersion blender**

2 tbsp	olive oil	30 mL
2	shallots, finely chopped	2
2	medium (about 8 oz/250 g) white or red-skinned boiling potatoes, peeled and finely diced	2
4 cups	vegetable or chicken broth	1 L
1	bunch (about 8 oz/250 g) watercress	1
8 oz	baby spinach	250 g
	Salt and freshly ground white pepper	
1 cup	crème fraîche (see Tips, left)	250 mL

1. In a large pot, heat oil over medium heat. Add shallots and potatoes and cook, stirring, for 5 to 6 minutes or until softened but not beginning to brown. Add broth, increase heat to high, bring to a boil and cook for about 1 minute.

2. Quickly add watercress and spinach. After they have cooked a few seconds, use a slotted spoon to transfer all the vegetables to a food processor. Pulse until relatively smooth but not watery.

3. Add about 1 cup (250 mL) of the cooking broth and pulse until soup is smooth. Return to saucepan. (If using an immersion blender, remove saucepan from heat and purée.) Season to taste with salt and white pepper. Gently reheat over medium heat.

4. Ladle into warmed individual serving bowls. Add a spoonful of crème fraîche to the center of each and serve immediately.

Potato & Two-Leek Soup

Here is a classic soup known in France as potage Parmentier. Served chilled, it becomes even more sophisticated, and acquires a new name too: vichyssoise. While vichyssoise is lovely on a sultry summer day, I think I prefer potato and leek soup as a winter warmer, served as I suggest here, with a tangle of sautéed leeks in the center.

Makes 4 to 6 servings

Tips

Make sure to wash leeks thoroughly by slitting them open lengthwise and spreading them apart while rinsing clean under cold running water.

While homemade vegetable broths can make a good base for this and other soups, make sure yours has enough flavor. If not, add a vegetable bouillon cube or two to help it along.

You can simply sauté skinny strands of leek as a garnish for this soup. Or use the chef's trick we employ at the Black Dog, which involves deep-frying strands of leek that have been lightly tossed with flour. This quick method (just a minute of deep-frying) will make them frizzled and produce a nice chef-style garnish.

• **Immersion blender, food processor or blender**

2 tbsp	butter	30 mL
1 tbsp	olive oil	15 mL
3	large leeks, light green and white parts only, trimmed and thinly sliced	3
1	clove garlic, minced	1
1	onion, finely chopped	1
3	large floury potatoes, peeled and diced	3
4 cups	chicken or full-flavored vegetable broth (approx.; see Tips, left)	1 L
1 cup	heavy or whipping (35%) cream	250 mL
	Salt and freshly ground black pepper	
	Milk (optional)	
	Sautéed or deep-fried leeks (see Tips, left)	

1. In a large pot, heat butter and oil over medium heat. Cook leeks, garlic and onion, stirring occasionally, for about 5 minutes or until softened but not beginning to brown. Increase heat to high, add potatoes and chicken broth and bring to a boil. Reduce heat to medium, cover and simmer, stirring occasionally, for about 25 minutes or until potatoes are tender.

2. Using an immersion blender, or a food processor or blender in batches, purée soup until relatively smooth and thick. Return to pot, if necessary, and stir in cream. Season to taste with salt and pepper. Reheat gently over medium heat, stirring and reducing heat slightly if necessary to maintain a gentle simmer, until heated through (if soup is too thick, add a little milk or broth). Ladle into warmed individual serving bowls. Garnish with sautéed or deep-fried leeks.

Variation

If you don't feel like sautéing leeks for a topping, garnish with finely snipped chives to taste.

Celeriac & Potato Vichyssoise

Knobbly old celeriac won't win any awards for beauty in the vegetable world but it is a wonderfully flavorful root that deserves more attention. Certainly chefs know the unmistakable flavor it can add to soups and purées. At the Black Dog we often add it to white vegetable purées that include potato, onion, parsnip and turnip, as it adds a wonderful earthiness to the overall flavor. This makes quite a bit of soup but it freezes well.

**Makes
10 servings**

Tips

Celeriac (or celery root, as it is also known) is always peeled to remove its rough, tough outer skin. Cut celeriac turns brown fairly quickly, so drop the pieces into acidulated water (add a squirt of lemon juice) if you are not working quickly.

Make sure to wash leeks thoroughly by slitting them open lengthwise and spreading them apart while rinsing clean under cold running water.

● **Food processor or immersion blender**

¼ cup	butter	60 mL
4	cloves garlic, chopped	4
I	Spanish onion, finely chopped	1
1	leek (white and light green parts only), finely chopped (see Tips, left)	1
2 lbs	floury or all-purpose potatoes, peeled and cut into 1-inch (2.5 cm) cubes	1 kg
2 lbs	celeriac, peeled and cut into 1-inch (2.5 cm) cubes	1 kg
6 cups	chicken or vegetable broth	1.5 L
	Salt and white pepper	
3 cups	whole milk	750 mL
2 cups	table (18%) cream	500 mL
½ cup	chopped fresh chives	125 mL

1. In a large pot, warm butter over medium heat. Cook garlic, onion and leek, gently stirring, for about 10 minutes or until softened but not beginning to brown.

2. Stir in potatoes and celeriac and cook for about 5 minutes or until well incorporated with the other ingredients. Increase heat to high and stir in broth. Season with salt and white pepper and bring to a boil. Reduce heat to medium-low and simmer, loosely covered, for about 30 minutes or until potatoes and celeriac are tender. Remove from heat and let cool slightly.

3. Using an immersion blender, or a food processor or blender in batches, purée soup until relatively smooth and thick. Return soup to a clean pot over medium heat. Stir in milk and cream and gently reheat (do not boil). Ladle into warmed individual serving bowls. Sprinkle with chives and serve immediately.

Potato Soup with Pesto Cream

This luxurious, silky smooth soup showcases a brilliant emerald mound of pesto floating on its surface — a good choice for St. Patrick's Day. Serve this elegant soup with thin slices of toasted baguette alongside.

Makes 4 to 6 servings

Tips

For convenience you can make the pesto ahead of time. Or, if you prefer, substitute a good-quality store-bought pesto.

Make sure to wash leeks thoroughly by slitting them open lengthwise and spreading them apart while rinsing clean under cold running water.

Crème fraîche is available in the dairy section of most large supermarkets. If you prefer, make your own, using the recipe on page 132.

- **Food processor or blender**

Pesto Cream

1	large clove garlic	1
1/2 tsp	salt	2 mL
2 cups	lightly packed fresh basil leaves	500 mL
1/2 cup	extra virgin olive oil (approx.)	125 mL
1 1/2 tbsp	pine nuts or walnuts	22 mL
1/2 cup	freshly grated Pecorino Romano or Parmesan cheese	125 mL
1 cup	crème fraîche (see Tips, left)	250 mL
	Salt and white pepper	

Soup

1/4 cup	butter	60 mL
4	cloves garlic, peeled and crushed	4
1	bay leaf	1
1	sprig fresh thyme	1
1	leek (white part only), chopped (see Tips, left)	1
1	small onion, chopped	1
1	stalk celery, chopped	1
3	large floury potatoes, peeled and sliced	3
2 cups	chicken broth	500 mL
1 1/2 cups	table (18%) cream	375 mL

1. *Pesto Cream:* On a cutting board, use the flat side of a knife blade to crush together garlic and salt. Add to food processor fitted with metal blade, along with basil, oil and pine nuts. Pulse, adding a little more oil if necessary to make a paste and scraping down sides occasionally, until finely puréed. Using a rubber spatula, scrape pesto into a bowl. Fold in cheese until blended. Carefully fold in crème fraîche until blended. Season to taste with salt and white pepper. Cover with plastic wrap and refrigerate until ready to use or for up to 1 week.

2. *Soup:* In a large saucepan, melt butter over medium heat. Add garlic, bay leaf, thyme, leek, onion and celery and cook, stirring, for 1 to 2 minutes. Reduce heat to medium and cook, stirring, for about 5 minutes or until vegetables are tender but not beginning to brown.

3. Add potatoes and chicken broth (add water, if necessary, to totally submerge potatoes) and simmer, loosely covered, for about 20 minutes or until potatoes are cooked through and tender. Using an immersion blender, or a food processor or blender in batches, purée soup until smooth.

4. Pour puréed soup through a fine-mesh sieve set over a large bowl, pressing down on any remaining solids and scraping purée from underside of sieve into the bowl (discard solids). Return soup to a clean pot. Stir in cream and reheat gently over medium heat. Season to taste with salt and white pepper.

5. Ladle hot soup into warmed individual serving bowls. Add a good dollop of pesto cream to the center of each bowl. Drag a toothpick through the dollop to spread pesto cream decoratively across surface of soup. Serve immediately.

Creamy Potato & Four-Onion Soup

White onion, leek, shallot, garlic and chives all lend their unmistakable characteristics to this creamy, comforting concoction. Make a few garlic and herb croutons to float in the center, as their crispness is a nice foil to the creaminess of the soup (see Tips).

Makes 4 to 6 servings

Tips

Make sure to wash leeks thoroughly by slitting them open lengthwise and spreading them apart while rinsing clean under cold running water.

To make croutons, cut a few slices of day-old French or Italian bread into cubes. Toss together with melted butter, garlic powder and a bit of dried basil, oregano or thyme (or a combination of herbs). Fry in a hot skillet until golden brown on all sides, or bake in a 375°F (190°C) oven, tossing once or twice.

- **Immersion blender, blender or food processor**

2 tbsp	butter	30 mL
1 tbsp	olive oil	15 mL
1	large white onion, finely chopped	1
1	leek (white and light green parts only), finely sliced (see Tips, left)	1
1	shallot, finely chopped	1
4	cloves garlic, finely chopped	1
4 cups	chicken broth	1 L
2 lbs	all-purpose or floury potatoes, peeled and cut into chunks	1 kg
2	sprigs fresh thyme	2
1 cup	table (18%) cream	250 mL
	Salt and white pepper	
12	chives, snipped in half	12

1. In a large saucepan, heat butter and oil over medium heat. Cook onion, leek, shallot and garlic, stirring, for 5 to 6 minutes or until softened but not beginning to brown.

2. Add broth, potatoes and thyme, increase heat to high and bring to a boil. Reduce heat to medium-low, cover loosely and gently simmer for about 20 minutes or until potatoes are tender and cooked through. Using tongs, remove thyme sprigs.

3. Using an immersion blender, or a food processor or blender in batches, purée soup until smooth. Return soup to a clean saucepan. Stir in cream and gently reheat over medium heat. Season to taste with salt and white pepper. Ladle into warmed individual serving bowls. Garnish with chives and serve immediately.

Potato & Roasted Garlic Soup with Cheese Toasties

This wonderfully warming concoction is a perfect supper for a frigid February evening. Easy to put together, this soup is flat-out delicious and quite substantial, especially with the floating cheese toasties. This is a favorite at our pub on St. Patrick's Day.

Makes 4 to 6 servings

Tips

Don't worry about the amount of garlic — once it is baked it becomes quite mellow.

To roast garlic: Preheat oven to 375°F (190°C). With a sharp chef's knife, carefully slice tip off each head of garlic, exposing the tops of the cloves. Place heads, tops up, in foil-lined roasting pan and drizzle with 2 tbsp (30 mL) olive oil. Roast in preheated oven for about 30 minutes or until softened. Set aside until cool enough to handle. Squeeze cloves out of their skins, coarsely chop and set aside.

● **Preheat oven to 400°F (200°C)**

2	heads roasted garlic (see Tips, left)	2
7 cups	chicken broth	1.75 L
4	large all-purpose potatoes, peeled and diced	4
	Salt and freshly ground black pepper	
½ cup	extra virgin olive oil	125 mL
1	baguette, cut diagonally into 1-inch (2.5 cm) slices	1
1½ cups	ricotta cheese	375 mL
1 cup	freshly grated Grana Padano or Parmesan	250 mL
¼ cup	chopped flat-leaf parsley leaves	60 mL

1. In a large pot, bring broth to a boil over high heat. Reduce heat to medium, add potatoes, cover and cook for 10 minutes. Add roasted garlic and season to taste with salt and freshly ground pepper. Simmer, uncovered, for about 15 minutes or until garlic is heated through.

2. In a large skillet, heat oil over medium-high heat. In batches, add baguette slices and toast, turning once, for about 1 minute per side or until golden brown. Transfer to a plate lined with paper towels and let drain.

3. Divide ricotta among toasts and spread over the tops. Transfer toasts to a baking sheet and sprinkle with Grana Padano. Bake for 5 minutes or until cheese is slightly golden. Remove from oven and sprinkle evenly with parsley.

4. Ladle soup into warmed serving bowls and center one cheese toastie, on each. Serve remaining toasties on the side.

Variation

If you prefer an even heartier soup, purée the finished soup and add 1 cup (250 mL) shredded sharp (aged) Cheddar.

Polish Potato & Porcini Soup

Packed as it is with an assortment of dried and fresh fungi, this good-for-what-ails-you soup would be perfect for a large gathering of mushroom lovers. Or you can plan on freezing some for one of those days when you just don't have time to cook.

Makes 10 servings

Tips

Dried porcini and other specialty mushrooms pack a lot of flavor. *To rehydrate the dried mushrooms for this recipe:* In a saucepan, combine dried mushrooms with 4 cups (1 L) water over high heat and bring to a boil. Reduce heat to low and simmer, uncovered, for 25 minutes or until softened. Remove from heat and let stand for 5 minutes. Place a sieve over a bowl and strain, collecting cooking liquid in bowl. Set liquid aside. Coarsely chop mushrooms and set aside.

Make sure to wash leeks thoroughly by slitting them open lengthwise and spreading them apart while rinsing clean under cold running water.

- Food processor

1 cup	dried porcini mushrooms (or mixture of dried porcini and dried chanterelle or other specialty mushrooms), rehydrated (see Tips, left)	250 mL
½ cup	butter	125 mL
2	large leeks (white and light green parts only), finely sliced (see Tips, left)	2
1	onion, finely chopped	1
2	stalks celery, chopped	2
1	large carrot, peeled and finely chopped	1
2 tsp	sweet paprika	10 mL
8 oz	cremini mushrooms, thinly sliced	250 g
8 oz	shiitake mushrooms, thinly sliced	250 g
4 cups	chicken or vegetable broth	1 L
6	large floury potatoes, peeled and cut into chunks	6
4 cups	whole milk	1 L
	Salt and freshly ground black pepper	

1. In a large saucepan, melt butter over medium heat. Cook leeks, onion, celery, carrot and paprika, stirring, for 5 minutes. Reduce heat slightly, stir in cremini and shiitake mushrooms and reserved dried mushrooms and cook for about 15 minutes or until vegetables are tender.

2. In another large saucepan, combine reserved mushroom cooking liquid, chicken broth and potatoes over high heat and bring to a boil. Reduce heat, cover loosely and cook for about 20 minutes or until potatoes are cooked through.

3. Transfer half the potatoes and some of their cooking liquid to a food processor and purée. Stir purée into mushroom mixture and add remaining potatoes and cooking liquid. Stir in milk and gently reheat over medium-low heat. Ladle into warmed serving bowls. Serve immediately.

Spices of India Soup

Because vegetable or chicken broth is not used in this soup — just water — it has a real clarity of potato and spice flavor. This is wonderful served with a savory flatbread such as Aloo Paratha (page 398) as an accompaniment.

Makes 6 to 8 servings

Tips

The mustard seeds will pop slightly when they hit the oil, so take care.

I prefer to use sea salt rather than refined table salt because it has a much cleaner, crisper taste and enhanced mineral content.

2 tbsp	vegetable oil	30 mL
2 tsp	yellow mustard seeds	10 mL
2 tbsp	chopped fresh gingerroot	30 mL
3 tbsp	tomato paste	45 mL
6	large all-purpose or floury potatoes, peeled and diced	6
4	fresh or canned large Roma (plum) tomatoes, peeled and chopped	4
1 tsp	salt	5 mL
1 tsp	turmeric	5 mL
2 tsp	cayenne pepper (approx.)	10 mL
6 cups	water	1.5 L
½ cup	fresh cilantro leaves	125 mL

1. In a large pot, heat oil over medium-high heat until shimmering. Reduce heat to medium, stir in mustard seeds and ginger and cook for 1 to 2 minutes. Stir in tomato paste to blend.

2. Add potatoes and tomatoes and cook, stirring, for about 10 minutes or until ingredients are well combined. Stir in salt, turmeric and cayenne, to taste.

3. Stir in water, scraping up any brown bits from bottom of pan, and cook for about 30 minutes or until potatoes have softened.

4. Using a slotted spoon, transfer a third of the potatoes to a bowl. Using a fork, mash coarsely, then return to pot. Stir, add cilantro and immediately ladle into warmed individual serving bowls. Serve immediately.

African Sweet Potato & Peanut Soup

This makes a rich soup that, with the addition of rice (see Tips), makes a one-dish meal.

Makes 4 to 6 servings

Tips

If you decide to accompany this soup with rice, keep the cooked rice warm. When ready to serve, place ½ cup (125 mL) rice in the center of each soup plate and pour the soup over and around it.

If you have leftover roast or grilled chicken, add it to the finished soup. In Africa peanuts would be pounded and added to the soup, but crunchy peanut butter makes a fine substitute.

2 tbsp	vegetable or peanut oil	30 mL
3	cloves garlic, finely chopped	3
1	onion, finely chopped	1
1 tsp	red pepper flakes (approx.)	5 mL
2	large sweet potatoes, peeled and cut into chunks	2
4 cups	chicken broth	1 L
⅔ cup	crunchy peanut butter (approx.)	150 mL
1 lb	spinach, stems removed, leaves cut into narrow strips	500 g
3 tbsp	freshly squeezed lemon juice	45 mL
	Salt and freshly ground black pepper	

1. In a large pot, heat oil over medium heat. Cook garlic and onion, stirring, for about 10 minutes or until softened. Stir in red pepper flakes and cook, stirring, for 1 minute.

2. Stir in sweet potatoes and cook for 1 to 2 minutes. Increase heat to high, stir in chicken broth, scraping up any brown bits from bottom of pot, and bring to a boil. Reduce heat to medium, cover loosely and simmer for about 20 minutes or until sweet potatoes are tender.

3. Stir in peanut butter until melted and blended (taste soup and, if desired, add a little more peanut butter; the flavor should be fairly prominent).

4. Add spinach, pushing it down into the soup, and cook for 1 to 2 minutes or until wilted. Stir in lemon juice. Season to taste with salt and pepper. Ladle into warmed individual serving bowls. Serve immediately.

Moroccan Spiced Soup

I have made a variation of this soup many times for customers of the Black Dog, and it is always very well received. One couple told me they had travelled all the way from Michigan in the hope that it was still on the menu (it wasn't, but, aiming to please, I made it for them the following day). I am not sure you would experience a soup exactly like this in North Africa, but certainly the spice mix is common. These spices are among those in a classic Moroccan spice blend called ras el hanout, which means "head of the shop." When this is cooking, your kitchen will smell amazing.

Makes 6 to 8 servings

Tips

To make the spice blend for this recipe: Combine 2 tsp (10 mL) ground turmeric, 1 tsp (5 mL) ground cinnamon, ½ tsp (2 mL) ground ginger, ¼ tsp (1 mL) each ground nutmeg, cardamom, freshly ground black pepper and cayenne pepper, and a pinch of ground cloves in a small bowl. Stir well.

You can use all sweet potato or all white potato in this soup. I like to use both, as it adds to the flavor of the finished product.

Use canned chickpeas (or other canned beans), or soak and cook about ¾ cup (175 mL) dried chickpeas.

¼ cup	olive oil (approx.)	60 mL
2	stalks celery, trimmed and chopped	2
2	carrots, peeled and chopped	2
1	large onion, chopped	1
4	cloves garlic, finely chopped	4
	Spice blend (see Tips, left)	
1	can (28 oz/796 mL) tomatoes, with juice, coarsely chopped	1
5 cups	chicken or vegetable broth	1.25 L
2	large all-purpose potatoes (about 1 lb/500 g), scrubbed and cut into ½-inch (1 cm) chunks	2
1	large sweet potato, peeled and cut into ½-inch (1 cm) chunks	1
	Salt (optional)	
1½ cups	cooked chickpeas, drained and rinsed	375 mL
1 cup	chopped fresh cilantro leaves	250 mL

1. In a large pot, warm oil over medium heat. Cook celery, carrots and onion, stirring, for about 10 minutes or until softened. Add garlic and cook for 1 to 2 minutes.

2. Stir in spice blend until vegetables are coated (if mixture looks too dry, splash in a little more oil). Reduce heat to medium-low (so as not to burn the spices) and cook, stirring, for about 5 minutes.

3. Stir in tomatoes with juice, broth, potatoes and sweet potato, scraping up any brown bits from bottom of pot, and bring to a boil. Cook, uncovered, over medium-low heat, stirring occasionally, for about 30 minutes or until vegetables are tender and soup has thickened slightly. Season to taste with salt (if using).

4. Stir in chickpeas and cook until heated through. Ladle into warmed serving bowls. Sprinkle with cilantro and serve.

Roasted Sweet Potato Soup with Smoked Cheddar & Herb Croutons

When sweet potatoes are baked or roasted, their flesh becomes very soft and rich-tasting, making them the perfect choice around which to build a soup. The smoked Cheddar and herb croutons are a lovely addition; they can be made while the sweet potatoes roast in the oven.

Makes 6 servings

Tips

Roasting the sweet potato adds depth to the vegetable, which is enhanced by the roasted garlic.

If you have one of those great little butane kitchen torches that are used to caramelize crème brûlée, it will save you having to turn on the broiler to melt the cheese on the croutons.

- Preheat oven to 450°F (230°C)
- Baking sheet, lined with parchment
- Immersion blender or food processor

2	large sweet potatoes (each about ¾ lb/375 g), peeled and cubed	2
4	cloves garlic, unpeeled	4
2 tbsp	extra virgin olive oil, divided	30 mL
½ tsp	salt, divided	2 mL
1	small onion, chopped	1
1	stalk celery, chopped	1
1	carrot, peeled and chopped	1
1 tsp	chopped fresh thyme leaves	5 mL
¼ tsp	white pepper	1 mL
4 cups	water	1 L
2 cups	chicken or vegetable broth	500 mL

Croutons

3 tbsp	extra virgin olive oil	45 mL
1 tbsp	melted butter	15 mL
1	clove garlic, minced	1
1 tbsp	chopped flat-leaf parsley leaves	15 mL
1 tbsp	chopped fresh thyme leaves	15 mL
6	slices Italian-style bread	6
6 oz	smoked Cheddar cheese, shredded	175 g

1. In a bowl, toss together sweet potatoes, garlic, 1 tbsp (15 mL) oil and ¼ tsp (1 mL) salt to coat. Transfer to prepared baking sheet. Roast in preheated oven for about 25 minutes or until sweet potatoes are tender and garlic is softened. Remove from oven and set aside until garlic is cool enough to handle. Squeeze garlic cloves out of their skins, finely chop and set aside.

2. In a large pot, heat remaining 1 tbsp (15 mL) oil over medium heat. Add onion, celery, carrot, thyme, remaining $1/4$ tsp (1 mL) salt and white pepper and cook, stirring, for about 10 minutes or until vegetables are tender.

3. Increase heat to high, stir in water, chicken broth and reserved roasted sweet potatoes and garlic and bring to a boil. Reduce heat, cover and simmer, stirring occasionally, for about 20 minutes or until vegetables are tender.

4. *Croutons:* Meanwhile, preheat broiler. In a small bowl, stir together oil, butter, garlic, parsley and thyme. Toast bread slices and, while still hot, spread with oil mixture and sprinkle evenly with cheese. Broil for about 1 to 2 minutes or until cheese has melted.

5. Using an immersion blender, or a food processor or blender in batches, purée soup until smooth. Ladle into warmed individual serving bowls and top each with one crouton. Serve immediately.

Coconut & Sweet Potato Soup

If you don't think you have time to make soup on a weeknight, try this recipe. The very definition of simplicity, it is composed of just four ingredients. This soup would be a nice starter for a Thai- or Indonesian-inspired meal, for instance, as a precursor to skewers of chicken or shrimp satay.

Makes 4 to 6 servings

Tips

I have used vegetable broth here, with the caveat that it must be of good quality (preferably homemade), as you will be relying on it to provide flavor. Or you can choose to use chicken broth or a combination of both.

Before opening a can of coconut milk, always give it a good shake, as the contents will have separated in the can.

● **Food processor or blender**

6 cups	vegetable or chicken broth (see Tips, left)	1.5 L
2 lbs	sweet potatoes, peeled and cut into chunks	1 kg
3 cups	canned coconut milk	750 mL
8	fresh basil leaves, cut into fine strips	8

1. In a large pot over high heat, bring vegetable broth to a boil. Add sweet potatoes and cook for 15 to 20 minutes or until tender.
2. Working in batches to keep the liquid from leaking out, transfer a third of the mixture (both liquid and solids) to a food processor or blender, add coconut milk and purée until smooth. Repeat with the remaining mixture, transferring the batches to a clean pot after puréeing. Reduce heat to medium and reheat gently, stirring to combine. Ladle into warmed individual serving bowls. Garnish with basil.

Sweet Potato Soup with Lentils & Curry

I made this substantial soup one evening with a couple of big sweet potatoes that had been baked the day before, but it works just as well with uncooked sweet potatoes. Like butternut squash, sweet potatoes respond well to a bit of curry and ginger seasoning. And the lentils add enough protein to make this almost a complete meal, especially if served with a whole-grain bread.

Makes 4 to 6 servings

Tips

Use split orange or red lentils, the kind used for making dal, the thick lentil purée that is so good when scooped up with an Indian flatbread such as paratha or naan. These lentils break down well, whereas brown or green lentils keep their shape.

If leftovers of this soup get too thick, just thin it out with a bit more broth or water.

- **Immersion blender or food processor**

¼ cup	vegetable oil	60 mL
3	cloves garlic, finely chopped	3
1	large onion, finely chopped	1
1	stalk celery, finely chopped	1
2 tbsp	chopped fresh gingerroot	30 mL
1 tbsp	curry powder or curry paste	15 mL
2	large sweet potatoes, peeled and diced	2
1½ cups	orange or red lentils	375 mL
5 cups	chicken or vegetable broth (approx.)	1.25 L
¼ cup	chopped flat-leaf parsley leaves	60 mL

1. In a large pot, heat oil over medium heat. Cook garlic, onion and celery, stirring, for about 10 minutes or until softened. Stir in ginger and curry powder and cook, stirring, for 4 or 5 minutes.

2. Stir in sweet potatoes and lentils to combine. Increase heat to high, stir in chicken broth and bring to a boil. Reduce heat to medium-low, cover loosely and cook gently for about 30 minutes or until potatoes and lentils have softened.

3. Using an immersion blender, or a food processor or blender in batches, purée soup until smooth. Return to a clean pot and gently reheat over medium heat (if soup is too thick, add a little more broth, water or milk). Ladle into warmed individual serving bowls. Sprinkle with parsley and serve immediately.

New Fulton Fish Market Chowder

This chowder pays homage to New York City's fabulous New Fulton Fish Market, where restaurant chefs and fishmongers go to stock up on some of the hundreds of species of fish and seafood sold there. The "new" in the name was added in 2005, when the market was moved to its current location in the Bronx. This Manhattan-style fish and potato soup is ultra-easy and can be put together quickly. So organize a kitchen party, pour everyone a glass of wine and get to it! Accompany with lots of good crusty bread.

**Makes
6 servings**

Tip
Accompany with a light-bodied red wine such as Gamay or Beaujolais.

6	strips bacon, diced	6
2	cloves garlic, minced	2
1	large onion, chopped	1
1	yellow or orange bell pepper, seeded and thinly sliced	1
2 tbsp	chopped flat-leaf parsley leaves	30 mL
1	can (28 oz/796 mL) tomatoes, with juice	1
2½ cups	clam juice	625 mL
1 cup	light-bodied red wine	250 mL
1 tbsp	chopped fresh thyme	15 mL
	Salt and freshly ground black pepper	
3	large waxy red-skinned potatoes, scrubbed and cut into chunks	3
8 oz	skinless salmon fillet, cut into small chunks	250 g
8 oz	small scallops	250 g
1 lb	small shrimp, shelled and deveined	500 g
½ cup	chopped fresh cilantro leaves	125 mL

1. In a large pot, sauté bacon over medium-high heat for about 10 minutes or until crisp. Reduce heat to medium and stir in garlic, onion, bell pepper and parsley. Cook, stirring often, until vegetables are softened.

2. Stir in tomatoes with juice and, using a wooden spoon, coarsely break up tomatoes. Stir in clam juice, wine and thyme. Season to taste with salt and pepper. Bring to a boil. Reduce heat and simmer uncovered for 15 to 20 minutes.

3. Add potatoes and cook until tender. Stir in salmon. Cover and cook for 5 minutes, then add scallops and shrimp and cook, covered, for 5 minutes. Ladle into warmed serving bowls. Sprinkle with cilantro and serve.

Variation

To spice things up a bit, add some chopped fresh chile peppers when you add the bell pepper.

Cullen Skink

This is Scotland's famous potato and smoked haddock soup. It's a featured favorite every January on the annual Robbie Burns Night at our restaurant, the Black Dog. *Skink* derives from the Gaelic word meaning "essence." I have also read that the word describes a thin oatmeal-based gruel, but I know you will enjoy this delicious preparation much more. Serve with good bread and butter.

**Makes
4 servings**

Tip
Dry-mashed potatoes are mashed without butter, milk or cream.

2 lbs	smoked haddock fillets	1 kg
4 cups	whole milk	1 L
1	onion, thinly sliced	1
1	stalk celery, trimmed and chopped	1
1 or 2	bay leaves	1 or 2
2 cups	dry-mashed potato (see Tip, left)	500 mL
½ cup	heavy or whipping (35%) cream	125 mL
3 tbsp	chilled butter, cut into small pieces	45 mL
	Salt and white pepper	
¼ cup	chopped flat-leaf parsley leaves	60 mL

1. Place haddock in a single layer in a large saucepan. Add milk, onion, celery and bay leaves and bring to a gentle boil over medium heat. Reduce heat to low and gently simmer for 5 to 10 minutes or until haddock is tender. Using a slotted spoon, transfer haddock to a plate and set aside until cool enough to handle.

2. Remove skin and bones from haddock, breaking meat into small chunks as you work. Set meat aside. Return skin and bones to saucepan and simmer for about 20 minutes. Set a sieve over a bowl and pour milk mixture through sieve. Discard solids. Wipe saucepan clean and return milk mixture to it. Place over low heat.

3. Whisk in mashed potato until smooth. Stir in haddock and cream and cook for 1 to 2 minutes or until heated through. Add butter. Season to taste with salt and white pepper. Sprinkle with parsley and serve immediately.

Cape Breton Clam Chowder

After a brisk walk through the Mabou Highlands and along the beautiful Ceilidh Trail in Cape Breton, Nova Scotia, I enjoyed this rich, creamy, thoroughly delicious chowder at the Glenora Inn and Distillery. One of the best chowders I have ever had, it was served with a basket of warm-from-the-oven whole wheat bread and butter. Perfect.

Makes 4 to 6 servings

Tips

If you don't want to blend the chowder, use 2 lbs (1 kg) firm, waxy potatoes, scrubbed and diced, in place of the all-purpose type.

Make sure to wash leeks thoroughly by slitting them open lengthwise and spreading them apart while rinsing clean under cold running water.

● **Food processor or blender**

3 dozen	small (littleneck or "pasta") clams, well scrubbed	1.25 kg
2 tbsp	dried dulse or other dried seaweed	30 mL
2	small onions, finely chopped, divided	2
1	leek (white and light green parts only), trimmed and chopped	1
1	small carrot, peeled and chopped	1
2	sprigs flat-leaf parsley	2
2	sprigs fresh thyme	2
2 cups	water	500 mL
1 cup	dry white wine	250 mL
2 tbsp	butter	30 mL
6	slices smoked bacon, diced	6
1 cup	clam juice or chicken broth	250 mL
2	large all-purpose potatoes, peeled and diced (see Tips, left)	2
1 cup	heavy or whipping (35%) cream	250 mL
	Salt and freshly ground black pepper	
2 tbsp	chopped flat-leaf parsley leaves	30 mL
1 tbsp	chopped fresh chives	15 mL

1. Rinse clams under cool running water, discarding any that do not close when tapped firmly. Set aside.
2. In a large, wide saucepan over high heat, combine dulse, half of the onions, leek, carrot, parsley, thyme and water and bring to a boil. Reduce heat to medium, cover loosely and simmer for 10 minutes. Turn off the heat and let stand for 20 minutes to infuse.
3. Stir in wine and return to a boil over high heat. Add clams, cover and cook, occasionally shaking pan vigorously back and forth, for 1 or 2 minutes or until clams have opened. Discard any clams that have not opened.

4. Set a colander over a large bowl. Using tongs, transfer clams to colander and pull meat from shells, collecting any liquid from the shells in bowl. Add meat to bowl along with vegetable mixture and cooking liquid, discarding sprigs of parsley and thyme. Set aside.

5. In a clean saucepan, melt butter over medium heat. Cook remaining onion and the bacon, stirring, for about 6 minutes or until onion has softened and bacon is just cooked. Stir in clam juice, scraping up any brown bits from bottom of pan, and bring to a gentle boil. Add potatoes and cook gently for about 15 minutes or until tender (add a little water, if necessary, to make sure potatoes have enough liquid to cook).

6. Transfer half of the potato mixture (liquid and solids) to a food processor or blender and purée. Return purée to saucepan along with reserved clam mixture. Reheat over medium heat for about 10 minutes or until heated through.

7. Reduce heat to low, stir in cream and simmer for 10 minutes. Season to taste with salt and pepper. Stir in parsley and chives. Ladle into warmed individual serving bowls and serve immediately.

Potato, Bacon & Mussels in Cider & Cream Soup

Three happy bedfellows — potatoes, bacon and fresh mussels — in a sea of cider, cream and garlic. This may not appear to be a conventional soup but it certainly is soup-like and can be offered as such. Make sure to have a couple of baguettes on hand to serve with this, and enjoy every spoonful.

Makes 4 servings

2½ lbs	fresh mussels, cleaned	1.25 kg
2 cups	dry apple cider (or dry white wine)	500 mL
2	cloves garlic, thinly sliced	2
1	leek (white and light green parts only), thinly sliced (see Tips, page 94)	1
1	stalk celery, thinly sliced diagonally	1
1 cup	table (18%) cream	250 mL
1 cup	heavy or whipping (35%) cream	250 mL
	Salt and white pepper	
10	saffron threads, soaked (see Tips, left)	10
¼ cup	finely chopped flat-leaf parsley leaves	60 mL

Tips

These days fresh mussels usually come de-bearded (that is, with the little bundle of brown fibers between the shells removed), but check to make sure they have been. If not, holding the mussel in the palm of your hand, use your other hand to grab hold of the fibers and give them a good tug; they should come away cleanly. Before using, rinse mussels under cool running water, using a small stiff brush if necessary to clean their shells. The shells should close when given a little tap; if they don't, discard the mussels. Similarly, discard any that do not open after cooking.

Soak the saffron in a small amount of hot water (or some of the cider) for 15 minutes before using.

Make sure the vegetables are very thinly sliced, as they have only a brief time in the cooking liquid.

1. Rinse mussels under cool running water, discarding any that do not close when tapped firmly. Set aside.

2. In large saucepan, warm cider over medium heat. Increase heat to high, add mussels, cover and cook, occasionally shaking pan vigorously back and forth, for about 5 minutes or until mussels have opened. Remove from heat and discard any unopened mussels.

3. Place a fine-mesh sieve over a bowl and pour mussels and cooking liquid from pan into sieve, collecting liquid in the bowl. Let cool for about 5 minutes. Working over sieve and bowl to catch any liquid from the shells, remove mussels from shells and set aside.

4. Wipe saucepan clean and return cooking liquid to it. Place over medium heat. Add garlic, leek, celery and all the cream. Season to taste with salt and white pepper and bring to a boil over high heat. Reduce heat to medium-low and simmer for about 8 to 10 minutes or until vegetables have softened.

5. Add mussels, saffron and soaking liquid (see Tips, left) and simmer until mussels are just heated through. Ladle into warmed individual serving bowls. Sprinkle with parsley and serve immediately.

St. Patrick's Day Potato Chowder

This hearty soup is full of chunky potatoes, cabbage and a little smoked sausage. It is bound to be especially well-received on St. Patrick's Day, when the mid-March winds often blow cold in my part of the world.

Makes 4 to 6 servings

Tip

I prefer to use sea salt rather than refined table salt because it has a much cleaner, crisper taste and enhanced mineral content.

1 tbsp	olive oil	15 mL
8 oz	smoked sausage (pork, chicken or turkey), thinly sliced or diced	250 g
3	cloves garlic, finely chopped	3
1	large onion, finely chopped	1
1	carrot, peeled and grated	1
½	head green cabbage (outer leaves trimmed), cored, shredded and chopped (about 3 cups/750 mL)	½
4	floury potatoes, peeled and cut into chunks	4
4 cups	chicken broth	1 L
	Salt and freshly ground black pepper	
¼ cup	chopped flat-leaf parsley leaves	60 mL

1. In a large pot, heat oil over medium heat. Add sausage and cook, stirring occasionally, for 10 to 15 minutes or until almost cooked through and fat has been released. Pour off all but 2 tbsp (30 mL) fat from pan.

2. Stir in garlic, onion and carrot and cook, stirring and scraping up any brown bits from bottom and sides of pan, for 10 minutes. Stir in cabbage and cook, stirring, for about 10 minutes or until vegetables and meat are starting to brown.

3. Toss in potatoes, then stir in chicken broth (add enough water, if necessary, to totally immerse solids) and bring to a boil. Reduce heat to medium, cover loosely and cook for 15 to 20 minutes or until potatoes and cabbage are tender. Season to taste with salt and pepper. Ladle into warmed individual serving bowls. Sprinkle with parsley and serve immediately.

Potato & White Bean Soup

The county where we live is famous for its pork and its beans. Every type of bean grows here and huge farms are devoted to their production. White beans, kidney beans, soybeans — you name it. The small white bean also known as a navy bean even has a festival dedicated to it in August. Inspired by their proliferation and quality, we have always featured bean soups on our menu at the Black Dog. This version features navy beans teamed with bacon, potatoes and red bell pepper.

Makes 4 to 6 servings

Tips

Soak the beans overnight in enough cold water to cover by a couple of inches. Drain and rinse under cold running water before cooking. If you prefer, substitute 4 cups (1 L) canned beans (drained and rinsed) and skip Step 1. If you do this, include additional water or broth to make up the difference — you need a total of 10 cups (2.5 L).

Make sure to wash leeks thoroughly by slitting them open lengthwise and spreading them apart while rinsing clean under cold running water.

1½ cups	dried navy or cannellini (white kidney) beans, soaked (see Tips, left)	375 mL
8 oz	slab bacon, diced	250 g
1 tbsp	olive oil	15 mL
1	onion, finely chopped	1
3	leeks, trimmed (white and light green parts only), thinly sliced (see Tips, left)	3
1	carrot, peeled and chopped	1
1	stalk celery, finely chopped	1
1	red bell pepper, diced	1
1 tsp	red pepper flakes (approx.)	5 mL
4 cups	chicken broth	1 L
	Salt and freshly ground black pepper	
3	large floury potatoes, peeled and cut into ½-inch (1 cm) dice	3

1. In a large pot, combine beans with 6 cups (1.5 L) cold water and bring to a boil. Reduce heat to medium-low and simmer, uncovered, for about 1 hour or until tender.

2. Meanwhile, in a large skillet, combine bacon and oil over medium heat and cook, stirring, until bacon is beginning to crisp. Using a slotted spoon, transfer to a plate lined with paper towels and let drain. Pour off all but 2 tbsp (30 mL) fat from pan. Add onion, leeks, carrot, celery, red bell pepper and pepper flakes and cook, stirring, until vegetables are softened and just beginning to brown.

3. Using a ladle, transfer some of the bean cooking water to skillet. Stir well, scraping up any brown bits from bottom of pan. Add skillet contents to beans and cooking liquid and stir to combine. Add reserved bacon and the potatoes and bring to a boil. Cover loosely and cook for about 15 minutes or until potatoes are tender. Season to taste with salt and freshly ground pepper. Ladle into warmed serving bowls and serve.

Mexican Tortilla Soup

Mexican tortilla soup with chicken is a very simple affair: good chicken broth with a bit of shredded chicken, tomatoes, oregano and chile pepper for heat. It is always finished with fried tortilla strips and some chunks of avocado. Inspired by that concoction, I have come up with my version, which naturally includes potatoes.

Makes 4 to 6 servings

Tips

You'll need about 2 cups (500 mL) diced potatoes for this recipe.

Mexican oregano is a little sweeter than traditional oregano. It is available in Latin or South American food shops. If you can't obtain it for this recipe, you can use half regular oregano and half dried marjoram, or use all regular dried (not ground) oregano but reduce the amount by half.

This is a good soup to prepare when you have leftover roast or grilled chicken.

Peeling tomatoes may sound like a tedious chore, but it is effortless if you follow this method: Make sure the tomatoes are firm. With a sharp paring knife, cut a small X in the base of the tomato, then plunge it into a large pot of boiling water for 2 minutes. Remove with a slotted spoon. Working from the base, peel off the skin with the paring knife.

- Blender or food processor
- Cast-iron or other heavy skillet

4 cups	chicken or vegetable broth	1 L
1 lb	all-purpose potatoes, peeled and diced	500 g
3	large ripe tomatoes, peeled and coarsely chopped (see Tips, left)	3
1	red onion, chopped	1
2	cloves garlic, finely chopped	2
2 tsp	dried Mexican oregano (see Tips, left)	10 mL
1	chipotle pepper in adobo sauce, chopped	1
1 cup	tomato sauce	250 mL
	Salt and freshly ground black pepper	
1½ cups	cooked chicken, coarsely chopped	375 mL
½ cup	vegetable oil	125 mL
8	corn tortillas, cut into ½-inch (1 cm) strips	8
1 cup	sour cream	250 mL
1 or 2	firm ripe avocados, cut into chunks or slices	1 or 2
1 cup	cilantro leaves, with a bit of stem, chopped	250 mL

1. In a large pot, combine broth, potatoes, tomatoes, onion, garlic, oregano and chipotle (with sauce). Bring to a boil over high heat. Reduce heat, cover loosely and cook until potatoes are tender.

2. Scoop out about 2 cups (500 mL) of the mixture and transfer to a blender or food processor. Purée. Return to pot along with tomato sauce. Season to taste with salt and pepper and bring to a boil. Reduce heat, add chicken and simmer, loosely covered, for about 15 minutes or until chicken is heated through.

3. In a skillet, heat oil over medium heat. Fry tortilla strips in batches, turning once, for 1 to 2 minutes or until golden. Transfer to a plate lined with paper towels and sprinkle with salt.

4. Ladle soup into warmed serving bowls. Garnish with tortilla strips, sour cream, avocado and cilantro.

Galician Soup

Northern Spain is famous for the quality of its potatoes, which are reputed to be the finest in the country. I can attest to that, having enjoyed a variety of potato dishes in that region. This is one of the best. Although here the treatment is classic Galician — known as *caldo Gallego* — a version of this soup is popular throughout the country. Serve with good crusty bread and make the meal even more Spanish by accompanying it with a selection of that country's fantastic cheeses, such as manchego, tetilla or the intense blue Cabrales. Don't forget to include a nice Spanish red wine such as Tempranillo to serve alongside.

Makes 6 to 8 servings

Tips

Although collard greens work especially well, you can use any substantial leafy green such as turnip tops or mustard greens.

Ham or pork hocks vary in size; try to find one that weighs about 2 lbs (1 kg) or two smaller ones. If the ham hock you are using is especially large and yields too much meat for this recipe, reserve the rest for another use, such as in sandwiches or omelets or combined with mashed potato and cabbage for a quick skillet supper. You could also use a meaty ham bone in its place.

You can save a bit of time here by cooking the ham hock the day before. Just be sure to reserve the cooking liquid.

1½ cups	dried white beans, soaked overnight in cold water and drained	375 mL
1	fresh ham hock (see Tips, left)	1
2 tsp	salt	10 mL
2 tsp	freshly ground black pepper	10 mL
2 tsp	sweet Spanish paprika	10 mL
3	large floury or all-purpose potatoes, peeled and diced	3
1	bunch collard greens or kale, trimmed and thick stems discarded, coarsely chopped	1
2	chorizo sausages, cut into small chunks	2

1. Place beans in a large pot and cover with 8 cups (2 L) cold water. Add ham hock, salt, pepper and paprika and bring to a boil over high heat. Reduce heat to medium-low, cover loosely and cook, occasionally skimming off any foam that rises to the surface, for 90 minutes.
2. Using tongs, remove ham hock and let cool slightly. Add potatoes, collard greens and chorizo to beans and cook for about 20 minutes or until potatoes are tender.
3. Meanwhile, remove skin, fat and bone from ham hock. Chop meat coarsely and add to bean mixture.
4. If the broth is not as thick as you would like, using a slotted spoon, transfer a few chunks of potato and some beans to a bowl, mash together with a fork, then stir back into the pot. Ladle into warmed individual serving bowls. Serve as described above.

Salads

For Warm Days and Cold Nights

Potatoes lend their particular magic to so many dishes, and salads are no exception, especially now, when the concept of a salad has expanded to include grains, grilled foods, fish and seafood, cheeses and meats. This chapter includes potato salads with attitude — to be enjoyed at lunch, as a light summer supper or as a seriously good main course for dinner in the dead of winter. Whether hot, warm or cold, potatoes have what it takes to inspire wonderful salad creations year-round.

Baked Potato Salad with Blue Cheese Drizzle

When you bake potatoes for longer than necessary, the exterior gets extra crispy and the flesh becomes even sweeter. That makes these potatoes great candidates for this side-dish salad, which my husband, Ted, loves to serve with pan-seared strip loin steaks.

Makes 4 servings

Tips

Gorgonzola is an especially creamy Italian blue cheese, but any blue cheese will work well here.

If the refrigerated dressing becomes too thick, blend in a little cream until it reaches the desired consistency.

I prefer to use sea salt rather than refined table salt because it has a much cleaner, crisper taste and enhanced mineral content.

- **Preheat oven to 450°F (230°C)**

4	large floury potatoes, scrubbed	4

Dressing

½ cup	crumbled Gorgonzola cheese (see Tips, left)	125 mL
¼ cup	mayonnaise	60 mL
¼ cup	sour cream	60 mL
¼ cup	table (18%) cream	60 mL
2 tsp	freshly squeezed lemon juice	10 mL
	Salt and freshly ground black pepper	
4 cups	baby spinach	1 L
3	green onions, finely chopped	3

1. Place potatoes directly on oven rack and bake in preheated oven for 90 minutes or until skin is crisp and crackly. Remove from oven and let stand for 1 to 2 minutes.

2. *Dressing:* Meanwhile, in a bowl, combine cheese, mayonnaise, sour cream, cream and lemon juice. Using a large fork, lightly mash cheese, leaving some chunks intact. Season to taste with salt and freshly ground pepper. Cover and refrigerate until ready to use or for up to 6 hours.

3. When you're ready to serve, divide spinach evenly among four individual serving plates. Using a sharp chef's knife, slice each potato in half, then quarters, and arrange over spinach on one plate. Generously top with dressing (see Tips, left). Sprinkle with green onions. Serve immediately, with any remaining dressing on the side.

Grilled Red Potatoes with Basil Aïoli

Food from the south of France wouldn't be the same without aïoli, that region's characteristically pungent garlic mayonnaise that is so ubiquitous it is also known as *beurre de Provence* (Provençal butter). Aïoli is wonderful with any grilled vegetables or seafood but, although not traditional, I think it is especially memorable with new potatoes.

Makes 4 to 6 servings

Tips

If you're in a hurry, pierce the potatoes in a few places with a fork and precook in the microwave for about 5 minutes on High before coating and grilling.

Wooden skewers work best here because the potatoes won't slip around, as they often do on metal skewers. However, they need to be soaked first — otherwise they will burn when heated. Before using, soak in cold water to cover until you're ready to use them, for at least 30 minutes or up to 8 hours.

After refrigeration, let aïoli stand at room temperature for 30 minutes, to allow the flavors to bloom.

You can serve the potatoes skewered or, if you prefer, remove them from the skewers before serving.

- **Barbecue or indoor grill**
- **Blender or food processor**
- **Soaked wooden skewers (see Tips, left)**

Basil Aïoli

4	cloves garlic, finely chopped	4
2	egg yolks	2
2 tbsp	freshly squeezed lemon juice	30 mL
1 tsp	salt	5 mL
¼ tsp	freshly ground black pepper	2 mL
¾ cup	extra virgin olive oil	175 mL
½ cup	chopped fresh basil leaves	125 mL

Potatoes

2½ lbs	small new red potatoes, scrubbed	1.25 kg
¼ cup	extra virgin olive oil	60 mL
1 tbsp	dried basil	15 mL
	Salt and freshly ground black pepper	

1. *Basil Aïoli:* In a blender, combine garlic, egg yolks, lemon juice, salt and pepper. With the motor running, add oil in a thin stream until mixture is creamy and thick. Transfer to a small serving bowl and stir in basil. Cover and refrigerate for up to 6 hours.

2. *Potatoes:* Preheat barbecue to medium-high. In a large bowl, toss potatoes with oil and basil to coat. Season to taste with salt and pepper. Divide evenly among skewers. Place skewered potatoes on preheated grill and cook, turning often, for 25 to 30 minutes or until potatoes are cooked through and skins are beginning to brown and crisp up. Serve Basil Aïoli on the side.

Variation

Use a combination of waxy, red and white-skinned potatoes.

Fingerling Potato Salad with Tarragon Cream

The secret to the success of this simple summer dish is to serve it just warm, or as soon as it's ready. If left to cool, these lovely knobby, waxy potatoes lose some of their characteristic interior stickiness, arguably one of their nicest features. This is a great salad to serve with cold chicken and a selection of crudités.

Makes 6 to 8 servings

Tip

If you find the tarragon cream too acidic, add a little extra virgin olive oil and a wee bit of granulated sugar.

3 lbs	fingerling potatoes, rinsed	1.5 kg
1 tsp	salt	5 mL
1	shallot, minced	1
3 tbsp	chopped fresh tarragon leaves	45 mL
1/4 cup	tarragon or regular white wine vinegar	60 mL
	Salt and freshly ground black pepper	
1/4 cup	mayonnaise	60 mL
3 tbsp	heavy or whipping (35%) cream	45 mL
1	large bunch arugula	1

1. Place potatoes in a large saucepan and add boiling water to barely cover. Add salt, cover loosely and bring to a boil. Reduce heat and cook for 20 minutes or until potatoes are tender. Drain well and transfer to a warmed bowl.
2. Add shallot, tarragon and vinegar to potatoes and toss gently. Season to taste with salt and freshly ground pepper. Set aside to cool slightly. Add mayonnaise and cream and toss gently to coat. Arrange arugula on a large serving platter, top with potato mixture and serve immediately.

Baby Yukon Gold Salad with Parsley & Crème Fraîche

Although I've specified Yukon Golds, any new potatoes can be used in this sweet little preparation, a very simple but elegant potato salad. This is especially nice when paired with a selection of colorful grilled vegetables — red onion, eggplant, zucchini, sweet peppers — and rib-eye steaks treated to a spicy dry rub before grilling.

Makes 4 to 6 servings

Tip

Crème fraîche is available in well-stocked supermarkets. If you prefer, make your own (see page 132), but be sure to start it a day or two before you make this salad.

2½ lbs	small new Yukon Gold potatoes, scrubbed	1.25 kg
1 tsp	salt	5 mL
¾ cup	heavy or whipping (35%) cream	175 mL
2	shallots, minced	2
1	large clove garlic, minced	1
	Salt and freshly ground black pepper	
¾ cup	crème fraîche (see Tip, left)	175 mL
2 tbsp	white wine vinegar	30 mL
¼ cup	chopped flat-leaf parsley leaves	60 mL
¼ cup	chopped fresh chives	60 mL

1. Place potatoes in a large saucepan and add boiling water to barely cover. Add salt, cover loosely and bring to a boil over high heat. Reduce heat and cook for 20 minutes or until potatoes are tender. Drain and set aside to cool.

2. If potato skins are easy to pull off, do so, discarding skins; if not, cut potatoes into ¼-inch (0.5 cm) slices. Return potatoes to clean saucepan and set aside.

3. In another saucepan, combine cream, shallots and garlic. Season to taste with salt and pepper. Gently warm over low heat, stirring, for about 10 minutes or until vegetables have softened. Remove from heat. Let stand for about 10 minutes, then stir in crème fraîche until smooth and well blended.

4. Add crème fraiche mixture to potatoes and toss to coat. Over low heat, gradually stir in vinegar and warm gently for about 5 minutes or until heated through. Transfer to a serving dish. Sprinkle with parsley and chives and serve immediately.

Variation

Vary the herbs to suit your taste. You can substitute an equal quantity of chervil or basil for the parsley or chives.

Rustic Summer Reds Salad with Garlic & Fresh Herbs

You might call this my "house" potato salad. My daughters and I make it often during the summer and at other times of the year too, whenever we want a big, garlicky hit of spuds and herbs. It's not delicate but it is very good, and also quite versatile as far as the cooking of the potatoes goes — you can steam, boil, bake or grill them. Just make sure to combine the other ingredients with the potatoes while they are still quite hot. These potatoes are great with grilled sausages and hot mustard or hefty burgers.

Makes 4 to 6 servings

Tip

I prefer to use sea salt rather than refined table salt because it has a much cleaner, crisper taste and enhanced mineral content.

3 lbs	large red-skinned potatoes, cooked, cooled and cut into bite-size chunks	1.5 kg
½ cup	extra virgin olive oil	125 mL
¼ cup	balsamic vinegar	60 mL
4	cloves garlic, finely chopped	4
¼ cup	chopped fresh chives	60 mL
¼ cup	chopped fresh mint leaves	60 mL
¼ cup	chopped flat-leaf parsley leaves	60 mL
	Salt and freshly ground black pepper	

1. In a large bowl, toss potatoes, oil, vinegar, garlic, chives, mint and parsley. Season to taste with salt and freshly ground pepper. Set aside, uncovered, for about 30 minutes to allow flavors to develop before serving.

Corn & Potato Salad with Grape Tomatoes & Fresh Oregano

A perfect salad to make when corn, tomatoes and new potatoes are bountiful at farmers' markets, this is just right with glazed barbecued ribs.

Makes 4 to 6 servings

Tips

This salad is especially pretty since it combines both white and red new potatoes.

Taste the vinaigrette to see if it needs more oil or vinegar. If it does, add, then shake again.

Speed up preparation by cooking extra ears of corn the day before. When you are ready to make this salad, scrape the kernels from the cobs with a sharp chef's knife.

Fresh oregano is nothing like the dried version. Almost sweet and very fragrant, it lends a special quality to this salad.

If your skillet will not accommodate all the potatoes, sauté them in batches or save time by using a second skillet.

- **Large jar with tight-fitting lid**

Vinaigrette

⅔ cup	extra virgin olive oil	150 mL
¼ cup	balsamic vinegar	60 mL
	Salt and freshly ground black pepper	

Salad

¼ cup	butter	60 mL
3 tbsp	olive oil	45 mL
1 lb	each small white and red new potatoes, scrubbed and halved	500 g
2½ cups	cooked corn kernels (about 5 cobs)	625 mL
2	shallots, finely chopped	2
2 cups	grape tomatoes	500 mL
½ cup	fresh oregano leaves, torn	125 mL
	Salt and freshly ground black pepper	
1 lb	salad greens, torn, if needed	500 g

1. *Vinaigrette:* In a large jar with a tight-fitting lid, combine oil and vinegar. Season to taste with salt and freshly ground pepper. Close lid and shake to blend thoroughly (see Tips, left). Set aside.

2. *Salad:* In a large skillet, heat butter and oil over medium heat. In batches if necessary, cook potatoes, turning occasionally, for about 25 minutes or until tender, crisp and golden. Stir in corn and cook for about 3 minutes or until heated through. Turn out into a large bowl, scraping in any brown bits from bottom of pan.

3. Add shallots, tomatoes and oregano to potatoes. Season to taste with salt and freshly ground pepper. Drizzle with vinaigrette and toss to coat.

4. Divide salad greens evenly among 4 to 6 individual serving plates. Top with potato mixture.

English Country Garden Herb & Potato Salad

I was once served a deliciously fragrant warm potato salad in a lovely old walled garden in southwest England. The potatoes and herbs had been picked just an hour or so before I enjoyed them. It was understated elegance at its British best.

Makes 4 to 6 servings

Tips

After tossing in the herbs, taste and add a little more olive oil or vinegar if desired.

This salad is wonderful served with slices of cold ham, tiny tomatoes and a few halves of hard-boiled egg.

2½ lbs	small waxy new potatoes, scrubbed	1.25 kg
1 tsp	salt	5 mL

Dressing

½ cup	extra virgin olive oil (approx.)	125 mL
3 tbsp	white wine vinegar (approx.)	45 mL
	Salt and freshly ground black pepper	
¼ cup	finely chopped fresh chives	60 mL
¼ cup	finely chopped fresh dill fronds	60 mL
¼ cup	finely chopped flat-leaf parsley leaves	60 mL
¼ cup	finely chopped fresh tarragon leaves	60 mL

1. Place potatoes in a large saucepan and add boiling water to barely cover. Add salt, cover loosely and bring to a boil. Reduce heat and cook for 15 to 20 minutes or until potatoes are just tender.
2. *Dressing:* Meanwhile, in a large bowl, whisk together oil and vinegar. Season to taste with salt and freshly ground pepper.
3. Drain potatoes and set aside until cool enough to handle. Using a paring knife and working quickly, peel off skins and discard. Add potatoes to bowl with dressing and toss gently to coat. Add chives, dill, parsley and tarragon (see Variation, below) and toss well. Serve immediately.

Variation

Always use some fresh dill, but vary the selection of other fresh herbs as you wish. Try chervil, regular or lemon thyme and marjoram.

Winter Warmer Potato Salad

On a cycling tour of wine country in German's Mosel region, I must have enjoyed *kartoffelsalat* at least once a day. Although this preparation may not be perceived as a salad in the strictest sense of the word — it is invariably served at room temperature — it comes across that way. It is particularly good with pork, whether in the form of a roast, sausages, ham or other cured products.

Makes 6 to 8 servings

Tips

If you can obtain low-sodium vegetable or chicken bouillon cubes, use them for the broth. Or just use the premade broth sold in resealable containers.

I prefer to use sea salt rather than refined table salt because it has a much cleaner, crisper taste and enhanced mineral content.

3 lbs	all-purpose potatoes, peeled	1.5 kg
2 tbsp	caraway seeds	30 mL
1 tsp	salt	5 mL
1	onion, finely chopped	1
½ cup	vegetable or chicken broth	125 mL
⅓ cup	white wine vinegar	75 mL
1 tsp	granulated sugar	5 mL
	Salt and freshly ground black pepper	
¼ cup	canola or sunflower oil	60 mL
¼ cup	chopped flat-leaf parsley leaves	60 mL

1. Place potatoes and caraway seeds in a large saucepan and add cold water to barely cover. Bring to a boil over high heat. Add salt and return to a boil. Cover loosely, reduce heat and cook for 25 to 30 minutes or until potatoes are tender. Drain potatoes through a sieve and set the caraway seeds aside. Rinse potatoes briefly under cold running water and drain well. Using a paring knife, peel off the skins, then slice potatoes directly into a large serving bowl. Add caraway seeds and scatter onion over potatoes.

2. In a saucepan, warm broth over medium-high heat and pour over potato mixture.

3. In a measuring cup, whisk together vinegar and sugar. Season to taste with salt and freshly ground pepper. Add to potato mixture and toss to coat. Set aside and let stand for about 20 minutes to allow flavors to develop. Just before serving, drizzle oil over potato mixture and toss in parsley.

Variation

You might want to add a bit of crumbled cooked smoked bacon or chunks of cooked ham to the salad, which moves it in the direction of a main course. In that case you could serve it with a side of cucumbers and sweet onions tossed in sour cream with dill.

Salade de Pommes de Terre

"Apples of the earth" is how the French refer to potatoes. Looking through my mum's vintage collection of recipes I came across this old French preparation. It is very simple and a lovely old-fashioned treatment for waxy potatoes. Here is what the introduction says: "Potato salad is usually eaten cold, but whether served cold or just warm, which is far preferable, it should always be dressed while still hot, so that the potatoes absorb the dressing." I agree.

**Makes
2 servings
(see Tips, below)**

Tips

This makes a small quantity, but if you're serving more people, simply double or triple the recipe.

When the original recipe was conceived, cookbooks simply called for "olive oil," not making a quality distinction. I have tweaked it a bit by using extra virgin olive oil.

1½ lbs	small waxy potatoes, scrubbed	750 g
2 tsp	salt, divided	10 mL
¼ cup	extra virgin olive oil (see Tips, left)	60 mL
2 tbsp	dry red or white wine	30 mL
1 tbsp	red or white wine vinegar	15 mL
1 tsp	Dijon mustard	5 mL
½ tsp	freshly ground black pepper	2 mL
1 tsp	chopped flat-leaf parsley leaves	5 mL
1 tsp	chopped fresh chives	5 mL

1. Place potatoes in a large saucepan and add boiling water to barely cover. Add 1 tsp (5 mL) salt, cover loosely and bring to a boil. Reduce heat and cook for 15 to 20 minutes or until potatoes are just tender (don't overcook).
2. Meanwhile, in a small bowl, whisk together oil, wine, vinegar, mustard, remaining 1 tsp (5 mL) salt, pepper, parsley and chives. Set aside.
3. Drain potatoes well. Using a paring knife, peel off skins. Thinly slice potatoes directly into a salad bowl. Add vinaigrette and gently toss. Serve warm.

Horseradish Potato Salad

Just made to be teamed with beef — roast, steaks, burgers or even short ribs — this easy-to-put-together salad should be served warm. You could also grill marinated flank steak, slice it thinly and make it the central component of the salad.

Makes 4 servings

Tips

I prefer to use sea salt rather than refined table salt because it has a much cleaner, crisper taste and enhanced mineral content.

If you can't obtain fresh horseradish, use the prepared variety. You may need to reduce the quantity of rice vinegar.

2 lbs	small waxy potatoes, scrubbed	1 kg
1 tsp	salt	5 mL
2 tbsp	grated fresh horseradish (see Tips, left)	30 mL
2 tbsp	rice vinegar	30 mL
2 tsp	fresh thyme leaves	10 mL
½ cup	extra virgin olive oil	125 mL
	Freshly ground black pepper	
2	stalks celery, finely chopped	2

1. Place potatoes in a large saucepan and add boiling water to barely cover. Add salt, cover loosely and bring to a boil. Reduce heat and cook for 20 minutes or until tender. Drain well. Set aside until potatoes are cool enough to handle. Cut each potato into quarters.

2. In a large serving bowl, whisk together horseradish, vinegar and thyme. Add oil in a thin stream, whisking to blend. Season to taste with salt and freshly ground pepper. Add warm potatoes and celery and toss to coat. Serve warm.

New Orleans–Style Potato Salad

I had a potato salad very like this one at an outdoor music festival in New Orleans years ago. It was flavored with typical Cajun/Creole spices and served on a paper plate next to the best fried chicken I have ever eaten.

**Makes
4 servings**

Tips

Cajun-Creole Spice Mix: In a bowl, whisk together ½ cup (125 mL) each sweet paprika and garlic powder, ¼ cup (60 mL) onion powder, 3 tbsp (45 mL) each dried oregano, thyme and freshly ground black pepper and 2 tsp (10 mL) each white pepper, cayenne, ground cumin and ground coriander. Transfer to a small jar with a tight-fitting lid. Set aside.

The spice mix will make much more than you need; store the extra in an airtight container, where it will keep well for up to a month. You will find lots of uses for it. It's great on oven fries and as a seasoning rub for chicken, pork or ribs, among other things.

Although most people don't have separate grinders, freshly ground white pepper is a preferable addition to this mixture. If you have a good mortar and pestle or a spice grinder, you can use that to grind the peppercorns finely. Or substitute freshly ground black pepper.

2 lbs	red-skinned waxy potatoes, scrubbed	1 kg
1 tsp	salt	5 mL
1	red onion, finely chopped	1
2	stalks celery, finely chopped	2
4	cloves garlic, minced	4
2 tsp	Cajun-Creole Spice Mix (see Tips, left)	10 mL
	Freshly ground black pepper	
1 cup	mayonnaise	250 mL
½ cup	German-style brown mustard	125 mL
2 to 3 tbsp	hot pepper sauce, or to taste	30 to 45 mL
1 tsp	packed light brown sugar	5 mL

1. Place potatoes in a large saucepan and add boiling water to barely cover. Add salt, bring to a boil and cover loosely. Reduce heat and cook for 20 to 30 minutes or until tender. Drain well. Set aside potatoes until cool enough to handle. Using a paring knife, peel off skins, if desired. Cut each potato into 1-inch (2.5 cm) chunks and transfer to a serving bowl.
2. Add onion, celery, garlic, 2 tsp (10 mL) of the spice mix and salt and freshly ground pepper to taste. Toss until potatoes are well coated with spice mix.
3. In a small bowl, whisk together mayonnaise, mustard, hot sauce and brown sugar. Add to potatoes and toss to coat. Serve warm or at room temperature.

Potato Salad with Madras Cream

The cream in this recipe is actually a blend of mayonnaise and yogurt. It does a good job of coating Yukon Gold potatoes and hard-boiled eggs for a nice light lunch or supper dish. If you are a fan of tandoori-style barbecued chicken, this is a good go-with.

Makes 4 to 6 servings

Tips

Black mustard seeds are available at specialty food shops or East Indian or Asian markets.

The curry paste I am referring to is Indian curry paste, which comes in mild, medium and hot. It is widely available in supermarkets; Patak's is the most common brand. It will keep for up to six months in the fridge.

3	large Yukon Gold potatoes, peeled and cut into 2-inch (5 cm) chunks	3
1 tsp	salt	5 mL
1 tbsp	canola or sunflower oil	15 mL
2 tsp	black mustard seeds	10 mL
1 tbsp	Madras or other hot curry paste (see Tips, left)	15 mL
1 cup	plain yogurt	250 mL
¼ cup	mayonnaise	60 mL
	Salt and freshly ground black pepper	
2	hard-boiled eggs, coarsely chopped	2
1	bunch green onions, trimmed and chopped	1
3	stalks celery, chopped	3

1. Place potatoes in a large saucepan and add cold water to barely cover. Add salt, cover loosely and bring to a boil. Reduce heat and cook for about 20 minutes or until tender. Drain well. Set aside to cool slightly.

2. In a skillet, warm oil over medium heat. Cook mustard seeds, stirring, for about 1 to 2 minutes or until they begin to pop. Stir in curry paste and cook, stirring, for no more than 2 minutes (otherwise it will dry out). Transfer into a large bowl and set aside to cool for 5 minutes.

3. Whisk yogurt and mayonnaise into mustard-seed mixture. Season to taste with salt and freshly ground pepper. Add potatoes, eggs, green onions and celery and stir to combine. Serve at room temperature.

Roasted Sweet Potato & Yukon Gold Salad with Mâche & Honey Mustard Vinaigrette

The toasted walnuts complement the slight nuttiness of the mâche and add a nice bit of crunch to this two-potato salad.

Makes 4 to 6 servings

Tips

To toast walnuts: Place in a dry skillet over medium heat and toast, stirring, for 6 to 8 minutes or until fragrant and just starting to darken (don't let them burn.)

Mâche is also known as lamb's lettuce. It is a lovely salad green that can now be found in most large supermarkets.

● **Preheat oven to 375°F (190°C)**

1 lb	sweet potatoes, peeled and cut into 2-inch (5 cm) chunks	500 g
1 lb	Yukon Gold potatoes, peeled and cut into 2-inch (5 cm) chunks	500 g
2 tbsp	olive oil	30 mL
	Salt and freshly ground black pepper	

Vinaigrette

2 tbsp	white wine vinegar	30 mL
2 tsp	liquid honey	10 mL
1 tsp	Dijon mustard	5 mL
⅓ cup	extra virgin olive oil	75 mL
8 oz	mâche or assorted salad greens (about 6 cups/1.5 L)	250 g
1 cup	walnut halves, toasted (see Tips, left) and coarsely chopped	250 mL
2 tbsp	chopped fresh chives	30 mL

1. On a rimmed baking sheet, toss together sweet potatoes, white potatoes and oil. Season to taste with salt and freshly ground pepper. Roast in preheated oven, stirring occasionally, for about 30 minutes or until cooked through. Set aside to cool for 5 minutes.
2. *Vinaigrette:* In a serving bowl, whisk together vinegar, honey and mustard. Add oil in a thin stream, whisking to blend. Season to taste with salt and freshly ground pepper and whisk to blend.
3. Add potatoes to vinaigrette and toss to coat. Toss in mâche, walnuts and chives. Serve immediately.

Variation

Vary the greens by using baby spinach, arugula or a mixture of your favorites.

Greek-Style Potato Salad

Roasted fingerling potatoes combine with all the ingredients of a classic Greek salad to make one memorable dish.

Tips

I prefer to use whole olives with pits in this recipe, but pitted ones are fine, if you prefer.

To make the vinaigrette for this recipe: After the garlic has been roasted (Step 1), squeeze the cloves out of their skins, transfer to a bowl and, using a fork, mash into a paste. Whisk in ¼ cup (60 mL) white wine vinegar, 1 tbsp (15 mL) each liquid honey and dried oregano, ½ tsp (2 mL) salt, 1 tbsp (15 mL) dried oregano and a pinch of dried red pepper flakes. Whisk in ¾ cup (175 mL) extra virgin olive oil. Taste and add vinegar or seasoning to taste, then whisk again.

- Preheat oven to 375°F (190°C)
- Shallow 11- by 7-inch (2 L) baking dish

1½ lbs	fingerling potatoes, scrubbed	750 g
6	cloves garlic, unpeeled	6
1 tbsp	dried oregano, divided	15 mL
¼ cup	olive oil	60 mL
	Salt and freshly ground black pepper	
1	red onion, thinly sliced	1
1	small seedless cucumber, peeled, halved and sliced into bite-size chunks	1
1 cup	kalamata olives (see Tips, left)	250 mL
8 oz	grape or cherry tomatoes	250 g
	Vinaigrette (see Tips, left)	
8	hearts of romaine lettuce	8
⅓ cup	chopped flat-leaf parsley leaves	75 mL
8 oz	feta cheese, broken into chunks	250 g

1. In a baking dish, toss together potatoes, garlic, oregano and olive oil to coat. Season to taste with salt and freshly ground pepper. Roast in preheated oven for 30 minutes or until potatoes are tender. Remove from oven and set aside until garlic is cool enough to handle.

2. In a large bowl, gently toss potatoes, onion, cucumber, olives and tomatoes. Drizzle with three-quarters of the vinaigrette and toss.

3. Slice each heart of romaine in half vertically. Place, cut side up, on a large platter. Arrange potato mixture evenly over lettuce. Sprinkle with parsley, then feta. Drizzle with remaining vinaigrette.

Variation

You can also grill the fingerlings: Parboil for about 10 minutes, toss in olive oil and place on preheated grill, turning once or twice, until golden brown and cooked through, about 8 minutes. The garlic cloves can be threaded onto a soaked wooden skewer, drizzled with a bit of olive oil and grilled alongside the potatoes for the same length of time, until browned and tender.

Potato & Chèvre Cakes with Sun-Dried Tomatoes

Rather like a potato sandwich, with goat cheese and sun-dried tomatoes acting as the filling, this makes a lovely starter when served over a bed of mixed greens.

Makes 6 servings

Tips

To make the vinaigrette for this recipe: In a small bowl, whisk together 2 tbsp (30 mL) freshly squeezed lemon juice and 1 tsp (5 mL) each white wine vinegar and Dijon mustard. Season to taste with salt, freshly ground pepper and a pinch of granulated sugar. Whisk in ¼ cup (60 mL) extra virgin olive oil and taste to see if it needs a little more vinegar or oil; if it does, add and whisk again.

Choose a goat cheese that comes in a log shape. If you like the flavor of anchovies, add a drained fillet to the sun-dried tomatoes before blending.

Don't keep the finished potato cakes in the oven too long or the cheese will start to melt and ooze out.

- Preheat oven to 140°F (60°C)
- Food processor or blender

2	large floury potatoes, each cut crosswise into 6 slices	2
3 oz	oil-packed sun-dried tomatoes, patted dry	90 g
2	cloves garlic, minced	2
¼ cup	extra virgin olive oil	60 mL
⅓ cup	capers, drained	75 mL
1 tbsp	freshly squeezed lemon juice	15 mL
13 oz	soft roll goat cheese, cut into six ¾-inch (2 cm) slices	370 g
½ cup	canola or sunflower oil	125 mL
6 cups	mixed salad greens	1.5 L
	Vinaigrette (see Tips, left)	

1. In a pot of boiling lightly salted water, blanch potato slices for 1 or 2 minutes, being careful not to cook through. Drain and set aside.
2. In a food processor fitted with metal blade, pulse sun-dried tomatoes, garlic, olive oil, capers and lemon juice just to spreadable consistency.
3. Using a metal spatula, spread a sixth of the garlic mixture on each chèvre slice, then sandwich each slice between two slices of potato. Set aside.
4. In a large skillet, heat canola oil over medium heat. Using a spatula, carefully transfer potato sandwiches, in batches if necessary, to pan. Fry, turning once, for about 2 minutes per side or until golden brown. Transfer to a baking sheet and keep warm in preheated oven as completed.
5. In a large bowl, toss together salad greens and vinaigrette. Divide evenly among six individual serving plates. Top each with a potato sandwich and serve immediately.

Variation

Substitute about 4 oz (125 g) black olive tapenade (your own or store-bought) for the sun-dried tomatoes.

Caesar's Spuds Salad

Like every man, young man and boy I know, my husband and eldest grandson adore Caesar salad. Left to their own devices, they would probably enjoy one every evening with dinner. But because I love potatoes as much as I love them both, I figured if I put Caesar salad and potatoes together, we'd all be very happy. My invention is wonderful with steaks, bacon-topped cheeseburgers and just about everything else.

Makes 4 to 6 servings

Tips

If you end up with more dressing than you need, place it in a container, refrigerate and use the next day.

Please don't omit the anchovy paste, as it really does give this dressing its characteristic flavor. Think of anchovies as seasoning — in a good Caesar dressing (and many other recipes) that is exactly what they are.

2½ lbs	small waxy new potatoes, scrubbed	1.25 kg
1 tsp	salt	5 mL
Dressing		
2	cloves garlic, minced	2
¾ cup	freshly grated Grana Padano or Parmesan cheese, divided	175 mL
¼ cup	canola or sunflower oil	60 mL
2 tbsp	extra virgin olive oil	30 mL
2 tbsp	white wine vinegar	30 mL
2 tsp	Dijon mustard	10 mL
2 tsp	anchovy paste	10 mL
½ tsp	salt	2 mL
½ tsp	freshly ground black pepper	2 mL
½ tsp	Worcestershire sauce	2 mL
3 tbsp	mayonnaise	45 mL
6	slices bacon, cooked until crisp, drained and crumbled	6
	Hearts of romaine lettuce	

1. Place potatoes in a large saucepan and add boiling water to barely cover. Add salt, cover loosely and return to a boil. Reduce heat and cook for 15 to 20 minutes or until potatoes are just tender.

2. *Dressing:* Meanwhile, in a bowl, whisk together garlic, ¼ cup (60 mL) cheese, canola oil, olive oil, vinegar, mustard, anchovy paste, salt, pepper and Worcestershire sauce. Whisk in mayonnaise until smooth and blended. Cover with plastic wrap and refrigerate until ready to use or up to 6 hours.

3. Drain potatoes and set aside until cool enough to handle. Cut into halves or chunks, as desired, and transfer to a bowl. Toss in enough dressing to coat thoroughly. Toss in bacon and remaining cheese. Line individual bowls with whole hearts of romaine. Divide potato mixture among bowls.

Fall Vegetable Roast with Sweet Potatoes

No fewer than seven vegetables make up this colorful roasted assortment, which complements many other foods. The roasted vegetables are treated to an Asian-style dressing that works its magic when left to soak in for a few hours. This is a good party piece as it makes quite a bit, and it's even better the next day.

Makes 8 to 10 servings

Tips

When the marinade has come to a boil, taste to see if it needs a little more salt, pepper or brown sugar; if it does, whisk it in and cook for another minute.

Make this ahead of time. While the vegetables are resting in the marinade, roast a chicken or pan-sear some pork chops. Or, if you're pressed for time, team it with a quick-cooking grain dish such as couscous, rice or bulgur.

- **Preheat oven to 400°F (200°C)**
- **Large rimmed baking sheet**

3	Japanese (long, slender purple) eggplants, halved lengthwise	3
3	carrots, peeled and halved lengthwise, if large	3
3	zucchini, quartered lengthwise	3
2	red bell peppers, cut into quarters and seeded	2
2	large Spanish onions, peeled and quartered	2
2	sweet potatoes, peeled and cut crosswise into 1/2-inch (1 cm) slices	2
1	head garlic, cloves separated and unpeeled	1
1/2 cup	extra virgin olive oil	125 mL
1 tbsp	ground cumin	15 mL
1 tbsp	ground coriander	15 mL
1 tbsp	ground ginger	15 mL
1 tsp	cayenne pepper	5 mL
	Salt and freshly ground black pepper	
1 1/2 cups	cherry tomatoes	375 mL

Marinade

1/4 cup	freshly squeezed lime juice	60 mL
1/4 cup	rice vinegar	60 mL
2 tbsp	soy sauce	30 mL
1 tbsp	sesame oil	15 mL
1 tbsp	lightly packed light brown sugar	15 mL
1/2 cup	chopped cilantro leaves	125 mL

1. On baking sheet, arrange eggplants, carrots, zucchini, red peppers, onions, sweet potatoes and garlic. Pour olive oil evenly over vegetables and, using your hands, toss to coat.

2. In a small bowl, whisk together cumin, coriander, ginger and cayenne. Season to taste with salt and freshly ground pepper and whisk to blend. Sprinkle over vegetables and toss to coat. Roast in preheated oven, stirring occasionally, for 30 minutes.

3. Slide out the rack with the baking sheet on it and evenly scatter tomatoes, tucking them down among the vegetables. Roast for 15 minutes longer or until vegetables are tender. Using tongs, transfer vegetables to a large serving platter.

4. *Marinade:* Pour accumulated juices from baking sheet into a saucepan. Stir in lime juice, vinegar, soy sauce, sesame oil and brown sugar and bring to a boil over medium heat (see Tips, page 114). Pour evenly over vegetables. Set aside to marinate, covering with plastic wrap when completely cooled, for 1 to 2 hours so flavors develop before serving. Sprinkle with cilantro just before serving.

Variation

If you have lemon- or chile-flavored oil, use a little to replace some of the olive oil used to coat the vegetables before roasting.

Classic Salade Niçoise

I have often seen contemporary versions of this salad made using fresh tuna as some chefs strive to give this dish a more modern appeal. While there is something to be said for creativity, I think the original version, based on good-quality canned tuna, remains the best. You can use small new potatoes if you wish; however, traditionally older (floury) potatoes are used, all the better to soak up the great vinaigrette. Serve with warmed baguette and a well-chilled Rosé or white wine such as Moselle.

Makes 4 servings

Tips

To make dressing: In a jar with a tight-fitting lid, combine ¼ cup (60 mL) each olive and canola oil, 2 tbsp (30 mL) white wine vinegar, 1 tsp (5 mL) each Dijon mustard, salt, freshly ground pepper and freshly squeezed lemon juice, ½ tsp (2 mL) dry mustard and ¼ tsp (1 mL) granulated sugar. Cover tightly and shake well. Taste, then add a little more vinegar, lemon juice or seasoning, if desired, and shake again.

Look for superior tuna packed in olive oil, preferably from Italy or Spain. However, any solid tuna can be used, so long as it isn't flaked.

The anchovies are traditional, but if you are not fond of the taste, omit them.

Use thin green beans, preferably those known as French or haricots verts, and cook until crisp-tender.

Prepare the lettuce ahead of time. Wrap rinsed leaves in paper towels, place in a plastic bag and refrigerate for up to 3 days.

2½ cups	diced, cooked and cooled floury or all-purpose potatoes (see page 17)	625 mL
2 cups	halved crosswise, cooked and cooled green beans (see Tips, left)	500 mL
1½ cups	drained canned tuna (about three 6 oz/170 g cans; see Tips, left)	375 mL
	Dressing (see Tips, left)	
1	head Boston lettuce (see Tips, left), separated	1
3	ripe tomatoes, peeled and quartered	3
4	hard-boiled eggs, quartered	4
8	anchovy fillets, cut in half lengthwise and crosswise and drained on a paper towel, optional	8
¾ cup	pitted black olives	175 mL
¼ cup	chopped flat-leaf parsley leaves	60 mL

1. In a large bowl, lightly toss potatoes, green beans and tuna. Add dressing and gently toss without breaking up tuna. Cover with a clean tea towel and set aside to marinate for 1 hour or up to 3 hours (room temperature is preferred unless your kitchen is very warm; if so, refrigerate).

2. Line a large platter or pasta serving bowl with lettuce leaves. Arrange tuna mixture on top. Arrange tomatoes and eggs on and around tuna mixture. Drape 2 pieces of anchovy, if using, over each egg quarter to form an X. Scatter olives and parsley evenly overtop.

Lemon Potato Salad with Shrimp

This recipe is perfect for a lazy summer afternoon, especially if you've spent part of it picking a basketful of lovely skinny green beans and new Yukon Golds from your garden and are wondering what to do with them. Here it is: the first Yukon Gold new potatoes cooked and treated to a lemony dressing and combined with tiny shrimp and those slender beans. This is very good summer eating. Team with grilled chicken or pork tenderloin.

Makes 4 to 6 servings

Tips

If the use of raw egg yolk is not recommended because of salmonella concerns, substitute 1 heaping tbsp (20 mL) good-quality mayonnaise for the egg yolk.

I prefer to use sea salt rather than refined table salt because it has a much cleaner, crisper taste and enhanced mineral content.

Salad

2 lbs	small Yukon Gold or other new potatoes, scrubbed and quartered	1 kg
1 tsp	salt	5 mL
8 oz	skinny green beans, stem ends trimmed	250 g
1	red onion, very thinly sliced	1
1 lb	small salad shrimp, cooked	500 g

Dressing

1	egg yolk (see Tips, left)	1
2 tbsp	Dijon mustard	30 mL
2 tsp	finely grated lemon zest	10 mL
¼ cup	freshly squeezed lemon juice	60 mL
	Salt and freshly ground black pepper	
½ cup	extra virgin olive oil	125 mL
⅓ cup	chopped flat-leaf parsley leaves	75 mL

1. *Salad:* Place potatoes in a large saucepan and add boiling water to barely cover. Add salt, cover loosely and bring to a boil. Reduce heat and cook for 15 to 20 minutes or until potatoes are tender. Using a slotted spoon and reserving the cooking water, quickly transfer potatoes to a colander and rinse under cool running water. Drain well, transfer to a large serving bowl and set aside.

2. Add beans to reserved cooking water and bring to a boil. Reduce heat to medium and cook for 5 minutes. Drain, rinse under cold running water and drain well. Add to potatoes along with onion and shrimp.

3. *Dressing:* In a small bowl, whisk together egg yolk, mustard and lemon zest and juice. Season to taste with salt and pepper. Add oil in a thin stream, whisking to blend (adjust seasoning if necessary). Stir in parsley. Add dressing to potato mixture and toss well. Serve, preferably while still warm.

Curried Shrimp & Potato Salad with Cucumbers & Chives

If you are a fan of England's famed Coronation Chicken Salad, you will want to make this similarly flavored dish. The original salad was created by the late Constance Spry, a sort of earlier, British version of Martha Stewart, and was served at the luncheon following the coronation of Queen Elizabeth II back in 1953. Curry powder was used in the original recipe, but I find curry paste works far better for blending with the mayonnaise. This special summer main course requires very little effort.

Makes 4 servings

Tips

If you're serving a large group, double the recipe and serve on one big platter. It would make a great prelude to a barbecue buffet.

You could easily substitute an equal amount of cooked chicken for the shrimp.

The curry paste I am referring to is Indian curry paste, which comes in mild, medium and hot. It is widely available in supermarkets; Patak's is the most common brand. It will keep for up to six months in the fridge.

2 lbs	waxy new potatoes, quartered	1 kg
1 tsp	salt	5 mL
1	seedless cucumber, lightly peeled (leave some green)	1
⅓ cup	mayonnaise	75 mL
2 tbsp	freshly squeezed lemon juice, divided	30 mL
1 tsp	mild curry paste (see Tips, left)	5 mL
	Salt and freshly ground black pepper	
12 oz	cooked deveined, peeled shrimp	375 g
2 cups	sweet green peas, thawed if frozen	500 mL
2 tbsp	chopped fresh chives	30 mL
1 tbsp	extra virgin olive oil (approx.)	15 mL
4	leaves Boston or leaf lettuce	4

1. Place potatoes in a large saucepan and add boiling water to barely cover. Add salt, cover loosely and bring to a boil. Reduce heat and cook for 15 to 20 minutes or until tender. Drain well. Set aside to cool slightly.
2. Meanwhile, slice cucumber lengthwise into 4 strips. Slice strips crosswise into fairly thick chunks. Transfer to a large bowl and add potatoes.
3. In another large bowl, whisk together mayonnaise, half of the lemon juice and curry paste. Season to taste with salt and freshly ground pepper and whisk to blend. Add to potato mixture.
4. In bowl used to whisk mayonnaise mixture, toss together shrimp, peas, remaining lemon juice and chives. Add up to 1 tbsp (15 mL) oil if mixture seems dry.
5. Line each of four individual serving bowls with a lettuce leaf. Top each with a quarter of the potato mixture and a quarter of the shrimp mixture.

Lobster & Potato Supper Salad

This salad is a great choice when lobsters are seasonably priced and more readily available. If fresh lobster is not an option, it will also happily come together with frozen (thawed and drained) or even canned lobster.

Makes 4 to 6 servings

Tip

Don't "over-mayo" the salad; you want to be able to really taste the lobster and potatoes.

5 cups	diced, cooked and cooled new potatoes	1.25 L
3 cups	cooked lobster meat, coarsely chopped	750 mL
8 oz	snow peas, cut diagonally into thin slices	250 g
4	green onions, trimmed and chopped	4
	Salt and freshly ground black pepper	
1 cup	mayonnaise (approx.)	250 mL
3 tbsp	freshly squeezed lemon juice	45 mL
½ cup	chopped fresh dill fronds	125 mL
1 to 2	heads red oak leaf lettuce, separated	1 to 2

1. In a large bowl, combine potatoes, lobster, snow peas and green onions. Season to taste with salt and freshly ground pepper. Toss to combine.
2. In another bowl, whisk together mayonnaise and lemon juice until blended. Add to potato mixture and toss to coat (if it needs more mayonnaise, add a little more and toss again). Add dill and toss again.
3. Cover with plastic wrap and refrigerate for 1 hour or up to 3 hours. Divide leaf lettuce evenly among individual serving plates and top with potato mixture.

Variation

Grill four or five lobster tails, cool, then remove the meat from the shells and chop coarsely. Substitute for the lobster.

Potato Latke Stacks with Smoked Trout & Watercress Salad

This makes a lovely first course — light, crisp-edged potato latkes topped with a smoked trout and sour cream combination, served on a bed of peppery watercress. Because this dish is rather filling, choose a main course that is not too demanding and don't make the latkes too large.

Makes 4 servings

Tips

Try to work quickly after shredding the potatoes, so they do not have a chance to discolor. Or add them to a bowl of cold water after shredding, and dry thoroughly before proceeding.

Be sure to buy dry (pressed) cottage cheese or farmer's cheese, which is sold wrapped in a package. Don't use the tub variety, because it is too loose and wet.

It is a good idea to spin or otherwise dry the salad greens after rinsing and trim and discard any tough or ragged stems. Allow enough time to refrigerate and chill the greens well before using.

- Preheat oven to 140°F (60°C)
- Food processor

12 oz	smoked trout fillets, skins removed	375 g
½ cup	pressed cottage cheese (see Tips, left)	125 mL
½ cup	sour cream	125 mL
2 tbsp	freshly squeezed lemon juice	30 mL
Pinch	cayenne pepper	Pinch
	Salt and freshly ground black pepper	

Vinaigrette

2 tbsp	extra virgin olive oil	30 mL
1 tbsp	balsamic vinegar	15 mL
1 tsp	Dijon mustard	5 mL

Latkes

2	large all-purpose potatoes, peeled	2
2	shallots, finely chopped	2
1	extra-large egg, beaten	1
¼ cup	all-purpose flour	60 mL
¼ cup	olive or vegetable oil, divided	60 mL
2	bunches watercress (see Tips, left)	2

1. In a food processor fitted with metal blade, pulse trout until coarsely chopped, about five times. Add cottage cheese and sour cream and purée until smooth. Add lemon juice and cayenne and season to taste with salt and freshly ground pepper. Pulse until just combined. Scrape into a bowl, cover and refrigerate until ready to use or up to 2 days.

2. *Vinaigrette:* In a small bowl, whisk together oil, vinegar and mustard. Season to taste with salt and freshly ground pepper and set aside.

3. *Latkes:* Using the coarse side of a box grater or a food processor fitted with shredding disk, shred potatoes and transfer to a colander. Using your hands, press potatoes to squeeze out as much liquid as possible (you can also tie them into a clean tea towel and wring out the liquid).

4. Transfer potatoes to a large bowl and stir in shallots, egg and flour. Season to taste with salt and pepper, stirring to combine thoroughly. Divide into eight equal portions.

5. In a large skillet, heat 1 tbsp (15 mL) oil over medium heat. Using a large spoon, add one portion of potato mixture. Pat lightly with the back of a spoon or a metal spatula to form a round (don't press mixture down or latkes will be heavy). Repeat, adding as many portions as skillet will accommodate comfortably without crowding, and cook, turning once or twice, for 3 to 4 minutes per side or until cooked through. Transfer to a plate lined with paper towels and keep warm in preheated oven as completed. Repeat until all portions have been fried, adding more oil to pan as necessary.

6. In a bowl, toss watercress with vinaigrette to coat. Divide evenly among four individual serving plates. Divide trout purée into eight portions. Dollop each of four latkes with a portion, then sandwich with another latke and top with remaining purée. Top each portion of watercress with one latke stack and serve immediately.

Smoked Salmon & Potato Salad

A different, refreshing treatment for smoked salmon, this preparation relies on a citrusy vinaigrette and lots of fresh herbs to lift the flavors of the smoked fish. Because the fresh herbs — parsley, chervil, tarragon, cilantro and basil — are left whole, they act as salad greens. If you like, you can also add some favorite salad greens to the mix.

Makes 4 servings

Tip

The cucumber may be peeled or not, as you prefer. If you are using a regular cucumber, make sure to peel it, and use a soup spoon to scrape out and discard the seeds.

2 lbs	small red-skinned waxy potatoes	1 kg

Vinaigrette

½ cup	freshly squeezed orange juice	125 mL
2 tbsp	freshly squeezed lime juice	30 mL
2 tbsp	rice vinegar	30 mL
¾ cup	extra virgin olive oil	175 mL
4 to 5	green onions, thinly sliced	4 to 5
	Salt and freshly ground black pepper	
½ cup	thinly sliced radishes	125 mL
½ cup	finely diced English cucumber (see Tip, left)	125 mL
¼ cup	flat-leaf parsley leaves	60 mL
¼ cup	fresh chervil leaves	60 mL
2 tbsp	fresh tarragon leaves	30 mL
2 tbsp	fresh cilantro leaves	30 mL
2 tbsp	fresh basil leaves	30 mL
12	slices smoked salmon	12

1. Place potatoes in a large saucepan and add boiling water to barely cover. Add 1 tsp (5 mL) salt, cover loosely and bring to a boil. Reduce heat and cook for 20 minutes until tender. Drain well. Set aside until cool enough to handle. Cut each potato into eight wedges and transfer to a large bowl.

2. *Vinaigrette:* In a small bowl, whisk together orange juice, lime juice and vinegar. Add oil in a thin stream, whisking to blend. Stir in green onions. Season to taste with salt and freshly ground pepper and stir to blend. Set vinaigrette aside.

3. Add radishes and cucumber to potatoes and toss to combine. Add half the vinaigrette, parsley, chervil, tarragon, cilantro and basil and toss well. Set aside.

4. On each of four individual serving plates, place three salmon slices, then top with a quarter of the potato mixture. Using a spoon, dot a little of the reserved vinaigrette on the plate around the edges of the salad. Serve immediately.

Potato, Green Bean & Mushroom Salad

Long quarters of fingerling potatoes, skinny green beans and pretty little mushrooms make for a visually and texturally attractive salad that works well alongside roast chicken. You can also use it to top cooked quinoa or bulgur for a vegetarian option. Delightful fingerling potatoes are the perfect choice for this salad because their lovely waxiness complements both the beans and the mushrooms.

Makes 4 servings

Tips

If you prefer a vegetarian version of this salad it can be made without the small amount of bacon in the ingredient list.

For a little crunch, toast approximately ½ cup (125 mL) walnuts, pecans or cashews in a skillet, lightly chop and add to the finished salad.

1½ lbs	fingerling potatoes, scrubbed	750 g
2 tsp	salt, divided	10 mL
⅓ cup	extra virgin olive oil, divided	75 mL
1 tbsp	red wine vinegar	15 mL
	Freshly ground black pepper	
6	slices bacon, diced, optional	6
8 oz	small cremini or button mushrooms, wiped clean (if larger, halved or quartered)	250 g
2	cloves garlic, thinly sliced	2
12 oz	skinny green beans, stem ends trimmed	375 g
¼ cup	basil leaves, cut into thin strips	60 mL

1. Place potatoes in a large saucepan and add boiling water to barely cover. Add 1 tsp (5 mL) salt, cover loosely and return to a boil. Reduce heat and cook for 15 to 20 minutes or until potatoes are tender.
2. Meanwhile, in a serving bowl, whisk together ¼ cup (60 mL) oil, vinegar and remaining 1 tsp (5 mL) salt. Season to taste with freshly ground pepper. Set aside.
3. Drain potatoes, reserving cooking water, and set aside until cool enough to handle. Using a paring knife, peel off skins. Cut potatoes into quarters, add to vinaigrette and toss to coat. Set aside.
4. In a skillet, heat remaining olive oil over medium-high heat. If using, cook bacon, stirring, for about 1 minute. Add mushrooms and cook, stirring, for about 15 minutes, until tender. Add garlic and cook, stirring gently, for about 2 minutes or until garlic has softened but is not beginning to brown. Add to potatoes and toss well.
5. Return reserved potato water to a boil. Add green beans and cook for 3 to 4 minutes or until tender-crisp. Drain and add to potato mixture along with basil. Toss to combine and serve immediately.

Bistro Sausage & Potato Salad

Very Parisian, this is a great little supper to put together when you don't have much energy but are feeling hungry. It's the sort of satisfying rustic preparation enjoyed by those interesting-looking people you see happily dining solo in Paris bistros. Serve the salad with a substantial strong mustard — traditional Dijon or hot English — fresh baguette and a good sturdy red wine, preferably from the south of France.

Makes 4 to 6 servings

Tips

Look for good-quality lean, garlicky sausage for this dish. Choose from bratwurst, farmer's, Polish, lamb or even sweet Italian sausage.

A nice variation is to grill the sausage. Heat a grill or barbecue over medium heat. Cook sausage for 10 minutes on one side, then turn over and continue cooking for a further 10 minutes or until cooked through. This is particularly good served with Skordalia (page 144) and a Greek salad.

To make the vinaigrette for this recipe: In a bowl, whisk together 3 tbsp (45 mL) each Dijon mustard and freshly squeezed lemon juice or white wine vinegar. Add ¾ cup (175 mL) extra virgin olive oil in a thin stream, whisking to blend. Season to taste with salt and freshly ground pepper.

6	large waxy white potatoes, scrubbed	6
1 tsp	salt	5 mL
2 lbs	fresh garlic sausage (see Tips, left)	1 kg
	Canola or sunflower oil, optional	
2	heads assorted leafy lettuce, such as red or green leaf or Boston, separated	2
1	onion, thinly sliced	1
4	ripe Roma (plum) tomatoes, quartered	4
6 to 8	gherkins	6 to 8
	Vinaigrette (see Tips, left)	

1. Place potatoes in a large saucepan and add boiling water to barely cover. Add salt, cover loosely and bring to a boil over high heat. Reduce heat and cook for 30 minutes or until potatoes are tender. Drain well, cover with a clean tea towel and pot lid and keep warm.

2. Meanwhile, prick sausage a few times with a fork and place in a saucepan. Add enough water to come halfway up the sides of the sausage and bring to a boil over high heat. Reduce heat to medium and cook gently, uncovered, for about 15 minutes or until water has evaporated. Cook for about 10 minutes more, adding a little oil if sausage is very lean, or until no hint of pink remains in center. Using tongs, transfer sausage to a cutting board. Set aside until cool enough to handle.

3. Arrange lettuce leaves on a large serving platter. Scatter with onion. Slice sausage on an angle into 1-inch (2.5 cm) chunks, slice potatoes into quarters and arrange both on top of lettuce. Arrange tomatoes and gherkins around edges. Drizzle with vinaigrette and serve immediately.

New Potatoes with Asparagus & Prosciutto

There is nothing sophisticated about this preparation, which I think is just as it should be. It relies on the freshness of the vegetables to make it special. Make this dish when the first potatoes and asparagus make their seasonal entrance. Serve with plenty of crusty bread and butter.

Makes 6 servings

Tips

To prepare asparagus, using a vegetable peeler, lightly peel asparagus spears, starting halfway down from the tip, to reveal the pale green. Trim off 2 inches (5 cm) from base of each. Using kitchen string, tie spears into a few bundles.

Save asparagus stalks for soups, stocks and risottos or as an omelet filling, if desired.

It's important to cover the pot only loosely when cooking the asparagus. If it's tightly covered, the asparagus will loose its bright green color.

- Deep pot (large enough to accommodate potatoes and upright asparagus)
- Large oval serving platter, warmed

2 lbs	fresh asparagus (see Tips, left)	1 kg
2 lbs	waxy new potatoes, scrubbed, halved if large	1 kg
4 oz	butter, melted	125 g
3 tbsp	freshly squeezed lemon juice	45 mL
2 tbsp	chopped fresh chives	30 mL
	Salt and freshly ground black pepper	
8 oz	thinly sliced prosciutto	250 g

1. Place potatoes in a large, deep pot and add boiling water to barely cover. Add 1 tsp (5 mL) salt and bring to a boil. Add asparagus bundles, setting upright around sides of pot. Cover loosely, reduce heat and cook for 10 to 12 minutes or just until asparagus is tender. Using tongs, remove asparagus from pot, drain well, and wrap loosely in a clean tea towel. Continue cooking potatoes until tender. Drain well. Return potatoes to pot over very low heat and shake the pot to dry them thoroughly. Cool slightly.

2. In a bowl, whisk together butter, lemon juice and chives. Season to taste with salt and pepper. Pour about half of the mixture over potatoes, carefully turning to coat.

3. Transfer potatoes to center of prepared serving platter. Arrange asparagus in bundles around potatoes, parallel to long edges of platter. Drizzle with remaining butter mixture. Loosely drape prosciutto slices over asparagus, folding them so they don't cover asparagus completely. Serve immediately.

Variation

If you would like to add a little more green to the plate, serve with a small salad of arugula dressed with a little lemon juice, olive oil, salt and pepper.

Parmesan Potato Gnocchi with Red Pepper, Chèvre, Sausage & Arugula

A complete dinner salad, this recipe really only needs some good bread to accompany it.

Tips

The amount of flour is approximate; add it gradually, as you might not need it all. Stop adding flour when the dough has lost most of its stickiness and is soft and smooth. The less flour, the lighter the gnocchi will be.

For the same reason, the potatoes are not peeled before boiling. If the potatoes are not peeled, they absorb less water; therefore they absorb less flour and the resulting dough will be less heavy.

You can use any favorite lean sausage. However, if you can obtain them, lamb sausages are particularly good.

Pick up roasted red peppers at the deli counter if you don't have time to roast and peel your own.

- **Rimmed baking sheet, lightly greased**

1½ lbs	floury potatoes, scrubbed and halved	750 g
1 tsp	salt	5 mL
1	egg yolk	1
½ cup	freshly grated Grana Padano or Parmesan cheese	125 mL
2 cups	all-purpose flour (approx.), divided	500 mL
4	large cooked sausages (see Tips, left)	4
½ cup	extra virgin olive oil, divided	125 mL
⅓ cup	pitted black olives, halved	75 mL
2	roasted red peppers, sliced	2
6 oz	arugula	175 g
8 oz	soft goat cheese (chèvre)	250 g
	Freshly ground black pepper	

1. Place potatoes in a large saucepan and add cold water to barely cover. Add salt, cover loosely and bring to a boil. Reduce heat and cook for 15 to 20 minutes or until potatoes are just tender. Drain well. Return potatoes to saucepan over very low heat and shake the pot back and forth to remove any traces of moisture (this step is important; if the potatoes are wet they will absorb too much flour, which in turn will produce heavier gnocchi). When potatoes are cool enough to handle, using a paring knife, peel off skins and discard. Transfer potatoes to a large bowl.

2. Add egg yolk, cheese and ½ cup (125 mL) flour and mash well. Continue adding flour ½ cup (125 mL) at a time, gently kneading until a soft dough forms. (You might not use all the flour; see Tips, left). Knead several times until dough is firm and pliable.

3. Divide dough into three parts and roll each into a sausage shape about ¾ inch (2 cm) in diameter. Working with one roll at a time, cut into pieces about 1 inch (2.5 cm) long. As you cut, transfer the pieces to a baking sheet or tray covered with a clean tea towel lightly dusted with flour — do not allow gnocchi to touch. (At this point the gnocchi can be covered with plastic wrap and refrigerated until ready to cook the same day).

4. Bring a large pot of salted water to a boil. Using a long-handled strainer or slotted spoon, add gnocchi to boiling water in batches (about eight at a time, depending on their size) and cook until they rise to the surface, about 3 minutes. Cook for 1 minute longer, then, using a slotted spoon, transfer to lightly greased baking sheet. Repeat until all gnocchi are cooked. Leave pot with cooking water over low heat.

5. Cut cooked sausages into ¼ inch (0.5 cm) slices. In a large skillet, ¼ cup (60 mL) of the oil over medium heat. Reheat the sausage, stirring occasionally, for about 10 minutes or until golden brown. Remove from heat and toss with olives and roasted red peppers.

6. Increase heat of gnocchi cooking water to high and bring to a gentle boil. Using a slotted spoon, return all the gnocchi to the cooking water and cook for 1 minute. Using slotted spoon, transfer to sausage mixture in skillet. Gently toss gnocchi with sausage mixture and cook, stirring, for about 1 minute or until gnocchi are beginning to brown. Transfer to a large serving bowl.

7. Add arugula, goat cheese and the remaining oil and toss gently. Season to taste with salt and freshly ground pepper. Serve immediately.

Smoked Sausage & Warm Potato Salad in Mustard Tarragon Vinaigrette

In the Alsace region of France, this salad reigns supreme. It is always made with *saucisson de Morteau*, a rich pork sausage that is slightly smoked over pine wood. You can substitute just about any large sausage here, lightly smoked or not.

Makes 4 servings

Tips

Andouille sausage and kielbasa are both good choices for this recipe, but any garlicky smoked sausage will do.

Removing the casing from the sausage makes for a much more elegant presentation and elevates what is essentially a rustic dish.

2 cups	chicken broth	500 mL
1	large sprig fresh thyme	1
1	bay leaf	1
3	cloves garlic, peeled, divided	3
10 to 12 oz	smoked sausage (see Tips, left)	300 to 375 g
1½ lbs	waxy new potatoes, scrubbed	750 g
1 tsp	salt	5 mL
1	shallot, finely chopped	1
1	large sprig fresh tarragon	1
1 cup	heavy or whipping (35%) cream	250 mL
2 tbsp	Dijon mustard	30 mL
	Salt and freshly ground white pepper	
¼ cup	finely chopped flat-leaf parsley leaves	60 mL

1. In a skillet, warm chicken broth over medium heat. Add thyme, bay leaf and 2 cloves garlic and bring to a boil. Reduce heat to medium, add sausage and simmer for about 15 minutes or until cooked through, with no trace of pink remaining. Using tongs, transfer sausage to a cutting board, reserving broth in pan. When cool enough to handle, remove skin from sausage and discard. Set sausage aside, keeping warm.

2. Place potatoes in a large saucepan and add boiling water to barely cover. Add salt, cover loosely and bring to a boil. Reduce heat and cook for about 15 minutes or until just tender. Drain well. Set aside until cool enough to handle. Using a paring knife, peel off skins. Transfer potatoes to a cutting board. Cut into 1-inch (2.5 cm) slices and transfer to a clean saucepan. Add chopped shallot and ladle in a little of the broth to keep warm.

3. In another saucepan, combine remaining broth, tarragon and remaining clove of garlic. Bring to a boil over high heat. Reduce heat to medium and gently boil until reduced to about $\frac{1}{2}$ cup (125 mL). Stir in cream and return to a boil. Reduce heat to medium and cook gently, stirring, for about 10 minutes or until thickened into sauce. Remove from heat and whisk in mustard and salt and white pepper to taste. Strain through a fine-mesh sieve, discarding herb sprigs, and return to pan. Keep warm (do not allow to boil again).

4. Evenly divide potatoes among four warmed individual serving plates. Using a sharp chef's knife, slice sausage evenly into rounds. Arrange sausage slices, overlapping slightly, over potatoes. Carefully spoon a quarter of the sauce around the potatoes on each plate. Sprinkle with parsley and serve immediately.

Char-Grilled Potato & Chorizo Salad

This dish works as well in the summer months as it does during the cooler times of the year, when an indoor grill could be used to great advantage.

Makes 4 to 6 servings

Tip

If fresh chorizo sausage is not available, use the spicy lamb sausage known as Merguez or hot Italian sausage.

● **Preheat grill to medium-high**

2 lbs	small waxy new potatoes, scrubbed and halved	1 kg
1 tsp	salt	5 mL
8 oz	fresh chorizo sausage (see Tips, left)	250 g
4	whole green onions, trimmed	4
¼ cup	extra virgin olive oil (approx.)	60 mL
1 tbsp	sherry wine vinegar	15 mL
1 tbsp	balsamic vinegar	15 mL
	Salt and freshly ground black pepper	
¼ cup	finely chopped fresh basil leaves	60 mL

1. Place potatoes in a large saucepan and add boiling water to barely cover. Add salt, cover loosely and bring to a boil. Reduce heat and parboil for 10 minutes. Drain well and set aside.

2. Cut each sausage in half lengthwise and place in a large bowl. Toss in parboiled potatoes, green onions and enough oil to coat.

3. Using tongs, transfer vegetables and sausage directly onto grill and cook, brushing with oil if necessary to prevent sticking, for 10 to 15 minutes or until vegetables are tender and everything is beginning to char nicely.

4. Using tongs, transfer potatoes to a serving bowl. Transfer sausage to a cutting board, slice crosswise into thirds and add to the potatoes. Using kitchen shears, snip green onions into pieces and add to potato mixture. While mixture is still warm, sprinkle with sherry and balsamic vinegars and toss to coat. Season to taste with salt and freshly ground pepper. Toss in basil and serve immediately.

Appetizers

Packed with flavor, these recipes showcase just how incredibly useful, versatile and delicious the potato can be. They include comforting, delectable snack-type nibblies, hors d'oeuvres for an elegant cocktail gathering, and heartier fare suitable for a group of sports fanatics. And, because we often think of sweet potatoes as a substitute or replacement for potatoes in general, we have made sure to include a few in these categories too.

Baked Baby Reds
with Crème Fraîche & Caviar

Watch the faces of your guests when you present these lovely little spuds. Here we have one perfect potato bite made even more special by a little crown of crème fraîche and a bit of caviar — I'll leave the type to you and your budget.

Makes 30 hors d'oeuvres

Tips

You can buy prepared crème fraîche in well-stocked supermarkets or specialty stores, or you can make your own. In a small saucepan, gently warm 1 cup (250 mL) heavy or whipping (35%) cream over medium heat; do not allow it to come to a boil. Remove from heat. In a glass or ceramic bowl combine cream and 2 tbsp (30 mL) buttermilk or sour cream. Mix well, cover and let stand at room temperature overnight (the top of the refrigerator is a good place, as it is slightly warm). Stir well. Cover and refrigerate until you're ready to use.

If you are making your own crème fraîche, be sure to start a day ahead of when you want to serve these potatoes. The recipe above makes more than you need for the potatoes, but it keeps for up to 10 days refrigerated. Use any extra in recipes such as Baby Yukon Gold Salad with Parsley & Crème Fraîche (page 101) or Watercress & Potato Soup (page 73).

- **Preheat oven to 375°F (190°C)**
- **Rimmed baking sheet, lightly greased**

30	small new red-skinned potatoes, lightly scrubbed	30
¾ cup	crème fraîche (see Tips, left)	175 mL
½ oz	caviar	15 g
	Sprigs of fresh chervil	

1. Using a sharp knife, cut a thin slice off one end of each potato to form a flat base. On the top, cut a small X. Place potatoes on prepared baking sheet so they don't touch (use two baking sheets if necessary) and bake in preheated oven for about 45 minutes, until tender.

2. Let cool slightly. Using your fingers, gently push in the sides of the potato (the precut X will help it open up like a little blossom). Top each with a bit of crème fraîche, a smidge of caviar and a chervil sprig. Serve immediately.

Variations

If you prefer, use finely chopped smoked salmon or trout, tiny shrimp or even crumbled crisp bacon in place of the caviar.

For a vegetarian option, blend a small piece of strong blue cheese, such as Stilton or a Danish blue, with a little of the crème fraîche.

Baby Potatoes with Salsa Verde

Salsa verde translates as "green sauce," and that is exactly what this fresh-tasting accompaniment to baby new potatoes is all about. This makes a great starter if you spear the potatoes on wooden skewers and grill them, then serve the salsa verde as a dipping sauce. These fragrant potatoes also make a great accompaniment, with the salsa verde on the side. Pair them with chicken that has been rubbed with olive oil, lemon juice and dried chiles before roasting, or team with pan-seared pork tenderloin or chops.

Makes 6 to 8 servings

Tips

Use both the parsley leaves and stems, but trim the stems before adding to the food processor.

Choose the smallest new potatoes you can find for this dish. Depending on the time of year, you may choose to steam, boil, bake or grill the potatoes. If you plan to grill them, parboil for a few minutes first.

- **Food processor**

1	bunch flat-leaf parsley (see Tips, left)	1
12	fresh basil leaves	12
6 to 8	pitted green olives, coarsely chopped	6 to 8
4	anchovy fillets, drained	4
2	cloves garlic, coarsely chopped	2
2 tbsp	drained capers	30 mL
1 tbsp	malt vinegar	15 mL
1	thick slice bread, crusts removed, torn into pieces	1
1 cup	extra virgin olive oil	250 mL
	Salt and freshly ground black pepper	
30	hot cooked baby potatoes (see Tips, left)	30

1. In a food processor fitted with metal blade, pulse parsley, basil, olives, anchovy fillets, garlic, capers, vinegar and bread, scraping down sides occasionally, until ingredients are well combined and a paste forms. With the motor running, add oil in a thin stream until blended. Season to taste with salt and freshly ground pepper.
2. Transfer potatoes to a serving bowl. Serve salsa verde on the side or scrape over potatoes and toss to coat. Serve immediately.

Hot Szechwan
Salt & Pepper Potatoes

You can hardly get more basic than potatoes and salt, but when the salt in question includes dried chiles, a little five-spice powder and Szechwan peppercorns, it's a whole different ballgame. Spear these on cocktail toothpicks and pass to your guests along with glasses of bubbly or a good cold lager.

Serves 4

Tips

This makes a large quantity (about 1 cup/250 mL) of Szechwan Salt and Pepper, but this spice mixture is great to have on hand for many things. Try it rubbed into shrimp or sprinkled over whole chicken or pork ribs. Look for Szechwan peppercorns in Asian supermarkets or specialty food shops.

If you prefer, parboil the potatoes (Step 2) up to one day ahead. Refrigerate until ready to use.

- Preheat oven to 140°F (60°C)
- Spice grinder or mortar and pestle
- Large heavy pot, Dutch oven or deep fryer
- Candy/deep-frying thermometer (if not using a deep fryer)

Szechwan Salt and Pepper

2 to 4	whole dried chiles	2 to 4
¼ cup	Szechwan peppercorns	60 mL
1 tbsp	coriander seeds	15 mL
1 tbsp	cumin seeds	15 mL
1 tbsp	fennel seeds	15 mL
½ cup	kosher or coarse sea salt	125 mL
1 tsp	Chinese five-spice powder	5 mL

Potatoes

2 lbs	small waxy new potatoes, rinsed and halved	1 kg
1 tsp	salt	5 mL
	Vegetable oil	
½ to 1 tsp	Szechwan Salt and Pepper (see above)	2 to 5 mL
½ cup	chopped fresh cilantro leaves	125 mL

1. *Szechwan Salt and Pepper:* In a spice grinder or using a mortar and pestle, grind dried chiles to a fine powder. Transfer to a small bowl. Place peppercorns and coriander, cumin and fennel seeds in grinder and grind to a fine powder. Add to ground chiles along with salt and five-spice powder. Mix well. Transfer to a jar with a tight-fitting lid and store for up to one month.

The oil should come a little over halfway up the sides of the pot. Do not overfill; leave at least 3 inches (7.5 cm) of headspace at the top.

2. *Potatoes:* Place potatoes in a large saucepan and add boiling water to barely cover. Add salt, cover loosely and return to a boil over high heat. Reduce heat and cook for 3 to 4 minutes, taking care not to cook the potatoes all the way through. Drain and set aside to cool.

3. Place 4 to 6 inches (10 to 15 cm) oil in a large, heavy pot (see Tips, left). Heat over medium-high until thermometer registers 375°F (190°C). (If you're using a deep fryer, follow the manufacturer's instructions.)

4. Divide potatoes into three batches. Pat the first batch dry, then carefully add to hot oil. Fry for just under 2 minutes (if potatoes are very small, $1\frac{1}{2}$ minutes should do it), until golden brown. Using a slotted spoon, transfer to a baking sheet lined with paper towels and keep warm in preheated oven. Let oil return to 375°F (190°C) before adding next batch. Repeat until all potatoes are cooked.

5. When all the potatoes have been fried, transfer to a large bowl. Sprinkle with Szechwan Salt and Pepper and cilantro and toss well. Serve immediately.

Grilled Potatoes with Creamy Aïoli

These potatoes look very pretty. After grilling, remove the skewers and pile the potatoes on a serving platter with the tangy dip in the center.

Serves 4

Tips

Because it contains mustard and dill, this aïoli is not exactly traditional, but it is delicious.

Small waxy potatoes, which are called for in this recipe, take very well to the grill if you parboil them first. Young floury or all-purpose potatoes don't have the right texture because they will break apart.

Don't parboil the potatoes longer than 5 minutes, as they will be cooked until tender on the grill.

Make sure to take time to grill the potatoes long enough that they get slightly charred, for extra flavor.

You can also oven-roast the parboiled potatoes with good results. Just toss with 2 tbsp (30 mL) olive oil and season with a little salt and pepper. After parboiling they won't take long to cook through, about 20 minutes or so.

- **Barbecue or grill**
- **Food processor**
- **Soaked wooden or metal skewers (see Tips, page 99)**

Creamy Aïoli

2	cloves garlic, crushed	2
2	egg yolks	2
3 tbsp	freshly squeezed lemon juice	45 mL
1¼ cups	extra virgin olive oil	300 mL
1½ tbsp	Dijon mustard	22 mL
	Salt and freshly ground black pepper	
¼ cup	chopped fresh dill fronds	60 mL

Potatoes

2½ lbs	small waxy potatoes, rinsed	1.25 kg
1 tbsp	olive oil	15 mL
	Freshly ground black pepper	

1. *Creamy Aïoli:* In a food processor fitted with metal blade, pulse garlic, egg yolks and lemon juice, then process for a minute or so until smooth. With motor running, add the olive oil in a thin stream until a thick, shiny sauce is formed. Add mustard and pulse two or three times to blend. Transfer to a bowl, season to taste with salt and pepper and stir in dill. Cover and refrigerate until ready to use.

2. *Potatoes:* Place potatoes in a large saucepan and add cold water to barely cover. Add 1 tsp (5 mL) salt, cover loosely and bring to a boil over high heat. Reduce heat and cook for 5 minutes (see Tips, left). Drain well and set aside to cool slightly.

3. Preheat barbecue. Thread 4 or 5 potatoes onto each skewer. Brush with olive oil and season with freshly ground pepper. Place on preheated barbecue. Grill for about 10 minutes in total, turning occasionally to cook evenly. Serve with aïoli.

Variations

These are also lovely as a side dish with grilled steak or fish.

Spanish Wrinkled Potatoes with Mojo Verde

It is thought that this way of cooking small new potatoes with coarse salt harks back to a time when people of the Canary Islands boiled their potatoes in seawater because fresh water was at a premium. The Canary Islands are also famous for their *mojos* — flavorful fresh sauces generally based on garlic, herbs, spices, peppers, olive oil and vinegar. This cilantro-based version is also wonderful with grilled fish.

Makes 4 to 6 servings

Tips

Use both the stems and leaves of the cilantro, but trim the stems a bit before processing.

While the amount of salt used here may seem extraordinary, the potatoes are cooked whole and the salt cannot penetrate their skin. Make sure you use only good-quality sea salt for this recipe.

- Mini food processor or mortar and pestle

¾ cup	coarse sea salt, such as *sel gris*	175 mL
2½ lbs	small new potatoes, scrubbed	1.25 kg

Mojo Verde

4	cloves garlic, peeled	4
1	bunch cilantro, leaves and stems	1
½	green bell pepper, seeded and coarsely chopped	½
½ tsp	salt	2 mL
¼ tsp	ground cumin	1 mL
¾ cup	extra virgin olive oil	175 mL
2 to 3 tbsp	red or white wine vinegar (approx.)	30 to 45 mL
	Freshly ground black pepper	

1. In a large saucepan, combine 4 cups (1 L) water and sea salt, stirring until salt is completely dissolved. Add potatoes — they should float; if they don't, add more salt. Cover loosely and bring to a rapid boil over high heat. Reduce heat to medium and boil for about 20 minutes or until potatoes are cooked through.

2. *Mojo Verde:* Meanwhile, in a food processor, pulse garlic, cilantro, green pepper, salt and cumin until blended. With the motor running, add oil in a thin stream, until blended into a thick paste. Still with the motor running, add vinegar and freshly ground pepper to taste. Scrape into a small bowl. Set aside.

3. Drain potatoes well. Return to saucepan over very low heat and shake the pot back and forth for 10 to 12 minutes to remove any trace of moisture, until skins are slightly wrinkled and coated with a film of dry salt. Serve with mojo on the side or drizzled overtop.

Patatas Bravas

If you have ever enjoyed tapas in Spain you will be familiar with these spicily sauced potatoes, which are often served with additional sauces of mayonnaise or aïoli.

Tips

An easy way to chop canned tomatoes is to snip them with kitchen shears while they're still in the can.

For the most authentic results, use Spanish olive oil and paprika. Look for them at specialty food shops.

Adjust the spiciness level to suit your tolerance by increasing the quantity of chile peppers or hot paprika.

2 lbs	small waxy potatoes, scrubbed	1 kg
1 tsp	salt	5 mL

Bravas Sauce

¼ cup	olive oil	60 mL
4	cloves garlic, thinly sliced	4
1	Spanish onion, finely chopped	1
1	green bell pepper, seeded and finely chopped	1
2	dried red chile peppers, crushed	2
1	bay leaf, crushed	1
1 cup	chopped canned tomatoes with juice (see Tips, left)	250 mL
½ cup	dry white wine	125 mL
1 tbsp	red wine vinegar	15 mL
1 tbsp	tomato paste	15 mL
1 tsp	hot paprika (see Tips, left)	5 mL
1 tsp	granulated sugar	5 mL
½ tsp	dried oregano	2 mL
½ tsp	dried thyme	2 mL
	Salt and freshly ground black pepper	

1. Place potatoes in a large saucepan and add boiling water to barely cover. Add salt, cover loosely and bring to a boil. Reduce heat and cook for 10 to 12 minutes or until potatoes are just tender. Drain well. Set aside until cool enough to handle. Cut in half and set aside.

2. *Bravas Sauce:* In a large skillet, heat oil over medium heat. Cook garlic and onion, stirring, for about 8 minutes or until softened but garlic is not beginning to color. Stir in bell pepper, chile peppers, bay leaf, tomatoes and juice, wine, vinegar, tomato paste, paprika, sugar, oregano and thyme and bring to a gentle boil. Reduce heat to low and simmer for about 10 minutes or until thickened. Season to taste with salt and freshly ground pepper.

3. Add potatoes and stir to coat. Cover and simmer for about 8 minutes or until potatoes are tender and completely cooked through. Serve immediately or slightly cooled to warm.

Valencian Patatas Bravas

This recipe features potatoes treated to a double dose of extra virgin olive oil. They are first lightly poached in hot oil; then, after a chilling, they are fried again, this time at a higher temperature. In the traditional recipe, larger, floury potatoes are shaped with a small knife into football shapes, a rather tricky maneuver. In this simplified version we just cut them into chunks. They can be served with Bravas Sauce (page 138) or with Creamy Aïoli (page 136). Or do as they do in Valencia, and offer both.

Makes 4 to 6 servings

Tips

Use the potato trimmings in soups or add to other potatoes to make hash browns or mash.

The oil should come a little over halfway up the sides of the pot. Do not overfill; leave at least 3 inches (7.5 cm) of headspace at the top.

If you don't have a thermometer, drop a small cube of dry bread into the oil. If it floats, the oil is hot enough.

For the most authentic results, use best-quality Spanish extra virgin olive oil.

- **Large heavy pot, Dutch oven or deep fryer**
- **Candy/deep-frying thermometer (if not using a deep fryer; see Tips, left)**

6	floury or all-purpose potatoes, peeled	6
	Extra virgin olive oil, preferably Spanish	
	Bravas Sauce, optional (see page 138)	
	Creamy Aïoli, optional (see page 136)	

1. Using a paring knife, halve potatoes crosswise, then cut each half into chunks a little less than 2 inches (5 cm) long and about 1 to 2 inches (2.5 to 5 cm) wide.

2. Place 1½ inches (4 cm) oil in a large, heavy pot (see Tips, left). Heat over medium-high heat until the thermometer registers 220°F (105°C). (If you're using a deep fryer, follow the manufacturer's instructions.) Add potatoes to oil and cook, turning occasionally, for 15 to 20 minutes or until tender and just beginning to color. Using a slotted spoon, transfer to a baking sheet lined with paper towels. Let cool slightly (if you have time, refrigerate for about 30 minutes). Remove pot from heat, reserving oil.

3. Return pot to medium-high heat, adding more oil if necessary. Heat until thermometer registers 350°F (180°C). Return cooled potatoes to hot oil and cook, turning occasionally, for 4 to 5 minutes or until just beginning to turn golden brown. Using a slotted spoon, transfer to a baking sheet lined with paper towels. Sprinkle with salt and serve immediately with Bravas Sauce and/or Creamy Aïoli.

Potato & Pepper Tortilla

A Spanish tortilla, cut into wedges or bite-size squares, is a traditional tapas dish. If the quantity of oil seems considerable, remember that this dish comes from the world's largest producer of olive oil, a country where it is used lavishly. The quality and amount of oil are central to the success of this dish, so make an effort to find good Spanish olive oil. Serve warm or at room temperature.

Serves 4 to 6

Tips

Look for jarred piquillo peppers imported from Spain, in specialty food shops, or use regular roasted red bell peppers.

Like Italian frittata, when cut into larger pieces, this tortilla also works well for brunch, lunch or dinner.

4	large Yukon Gold potatoes, peeled and thinly sliced	4
1	onion, finely chopped	1
¾ cup	extra virgin olive oil	175 mL
	Salt and freshly ground black pepper	
6	large eggs	6
3	piquillo peppers, cut into strips (or 1 large roasted red bell pepper, peeled and cut into strips; see Tips, left)	3

1. In a large bowl, combine potatoes and onion. Mix well.

2. In a skillet, heat oil over medium-high heat. Add potato mixture and season to taste with salt and freshly ground pepper. Shake the pan a little to help the mixture settle and even out into a layer, then flatten with a metal spatula. Using the spatula, divide into sections and turn over, flattening again.

3. Reduce heat to medium-low. Cook, turning often and being careful not to overly brown, for 15 to 20 minutes or until potatoes are tender.

4. Use a slotted spoon to transfer to a plate lined with paper towels, patting with more paper towels to remove excess oil. Set aside to cool slightly. Transfer oil to a small bowl and set aside.

5. In a large bowl, whisk eggs with salt to taste. Stir in pepper strips and cooled potatoes. Set aside at room temperature for 10 minutes.

6. Wipe skillet clean. Add 2 tbsp (30 mL) reserved oil and heat over medium heat. Add egg mixture and cook, shaking skillet occasionally, for about 4 minutes, or until tortilla is lightly brown on the bottom.

7. Invert a large plate over the skillet. Flip tortilla onto plate, then slip it back into the skillet, bottom side up. Cook, pressing down on tortilla and shaking skillet a little, for another 4 minutes, until tortilla is lightly brown on the bottom. Transfer to a plate and serve warm or at room temperature, cut into wedges or small squares.

Italian Frico with Potatoes

In Italy a *frico* is a sort of cheese pancake, fried — *really* fried — until quite firm and very crisp. While some are made with cheese only, this version includes thinly sliced potatoes.

Serves 8

Tips

A good cheese shop should have medium-aged montasio cheese, which comes from the alpine region of Italy known as Friuli. If you can't find it, substitute Grana Padano, Asiago or fontina.

If a great deal of fat has been released from the cheese after the frico is cooked, carefully pour most of it off before serving, leaving just a bit behind.

- 10- or 12-inch (25 or 30 cm) skillet, preferably nonstick
- Mandoline or food processor with slicing blade

2 tbsp	butter	30 mL
1	large onion, chopped	1
4	floury potatoes, peeled and thinly sliced (or cut into matchsticks)	4
1½ cups	chicken, beef or vegetable broth	375 mL
1 lb	montasio cheese, shredded (see Tips, left)	500 g

1. In a large skillet over medium-high heat, melt butter. Add onion and sauté until softened, about 2 minutes. Add potato slices, turning them a few times to coat with onion. Continue cooking for 2 minutes.
2. Add broth and shake the pan a few times to settle the slices into the liquid. Gently cook potatoes over medium heat, uncovered, until they are tender and broth has been completely absorbed, about 20 minutes.
3. Cover potatoes with the cheese, spreading it over them evenly. Allow mixture to cook, melting the cheese and browning it around the edges. Invert a large plate over the skillet and slide frico onto it, then gently slide it back into the pan, bottom side up. Continue to cook for a few minutes, until cheese has melted and is brown around the edges and in dots on the surface.
4. At this point, if you like, you can slip the skillet beneath a hot broiler for a minute to brown the frico further. Cut into wedges and serve hot.

Variation

The addition of potatoes makes this substantial enough to serve as a light supper with a green vegetable and lots of good crusty bread.

Kingsmill's Potato Rafts

From my good buddy David Kingsmill, restaurant consultant and cookbook author, comes this lovely creation. His words: "Life is full of mistakes. I was once asked on very short notice to invent a snack for a sports event, so I thought I would reinvent the potato chip. I figured if I got the rounds of potatoes extremely thin, I wouldn't have to go through the bother of frying twice. So, using the potato peeler, I started slicing a peeled potato directly into the hot oil. Well, the slices stuck together. Couldn't get them to separate to save my life. Finally, I gave up. The result was an attractive irregularly shaped 'raft' of delicately fried spuds." See what I mean about potatoes? Even when a preparation doesn't work out exactly as planned, you can still enjoy eating it — and sometimes you come up with a new creation altogether.

Serves 2 (see Tips, below)

Tips

We've specified two servings here but, working with one potato at a time, you can prepare as many as you like, keeping the cooked rafts warm until you're ready to serve.

The oil should come a little over halfway up the sides of the pot. Do not overfill; leave at least 3 inches (7.5 cm) of headspace at the top.

Be sure to use good sea salt, such as *fleur de sel*, to finish your raft. Refined table salt has a bitter, acrid taste.

- Preheat oven to 140°F (60°C)
- Large heavy pot, Dutch oven or deep fryer
- Candy/deep-frying thermometer (if not using a deep fryer)

2	large floury or all-purpose potatoes, peeled	2
	Vegetable oil	
	Salt (see Tips, left)	

1. Place 4 to 6 inches (10 to 15 cm) oil in a large, heavy pot (see Tips, left). Heat over medium-high heat until thermometer registers 375°F (190°C). (If you're using a deep fryer, follow the manufacturer's instructions.)

2. Using a potato peeler that produces very thin slices and working with one potato at a time, peel slices crosswise directly into the hot oil, as if you were flipping playing cards into a hat. They will stick together in a raft as they fry. When potato is all sliced, flip raft and brown the other side, about 2 minutes. Transfer to plate lined with paper towels to drain, sprinkle with salt and keep warm. Repeat with second potato. Serve immediately.

Variation

According to its creator, in addition to being a sumptuous starter or snack, these rafts look — and taste — fab next to a slab of rare prime rib.

Garlic Saratogas

Saratoga chips are so named because they were invented in 1854 by a chef named George Crum in Saratoga Springs, New York. Not long afterward, you could find vendors selling paper cones filled with warm potato chips all over New York City — oh, to have lived there then! Many years later, Chef Michael Romano, of New York City's Union Square Café, wowed customers with his version, treated to a little garlic.

Serves 6 to 8

Tips

Use a mandoline or the slicing blade of a food processor to slice the potatoes. The slices should be about $1/16$ inch (1.5 mm) thick.

You'll notice that the oil temperature is lower than for most other recipes. This is so that the chips can cook a wee bit longer and really crisp up.

Use a garlic press or a sharp-toothed grater such as a Microplane to purée the garlic instead of mincing it.

If necessary, when drying the sliced potatoes, replace the tea towel when it gets wet. The potatoes should be very dry.

- Preheat oven to 140°F (60°C)
- Large heavy pot, Dutch oven or deep fryer
- Candy/deep-frying thermometer (if not using a deep fryer)
- Mandoline or food processor

6	large floury potatoes, peeled and thinly sliced (see Tips, left)	6
	Vegetable oil	
2	cloves garlic, minced	2
1 tbsp	olive oil	15 mL
3 tbsp	butter	45 mL
2 tbsp	very finely chopped flat-leaf parsley	30 mL
	Salt and freshly ground black pepper	

1. Place 4 cups (1 L) ice water in a large bowl, add 1 tbsp (15 mL) salt and stir well. As potatoes are sliced, transfer to the ice water as completed.
2. Meanwhile, place 4 to 6 inches (10 to 15 cm) oil in a large, heavy pot (see Tips, page 142). Heat over medium-high heat until thermometer registers 325°F (160°C). (If using a deep fryer, follow the manufacturer's instructions.)
3. Drain potatoes and rinse thoroughly under cold water until the water runs clear, with no trace of cloudiness. Using a clean tea towel, dry potatoes thoroughly (see Tips, left).
4. In three batches, carefully add potatoes to the hot oil and fry until light brown and crisp, stirring frequently to ensure even cooking. Using a slotted spoon, transfer to a plate lined with paper towels. Keep warm in preheated oven.
5. When all the potatoes are cooked, in a small saucepan over low heat, combine garlic, oil and butter. Cook, stirring, until butter melts and is infused with garlic, about 1 minute. Don't let the garlic brown. Transfer chips to a large serving bowl, drizzle with butter, add parsley and season to taste with salt and pepper. Very gently turn chips until well coated. Serve hot.

Skordalia with Grilled Pita Points & Black Olives

Skordalia is a very old Greek dish, traditionally eaten on Palm Sunday but also enjoyed throughout the year. It is basically a luxurious blend of garlic, mashed potatoes and olive oil, served as a dip or spread. Variations on the theme can include liquid-soaked bread in place of the potatoes, or ground walnuts — in this case, almonds — to provide an interesting texture. This is very good with batter-fried vegetables such as eggplant or zucchini and wonderful with fried fish or shrimp. Or just enjoy it with a selection of fresh-cut vegetables or pita triangles.

Makes about 6 cups (1.5 L)

Tips

Dry-mashed potatoes are mashed without butter, milk or cream. Use fresh mashed potatoes that are still warm — they will absorb the ingredients better.

It would be nice to use a good-quality extra virgin olive oil from Greece for this. Make ahead of time to allow flavors to develop.

I prefer to use sea salt rather than refined table salt because it has a much cleaner, crisper taste and enhanced mineral content.

- **Food processor**

6	floury potatoes, peeled, boiled and dry mashed	6
¾ cup	ground almonds	175 mL
6	cloves garlic, minced	6
1 tsp	honey	5 mL
1 tsp	salt	5 mL
¼ cup	white wine vinegar	60 mL
½ cup	extra virgin olive oil (approx.)	125 mL
	Salt and freshly ground black pepper	
6	pita breads, grilled and cut into wedges	6
6	kalamata olives, pitted or unpitted	6
3 tbsp	extra virgin olive oil	45 mL

1. In a food processor fitted with the metal blade, process potatoes, almonds, garlic, honey, salt and vinegar until ingredients are well combined and mixture is smooth. With the motor running, gradually add olive oil through the feed tube until you have attained a smooth texture; it should not be lumpy. Taste to see if it needs a little more oil or vinegar — it shouldn't be dry. Pulse to blend. Finally, season to taste with salt and pepper and pulse again.

2. Transfer to a serving bowl and garnish with olives. Drizzle with a little more olive oil. Set aside for at least 15 minutes to let the flavors develop. Serve at room temperature, accompanied by pita triangles.

Brandade with Toasted Pita

Brandade is French in origin, a blend of salt cod, potato and olive oil. Also popular in Spain and Portugal, it is slightly rich, smooth and satisfying. The crisped pita breads provide the right textural contrast, but brandade also works well with crudités.

Serves 8

Tips

When choosing salt cod, try to obtain thicker pieces, from the center of the fish. Start preparation a day ahead of time in order to rehydrate the cod.

Use the broad side of a chef's knife to crush each garlic clove, then remove the bitter pith and discard.

To toast pitas: Preheat oven to 400°F (200°C). Brush pitas with a little olive oil, place on a baking sheet and bake until crisp around the edges.

If you prefer, instead of baking the pitas, brush them with a little olive oil and toast in a hot skillet over medium-high heat until crisped.

- **Food processor**

1 lb	salt cod fillets	500 g
2½ cups	whole milk	625 mL
1	bay leaf	1
3	large floury potatoes, peeled	3
3	cloves garlic, crushed (see Tips, left)	3
½ cup	coarsely chopped flat-leaf parsley leaves	125 mL
3 tbsp	freshly squeezed lemon juice	45 mL
	Freshly ground black pepper	
1 cup	extra virgin olive oil + additional for brushing pitas	250 mL
6	whole wheat pita breads	6

1. Rinse cod well under cold running water. Cut into five or six pieces and place in a large bowl. Cover with cold water and soak overnight, changing the water twice.

2. Drain cod and discard water. Place in a saucepan and add milk, bay leaf and, if necessary, enough water to ensure fish is submerged in liquid. Bring to a simmer over medium heat and poach for 15 minutes or until fish falls apart easily when pierced with a sharp knife. Using a slotted spoon, transfer to a bowl to cool. Set cooking liquid aside. When fish has cooled, remove and discard any skin and bones.

3. Meanwhile, place potatoes in another saucepan and add cold water to barely cover. Add a pinch of salt, cover loosely and bring to a boil over high heat. Reduce heat and cook for 20 minutes or until potatoes are tender. Drain well and set aside to cool.

4. In a food processor fitted with metal blade, pulse cod, potatoes, garlic, parsley, lemon juice and pepper to taste, just until blended, about 10 times. With motor running, add ¼ cup (60 mL) reserved fish-poaching liquid. Then slowly add olive oil through the feed tube, processing until mixture is a smooth consistency.

5. Transfer brandade to a serving bowl. Drizzle with extra olive oil, if you like. Serve warm or at room temperature with crisped pitas.

Spiced Potato Ribbons

These chips and the Garlic Saratogas (page 143) are almost too good to share, but the quantity does provide for that generosity. Enjoy them with a good-quality beer and an old black-and-white movie. Choose the longest baking potatoes you can find for this recipe, and pick up a container of tzatziki to serve alongside as a cooling dip. These are truly potatoes for couch potatoes!

Serves 6 to 8

Tip

The oil should come a little over halfway up the sides of the pot. Do not overfill; leave at least 3 inches (7.5 cm) of headspace at the top.

- **Preheat oven to 140°F (60°C)**
- **Large heavy pot, Dutch oven or deep fryer**
- **Candy/deep-frying thermometer (if not using a deep fryer)**
- **Vegetable peeler**

4 cups	ice water	1 L
1 tbsp + 1 tsp	salt, divided	20 mL
6	large floury potatoes, scrubbed	6
	Vegetable oil	
1 tbsp	chili powder	15 mL
½ tsp	cayenne pepper	2 mL

1. Place ice water in a large bowl. Add 1 tbsp (15 mL) salt and stir well. Using a vegetable peeler, peel lengthwise strips from the potatoes, allowing the strips to fall into the water as you work. Set aside.

2. Meanwhile, place 4 to 6 inches (10 to 15 cm) oil in a large, heavy pot (see Tip, left). Heat over medium-high heat until thermometer registers 375°F (190°C). (If you're using a deep fryer, follow the manufacturer's instructions.)

3. In a small bowl, combine chili powder, remaining 1 tsp (5 mL) salt and cayenne pepper. Mix well.

4. Drain potatoes and, using a clean tea towel, dry thoroughly, replacing towel if necessary. Drop strips, a few at a time, into hot oil and fry until crisp and golden, stirring to encourage even cooking, about 1 minute. Using a slotted spoon, transfer to a baking sheet lined with paper towels. Keep warm in preheated oven as completed. Repeat until all potatoes are cooked.

5. Transfer chips to a large bowl, add spice mixture and toss well. Head for the couch and enjoy immediately.

Grilled French Fries with Spicy Ketchup

Unless you are planning to grill other items on your barbecue, an indoor grill would be a good idea for these hefty fries. Make sure to cut them large enough that they don't fall through the grill openings.

Serves 4

Tips

I like to use sriracha, a garlicky Thai hot sauce, in this ketchup. It is widely available, usually in the Asian foods section of supermarkets, but if you can't obtain it, any hot sauce may be used. Use less or more as you prefer.

Make these when you are already planning on barbecuing or grilling. They can be offered with so many dipping accompaniments besides the spicy ketchup: salsa, guacamole, aïoli or even a smoky barbecue sauce.

- **Preheat barbecue or grill to medium high**

Spicy Ketchup

¼ cup	ketchup	60 mL
½ tsp	hot pepper sauce (approx.; see Tips, left)	2 mL
½ tsp	balsamic vinegar	2 mL
3	large floury potatoes, scrubbed and patted dry	3
1 tbsp	olive oil	15 mL
1 tbsp	finely chopped garlic	15 mL
	Salt and freshly ground black pepper	

1. *Spicy Ketchup:* In a small bowl, combine ketchup, hot sauce and vinegar and mix well. Set aside.
2. Cut potatoes lengthwise in half, then cut each half into four to make eight wedges ¼-inch (0.5 cm) thick. Transfer to a bowl and toss with olive oil, garlic and salt and pepper to taste.
3. Lightly grease the grill. Place potato wedges on preheated grill and cook until golden brown, turning once or twice, about 12 minutes. Serve immediately, accompanied by Spicy Ketchup.

Chips & Aïoli

Goodness knows how many portions of our hand-cut chips and aïoli we have served at our restaurant, the Black Dog Village Pub & Bistro, since we opened six years ago. Let's just say lots. They are always good — and good to share. Serve these golden chips in paper cones for a stylish and very au courant appetizer.

Serves 4

Tips

If you have concerns about using raw egg yolks because of salmonella, use pasteurized eggs instead.

This recipe for aïoli makes more than you need. It stores well for up to three days in a container with a tight-fitting lid.

Substitute chives or tarragon for the parsley, or omit herbs altogether for a truly authentic aïoli.

To prepare the potatoes for this recipe, cut them into slices about 2 inches (5 cm) long and ½ inch (1 cm) wide. Place in a large bowl of cold water as completed. Set aside for at least 15 minutes or up to 2 hours.

- Large heavy pot, Dutch oven or deep fryer
- Candy/deep-frying thermometer (if not using a deep fryer)

Aïoli

4	egg yolks (see Tips, left)	4
4	cloves garlic, minced	4
1 tbsp	freshly squeezed lemon juice	15 mL
½ tsp	salt	2 mL
¼ tsp	freshly ground black pepper	1 mL
2 cups	extra virgin olive oil	500 mL
½ cup	chopped fresh flat-leaf parsley leaves	125 mL
6	large floury potatoes, cut for chips (see Tips, left)	6
	Vegetable oil	

1. *Aïoli:* In a food processor fitted with the metal blade, process egg yolks, garlic, lemon juice, salt and pepper until smoothly blended, about 1 minute. With motor running, slowly add olive oil through the feed tube until mixture becomes creamy and thick. Transfer to a bowl and stir in parsley. Cover and refrigerate until chilled, at least 30 minutes.

2. Add 4 to 6 inches (10 to 15 cm) oil to a large, heavy pot. It should come a little over halfway up the sides of the pot; do not overfill, making sure to leave at least 3 inches (7.5 cm) of space at the top. Place over medium-high heat until thermometer registers 350°F (180°C). (If you are using a deep fryer, follow the manufacturer's instructions.)

3. Drain potatoes and pat dry. In batches, carefully add to the hot oil. Fry until they are just beginning to color and are soft. Using a slotted spoon, transfer to a baking sheet lined with paper towels. Set aside for at least 10 minutes or up to 2 hours.

4. When you are ready to serve, heat oil again until thermometer registers 400°F (200°C). Return chips to oil, in batches, and cook until crisp and golden, 3 to 5 minutes. Serve immediately, accompanied by aïoli.

Maxwell's All-Ireland Baked Potato French Fries

Allen's, a lovely wood-paneled bar/restaurant, is an institution on Toronto's Danforth Avenue. Allen's is renowned for many things: food, ale, spirits . . . and spirit, most of which emanates from owner John Maxwell, who I am blessed to describe as a friend. I have devoured many a plate of spuds at Allen's, including these honking great beauties.

Serves 4

Tips

To bake potatoes for this recipe: Preheat oven to 425°F (220°C). Place potatoes in center of preheated oven, directly on the rack, and bake for 1 hour, until golden brown. Remove from oven and allow to cool slightly.

The oil should come a little over halfway up the sides of the pot. Do not overfill; leave at least 3 inches (7.5 cm) of headspace at the top.

Serve with sour cream blended with snipped fresh chives or a spicy ketchup, homemade if you prefer (see page 147).

- Preheat oven to 425°F (220°C)
- Baking sheet lined with parchment paper
- Large heavy pot, Dutch oven or deep fryer
- Candy/deep-frying thermometer (if not using a deep fryer)

2 cups	all-purpose flour	500 mL
1 tbsp	cayenne pepper	15 mL
1 tsp	freshly ground black pepper	5 mL
1 tsp	salt	5 mL
2 cups	buttermilk	500 mL
4	large floury or all-purpose potatoes, scrubbed and baked (see Tips, left)	4
	Vegetable oil	

1. In a shallow bowl, combine flour, cayenne, pepper and salt and mix well. Pour buttermilk into another shallow bowl.
2. Slice each potato in half lengthwise, then slice each half lengthwise into four wedges — you'll have eight wedges per potato. One at a time, dip each wedge in buttermilk and then dredge in seasoned flour. Transfer to prepared baking sheet as completed. When all the potatoes have been dipped once, repeat the process. Cover loosely with plastic wrap and set aside at room temperature for about 6 hours.
3. When you are ready to cook, preheat oven to 140°F (60°C). Place 4 to 6 inches (10 to 15 cm) oil in a large, heavy pot (see Tips, left). Place over medium-high heat until thermometer registers 375°F (190°C). (You can also do this in a deep fryer, following the manufacturer's instructions.)
4. Add potatoes in batches and fry, stirring occasionally, until crisp and golden on all sides, about 3 minutes per batch. Transfer to a tray lined with paper towels and keep warm in preheated oven while you complete frying. Serve immediately.

Sweet Potato–Crusted Shrimp

Make these shrimp as a special hors d'oeuvre — crispy, colorful and very pretty. They have a nice balance of sweet and spicy and go very well with a dry bubbly. A cooling creamy dip such as tzatziki would be nice as an accompaniment.

Makes about 25 shrimp

Tips

The oil should come a little over halfway up the sides of the pot. Do not overfill; leave at least 3 inches (7.5 cm) of headspace at the top.

If you don't have a thermometer, drop a small square of dry bread into the oil; if it floats, the oil is hot enough.

If you prefer, use a garlic press or a sharp-toothed grater, such as those made by Microplane, to purée the garlic and ginger.

You can prepare the shrimp ahead of time; they are quite good even when reheated in the oven. If reheating, place in a 400°F (200°C) oven for about 5 minutes. Serve hot.

- **Large heavy pot, Dutch oven or deep fryer**
- **Candy/deep-frying thermometer (if not using a deep fryer)**

2 lbs	sweet potatoes, peeled and shredded	1 kg
¾ cup	chopped fresh cilantro leaves	175 mL
6	green onions, finely chopped	6
2 tbsp	minced gingerroot	30 mL
3	cloves garlic, minced	3
1 tsp	curry powder	5 mL
¼ cup	soy sauce	60 mL
1 tsp	sesame oil	5 mL
	Salt and freshly ground black pepper	
1¼ cups	all-purpose flour, divided (approx.)	300 mL
1 lb	large shrimp, peeled, deveined and patted dry	500 g
	Vegetable oil	

1. In a large bowl, combine sweet potato, cilantro, green onions, gingerroot, garlic and curry powder. Mix well. Stir in soy sauce and sesame oil. Season to taste with salt and pepper. Add 1 cup (250 mL) flour and mix well.

2. Place remaining flour in a resealable plastic bag and toss the shrimp to coat, shaking off excess. Place shrimp, a few at a time, in sweet potato mixture and pat mixture onto shrimp, coating them well. As you work, transfer shrimp to a parchment-lined baking sheet. Repeat until all shrimp are coated. Cover with plastic wrap and set aside at room temperature for at least 15 minutes or up to 1 hour.

3. Add 4 to 6 inches (10 to 15 cm) oil to a large, heavy pot (see Tips, left). Place over medium-high heat until thermometer registers 350°F (180°C). (If you are using a deep fryer, follow the manufacturer's instructions.)

4. Carefully add shrimp to hot oil, a few at a time, and cook, turning once, until golden, about 2 minutes. Transfer to a platter lined with paper towels as completed. Repeat until all shrimp are cooked. Serve warm.

Potato Cakes with Pancetta & Fontina

There is something about mashed potato–bound cakes crisped up in hot fat that is very satisfying. Different from potato latkes (page 120), these little cakes can be made from leftover or freshly boiled potatoes, and they are the perfect vehicle for good-quality Italian bacon and warm, melting fontina cheese. They are particularly nice finished with a bit of dark, fruity chutney.

Makes 8 potato cakes

Tips

Pancetta is unsmoked Italian bacon. Because it comes in rounds, it makes a perfect topping for these savory cakes. It is widely available in supermarkets and at deli counters.

The easiest way to prepare the potatoes for this recipe is to boil them in their skins, then place them in the refrigerator to cool. When they are chilled, remove the skins and shred the potatoes.

Undercooking the potatoes slightly will make them easier to shred.

- **Preheat oven to 140°F (60°C)**

8	thin slices pancetta (see Tips, left)	8
4	large boiled Yukon Gold (or other all-purpose or floury) potatoes, peeled (see Tips, left)	4
	Salt and freshly ground black pepper	
2 tbsp	butter (approx.)	30 mL
2 tbsp	olive oil (approx.)	30 mL
8	fresh sage leaves	8
8	thin slices fontina cheese	8

1. In a large skillet over medium-high heat, sauté pancetta until just cooked and barely crisp; do not overcook. Transfer to a plate and set aside.

2. Using the coarse side of a box grater, shred potatoes into a shallow dish. Season with salt and freshly ground pepper, then shape into eight flattish patties.

3. In the same skillet used to sauté pancetta, melt butter with olive oil over medium-high heat. When the butter begins to froth, slide in four of the potato cakes, using a metal spatula. (If you are working with a smaller skillet, cook the potato cakes in batches, keeping the cooked cakes warm in preheated oven as you work.) Cook for 3 to 4 minutes per side or until golden brown and heated through.

4. When all the potato cakes have been cooked, return as many as will comfortably fit in one layer to the skillet, adding more oil and butter if necessary. Place a piece of pancetta on each cake, followed by a sage leaf and a slice of fontina. Cover the skillet with a lid and cook just until the cheese has melted, 1 to 2 minutes. Repeat with any remaining cakes. Serve immediately.

Crisp Potato Pakoras with Mint-Cilantro Chutney

Fans of East Indian food know all about pakoras: crisp little fritters composed of vegetables such as spinach and onion and, best of all, potato. Pakoras are quite easy to prepare, and great as a prelude to a summer barbecue or for enjoying around the fire during the winter. They are also ideal for serving alongside a hearty Indian-spiced lentil soup or as cocktail fare along with samosas (page 168).

Serves 4

Tips

Start by making the chutney, to allow the flavors to develop fully.

Be sure to get the oil hot enough to ensure that the interior of the potato is cooked and the exterior is crunchy-crisp.

Look for chickpea flour in East Indian food shops, where it may also be labeled *besan*. Chickpea flour is also used extensively in Sicilian cuisine, so you may find it in some Italian supermarkets or food shops.

If you slice the potatoes ahead of time, cover them with cold water until you're ready to cook, but make sure to dry thoroughly before dipping in the batter and frying.

- Food processor or blender
- Large heavy pot, Dutch oven or deep fryer
- Candy/deep-frying thermometer (if not using a deep fryer)

Mint-Cilantro Chutney

2 cups	fresh mint leaves	500 mL
1 cup	fresh cilantro leaves, with some stems	250 mL
1/2 cup	unsweetened dried coconut	125 mL
1/4 cup	water	60 mL
2 tbsp	freshly squeezed lime juice	30 mL
1 tsp	brown sugar	5 mL
1 tsp	salt	5 mL
1/2 tsp	hot red pepper flakes	2 mL
2 tsp	vegetable oil	10 mL

Pakora Batter

1 cup	chickpea flour (see Tips, left)	250 mL
2 tbsp	rice flour	30 mL
1 tbsp	freshly squeezed lime juice	15 mL
1/2 tsp	chili powder	2 mL
1/2 tsp	salt	2 mL
1/2 tsp	turmeric	2 mL
1/2 cup	water	125 mL
1/8 tsp	baking soda	0.5 mL

Potatoes

	Vegetable oil	
3	large floury potatoes, peeled and sliced 1/8 inch (3 mm) thick	3

1. *Mint-Cilantro Chutney:* In a food processor fitted with metal blade, pulse mint, cilantro, coconut, water, lime juice, brown sugar, salt and hot pepper flakes until smoothly blended.

2. In a small saucepan, heat oil over medium heat. Add chutney mixture (be wary of spitting oil) and stir-fry until fragrant, about 10 minutes. Scrape into a small bowl and set aside to cool. Cover with plastic wrap and refrigerate until ready to serve, about an hour ahead of time.

3. *Pakora Batter:* In a bowl, sift together chickpea and rice flours. Add lime juice, chili powder, salt and turmeric, then gradually whisk in water until mixture is consistency of heavy cream. Cover and let stand for 10 minutes. Just before you're ready to cook, add baking soda, whisking for about a minute to fully incorporate into batter.

4. Preheat oven to 140°F (60°C). Add 4 to 6 inches (10 to 13 cm) oil to a large, heavy pot. It should come a little over halfway up the sides of the pot; do not overfill, making sure to leave at least 3 inches (7.5 cm) of space at top of pot. Place over medium-high heat until thermometer registers 360°F (185°C). (If you are using a deep fryer, follow the manufacturer's instructions.)

5. Working with six slices at a time, pat potatoes dry and dip each in batter until well coated, letting excess drip back into bowl. Carefully slip into hot oil. Fry, turning once or twice, until golden on both sides, about 5 minutes. Once cooked, transfer to a baking sheet lined with paper towels and keep warm in the oven. Serve with Mint-Cilantro Chutney.

Onion & Potato Cake

This simple yet satisfying potato cake is based on mashed potato. It is particularly good for serving when you have company, as it can be made ahead up to the point where you brown and crisp it beneath the broiler.

Serves 4 to 6

Tip

Emmental is the original Swiss cheese. Gruyère or fontina is a good substitution in this recipe.

- **Cast-iron pan or heavy ovenproof skillet**

5	large floury potatoes, peeled and quartered	5
1 tsp	salt	5 mL
¼ cup + 2 tbsp	butter, divided	90 mL
2 tbsp	olive oil	30 mL
3	large onions, thinly sliced	3
1 cup	shredded Swiss Emmental cheese	250 mL
	Salt and freshly ground black pepper	

1. Place potatoes in a large saucepan and add cold water to barely cover. Add salt, cover loosely and bring to a boil over high heat. Reduce heat and cook for 20 minutes or until potatoes are tender. Drain well. Return potatoes to saucepan over very low heat and shake the pot back and forth to remove any trace of moisture. Using a large fork, mash potatoes roughly. Set aside.

2. In cast-iron pan, heat ¼ cup (60 mL) butter with the oil over medium-high heat. Add onions and sauté until soft and lightly browned, about 15 minutes. Add to potatoes, along with cheese and salt and freshly ground pepper to taste, and mix well.

3. In same skillet, melt remaining 2 tbsp (30 mL) butter over medium heat. Add potato mixture. Pressing down firmly with a metal spatula, shape mixture into a cake. Cover and cook until bottom of cake is browned, 10 to 15 minutes.

4. Preheat broiler to high. Place skillet 5 to 6 inches (12 to 15 cm) below broiler until top is crisped and brown, watching carefully to ensure it doesn't burn. Remove from oven and let stand for 10 minutes before serving.

Variation

This is another of those recipes that you can enjoy any time. It also makes a great accompaniment to marinated flank steak or pork tenderloin.

Meze Polpettes

Like tapas in Spain, Greek meze are usually simple to prepare and work well as part of a selection of Mediterranean dishes. Round out the meze experience by serving them with small plates of black olives, marinated calamari, shrimp sautéed with garlic and lemon, warm salted almonds, grilled peppers and a cooling salad such as cucumbers in yogurt with fresh dill.

Serves 6 to 8

Tips

These little Greek-style potato patties can be put together ahead of time and fried just before serving.

Be cautious when salting the potato mixture, because feta cheese is quite salty already.

2 lbs	floury potatoes, peeled and quartered	1 kg
1 tsp	salt	5 mL
8 oz	feta cheese, crumbled	250 g
8	pitted black olives, finely chopped	8
4	green onions, finely chopped	4
1	large egg, lightly beaten	1
¼ cup	chopped fresh dill fronds	60 mL
	Grated zest and juice of 1 lemon	
	Salt and freshly ground black pepper	
½ cup	all-purpose flour (approx.)	125 mL
¼ cup	olive oil, divided	60 mL

1. Place potatoes in a large saucepan and add cold water to barely cover. Add salt, cover loosely and bring to a boil over high heat. Reduce heat and cook for 20 minutes or until potatoes are tender. Drain well. Return potatoes to saucepan over very low heat and shake pot back and forth to remove any trace of moisture. Transfer to a large bowl and mash roughly.

2. Add feta, olives, onions, egg, dill, lemon zest and juice and season to taste with salt and pepper. Using your hands, mix gently, trying not to break up the cheese pieces too much. Cover with plastic wrap and refrigerate for at least 1 hour or overnight.

3. When you're ready to cook, with lightly floured hands, form potato mixture into balls about the size of a ping-pong ball. Roll them in a little of the flour, shaking off the excess. Transfer to a baking sheet when completed.

4. In a skillet, heat 2 tbsp (30 mL) oil over medium-high heat. Add the balls to the pan, a few at a time (being careful not to crowd them), flatten slightly with a metal spatula to form a round patty shape, and fry until golden brown on both sides, flipping once or twice, about 5 minutes.

5. Transfer to a baking sheet lined with paper towels and keep warm in preheated oven until all polpettes are cooked. Serve immediately or just warm.

Saffron Potato Cakes

Spain comes naturally to mind when we think of saffron, but this preparation is inspired by little potato cakes I was served by a chef from the north of Italy. A modicum of saffron — the world's most expensive spice — is put to great use in these crispy little bites, which have a vibrant golden crust and creamy interior. They make lovely appetizers on their own or can be jazzed up with any number of toppings. Consider a sliver of black olive and a parsley leaf, a bit of roasted red pepper and crème fraîche, or baby shrimp and a sprig of fresh dill.

Makes about 15 cakes

- **Preheat oven to 140°F (60°C)**

⅓ cup	extra virgin olive oil, divided (approx.)	75 mL
1 tsp	saffron	5 mL
2 lbs	floury potatoes, peeled and quartered	1 kg
1 tsp	salt	5 mL
2	large eggs, lightly beaten	2
2 tbsp	chopped fresh flat-leaf parsley leaves	30 mL
	Salt and freshly ground black pepper	
½ cup	all-purpose flour (approx.)	125 mL

1. In a small bowl, combine 3 tbsp (45 mL) olive oil and saffron. Set aside.

2. Place potatoes in a large saucepan and add cold water to barely cover. Add salt, cover loosely and bring to a boil over high heat. Reduce heat and cook for 20 minutes or until potatoes are tender. Drain well. Return potatoes to saucepan over very low heat and shake pot back and forth to remove any trace of moisture.

3. Transfer potatoes to a large bowl and mash roughly. Add eggs, parsley, salt and freshly ground pepper and reserved saffron oil. Stir well. Gradually add half the flour, mixing to form a soft dough. At this point, decide whether you need a little more flour, depending on how the mixture feels — it should be soft and not sticky.

4. With floured hands, shape large spoonfuls of the mixture into plump little cakes about 2½ inches (6 cm) across and ¾ inch (2 cm) thick.

5. In a large skillet over medium heat, heat remaining olive oil. Add cakes in batches and fry until golden brown and crispy on both sides, about 6 minutes total for each batch. Keep warm in oven as prepared. Repeat until all cakes have been fried. Serve hot.

Florentine Potato Cakes

We don't usually associate potatoes with Italian cuisine but I have eaten some fabulous potato dishes in that country. This recipe is styled after one I had in Umbria, Italy's heartland, where I enjoyed it for lunch with a salad of bitter greens. You can make the cakes a little smaller and serve them as an appetizer.

Serves 4

Tips

Pancetta is unsmoked Italian-style bacon and is widely available.

This is another simple potato cake recipe that uses potatoes that are parboiled, not cooked completely through, making them easier to shred.

I prefer to use sea salt rather than refined table salt because it has a much cleaner, crisper taste and enhanced mineral content.

- **Preheat oven to 140°F (60°C)**

1 lb	floury potatoes, scrubbed	500 g
1 tsp	salt	5 mL
4	slices pancetta, diced	4
1	small red onion, diced	1
3 tbsp	finely chopped flat-leaf parsley leaves	45 mL
	Salt and freshly ground black pepper	
3 tbsp	olive oil	45 mL

1. Place potatoes in a large saucepan and add cold water to barely cover. Add salt, cover loosely and bring to a boil over high heat. Reduce heat, cover and cook until potatoes are tender around the edges but relatively firm in the center, about 10 minutes. Drain well and set aside until cool enough to handle. Using a sharp paring knife, peel the skins. Using the coarse side of a box grater, shred potatoes into a large bowl. Set aside.

2. In a skillet over medium heat, cook pancetta and onion, stirring, until softened, about 6 minutes. Add to potato mixture, making sure to scrape up any brown bits from bottom of pan and the accumulated pan drippings. Add parsley and salt and freshly ground black pepper to taste. Mix well.

3. Shape mixture into 3-inch (8.5 cm) round cakes. (Cakes may be made ahead to this point, covered with plastic wrap and refrigerated for up to two days.)

4. In same skillet, heat oil over medium-high heat. Add potato cakes in batches (unless skillet is very large) and cook until golden brown on both sides, about 10 minutes a batch. Transfer to a platter and keep warm in preheated oven as completed. Serve hot.

Marian's Leftover Mash Croquettes

Remember TV's Archie Bunker and the way he used to complain about his long-suffering wife Edith's chicken croquettes? Perhaps he would have preferred this simple but delicious version, which comes from my friend Marian Kingsmill. I couldn't resist adding a bite-size chunk of gorgeous Taleggio cheese to the center of each one. Croquettes are called *kroketten* in Holland, where they are ubiquitous and usually have a meat filling — in that country, even McDonald's offers a *kroket*!

Makes about 6

Tip

This recipe is flexible. If you have a larger quantity of leftover potatoes that you would like to use up, just add a little more of the other ingredients and make more croquettes.

- **Baking sheet lined with parchment paper**

2 cups	leftover mashed potatoes (see Tip, left)	500 mL
2 tbsp	all-purpose flour	30 mL
2	eggs, divided	2
1	small onion or large shallot, finely chopped	1
Pinch	ground nutmeg	Pinch
	Freshly ground white pepper	
4 oz	Taleggio or mozzarella cheese, cut into bite-size chunks	125 g
1½ cups	dry bread crumbs	375 mL
⅓ cup	vegetable oil	75 mL

1. In a bowl, combine potato, flour, 1 egg, onion, nutmeg and pepper. Using your hands, mix well.
2. With lightly floured hands, scoop up a handful of potato mixture, add a piece of cheese and shape potato mixture into a 2-inch (5 cm) log with cheese in the center. Repeat until all potatoes and cheese are used up.
3. In a small, shallow bowl, lightly beat remaining egg with 1 tbsp (15 mL) water.
4. Place breadcrumbs in another shallow bowl. Dip potato logs first in egg mixture and then in breadcrumbs, transferring to prepared baking sheet as completed.
5. When croquettes are all made, cover with plastic wrap and refrigerate to allow them to set up for about an hour.
6. When you're ready to cook, heat oil in a skillet over medium-high heat. Add croquettes and fry, turning often, until golden brown all over, about 6 minutes. Serve hot.

Aloo Tikki

Aloo means potato and *tikki* means croquette. These delicious little East Indian potato patties are the perfect solution to your entertaining needs. They are simple to prepare, quite different and can easily be made ahead and kept warm in a low oven.

Makes about 14

Tips

This is a great use for leftover mashed potatoes, or you can plan to make them with freshly made potatoes. If you are using leftover mash that was prepared with lots of butter and cream, add a little flour to the mixture, enough to form a soft dough. One pound (500 g), or 2 large potatoes, makes about 2½ to 3 cups (625 to 750 mL) mashed potatoes.

I prefer to use sea salt rather than refined table salt because it has a much cleaner, crisper taste and enhanced mineral content.

4	large floury potatoes, peeled	4
2 tsp	salt, divided	10 mL
2	onions, finely chopped	2
3	cloves garlic, finely chopped	3
2 tsp	chopped fresh gingerroot	10 mL
1 cup	chopped fresh cilantro, leaves and some stem	250 mL
1 tsp	freshly ground black pepper	5 mL
½ tsp	ground cinnamon	2 mL
¼ cup	vegetable oil	60 mL

1. Place potatoes in a large saucepan and add cold water to barely cover. Add 1 tsp (5 mL) salt, cover loosely and bring to a boil over high heat. Reduce heat and cook for 20 minutes or until potatoes are tender. Drain well. Using a large fork, mash potatoes roughly.

2. In a large bowl, combine potatoes, onions, garlic, ginger, cilantro, remaining 1 tsp (5 mL) salt and freshly ground pepper. Mix well. Divide into balls the size of ping-pong balls, then flatten into disks.

3. In a skillet, heat oil over medium-high heat. Add patties, in batches, and fry until golden brown and crisp, about 2 minutes a side. Serve with Spicy Ketchup (page 147) or Mint-Cilantro Chutney (page 152).

Sweet Potato Hush Puppies

In the southern United States, the savory little fritters known as hush puppies, served in a napkin-lined basket, are always part of the menu at outdoor fish fries. These "pups" (as Southerners refer to them) are fine with good ham, fried chicken or ribs, collard greens and rice, but they also make perfect cocktail fare. While Southerners do not traditionally use sweet potatoes in the mix, I like the texture and flavor they add. Usually hush puppies are deep-fried, but I prefer this pan-fried version.

Makes 20 to 24 pieces

● **Preheat oven to 140°F (60°C)**

1 cup	dry-mashed sweet potatoes	250 mL
1	small onion, finely chopped	1
3	eggs	3
½ cup	cornmeal	125 mL
½ cup	all-purpose flour	125 mL
1 tsp	salt	5 mL
½ to 1 tsp	cayenne pepper	2 to 5 mL
	Freshly ground black pepper	
¼ cup	vegetable or olive oil, divided (approx.)	60 mL

1. In a bowl, combine sweet potatoes and onion and mix well. Add eggs one at a time, beating well after each addition. Add cornmeal, flour, salt, cayenne and freshly ground pepper to taste. Mix well.

2. In a heavy skillet, heat 2 tbsp (30 mL) oil over medium-high heat. Drop potato mixture by tablespoons into the skillet and fry, turning once, until nicely browned, about 3 minutes a side. Transfer to a platter lined with paper towels as completed and keep warm in preheated oven. Repeat until potato mixture is used up, adding oil as necessary and reheating it between batches. Serve hot.

Cantal & Potato Purée with Parsley Garlic Butter (page 53)

Frites à La Kingsmill (page 65)

Spring Vegetable Soup with New Potatoes & Gruyère Toasts (page 72)

Lemon Potato Salad with Shrimp (page 117)

Hot Szechwan Salt & Pepper Potatoes (page 134)

Mum's Potato Breads (page 161)

Classic Twice-Baked Jacket Potato (page 172)

Pan-Fried Sweet Potato with Gremolata (page 235)

Mum's Potato Breads

These little breads, which are a specialty of Northern Ireland, are not really bread in the strictest sense of the word. In Ulster they are also known as fadge, but in my family they were always called potato bread and anticipated with great delight. We even make them in batches for Christmas gift-giving. They are the backbone of the traditional Northern Irish breakfast (often known as an Ulster fry), which is usually composed of black pudding (sausage), bacon, tomato, mushrooms, eggs and fried soda bread — no lunch required! Put on hold any reservations you may have about using butter or salt — slather and sprinkle at will.

Makes 25 to 30 pieces

Tips

This is a hands-on recipe — don't use a food processor or electric mixer, because you are likely to overwork the dough, which will make it gummy. Also, you need to feel the dough to know when to add (or stop adding) more flour.

The amounts of butter and flour given here are meant to be guidelines. Sometimes you may use a little less of each and at other times you may need to use more to achieve a nice unsticky dough that rolls out beautifully. Don't worry about the amount of butter but be careful not to add too much flour, to keep the finished breads light. You can reroll scraps of this dough with no worries.

Make sure the mashed potatoes are warmed before using so they will absorb the butter and flour properly. If leftover mash is used, reheat in the microwave to just warm.

- **Griddle or cast-iron pan**
- **Preheat oven to 140°F (60°C)**

5 cups	mashed potatoes, warmed slightly	1.25 L
1 cup + 1 tbsp	all-purpose flour, divided	250 mL + 15 mL
½ cup	butter, softened, divided	125 mL
	Salt	

1. In a bowl, combine potatoes with ½ cup (125 mL) flour and ¼ cup (60 mL) butter. Use your hands or a wooden spoon to blend the ingredients thoroughly. Then switch to your hands so you can feel the dough.

2. While mixture is still a little sticky, turn it out onto a lightly floured surface. Add remaining ½ cup (125 mL) flour and work it into mixture. When it is no longer sticky and a dough has formed, knead lightly a few times. Use a little more flour to dust work surface, then roll out dough to about ½ inch (1 cm) thick (divide dough in half or thirds if too large for work surface). Cut dough into small circles, squares or triangles.

3. Heat griddle over medium-high heat and add a little of the remaining butter. Fry pieces in batches, turning once or twice, until golden and speckled with brown on both sides, 2 minutes per side. Repeat until all the dough has been used up, adding more butter as necessary. Keep warm in preheated oven until all bread has been fried. Serve hot, topped with a pat of butter and sprinkled with salt.

Potato Blini

Blini are sweet little pancakes with roots in Russia and Eastern Europe. Because they are often used as a base for expensive caviar, they have become associated with elegance. Another traditional topping is crème fraîche and smoked salmon garnished with snipped chives. However, there are many ways to crown them — roasted eggplant and hummus, Brie and a slice of black olive, ham with smoky whole-grain mustard, or even something sweet such as strawberries and cream cheese.

Makes about 3 dozen blini

Tips

This is a perfect recipe for a party because you can make them ahead of time, then reheat and top them when it suits you best.

Crème fraîche is available in well-stocked supermarkets, or you can make your own (page 132).

The finished batter will be a little thinner than conventional pancake batter and, just as with pancakes, the first one you make will probably not be a keeper.

The blini can be made larger — just increase the amount of batter you use for each.

- Preheat oven to 140°F (60°C)
- Potato ricer or colander
- Nonstick griddle or skillet

1 lb	floury or all-purpose potatoes, peeled and quartered	500 g
1 tsp	salt	5 mL
3 tbsp	all-purpose flour	45 mL
3 tbsp	crème fraîche or sour cream at room temperature (see Tips, left)	45 mL
2	large eggs, divided	2
	Salt and freshly ground pepper	

1. Place potatoes in a large saucepan and add cold water to barely cover. Add salt, cover loosely and bring to a boil over high heat. Reduce heat and cook for 20 minutes or until potatoes are tender. Drain well. Return potatoes to saucepan over very low heat and shake the pot back and forth to remove any trace of moisture.

2. While potatoes are still hot, put them through a ricer or rub through a colander into a mixing bowl. With a wooden spoon, mix in flour, crème fraîche and 1 egg. Blend all the ingredients together, then add remaining egg and continue whisking until mixture is smooth. Season to taste with salt and freshly ground pepper.

3. Preheat lightly greased griddle or pan to medium-high. Drop 1 tbsp (15 mL) batter per blini on griddle, leaving 1 inch (2.5 cm) between them, and cook until tiny bubbles form on the surface, about $1\frac{1}{2}$ minutes. Carefully flip and cook on the other side for about 1 minute, until golden brown. Transfer to a baking sheet as completed and keep warm in preheated oven. Grease pan and adjust heat between batches as necessary. Continue until all the batter is used up. Serve warm with suggested toppings.

Sweet Potato Wontons

These make great little cocktail snacks, especially if accompanied with a simple soy sauce dip (see Tips, below).

Serves 4

Tips

These wontons don't take long to cook in the hot oil. Just make sure it is good and hot so that they don't absorb much of it.

To make dip: In a bowl, combine ½ cup (125 mL) soy sauce, 3 tbsp (45 mL) sesame oil, 1 tbsp (15 mL) each minced gingerroot and chopped fresh cilantro leaves, and 1 tsp (5 mL) hot Asian chile sauce. Mix well.

You can also serve these as the focal point of a lunch or supper, alongside a mixed green salad tossed with an Asian-style vinaigrette.

- Preheat oven to 400°F (200°C)
- Deep skillet or wok
- Baking sheet lined with parchment paper

2	sweet potatoes, scrubbed	2
2 tbsp	minced gingerroot	30 mL
½ cup	chopped fresh cilantro, leaves and some stems	125 mL
1 to 2	jalapeño peppers, seeded and minced	1 to 2
	Salt and freshly ground black pepper	
20 to 24	round wonton wrappers	20 to 24
	Vegetable oil	

1. Prick sweet potatoes with tines of a fork. On parchment-lined baking sheet, bake sweet potatoes in preheated oven until tender when tested with a skewer, 45 minutes to 1 hour. Set aside until cool enough to handle, about 15 minutes. Using a large spoon, scrape out cooked potato flesh and transfer to a bowl. Add ginger, cilantro, jalapeño and salt and pepper to taste. Mix well.

2. Working with one wonton wrapper at a time, place wrapper in the palm of your hand and spoon about 1 tbsp (15 mL) filling in the center. Dip your finger in water and run along the edges of the wrapper. Fold opposite edges over filling to make a half-moon shape and press together to seal. Transfer to parchment-lined baking sheet as completed and cover with a damp tea towel to prevent drying out. Repeat until completed.

3. Place about ½ inch (1 cm) oil in a wok and heat over medium-high. Using tongs, carefully add wontons, a few at a time. Reduce heat slightly and fry until golden and beginning to puff up, about 1 minute. Turn and fry on other side until golden and puffed. Transfer to a baking sheet lined with paper towels to drain as completed. Repeat until all wontons have been fried, adding more oil as needed. Serve hot, accompanied by dip.

Variations

If you have a bit of leftover cooked pork or chicken, chop it finely and add to the filling.

Potato, Bean & Corn Empanaditas

When empanadas, the savory turnovers made popular by Latin American and Spanish cooks, are made smaller than usual, they become empanaditas — dainty little versions of themselves that make perfect party fare. The Black Dog has hosted many a wedding reception, including one where the South American groom especially requested these be served. They are not unlike East Indian samosas (page 168), which are deep-fried. Empanaditas can be deep-fried too, but I particularly like this baked version.

Makes about 18

Tips

Canned or frozen corn and lima beans are fine for the filling. Make sure to drain them well; if using frozen vegetables, thaw first.

If you're heat-averse, seed the chile pepper and remove the veins before chopping.

Be sure to buy dry (pressed) cottage cheese, which is sold wrapped in a package.

- **4-inch (10 cm) round cutter**
- **Baking sheet lined with parchment paper**

2 cups	all-purpose flour	500 mL
¼ tsp	salt	1 mL
¾ cup	cold butter	175 mL
⅓ cup	ice water	75 mL
2	waxy potatoes, scrubbed and diced	2
1 tsp	salt	5 mL
2	green onions, finely chopped	2
1	small green chile pepper, minced (see Tips, left)	1
¼ cup	corn kernels	60 mL
¼ cup	small cooked lima beans, thawed if frozen	60 mL
3 tbsp	pressed cottage cheese, crumbled	45 mL
¼ cup	chopped fresh cilantro leaves	60 mL
	Salt and freshly ground black pepper	
	Melted butter for brushing on the pastry	

1. In a bowl, combine flour and salt. Mix well. Using a pastry blender, fork or your fingers, cut in butter until mixture is uniform and resembles coarse breadcrumbs. Sprinkle with water, a little at a time, mixing lightly after each addition (add just enough to hold the dough together). Mix together to form a dough. Form into two disks and wrap tightly in plastic wrap; set aside for about 30 minutes at room temperature.

2. Place potatoes in a small saucepan and add boiling water to barely cover. Add salt, cover loosely, return to a boil and boil for 5 minutes, until potatoes are almost cooked through. Drain well and set aside to cool.

3. In a bowl, combine onions, chile pepper, corn, beans, cottage cheese and cilantro. Season to taste with salt and freshly ground pepper. Add cooled potatoes and toss together to blend well.

4. Preheat oven to 400°F (200°C). On a lightly floured surface, working with one disk at a time, roll out dough to $1/8$ inch (3 mm) thick. Using a cutter dipped in flour, cut out nine circles. Transfer to prepared baking sheet when completed.

5. Place about 1 tbsp (15 mL) filling off-center on each pastry round. Dip your finger in a little water and run it around the edge of each round. Fold in half and seal the edges by pressing together with the tines of a fork. Repeat until remaining pastry and filling are used up. Lightly brush empanaditas with melted butter and bake in preheated oven for about 20 minutes, until golden brown. Serve warm or at room temperature.

Zenia's Potato Pyrohy

My best friend, Zenia Curzon, is of Ukrainian heritage, and she kindly gave me her special recipe for real pyrohy, also called varenyky (in Poland these are known as perogy). Not only are these plump little dumplings filled with potato, the dough is also made of potato, giving them a one-two potato punch. Zenia says, "This is a pretty basic recipe for pyrohy, and there are probably as many versions as there are Ukrainian moms. My mom didn't use mashed potatoes in her dough, but this recipe has always worked really well for me." Serve topped with fried mushrooms and onions and sour cream.

Serves 4

Tip

One pound (500 g) of potatoes makes 2½ to 3 cups (625 to 750 mL) mashed potatoes, a little more than you will need for this recipe.

- **3-inch (7.5 cm) round cutter**

Filling

2 tbsp	butter	30 mL
1	small onion, finely chopped	1
2 cups	warm dry-mashed potatoes	500 L
¾ cup	shredded sharp (aged) Cheddar cheese	175 mL
	Salt and freshly ground black pepper	

Dough

2 cups	all-purpose flour	500 mL
1 tsp	salt	5 mL
2	egg yolks	2
½ cup	cold mashed potatoes	125 mL
1 tbsp	melted butter	15 mL
½ cup	cool water (approx.)	125 mL
	Melted butter	
	Sour cream, optional	

1. *Filling:* In a skillet, melt butter over medium heat. Add onion and cook, stirring, until softened, about 5 minutes. Remove from heat and set aside to cool slightly.
2. In a bowl, combine onion, potatoes, cheese and salt and pepper to taste. Mix well. Set aside to cool thoroughly. (The filling can be made a day ahead and refrigerated. Bring to room temperature before using.)
3. *Dough:* In a bowl, mix together flour and salt. Add egg yolks, mashed potatoes and melted butter. Mix well. Continue mixing, adding just enough water to form a medium-soft dough. Transfer to a lightly floured surface and knead until smooth, being careful not to over-knead, which will toughen the dough.

4. Divide dough in half, shape into two disks and cover each disk with an inverted bowl. Let stand for 10 minutes. Working with one disk at a time, on a lightly floured surface, roll out dough until it is quite thin, about $1/16$ inch (2 mm) thick. Using cutter dipped in flour, cut into rounds. Repeat with remaining dough.

5. Bring a large pot of salted water to a boil over high heat.

6. Meanwhile, working with one round at a time, place a tablespoon of filling in the middle of each. Fold dough over to form a half-circle. Press edges together with your fingers, making sure they are well sealed. Transfer to a lightly floured baking sheet and cover with a clean tea towel so pryohy don't dry out while you complete the remainder.

7. When all pyrohy are prepared, carefully add them, a few at a time, to the boiling water, stirring gently to separate, if necessary, and to prevent sticking to bottom of pot. Boil until they puff up and bob to the surface, 3 to 4 minutes (the thinner the dough, the faster they will cook).

8. Using a slotted spoon, transfer to a colander as completed. Drain thoroughly and place in a warmed serving dish. Drizzle with a little melted butter and toss gently to keep them from sticking together. Cover and keep warm. Repeat until all pyrohy are cooked. Serve hot with a little sour cream, if desired.

Potato & Pea Samosas

It seems that almost every culture makes something savory that is wrapped in dough and boiled, baked or fried. Samosas are an example from India. These popular snacks are traditionally filled with potato, peas and sometimes spinach and seasoned with classic Indian spices. They are delicious with Mint-Cilantro Chutney (page 152) or a good mango chutney.

Makes 24

Tips

This is a great way to use leftover boiled potatoes or even mashed potatoes. The same amount of sweet potato would also work very well.

Garam masala is an Indian spice mixture. It is available in specialty stores and East Indian food shops. If you can't obtain it easily, substitute an equal quantity of curry powder or make your own (see Tips, page 234).

When making the pastry you may not use may not use all the milk, which is fine. Process just until a ball is about to form.

- Preheat oven to 140°F (60°C)
- Food processor
- Large, heavy pot, Dutch oven or deep fryer
- Candy/deep-frying thermometer (if not using a deep fryer)

2 cups	all-purpose flour	500 mL
½ tsp	salt	2 mL
½ cup	cold vegetable shortening or butter, cut into small pieces	125 mL
½ cup	whole milk (approx.), divided	125 mL
5	medium Yukon Gold or other all-purpose potatoes, peeled and cut into small chunks	5
1 tsp	salt	5 mL
4 tbsp	vegetable oil	60 mL
1	onion, finely chopped	1
1 tbsp	minced gingerroot	15 mL
2	cloves garlic, minced	2
1 tsp	ground coriander	5 mL
1 tsp	ground cumin	5 mL
1 tsp	garam masala (see Tips, left)	5 mL
1 cup	green peas, thawed if frozen	250 mL
3 tbsp	chopped fresh cilantro leaves	45 mL
	Salt and freshly ground black pepper	
	Vegetable oil	

1. In a food processor fitted with metal blade, pulse flour and salt to blend. Add shortening and pulse until mixture resembles coarse crumbs, about ten times. Add half the milk and pulse just until incorporated. Pinch mixture between your thumb and fingers — if it doesn't hold together, add 1 tbsp (15 mL) milk and pulse three times. Pinch again and if necessary, add more milk and pulse (see Tips, left).

Tips

The oil should come a little over halfway up the sides of the pot. Do not overfill; leave at least 3 inches (7.5 cm) of headspace at the top.

If you don't want to deep-fry the samosas, you can brush them lightly with butter and bake at 400°F (200°C) for 15 minutes, until golden brown.

2. Transfer dough to a lightly floured surface and knead for about 5 minutes, until smooth and pliable. Set aside, covered, while you prepare the filling.

3. Place potatoes in a large saucepan and add cold water to barely cover. Add salt, cover loosely and bring to a boil over high heat. Reduce heat and cook for 20 minutes or until potatoes are tender. Drain well and set aside.

4. In a large skillet, heat oil over medium-high heat. Add onion, ginger and garlic and sauté until softened, about 2 minutes. Add coriander, cumin and garam masala and stir well. Cook, stirring, until mixture becomes fragrant, about 3 minutes. Add potatoes, peas and cilantro and mix well, using a wooden spoon to crush the potatoes (but keep them chunky). Season to taste with salt and freshly ground pepper. Set aside to cool.

5. Divide dough into 12 equal pieces and form each into a ball. On a lightly floured surface, roll out one ball to make a 6-inch (15 cm) circle. (For a perfect circle, place a 6-inch/15 cm plate on top of the pastry and, using a sharp knife, cut around it.) Cut circle in half. Repeat until all the dough is rolled out, yielding 24 half-circles.

6. Working with one half-circle at a time, moisten half of the straight edge with water. Fold in half, matching the dry straight edge with the wet one and keeping rounded edge open to form a cone. Pinch straight edge to seal. Holding the cone upright, fill with about 2 tbsp (30 mL) filling. Moisten inside edge of one side of cone with water, pinch edges together and press firmly to seal. Transfer to a baking sheet lined with parchment paper. Repeat until dough and filling are used up. Cover with plastic wrap and refrigerate prepared samosas for up to 8 hours.

7. Place 4 to 6 inches (10 to 15 cm) oil in a large, heavy pot (see Tips, left). Heat over medium-high until thermometer registers 375°F (190°C). (If you're using a deep fryer, follow the manufacturer's instructions.) Using tongs or a wire-mesh strainer, lower the samosas, a few at a time, into the hot oil and cook until golden brown, about 4 minutes on the first side. Flip and cook for 1 minute or just until golden brown. Place on a baking sheet and keep warm in preheated oven. Repeat until all samosas are cooked.

Middle Eastern Roasted Minis & Cauliflower with Tahini

My daughter Jenna introduced me to the pleasure of roasted cauliflower when she popped a pan in the oven, then presented it with luscious lemony tahini sauce. One day I thought, *Let's add some small red potatoes and treat them to the same delightful dip.* This makes a wonderful appetizer, particularly with a vegetarian meal. Enjoy as a slightly messy finger food or as part of the main meal.

Serves 6 to 8

Tips

You need to roast the cauliflower separately because you need a very high temperature to achieve the nice toasted bits.

Look for tahini in specialty food shops, some supermarkets and health food outlets.

● **Preheat oven to 500°F (260°C)**

2	heads cauliflower, cored and cut into 1½-inch (4 cm) florets	2
½ cup	extra virgin olive oil, divided	125 mL
3 tbsp	ground cumin, divided	45 mL
	Salt and freshly ground black pepper	
3 lb	very small waxy or all-purpose potatoes, lightly scrubbed and dried	1.5 kg
1 cup	tahini paste	250 mL
4	cloves garlic, minced	4
3 tbsp	freshly squeezed lemon juice	45 mL
1 cup	water	250 mL

1. In a large bowl, toss cauliflower with half the olive oil and cumin, plus salt and freshly ground pepper to taste. Mix well to coat. Transfer to two baking sheets, spreading evenly. Bake in preheated oven, switching baking sheets from front to back and top to bottom until cauliflower is tender and nicely browned in places, 25 to 30 minutes. Remove from oven and transfer to a bowl. Cover and keep warm.

2. Reduce oven temperature to 400°F (200°C). In same bowl, toss potatoes with remaining olive oil and cumin, plus additional salt and pepper to taste. Mix well to coat. Transfer to the same baking sheets (you may need only one, but make sure not to crowd), spreading evenly. Bake in preheated oven until tender and beginning to crisp, 20 to 30 minutes. Remove from oven and keep warm.

3. In another bowl, whisk tahini, garlic, lemon juice and water. Season to taste with salt and whisk again. Serve on the side with cauliflower and potatoes.

Snacks, Small Plates & Light Meals

This chapter features recipes that fill the bill perfectly when a lighter touch is required. You will find something here for brunch, lunch, simple suppers and maybe even late-night noshing. Smaller plates with big flavor appeal, they feature a variety of potatoes and sweet potatoes in ways you may never have thought of before.

Twice-Baked Jacket Potato

In the U.K., jacket potatoes — a.k.a baked potatoes — are a huge lunchtime favorite. They are sold in pubs, at outdoor market stalls and by vendors who specialize in "naught else," as my favorite characters on *Coronation Street* like to say. Many ingredients work well as the filling, such as shrimp and cilantro, mushrooms and Gruyère, baked beans and bacon. Here is one version to get your motor running. Serve it with just a bit of butter and, some would say, sour cream. The number of servings depends on whether the diners consume a whole potato or a half (they are quite substantial).

Makes 4 to 8 servings

Tips

Pat scrubbed potatoes dry with a clean tea towel or paper towels; if they still seem damp, let air-dry for about 10 minutes.

Taleggio is an absolutely delicious semi-soft northern Italian cheese of some pungency but with a relatively mild, nut-sweet flavor. If you can't obtain it easily, substitute fontina, which also melts beautifully.

If you like, you can spoon out some of the baked potato flesh and blend it with the topping mixture, which will give you more of a cavity to hold the filling.

- Preheat oven to 375°F (190°C)
- Small baking dish
- Rimmed baking sheet

4	large floury or all-purpose potatoes (each 8 to 10 oz/250 to 300 g), scrubbed and thoroughly dried (see Tips, left)	4
¼ cup	olive oil, divided	60 mL
	Salt	
1	onion, sliced	1
4	cloves garlic	4
6	slices back (Canadian) bacon, cooked and chopped	6
½ cup	shredded sharp (aged) Cheddar cheese	125 mL
½ cup	diced Taleggio cheese (see Tips, left)	125 mL
⅓ cup	butter, softened	75 mL
¼ cup	sour cream	60 mL
¼ cup	finely chopped fresh chives	60 mL
2 tsp	chili powder	10 mL
	Freshly ground black pepper	

1. Using a fork, prick each potato a few times, then rub with 1 tbsp (15 mL) oil and a little salt. Place potatoes directly on oven rack.

2. In a small baking dish, combine onion, garlic and remaining oil and toss to coat. Place in the oven along with the potatoes and roast for 30 to 40 minutes or until onion is slightly charred. Remove onion and garlic from oven and set aside until cool enough to handle. Continue to bake potatoes for a total of $1\frac{1}{2}$ to 2 hours or until cooked through and skin is super-crisp. Transfer to a cutting board and set aside until cool enough to handle.

3. Finely chop roasted onions and garlic and transfer to a bowl. Stir in bacon, Cheddar, Taleggio, butter, sour cream, chives and chili powder until thoroughly combined. Set aside.

4. Preheat broiler to high. Slit each potato open lengthwise (don't cut through the bottom skin). Using a fork, rough up the flesh a bit. Transfer potato, cut side up, to baking sheet and top with a quarter of the onion mixture. Repeat until all potatoes have been topped. Broil for 1 to 2 minutes or until potatoes are heated through and cheese is slightly melted. Serve immediately.

Four Cheese & Onion Jacket Potato

This is one of the original combinations for jacket potatoes and still one of the best. Serve half or whole potatoes to accommodate individual appetites.

Makes 4 to 8 servings

Tips

Pat scrubbed potatoes dry with a clean tea towel or paper towels; if they still seem damp, let air-dry for about 10 minutes.

Vary the cheeses as you wish or just use one or two of your favorites, but keep the total amount the same.

If you like, you can spoon out some of the baked potato flesh and blend it with the topping mixture, which will give you more of a cavity to hold the filling.

If you want to pump up the onion flavor, use finely chopped red or white onion in place of the green onions.

● **Preheat oven to 375°F (190°C)**

4	large floury or all-purpose potatoes (each 8 to 10 oz/250 to 300 g), scrubbed and thoroughly dried (see Tips, left)	4
¼ cup	olive oil, divided	60 mL
	Salt	

Topping

⅓ cup	butter, softened	75 mL
¼ cup	shredded sharp (aged) Cheddar cheese	60 mL
¼ cup	shredded fontina cheese	60 mL
¼ cup	freshly grated Grana Padano cheese	60 mL
¼ cup	crumbled Gorgonzola cheese	60 mL
3	finely chopped green onions, trimmed	3
¼ cup	finely chopped flat-leaf parsley leaves	60 mL
	Salt and freshly ground black pepper	

1. Using a fork, prick each potato a few times, then rub with 1 tbsp (15 mL) oil and a little salt. Place directly on oven rack and roast in preheated oven for 1½ to 2 hours or until flesh is cooked through and skin is super-crisp.
2. *Topping:* Meanwhile, in a bowl, using a fork, blend together butter, Cheddar, fontina, Grana Padano, Gorgonzola, green onions and parsley. Season to taste with salt and pepper.
3. Remove potatoes from oven and set aside until cool enough to handle.
4. Preheat broiler to high. Slit each potato open lengthwise (don't cut through the bottom skin). Using a fork, rough up the flesh a bit. Transfer potato, cut side up, to a rimmed baking sheet and top with a quarter of the onion mixture. Repeat until all potatoes have been filled. Broil for 1 to 2 minutes or until potatoes are heated through and cheese is slightly melted. Serve immediately.

Jacket Potato with Baby Shrimp & Marie Rose Sauce

I first had this combination in a café in the Scottish Highlands, in a lovely little town called Grantown on Spey. The potato was massive and topped with an enormous quantity of tiny shrimp in the very popular sauce known as Marie Rose. It may seem rather pedestrian but it was delish nonetheless!

Makes 4 to 8 servings

Tip

Pat scrubbed potatoes dry with a clean tea towel or paper towels; if they still seem damp, let air-dry for about 10 minutes.

● **Preheat oven to 375°F (190°C)**

4	large floury or all-purpose potatoes (each 8 to 10 oz/250 to 300 g), scrubbed and thoroughly dried (see Tip, left)	4
¼ cup	olive oil, divided	60 mL
	Salt	

Topping

½ cup	mayonnaise	125 mL
2 tbsp	ketchup	30 mL
Pinch	cayenne pepper	Pinch
1 tbsp	freshly squeezed lemon juice	15 mL
	Salt and freshly ground black pepper	
2 cups	cooked salad shrimp	500 mL
¼ cup	butter, divided	60 mL
1	small bunch watercress, rinsed and thoroughly dried	1

1. Using a fork, prick each potato a few times, then rub with 1 tbsp (15 mL) oil and a little salt. Place directly on oven rack and roast in preheated oven for 1½ to 2 hours or until flesh is cooked through and skin is super-crisp.
2. *Topping:* Meanwhile, in a bowl, whisk together mayonnaise, ketchup, cayenne and lemon juice to blend. Season to taste with salt and pepper. Stir in shrimp to coat.
3. Remove potatoes from oven and set aside until cool enough to handle.
4. Slit each potato open lengthwise (don't cut through the bottom skin). Using a fork, rough up the flesh a bit and transfer potatoes, cut side up, to a serving platter. Top each with 1 tbsp (15 mL) butter and a quarter of the topping. Garnish with watercress and serve immediately.

Chili & Bacon–Topped Jacket Potato

Here is one of the very best combinations for a jacket potato. It makes for a satisfying, substantial meal when paired with a salad of avocado, tomato, cucumber and green onion tossed with a creamy dressing and fresh dill.

Makes 4 to 8 servings

Tips

Pat scrubbed potatoes dry with a clean tea towel or paper towels; if they still seem damp, let air-dry for about 10 minutes.

You can use the excellent recipe for Smokin' Chili (page 186) for this hefty dish or, if time is short, pick up a good-quality prepared version. You can also substitute baked beans (canned, if you prefer) with great results.

- **Preheat oven to 375°F (190°C)**

4	large floury or all-purpose potatoes (each 8 to 10 oz/250 to 300 g), scrubbed and thoroughly dried (see Tips, left)	4
$\frac{1}{4}$ cup	olive oil, divided	60 mL
	Salt	

Topping

6	slices double-smoked bacon, chopped	6
$2\frac{1}{2}$ cups	chili (see Tips, left)	625 mL
$\frac{1}{2}$ cup	shredded sharp (aged) Cheddar cheese	125 mL
$\frac{1}{2}$ cup	shredded mozzarella cheese	125 mL

1. Using a fork, prick each potato a few times, then rub with 1 tbsp (15 mL) oil and a little salt. Place directly on oven rack and roast in preheated oven for $1\frac{1}{2}$ to 2 hours or until flesh is cooked through and skin is super-crisp.

2. *Topping:* Meanwhile, in a small skillet over medium-high heat, cook bacon, stirring frequently, for about 10 minutes or until almost crisp (don't overcook). Using a slotted spoon, transfer to a plate lined with paper towels to drain.

3. In a saucepan, heat chili, stirring occasionally, over medium-high heat. Reduce heat to low and keep hot.

4. Remove potatoes from oven and set aside until cool enough to handle.

5. Preheat broiler to high. Slit each potato open lengthwise (don't cut through the bottom skin). Using a fork, rough up the flesh a bit. Transfer potato, cut side up, to a rimmed baking sheet and top with a quarter each of the chili, bacon, Cheddar and mozzarella. Repeat until all potatoes have been topped. Broil for 1 to 2 minutes or until potatoes are heated through and cheese is slightly melted. Serve immediately.

Smoked Salmon, Cream Cheese & Capers Jacket Potato

Forget bagels and treat the classic combination of smoked salmon and cream cheese to a baked potato. In this easy preparation, the cream cheese is combined with the flesh of the baked potato and returned to the potato skin before being topped with lengths of smoked salmon, crème fraîche and chives.

Makes 4 to 8 servings

Tips

Pat scrubbed potatoes dry with a clean tea towel or paper towels; if they still seem damp, let air-dry for about 10 minutes.

I prefer to use sea salt rather than refined table salt because it has a much cleaner, crisper taste.

Most large supermarkets and cheese shops now sell crème fraîche. If you can't find it, it's easy to make your own (page 132).

- **Preheat oven to 375°F (190°C)**

4	large floury or all-purpose potatoes (each 8 to 10 oz/250 to 300 g), scrubbed and thoroughly dried (see Tips, left)	4
¼ cup	olive oil, divided	60 mL
	Salt	

Topping

8 oz	cream cheese, softened	250 g
2 tbsp	butter, softened	30 mL
¼ cup	capers, rinsed and dried	60 mL
	Freshly ground white pepper	
8 oz	smoked salmon, sliced	250 g
½ cup	crème fraîche (see Tips, left)	125 mL
¼ cup	chopped fresh chives	60 mL

1. Using a fork, prick each potato a few times, then rub with 1 tbsp (15 mL) oil and a little salt. Place directly on oven rack and roast for $1\frac{1}{2}$ to 2 hours or until flesh is cooked through and skin is super-crisp.

2. *Topping:* Meanwhile, in a bowl, combine cream cheese and butter to blend. Stir in capers and white pepper.

3. Remove potatoes from oven and set aside until cool enough to handle.

4. Slit each potato open lengthwise (don't cut through the bottom skin). Using a fork, rough up the flesh a bit and scoop out a generous portion. Add to cream cheese mixture. Repeat until all potatoes have been scooped. Top each potato with a quarter of the cream cheese mixture and transfer to individual serving plates. Drape slices of salmon decoratively over each. Top with a dollop of crème fraîche and sprinkle with chives. Serve immediately.

Creamed Mushroom & Shallot–Topped Jacket Potato

A wonderful choice to serve alongside grilled steaks, or as a main course accompanied by salad, these rich-tasting spuds feature those flavorful little brown mushrooms called cremini, although you can use any assortment you like. You will find many uses for this topping, but I think it shines brightest when used on a freshly baked potato, which you could also garnish with your favorite blue cheese.

Makes 4 to 8 servings

Tip

Pat scrubbed potatoes dry with a clean tea towel or paper towels; if they still seem damp, let air-dry for about 10 minutes.

● **Preheat oven to 375°F (190°C)**

4	large floury or all-purpose potatoes (each 8 to 10 oz/250 to 300 g), scrubbed and thoroughly dried (see Tip, left)	4
¼ cup	olive oil, divided	60 mL
	Salt	

Topping

2 tbsp	butter	30 mL
1 tbsp	olive oil	15 mL
3	shallots, peeled and finely chopped	3
1	clove garlic, peeled and finely chopped	1
1 lb	cremini mushrooms, finely chopped	500 g
1 tbsp	all-purpose flour	15 mL
⅓ cup	dry white wine	75 mL
½ cup	whole milk (approx.)	125 mL
½ cup	half-and-half (10%) cream	125 mL
Pinch	ground nutmeg	Pinch
	Salt and freshly ground white pepper	
1 tbsp	chopped fresh thyme leaves	15 mL
	Crumbled blue cheese, optional	

1. Using a fork, prick each potato a few times, then rub with 1 tbsp (15 mL) oil and a little salt. Place directly on oven rack and roast in preheated oven for 1½ to 2 hours or until flesh is cooked through and skin is super-crisp.

2. *Topping:* Meanwhile, in a large skillet, heat butter and oil over medium heat. Cook shallots and garlic, stirring, for about 10 minutes or until just softened (do not let brown). Add mushrooms and cook, stirring, for about 15 minutes or until softened. Sprinkle with flour and, using a wooden spoon, work flour into mushroom mixture until all traces have been absorbed.

3. Stir in wine and cook for 1 to 2 minutes. Gradually stir in milk and cream and cook, stirring constantly, for about 5 minutes or until thickened (if sauce looks too thick, stir in a little more milk or water). Stir in nutmeg. Season to taste with salt and white pepper. Stir in thyme. Reduce heat to low and keep warm.

4. Remove potatoes from oven and set aside until cool enough to handle.

5. Slit each potato open lengthwise (don't cut through the bottom skin). Using a fork, rough up the flesh a bit. Transfer potato, cut side up, to an individual serving plate. Top with a quarter of the mushroom mixture. Sprinkle with blue cheese to taste, if using. Repeat until all potatoes have been filled. Serve immediately.

Variations

This mushroom sauce is very versatile and makes a great accompaniment to many foods. It can be paired with seared pork tenderloin or boneless chicken breasts, used to fill mini pastry shells for an appetizer or even just spooned over hot buttered toast and then topped with your favorite blue cheese. At the Black Dog we have served an appetizer of this mushroom mixture with a little fresh tarragon added and topped with melting Brie — yum.

Jacket Potato Bolognese

Designed for the meat-and-potatoes lover, this is a great way to use up leftovers of your favorite homemade meat sauce — or use this foolproof and delicious recipe. If you don't eat meat, a mushroom-tomato sauce would be a nice option.

Makes 4 servings

Tip

Pat scrubbed potatoes dry with a clean tea towel or paper towels.

- **Preheat oven to 375°F (190°C)**

4	large floury or all-purpose potatoes (each 8 to 10 oz/250 to 300 g), scrubbed and thoroughly dried (see Tip, left)	4
¼ cup	olive oil, divided	60 mL
	Salt	

Bolognese Sauce

¼ cup	olive oil	60 mL
2	cloves garlic, finely chopped	2
1	onion, finely diced	1
2	stalks celery, finely diced	2
1	carrot, finely diced	1
12 oz	extra-lean beef	375 g
12 oz	lean ground pork	375 g
4 oz	pancetta, finely chopped	125 g
Pinch	freshly grated nutmeg	Pinch
1 cup	red wine (approx.)	250 mL
1 tbsp	tomato paste	15 mL
½ cup	warm water	125 mL
½ tsp	salt	2 mL
¼ tsp	freshly ground black pepper	1 mL
1 cup	freshly grated Grana Padano or Parmesan cheese	250 mL

1. Using a fork, prick each potato a few times, then rub with 1 tbsp (15 mL) oil and a little salt. Place directly on oven rack and roast for 1½ to 2 hours or until flesh is cooked through and skin is super-crisp.

2. *Bolognese Sauce:* Meanwhile, in a large skillet, heat oil over medium heat. Cook garlic and onion, stirring, for 3 minutes or until softened. Stir in celery and carrot and cook, stirring occasionally, for 10 minutes or until softened. Add beef, pork, pancetta and nutmeg and cook, stirring to break up meat, for 10 minutes or until browned. Stir in wine, bring to a boil and cook for 5 minutes.

3. In a bowl, combine tomato paste and water. Stir into meat mixture and return to a boil. Reduce heat to low and stir in salt and freshly ground pepper. Cover and cook, stirring occasionally, for $1\frac{1}{2}$ to 2 hours or until sauce is thickened (if mixture looks too dry, add a little more water or wine during cooking). Set aside and keep warm on very low heat.

4. Remove potatoes from oven and set aside until cool enough to handle.

5. Slit each potato open lengthwise (don't cut through the bottom skin). Using a fork, rough up the flesh a bit. Transfer potato, cut side up, to an individual serving plate, top with a quarter of the Bolognese sauce and sprinkle with a quarter of the cheese. Repeat until all potatoes and filling have been used. Serve immediately.

Southwestern Jacket Potato

The foods and flavors we associate with Tex-Mex cuisine are all here — avocado, salsa, lime juice, spicy beans, cilantro and pepper Jack cheese. This combination works very well with baked sweet potatoes too (see Tips, below).

Makes 4 to 8 servings

Tips

Pat scrubbed potatoes dry with a clean tea towel or paper towels; if they still seem damp, let air-dry for about 10 minutes.

Look for chili beans or spicy beans — a meatless mixture of beans in a spicy sauce — right next to the regular canned baked beans on your grocer's shelf.

You can make this using sweet potatoes, but reduce the baking time of the potatoes. Depending on their size, sweet potatoes should take 45 to 55 minutes in the oven.

Lining the baking sheet with parchment paper will save on cleanup.

• **Preheat oven to 375°F (190°C)**

4	large floury or all-purpose potatoes (each 8 to 10 oz/250 to 300 g), scrubbed and thoroughly dried (see Tips, left)	4
¼ cup	olive oil, divided	60 mL
	Salt	

Topping

2½ cups	chili beans (see Tips, left)	625 mL
2 cups	medium-hot salsa	500 mL
3	firm ripe avocados, cut into small chunks	3
2 tbsp	freshly squeezed lime juice	30 mL
1	red onion, finely diced	1
½ cup	coarsely chopped cilantro leaves	125 mL
	Salt and freshly ground black pepper	
2 cups	shredded pepper Jack cheese	500 mL

1. Using a fork, prick each potato a few times, then rub with 1 tbsp (15 mL) oil and a little salt. Place directly on oven rack and roast for 1½ to 2 hours or until flesh is cooked through and skin is super-crisp.
2. *Topping:* Meanwhile, in a saucepan, combine beans and salsa over medium heat and cook, stirring, for about 10 minutes or until heated through. Reduce heat to low and keep warm.
3. In a bowl, stir together avocado, lime juice, onion and cilantro. Season to taste with salt and pepper. Set aside.
4. Remove potatoes from oven and set aside until cool enough to handle.
5. Preheat broiler to high. Slit each potato open lengthwise (don't cut through the bottom skin). Using a fork, rough up the flesh a bit. Transfer potato, cut side up, to a rimmed baking sheet and top with a quarter of the chili mixture, then a quarter of the cheese. Broil for 1 to 2 minutes or until potatoes are heated through and cheese is melted. Transfer to individual serving plates. Top each with a quarter of the avocado mixture. Serve immediately.

Potato-Nest Eggs with Bacon & Cheddar

Once cooked and hollowed out, a big baked potato provides a great vehicle for many good things: mushrooms, chopped asparagus, sun-dried tomatoes, smoked fish, ham or salami, a variety of cheeses, fresh herbs. Think of this recipe as just the starting point. It's great for brunch or a late-night bite.

Makes 4 servings

Tip

If your potatoes are really large, you may have a bit too much potato flesh to fit both it and the egg in the hollowed-out skin. If so, reserve the extra potato for another use (or do as I did, and just eat it — chef's perk!).

- **Preheat oven to 400°F (200°C)**
- **Baking dish, large enough to hold 4 potatoes**

4	large floury potatoes, scrubbed	4
¼ cup	butter	60 mL
6	strips bacon, cooked until crisp, then crumbled	6
1 cup	shredded sharp (aged) Cheddar cheese	250 mL
¼ cup	chopped fresh chives or finely chopped green onions	60 mL
	Salt and freshly ground black pepper	
4	large eggs	4

1. With the tines of a fork, pierce each potato a few times. Place potatoes directly on center rack and bake in preheated oven for 1 hour or until cooked through (if very large, they will take longer to cook). Remove from oven and set aside until cool enough to handle. Reduce oven temperature to 350°F (180°C).

2. Using a small, sharp knife, cut off a "lid" lengthwise along each potato and set lids aside. Working with one potato at a time, using a small spoon, carefully scoop out as much potato flesh as possible and transfer to a bowl. Set skin aside. Repeat with remaining potatoes.

3. Add butter to potato flesh and mash well. Add bacon, cheese and chives and mix well. Season to taste with salt and freshly ground pepper.

4. Spoon potato mixture into skins, making a well in the center of each. Transfer to baking dish. Crack one egg into each well. Top with reserved lids and bake for about 20 minutes or until whites are set. Serve immediately.

Grilled Potato Wedges with Smoky Tomato & Chiles

These wedges make great casual hors d'oeuvres passed around like finger food. However, when your in-house grill king is bent on enjoying some great homemade chips or oven-fries to accompany his masterful porterhouse steak, tell him these grilled spud wedges are the way to go. Even the ingredients for the accompanying chili sauce can be grilled, making this the perfect summer preparation. Get fired up and make the chili sauce first. It has a nice bit of heat and is also outstanding with grilled jumbo shrimp.

Serves 6 to 8

Tips

Long red chile peppers or Thai bird's-eye chiles are good choices.

An easy way to grill garlic is to thread individual cloves on presoaked wooden skewers, or grill an entire head of garlic and keep some for another use.

You don't need to peel the grilled tomatoes, chiles or bell pepper. When the vegetables are puréed, the skins help give body to the finished sauce.

- Preheat barbecue or broiler to medium-high
- Food processor

Chili Sauce

6	large ripe plum tomatoes	6
1	onion, unpeeled and halved	1
1	small red bell pepper	1
4	cloves garlic, unpeeled (see Tips, left)	4
3	fresh red chile peppers (see Tips, left)	3
3 tbsp	extra virgin olive oil	45 mL
3 tbsp	finely chopped fresh cilantro leaves	45 mL
2 tsp	brown sugar	10 mL
2 tsp	tomato paste	10 mL
	Juice of 1 lime	
	Salt and freshly ground black pepper	

Potatoes

6	large floury potatoes, scrubbed	6
3 tbsp	olive oil	45 mL
2 tsp	sweet paprika	10 mL
	Salt and freshly ground black pepper	

1. *Chili Sauce:* Place tomatoes, onion, bell pepper, garlic and chiles on preheated, lightly greased grill (or beneath a hot broiler) and grill, turning, until charred and softened. Transfer to a baking sheet as completed and set aside to cool slightly. Squeeze garlic out of its skin and peel onion; discard skins. Scrape seeds from the bell pepper.

2. In a food processor fitted with metal blade, process grilled tomatoes, onion, bell pepper, garlic and chiles along with olive oil, cilantro, sugar, tomato paste and lime juice, until smooth and blended. Season to taste with salt and pepper and set aside to allow flavors to develop.

3. *Potatoes:* Slice potatoes in half lengthwise and cut each half lengthwise into thirds (or quarters if potatoes are really large). In a large bowl, toss potato wedges, olive oil, paprika and salt and freshly ground pepper until well coated. Place on preheated, lightly greased grill (or under a preheated broiler) set about 4 to 6 inches (10 to 15 cm) above the fire so the potatoes will cook through internally before coloring too much on the outside. Cook the potatoes, turning every 5 minutes or so, until they are crisp and cooked through. Serve with the chili sauce.

Smokin' Chili Spuds

We don't often put potatoes and chili together but they seem pretty natural bedfellows to me. Enjoy this as an appetizer, a snack or a full meal, depending on the number of people you are serving. This is especially good fare for a busy cold winter weekend.

Serves 4 to 6

Tips

This meaty chili contains no beans, but feel free to add some if you wish.

Cutting the potatoes crosswise creates two small, thick halves, which make nice little cups to fill with the chili.

If you have a chili recipe of which you are particularly fond, by all means use it here.

Make the chili the day before you plan to serve it. When you're ready to serve, put the potatoes in the oven and head out for a walk while they bake.

Smokin' Chili

2 tbsp	olive oil	30 mL
1 lb	lean ground beef	500 g
½ lb	lean ground pork	250 g
1	large onion, finely chopped	1
2	cloves garlic, chopped	2
1 to 2	small fresh red chiles, finely chopped	1 to 2
1 tbsp	ancho chile powder	15 mL
4 tsp	ground cumin	20 mL
1 tbsp	dried oregano	15 mL
2 tsp	cayenne pepper (or to taste)	10 mL
4 cups	chopped canned plum tomatoes, with juice	1 L
¼ cup	tomato paste	60 mL
	Salt and freshly ground black pepper	
½ cup	chopped fresh cilantro leaves	125 mL

Spuds

4	large floury potatoes, scrubbed	4
1 cup	sour cream	250 mL

1. *Chili:* In a large saucepan, heat oil over medium-high heat. Add ground meats and sauté, breaking up with the back of a spoon until no trace of pink remains, about 15 minutes. Pour off all but 1 tbsp (15 mL) of the fat.

2. Lower heat slightly. Add onion, garlic, chiles, chile powder, cumin, oregano and cayenne and cook, stirring, for 2 minutes. Add tomatoes, bring to a boil and cook, stirring frequently, for 10 minutes. Stir in tomato paste and season to taste with salt and pepper. Reduce heat and simmer for about 1 hour, until thickened. Stir in cilantro.

3. *Spuds:* Meanwhile, preheat oven to 375°F (190°C). Place potatoes on oven rack and bake in preheated oven until skins are crisped and potatoes are cooked through, 1 to 1¼ hours. Remove from oven and set aside until cool enough to handle.

4. Cut potatoes in half crosswise; scoop out the flesh and stir into chili. Arrange potato skins on a plate and fill with chili. Top each with sour cream and serve.

Spinach & Potato Gnocchi

Serve these as they would in Italy, as a light first course before a main of meat, fish or poultry. Or you can serve a few more per person for a main course. All these rich little dumplings need is a gloss of melted butter, a squirt of lemon and freshly ground black pepper.

Serves 6

Tips

If your spinach has not been prewashed, swish the leaves around in a basin of lukewarm water before placing in colander and rinsing. Otherwise it is likely to be gritty.

When making gnocchi, remember, the less flour and handling the dough receives, the lighter the gnocchi will be.

● **Food processor or food mill**

1½ lbs	floury potatoes, scrubbed and halved (about 2 large)	750 g
2 tsp	salt, divided	10 mL
12 oz	fresh spinach, stems removed, cooked (see Tips, left)	375 g
2 cups	all-purpose flour (approx.)	500 mL
2	egg yolks, divided	2
¼ cup	melted butter	60 mL
3 tbsp	freshly squeezed lemon juice	45 mL
	Salt and freshly ground black pepper	

1. Follow Step 1 (page 188), adding 1 tsp (5 mL) salt to the cooking water but mash potatoes roughly once cooked.
2. In a food processor fitted with metal blade, pulse cooked potatoes and spinach just until blended, 6 to 8 times. (Alternatively, work the mixture together by hand in a large bowl or put through a food mill until blended.) Transfer to a work surface lightly dusted with flour. Add ½ cup (125 mL) flour and work it into the potato and spinach mixture with your hands. Add one of the egg yolks and work well into the mixture, then add another ½ cup (125 mL) flour. Repeat, kneading remaining egg yolk and another ½ cup (125 mL) flour into the dough. Continue to work in flour, if necessary, until the dough has lost its stickiness and is firming up.
3. Follow instructions for rolling and cooking gnocchi (steps 3, 4 and 5) on page 189.
4. When all the gnocchi have been cooked, drizzle with melted butter and lemon juice and season to taste with salt and freshly ground pepper. Serve immediately.

Potato Gnocchi with Gorgonzola Cream

Gnocchi make an excellent light main course. While this classic, relatively simple version consists of nothing more than potato and flour, finishing it with a luxuriously creamy Gorgonzola sauce makes it quite impressive. This is also an excellent starter for a simple main dish of seared veal, chicken or fish. Serve with good crusty bread to soak up the lovely sauce.

Serves 6

Tips

The amount of flour is approximate; add it gradually, as you may not use it all. Stop adding flour when the dough has lost most of its stickiness and is soft and smooth. The less flour, the lighter the gnocchi will be.

For that same reason, the potatoes are not peeled before boiling. If the potatoes are not peeled, they absorb less water, so they absorb less flour and the resulting dough will be lighter.

When shopping for Gorgonzola, first make sure it is Italian. If you love strong blue cheese, look for *piccante* on the label. If you would like Gorgonzola with less punch, *dolcelatte* ("sweet milk") is the way to go.

Gnocchi

1½ lbs	floury potatoes, scrubbed and halved (about 2 large)	750 g
1 tsp	salt	5 mL
2 cups	all-purpose flour (approx.)	500 mL

Gorgonzola Cream

¼ cup	butter	60 mL
4 oz	Gorgonzola cheese, roughly chopped (see Tips, left)	125 g
⅔ cup	heavy or whipping (35%) cream	150 mL
	Salt and freshly ground black pepper	
½ cup	freshly grated Grana Padano or Parmesan cheese	125 mL

1. *Gnocchi:* Place potatoes in a large saucepan and add cold water to barely cover. Add salt, cover loosely and bring to a boil over high heat. Reduce heat and cook for 20 minutes or until potatoes are tender. Drain well, reserving water. Return potatoes to saucepan over very low heat and shake the pot back and forth to remove any trace of moisture. (This step is important because if they are wet, the potatoes will absorb too much flour, which in turn will produce heavier gnocchi.) When potatoes are cool enough to handle, peel, transfer to a bowl and mash until smooth. Set aside to cool slightly.

2. Transfer potatoes to a work surface lightly dusted with flour. Gradually add the flour ½ cup (125 mL) at a time, kneading gently until a soft dough forms. (You may not need all the flour; see Tips, left). Knead several times, until dough is firm and pliable.

3. Divide dough into thirds and, using your palms, roll each third into a long sausage about ³⁄₄ inch (2 cm) in diameter. Working with one roll at a time, cut into pieces about 1 inch (2.5 cm) long and transfer, as cut, to a clean tea towel lightly dusted with flour. Do not allow gnocchi to touch. Cover with another clean tea towel. (At this point gnocchi and towels can be covered with plastic wrap and refrigerated until ready to cook the same day.)

4. Bring a large pot of salted water to a boil.

5. Using a long-handled strainer or slotted spoon, add gnocchi to boiling water in batches (about eight at a time, depending upon their size) and cook until they rise to the surface, about 3 minutes. Cook for 1 minute longer, then, using a slotted spoon, transfer to a warm, lightly buttered serving dish. Repeat until all gnocchi have been cooked.

6. *Gorgonzola Cream:* Meanwhile, in a heavy skillet over medium heat, melt butter, watching carefully to ensure it doesn't start to brown. Add Gorgonzola and stir until melted. Reduce heat to medium low. Add cream and cook gently until sauce has thickened, about 5 minutes. Pour over gnocchi, season with salt and freshly ground pepper to taste and scatter Grana Padano evenly overtop. Serve immediately.

Variations

A lovely variation is to add steamed or sautéed asparagus and toasted walnuts to the gnocchi and sauce.

These gnocchi are also very good with your favorite tomato sauce instead of the Gorgonzola cream.

Sweet Potato Gnocchi with Sage Brown Butter

Brown butter and fresh sage is a classic accompaniment for conventional gnocchi. As good as that combination is, it really sings when the gnocchi are made with sweet potatoes. If you think making gnocchi is beyond your capabilities, let me just say that, armed with this recipe, my husband, Ted — a gnocchi-making novice — pulled this off without a hitch. With their lovely bright color and appealing texture, these make an attractive choice for serving to company, as you can make them ahead up to the point where you toss them to brown in the skillet.

Serves 6

Tips

Make the gnocchi ahead of time and toss with the butter sauce just before serving.

Let the ricotta cheese sit in a small strainer over a bowl to drain for a few minutes if it seems quite wet. Then place in a clean tea towel, wrap tightly and, using your hands, press against the fabric until excess moisture is absorbed. Draining the ricotta helps prevent the dough from absorbing too much flour and creating heavy gnocchi.

The amount of flour you use will depend on the moisture content of the sweet potato, so add it gradually, following the recipe instructions, to avoid making heavy gnocchi.

This recipe can be served as a first-course appetizer or a main course, perhaps with the addition of leaf spinach, steamed or in a salad.

- **Preheat oven to 400°F (200°C)**

Gnocchi

2 lbs	sweet potatoes, scrubbed (about 2 large or 3 medium)	1 kg
½ cup	ricotta cheese, drained of excess moisture (see Tips, left)	125 mL
½ cup	freshly grated Grana Padano or Parmesan cheese (approx.)	125 mL
1 tsp	salt	5 mL
¼ tsp	freshly ground black pepper	1 mL
¼ tsp	ground nutmeg	1 mL
1	egg yolk	1
1½ to 2 cups	all-purpose flour	375 to 500 mL

Sage Brown Butter

½ cup + 2 tbsp	butter, divided	155 mL
⅓ cup	chopped fresh sage	75 mL
	Finely grated zest of 1 lemon	

1. *Gnocchi:* Prick sweet potatoes with the tines of a fork. On a baking sheet lined with parchment paper, bake in preheated oven until tender when tested with a skewer, 45 minutes to 1 hour. Set aside for about 15 minutes, until cool enough to handle.

2. Using a large spoon, scrape out cooked sweet potato flesh and transfer to a large bowl. Add drained ricotta, Grana Padano, salt, pepper, nutmeg and egg yolk and mix well. Gradually add 1 cup flour, $\frac{1}{2}$ cup (125 mL) at a time, mixing gently but thoroughly until a soft dough forms. Transfer to a lightly floured surface and knead in additional flour $\frac{1}{4}$ cup (60 mL) at a time, kneading lightly as you work until it is no longer sticky and a smooth dough has formed.

3. Divide dough into eight equal portions. Working with one portion at a time and using your hands, roll into a long sausage shape about $\frac{3}{4}$ inch (2 cm) in diameter. Cut into pieces about $\frac{3}{4}$ inch (2 cm) long. Lightly flour your hands and roll each piece into a ball, using a little additional flour if necessary. Press each gnocchi with the tines of a fork, creating indentations on one side, then press down lightly with your thumb to indent the opposite side. Transfer gnocchi to a parchment-lined baking sheet as completed. Repeat until all dough is used up.

4. Bring a large pot of salted water to a boil.

5. *Sage Brown Butter:* Meanwhile, in a skillet, heat $\frac{1}{2}$ cup (125 mL) butter over medium-high heat until it begins to brown, about 4 minutes. Add sage and lemon zest, season with salt and pepper to taste, stir well and set aside.

6. Add gnocchi to boiling water in batches. Cook, uncovered, until they bob to the surface, then cook for 1 minute longer, for a total of 3 to 4 minutes. Using a slotted spoon, transfer to a baking sheet lined with a clean tea towel. Repeat until all gnocchi have been cooked.

7. In a large skillet, melt remaining 2 tbsp (30 mL) butter over medium-high heat. Add drained gnocchi and sauté gently until just beginning to brown at the edges, stirring occasionally. Add reserved brown butter sauce and toss gently to coat and warm through, about 1 minute. Transfer to warmed pasta bowls and sprinkle with additional Grana Padano, if desired.

Variation

Instead of finishing the gnocchi with brown butter and sage, try the creamy Gorgonzola sauce on page 188. Fresh spinach, quickly sautéed with a smidge of garlic, is a nice accompaniment to this pairing.

Potato Croutons with Linguine & Pesto

The word *crouton* derives from the French word for crust, which got me thinking, Why couldn't a potato chunk be a crouton, if it was nice and crispy like its bread counterpart? You may never have thought of putting potatoes and pasta together, but the Italians have. Here it is, with ripe tomatoes and a blend of fresh basil and parsley to round things out nicely.

Makes 4 servings

Tip

I prefer to use sea salt rather than refined table salt because it has a much cleaner, crisper taste and enhanced mineral content.

- **Rimmed baking sheet, lightly greased**
- **Mini food processor or blender**

3	all-purpose or floury potatoes, scrubbed	3
1 tsp	salt	5 mL
½ cup	olive oil, divided	125 mL
	Salt and freshly ground black pepper	
½ cup	tightly packed flat-leaf parsley leaves	125 mL
½ cup	tightly packed basil leaves	125 mL
2	cloves garlic	2
5	ripe tomatoes, cut in half	5
1 lb	linguine	500 g
1 cup	freshly grated Grana Padano or Parmesan cheese	250 mL

1. Place potatoes in a large saucepan and add cold water to barely cover. Add salt, cover loosely and bring to a boil over high heat. Reduce heat and cook for 20 minutes or until potatoes are tender. Drain well. Set aside until cool enough to handle.

2. Peel potatoes, cut into ¼-inch (0.5 cm) cubes and return to clean saucepan. Toss in 2 tbsp (30 mL) oil. Season to taste with salt and freshly ground pepper. Arrange in a single layer on prepared baking sheet. Set aside.

3. Bring a large pot of salted water to a boil and preheat broiler.

4. Meanwhile, in a mini food processor, pulse parsley, basil and garlic until chopped, scraping down sides of the bowl as necessary. With motor running, add remaining oil in a thin stream until blended and smooth. Season to taste with salt and freshly ground pepper and pulse once. Scrape into a large bowl and set aside.

5. Working over a bowl to catch the juice, and using a small spoon, scoop out and discard as many of the tomato seeds as possible. Slice tomatoes into small chunks and add to basil mixture. Set aside.

6. Place potato cubes under preheated broiler for 5 to 7 minutes, turning frequently, until golden brown and crisp.

7. Meanwhile, add linguine to boiling water and cook for about 8 minutes or until tender but firm. Drain and toss into pesto mixture along with half the potato croutons and half the cheese. Divide among four warmed individual pasta bowls. Garnish with the remaining potato croutons. Serve remaining cheese on the side.

Variation

If you prefer, instead of browning the parboiled potatoes under the broiler, you can toss them into a large skillet and sauté over high heat until crispy.

Herb & Garlic Roasted Mini Potatoes with Penne

When you spy those really small waxy potatoes at your local market, snap them up and plan to make this dish. It's a brand-new way to enjoy them.

Makes 4 servings

Tips

Use the best balsamic vinegar you can afford.

The little bit of cooking water left clinging to the penne will combine with the oil and vinegar to make a bit of a sauce.

Ricotta comes in varying degrees of wetness; check the moisture content on your package. Dry ricotta, which has a moisture content of about 65% (compared to the usual 72% to 80%) is preferred here because you won't have to drain it. However, draining is easy to do. Place a double layer of cheesecloth in a strainer, place the strainer over a mixing bowl and add ricotta. Cover with plastic wrap and place a plate over the plastic to press down the cheese. Refrigerate for about 8 hours. Discard liquid that has accumulated in the bowl.

Be sure to use a baking dish large enough to accommodate the potatoes in a single layer.

- Preheat oven to 400°F (200°C)
- Large baking dish

1 lb	mini red or yellow new potatoes (or a mixture), scrubbed and quartered	500 g
4	cloves garlic, minced	4
⅓ cup	extra virgin olive oil, divided	75 mL
6	fresh sage leaves, chopped	6
1 tbsp	chopped fresh thyme leaves	15 mL
	Salt and freshly ground black pepper	
2 tbsp	balsamic vinegar	30 mL
1 lb	penne	500 g
2 tbsp	chopped flat-leaf parsley leaves	30 mL
2 tbsp	chopped fresh mint leaves	30 mL
1 cup	ricotta cheese, drained if necessary (see Tips, left)	250 mL

1. In baking dish, toss potatoes, garlic, 3 tbsp (45 mL) oil, sage and thyme to coat. Season to taste with salt and pepper. Roast in preheated oven, turning occasionally, for 30 to 40 minutes or until golden.

2. Bring a large pot of salted water to a boil. When potatoes are almost finished, add pasta to water and cook for about 8 minutes or until tender but firm. Drain, leaving a little of the cooking water clinging to the pasta (see Tips, left).

3. Transfer potatoes to a large warmed serving bowl, scraping in any bits or oil from bottom of baking dish. Toss in vinegar and remaining oil and, if necessary, season to taste with additional salt and pepper. Toss in pasta, parsley, mint and cheese. If you prefer a glossy finish, drizzle with extra virgin olive oil. Serve immediately.

Variation

The fresh herbs in this recipe contribute to making it what it is. You may vary them as you wish — sage, rosemary, thyme (or lemon thyme), marjoram and oregano are all good choices.

Glaswegian Chips in Curry Sauce

Strictly an Anglo invention, this is the ultimate antidote after a pub crawl — "good for soakage," as one Scotsman I know puts it. It may sound like an unlikely combination until you realize just how fond of curry people in the U.K. are. It was only a matter of time before someone put these two favorites together, and I, for one, am very glad they did.

Serves 4

Makes about 3 cups (750 mL) sauce

Tips

When using canned coconut milk, be sure to shake the can well before opening, as the cream tends to settle on sitting.

Use more or less curry powder to accommodate your desire for heat.

You'll have leftover sauce, but it makes a great curry base. Sear chunks of boneless chicken, beef, lamb or shrimp and add the sauce. Cook gently along with thinly sliced onion, mushrooms and sweet peppers. Serve over basmati rice.

If you really want to go over the top, for a great snack, serve the chips in sauce rolled up in an Indian bread such as paratha or chapati — a curried chip butty!

- **Immersion blender or food processor**

1 tsp	unsalted butter	5 mL
1	small onion, chopped	1
Pinch	salt	Pinch
2 tbsp	all-purpose flour	30 mL
2	cloves garlic, minced	2
1	large apple (not Granny Smith), cored, peeled and chopped	1
1	ripe tomato, chopped	1
3 cups	chicken broth	750 mL
1 cup	unsweetened coconut milk (see Tips, left)	250 mL
¼ cup	ground almonds	60 mL
4 to 5 tbsp	curry powder (see Tips, left)	60 to 75 mL
2 tbsp	chopped fresh gingerroot	30 mL
1 tsp	tomato paste	5 mL
1	batch/recipe Real English Chips (page 64)	1

1. Heat butter in a large saucepan or skillet over medium-high heat. Add onion and salt and sauté until onion is softened, about 2 minutes. Add flour, stir well and cook for 2 minutes. Add garlic, apple, tomato, chicken broth, coconut milk, ground almonds, curry powder, ginger and tomato paste and stir well. Reduce heat, cover loosely and simmer for 1½ hours, stirring often, until mixture has thickened and flavors have developed.

2. Using an immersion blender, purée (you can also do this, in batches, in a food processor fitted with metal blade). Serve immediately with fresh-cooked Real English Chips, either on the side or poured lavishly over the chips. If you prefer, cover and refrigerate sauce for up to 4 days. When you're ready to serve, make chips and reheat sauce.

Poutine à la Montreal

What can be said about poutine — that French-Canadian extravaganza of fried potatoes, cheese curds and gravy — that hasn't already been said? Well, I can say that there are umpteen restaurants in Montreal serving poutine, from the perfect classic at Ma-am-m Bolduc to a vegan offering at Aux Vivres. At La Banquise they serve more than 25 varieties, with ingredients such as spicy merguez sausage, bacon, ground beef, chicken, turkey, guacamole, pepperoni and hot peppers. But for sheer over-the-topness, I don't think any of them can compete with the version at Au Pied du Cochon: their *haute poutine* is served topped with a hefty slab of foie gras — wow! It makes this classic version sound rather pedestrian, but it's delicious nonetheless.

Serves 4 to 6

Tips

Cheese curds are small, slightly rubbery chunks that have been separated from the natural whey present in milk but have not yet been pressed into molds to make cheese. They are available at some supermarkets and cheesemongers and usually anywhere cheese is produced.

If you don't want to go to the trouble of making the gravy, you can always rely on a packaged or canned product, which would capture the spirit of the original poutine.

The oil should come a little over halfway up the sides of the pot. Do not overfill; leave at least 3 inches (7.5 cm) of headspace at the top.

If you don't have a thermometer, drop a small square of dry bread into the oil; if it floats, the oil is hot enough.

- Large heavy pot, Dutch oven or deep fryer
- Candy/deep-frying thermometer (if not using a deep fryer)

6	large floury or all-purpose potatoes	6
2 tbsp	butter	30 mL
2 tbsp	all-purpose flour	30 mL
1½ cups	beef broth	375 mL
1 tsp	Worcestershire sauce	5 mL
Pinch	ground cloves	Pinch
Dash	hot pepper sauce	Dash
	Salt and freshly ground black pepper	
	Vegetable oil	
14 oz	white cheese curds (see Tips, left)	400 g

1. Peel potatoes and cut into fat slices about 2 inches by ½ inch (5 by 1 cm). As you slice, drop into a bowl of cold water. Once all the potatoes are sliced, set aside in the water for at least 15 minutes or up to an hour, sloshing them about a bit to help release their surface starch. When you're ready to cook, drain potatoes and dry thoroughly on a clean tea towel or two, or paper towels. They must be completely dry.

2. Meanwhile, in a saucepan, melt butter over medium-high heat. Whisk in flour and cook for a minute or two until a paste forms. Add beef broth slowly, whisking constantly to prevent lumps. Add Worcestershire sauce, cloves and hot pepper sauce and whisk again. Season to taste with salt and pepper. Cook, whisking, until thickened, about 10 minutes. Keep warm while you prepare the chips.

3. Place 4 to 6 inches (10 to 15 cm) oil in a large, heavy pot (see Tips, page 196). Heat over medium-high until thermometer registers 375°F (190°C). (If you're using a deep fryer, follow the manufacturer's instructions.)

4. Carefully add the dried potato slices, in batches, and fry until they are just beginning to color and are soft, 5 to 6 minutes. Using a slotted spoon, transfer to a plate lined with paper towels. They should sit for at least 10 minutes or up to 3 hours before the second fry.

5. When you are ready to serve, heat oil until thermometer registers 400°F (200°C). Return chips to oil, in batches, and cook until crisp and golden, 3 to 5 minutes. Using a slotted spoon, transfer to a plate lined with paper towels. When all the chips are cooked, transfer to a bowl, sprinkle with salt and toss.

6. Pile the chips on a serving platter. Distribute cheese curds evenly overtop and finish with the hot gravy, which will encourage the curds to melt slightly. Serve hot.

Variation

If you like, you can serve individual plates of poutine, but one big platter is fun to share.

Potato-Wafer Club Sandwich

Using ultra-thin slices of potato in place of bread makes for an inspired creation that I first enjoyed years ago, at a little restaurant in New York City. They didn't call it a sandwich but I couldn't help but think how sandwich-like it was, especially when combined with all the ingredients for a traditional club sandwich. This is a great dish for weekend brunch.

Serves 4

Tips

You need to use a mandoline for this recipe because the potatoes must be exceedingly thin.

Don't slice the avocado until you're ready to use it; otherwise it will turn brown.

- **Mandoline**
- **Seasoned cast-iron pan, nonstick skillet or griddle**
- **Preheat oven to 140°F (60°C)**

4	large floury potatoes, peeled	4
½ cup	extra virgin olive oil	125 mL
8	pieces leaf lettuce, rinsed, dried and torn to match potato slices in size and shape	8
3	large tomatoes, thinly sliced	3
4	slices cooked back (Canadian) bacon	4
1 lb	cooked chicken or turkey, thinly sliced	500 g
2	ripe avocados, thinly sliced (see Tips, left)	2

1. Using a mandoline, slice potatoes lengthwise as thinly as possible. As you work, transfer slices to a bowl containing the olive oil. When all have been sliced, toss well.

2. Over medium-high heat, preheat pan or griddle until fairly hot. Working in batches, arrange potato slices in one layer without crowding, and fry, turning frequently, until golden brown and beginning to crisp around the edges, about 10 minutes. Keep the cooked slices warm while you fry the remainder.

3. Place a slice of potato on a serving plate, add a piece of lettuce and a tomato slice and top with a slice of potato. Add a slice of bacon, a portion of chicken and another slice of potato. Top with more lettuce, avocado and another slice of potato. Serve immediately with remaining potato slices on the side.

Variations

You can also bake the potato slices in a 400°F (200°C) oven for 10 to 15 minutes, turning them once or twice.

Try spreading each fried potato slice with Aïoli (page 148) or a good-quality mayonnaise.

Rösti with Fresh Herbs

For rösti, Switzerland's famed potato dish, you must begin preparation the night before you plan on serving it — or at least first thing in the morning of the same day — because the potatoes need to chill before you can successfully shred them. Rösti makes a great late-night snack, lunch or brunch item. Cut into wedges and topped with smoked salmon and crème fraîche, it is quite divine.

Serves 4 to 6

Tips

Don't cook the potatoes until they are completely tender, or they will be difficult to grate.

Rösti is one of those dishes you can enjoy morning, noon or night. Try using it as a base for smoked salmon and scrambled eggs and serve for brunch. If you make four individual rösti instead of one large one, they make a wonderful foundation for poached or fried eggs.

It's easy to improvise with this dish (as I have done here), adding different herbs or other ingredients from the onion family (shallots, leeks, chives) as you wish. Of course, you can also throw caution to the wind and include crumbled cooked bacon or bits of smoked ham.

- **Grater or food processor with shredding disk**
- **12-inch (30 cm) skillet, preferably nonstick**

6	large floury potatoes, scrubbed	6
1 tsp	salt	5 mL
1	medium red onion, minced	1
½ cup	chopped fresh flat-leaf Italian parsley	125 mL
¼ cup	chopped fresh sage	60 mL
	Salt and freshly ground black pepper	
¼ cup	butter, divided	60 mL
2 tbsp	olive oil, divided	30 mL

1. Place potatoes in a large saucepan and add cold water to barely cover. Add salt, cover loosely and bring to a boil over high heat. Reduce heat and cook for 12 to 15 minutes, until potatoes are still firm at the center when prodded with a sharp knife; do not overcook (see Tips, left). Drain and rinse under cold water. Cover and refrigerate overnight or for at least 6 hours.

2. When potatoes are cold, peel skins and, using either the largest side of a box grater or a food processor fitted with the shredding disk, shred potatoes. Transfer to a mixing bowl. Add onion, parsley, sage and salt and pepper to taste and mix well.

3. In a skillet, heat 2 tbsp (30 mL) butter and 1 tbsp (15 mL) oil over medium-high heat. Add potato mixture, spreading it out evenly in the pan, and use a metal spatula to press down firmly. (At this point some cooks add more melted butter to the pan, but I'll leave that to your discretion.) Cook over medium heat until the bottom is golden brown. Remove pan from heat.

4. Invert a large plate over the skillet and slip rösti onto it. Return pan to medium-high heat. Add remaining butter and oil and slide rösti, uncooked side down, back into pan. Cook until bottom is golden brown, about 10 minutes, pressing down with spatula to flatten. Turn out onto a heated platter, cut into wedges and serve.

Julie's Potato Burritos

It's debatable, but my good friend Julie Cohen maintains that she loves potatoes as much as I do. True fellow potato-heads, we have shared many a plate of garlic mash, frites and skins and massive bags of Lay's potato chips (plain only, please). Here is Julie's recipe for terrific handheld burritos filled with sautéed potato and other good things. Sliced and presented on a platter, they make a great appetizer or snack.

Serves 6 to 8

Tips

I prefer to use sea salt rather than refined table salt because it has a much cleaner, crisper taste and enhanced mineral content.

If you prefer a knife-and-fork meal, you can line up the finished burritos in a baking dish, seam side down, cover with additional taco sauce and shredded cheese of your choice, and bake in the oven for a few minutes to melt the cheese.

- **Preheat oven to 140°F (60°C)**

2 lbs	floury potatoes, peeled and diced	1 kg
1 tsp	salt	5 mL
2 tbsp	olive oil	30 mL
1	large onion, finely chopped	1
2	cloves garlic, finely chopped	2
1½ tsp	chili powder	7 mL
1½ tsp	ground cumin	7 mL
8	flour tortillas (6-inch/15 cm)	8
1 cup	shredded sharp (aged) Cheddar or Monterey Jack cheese	250 mL
1 cup	hot or mild salsa or taco sauce	250 mL

1. Place potatoes in a large saucepan and add cold water to barely cover. Add salt, cover loosely and bring to a boil over high heat. Reduce heat and cook for 15 minutes (potatoes should not be completely cooked through). Drain and cool.

2. In a large skillet, heat oil over medium-high heat. Add onion and garlic and cook, stirring, until onion becomes translucent, about 6 minutes. Add potatoes and cook until golden brown, about 15 minutes, stirring occasionally to ensure they brown on all sides. Add chili powder and cumin and stir well. Reduce heat to low and cook for another minute or so. Transfer to a bowl and keep warm in preheated oven.

3. Wipe skillet clean and return to heat. Increase heat to high and dry-fry tortillas until lightly browned, flipping once, about 30 seconds a side.

4. To assemble, place one tortilla on a plate, top with ½ cup (125 mL) potato mixture, about 2 tbsp (30 mL) cheese and 1 to 2 tbsp (15 to 30 mL) salsa. Fold ends over the filling and roll up. Using a sharp knife, cut in half on the diagonal. Repeat with remaining tortillas and filling. Serve immediately, accompanied by any remaining salsa.

Rustic Country Potato Tart

Garlic, fresh herbs, shallots, potatoes and cream combine to make a sumptuous filling for golden puff pastry. This is an impressive dish. It is particularly delicious as an accompaniment to meat dishes such as braised beef, roast lamb or roast pork.

Makes 6 to 8 servings

Tip

If you prefer, line a 9- or 10-inch (23 or 25 cm) glass baking dish with the pastry, or use the collar (ring part) of a 9-inch (23 cm) springform pan to support it, but I like the rustic look that comes from baking it freeform.

- **Preheat oven to 375°F (190°C)**

4	shallots, finely diced	4
3	large floury potatoes, peeled and cut into ¼-inch (0.5 cm) slices	3
3	cloves garlic, finely chopped	3
2 tbsp	chopped flat-leaf parsley leaves	30 mL
1 tsp	fresh thyme leaves	5 mL
1 tsp	chopped fresh rosemary leaves	5 mL
	Salt and freshly ground black pepper	
1 tbsp	cornmeal	15 mL
8 oz	frozen puff pastry dough, thawed	250 g
1 cup	heavy or whipping (35%) cream	250 mL
1 cup	half-and-half (10%) cream	250 mL

1. In a large bowl, toss together shallots, potatoes, garlic, parsley, thyme and rosemary. Season to taste with salt and freshly ground pepper. Set aside.

2. Lightly dust a baking sheet with cornmeal. On a lightly floured surface, roll out puff pastry dough into a rectangle about ¼ inch (0.5 cm) thick and about 9 inches (23 cm) square. Transfer to prepared baking sheet. Using your hands, pile potato mixture in center of dough, leaving a 3-inch (8 cm) border around the edge. Fold up edges of dough to form a substantial rim.

3. Pull out middle oven rack and transfer baking sheet to rack. Before pushing in rack, pour equal amounts of cream and half-and-half over filling, almost to top of pastry rim. You may not be able to use all the cream and half-and-half; if so, reserve and add to tart after 15 minutes of baking. Carefully push in rack and bake in preheated oven for about 1 hour or until potatoes are tender and pastry is golden brown. Let stand on a cooling rack for 15 minutes before serving.

Twice-Baked Potato Soufflé with Cashel Blue Cheese

Cashel blue is a creamy, blue-veined cheese from Ireland. It is my absolute favorite blue cheese. Great for company, these little soufflés go well with lightly dressed salad greens. They are perfect for brunch or as a first course of a sit-down dinner.

Serves 4

Tips

To cook the potatoes for this recipe, follow Step 1, Classic Mash Deluxe (page 50) adding 1 tsp (5 mL) salt to the cooking water.

You may use any good-quality blue cheese.

These are not delicate, fragile little soufflés but rather a more substantial version that receives an initial baking and then another, topped with extra cheese. You can do the first baking ahead of time and the final one just before serving.

Allowing the egg whites to come to room temperature will make them whip up more quickly.

- 4 ramekins or custard cups (¾ cup/175 mL), brushed with melted butter
- Electric mixer or eggbeater

3	medium floury potatoes, peeled, quartered and cooked (see Tips, left)	3
3	eggs, separated	3
½ cup	all-purpose flour	125 mL
¾ tsp	baking powder	4 mL
¼ tsp	salt	1 mL
8 oz	Cashel blue cheese, crumbled and divided (see Tips, left)	250 g
	Salt and freshly ground black pepper	
1 cup	loosely packed baby spinach leaves, finely chopped	250 mL

1. Preheat oven to 400°F (200°C). Using a large fork, mash cooked potatoes roughly. Add egg yolks and continue to mash.
2. In a bowl, combine flour, baking powder and salt. Mix well. Add half the cheese and all of the flour mixture to the mashed potatoes, mixing well. Season to taste with salt and freshly ground pepper. Fold spinach into potato mixture and set aside.
3. Using an electric mixer at high speed, beat egg whites in a bowl until they form soft peaks. Gently fold into potato mixture, being careful not to overmix. Divide potato mixture equally among ramekins, place on a baking sheet and cook in preheated oven for 20 minutes.
4. Remove ramekins from oven and let cool. Just before you're ready to serve, line a baking sheet with parchment paper and preheat oven, if necessary. Run a thin knife around the edges of each soufflé and turn them out onto the sheet. Sprinkle remaining cheese evenly over soufflés and return to oven. Bake until cheese melts and they are heated through, about 8 minutes. Serve immediately.

Irish Greens with Bacon & Potatoes

Now here is something to sustain you on a cold winter's night. Bacon, potatoes and any hearty green — regular cabbage, Savoy cabbage or kale, as we have used here — are very compatible bedfellows. They are often found together in one dish or another in Ireland.

Makes 4 to 6 servings

Tip

The mustard pickle piccalilli makes a great accompaniment to this dish.

- **Large skillet with lid**
- **Preheat oven to 140°F (60°C)**

1 tbsp	olive oil	15 mL
6	slices thick-cut back (Canadian) bacon	6
2 tbsp	butter	30 mL
1	onion, chopped	1
¾ cup	chicken broth (approx.)	175 mL
1 lb	kale, coarse stems trimmed, coarsely chopped	500 g
3	large all-purpose potatoes, scrubbed and diced	3
3 tbsp	malt vinegar	45 mL
	Salt and freshly ground black pepper	
¼ cup	finely chopped fresh chives	60 mL

1. In a large skillet over medium-high heat, warm the olive oil. Add the bacon and cook for 10 to 12 minutes, until cooked through. Slice bacon into strips. Set aside and keep warm in preheated oven.

2. In the same skillet, melt butter over medium-high heat. Sauté onion for about 5 minutes or until softened. Stir in chicken broth, kale and potatoes and bring to a boil. Reduce heat slightly, cover and cook, checking occasionally and adding a little more broth or water if necessary, for 15 to 20 minutes or until potatoes are tender and most of the liquid has evaporated.

3. Remove from heat and stir in vinegar. Toss in reserved bacon strips. Season to taste with salt and freshly ground pepper. Sprinkle with chives just before serving.

Variations

Substitute cabbage — regular or Savoy — collard greens or beet tops for the kale.

You can vary the meat component by using thick-cut strip (side) bacon or chunks of cooked ham.

Gail's Aberdeen Stovies

Stovies, a much-beloved potato-centric dish from Scotland, is one about which Scots have strong — really strong — opinions. There are some who maintain that it consists of nothing but potatoes, onions, a bit of fat and meat broth, asserting that it was invented because "There was nae beef tae be had!" My Scottish friend Gail is from Aberdeen, and she says that when she was growing up, stovies always appeared a couple of days after Sunday dinner. "It was simply a combo of Sunday's leftover meat (normally a roast), the meat fat and potatoes (also left over from Sunday). Add onions — the only other vegetable — and some stock and the obligatory salt and pepper. It cooks slowly, for about an hour, on the stove. Some recommend that they be served with oatcakes and beetroot. I've never had stovies with beetroot but I've heard that it works, and being a lover of beetroot, I would give it a try." And, I might add, perhaps a wee dram of your favorite single malt.

Makes 4 to 6 servings

Tips

Beef fat is the preferred fat to use for cooking this dish. Roast a piece of fat alongside your beef. Pour it off and refrigerate.

I have called for 1 lb (500 g) of meat, but if you have less, don't let that stop you from making this dish — it's really all about the potatoes and the cooking method.

Keep the pan on the stove long enough for a lovely dark crust to form on the bottom; for many, that's the best part.

Oatcakes are very thin and cracker-like and come in triangular or round shapes. Look for them in the supermarket.

• **Heavy skillet with lid**

3 to 4 tbsp	beef dripping, lard or butter	45 to 60 mL
2	small onions, chopped	2
1 lb	leftover roasted meat (beef, lamb or pork, or sausages), chopped (see Tips, left)	500 g
4	large floury potatoes, cooked, peeled and diced (not too small)	4
1/4 to 1/2 cup	beef broth	50 to 125 mL
	Salt and freshly ground black pepper	

1. In a heavy skillet, melt fat over medium heat. Cook onions, stirring, for about 5 minutes or until softened. Stir in meat and cook, stirring, for another 5 minutes.

2. Stir in potatoes and broth. Season to taste with salt and pepper. Reduce heat to medium, cover and cook gently, shaking pan occasionally to prevent sticking, for about 20 minutes or until cooked through. Increase heat to medium-high and cook for 15 to 20 minutes or until bottom of mixture is crusty and dark brown (at this point some cooks like to turn over the mixture and cook for another 10 minutes or so, to brown both sides). Serve immediately.

Pan Haggerty

What a wonderful name for an equally wonderful dish! Pan haggerty is an old British recipe that originated during the Industrial Revolution in northern England. It is thought that the name derives — as does that of Scotland's haggis — from the French word *hacher*, meaning to chop (also the root of hash). It is simple, filling and comforting and will work as well for lunch as it does for brunch or a midnight snack. A restaurant in the north of England called, appropriately, Pan Haggerty serves a dinner version of the dish, which includes a poached duck egg and hollandaise sauce. Fantastic! Traditionally this dish is enjoyed straight from the skillet.

Serves 4

Tip

You can use either all-purpose potatoes or firm waxy potatoes — varying results, both delicious.

- **Mandoline**
- **Heavy ovenproof skillet**

1 tbsp	olive oil	15 mL
2	large onions, thinly sliced	2
1 lb	medium waxy all-purpose potatoes, peeled and thinly sliced	500 g
3 tbsp	melted butter	45 mL
6 oz	shredded sharp (aged) Cheddar, Cheshire or Lancashire cheese, divided	175 g
	Salt and freshly ground black pepper	

1. In a heavy ovenproof skillet, heat oil over medium-high heat. Add onions and sauté until softened, about 6 minutes. Transfer to a bowl and set aside.
2. Preheat oven to 375°F (190°C). In the same pan, off the heat, arrange a layer of slightly overlapping potatoes. Brush with melted butter and season to taste with salt and pepper. Scatter a thin layer of cheese and onions overtop. Repeat this layering, making sure to end with a layer of cheese-topped potatoes.
3. Return pan to medium-high heat and cook until bottom is golden brown, about 3 minutes. Transfer to preheated oven and bake for about 25 minutes or until potatoes are tender when probed with a sharp knife. If the cheese is not browned in places, place under a preheated broiler, watching carefully so as not to burn the top.
4. Remove from the oven and let sit for 5 minutes or so before serving — straight from the pan if you like.

Potato & Pepper Breakfast Plate

There is a bit of a culinary tradition in Rochester, NY. It's called the "garbage plate" and it originated at a diner called Nick Tahou Hots. Apparently it came about during the Depression, when you could get a plate of cold baked beans and home fries topped with a couple of split red hots. Over the years the restaurant's collegiate crowd, noticing these odd piled-high plates going by but not knowing what they were called, would order them as "one of those plates with all the garbage on it." Thus was born this dish — a full three pounds of food, dubbed the fattiest in New York State. This recipe, which is a tad more user-friendly than the over-the-top versions served at Nick's, works any time of day or night.

Makes 2 to 4 servings

Tip

Use the coarse side of a box grater or the shredding disk on your food processor to shred the potatoes.

3 tbsp	vegetable oil	45 mL
4	hot or mild Italian sausages, casings removed, chopped	4
1	onion, diced	1
1	green bell pepper, diced	1
1	small jalapeño pepper, seeded and diced	1
4 cups	shredded potatoes (see Tip, left)	1 L
6	eggs	6
2	tomatoes, diced	2
1 cup	shredded sharp (aged) Cheddar cheese	250 mL
	Salt and freshly ground black pepper	
	Hot buttered toast	

1. In a large skillet, heat oil over medium-high heat. Stir in sausage, onion, green and jalapeño peppers and potatoes and sauté, tossing occasionally, for about 20 minutes or until sausage is cooked through.

2. Using a metal spatula, break mixture into chunks and flip over. Add eggs and tomatoes, breaking up eggs with spatula blade and cutting them into mixture. Cook, stirring, for about 10 minutes or until eggs are well blended and cooked.

3. Add cheese. Season to taste with salt and freshly ground pepper. Cook, using spatula blade to chop mixture together, just until cheese has melted. Serve with hot buttered toast.

Peruvian Potatoes

From the original home of the potato comes this quick-to-make recipe, which features potatoes, cheese and a little chile pepper. This makes a great brunch dish or late-night light meal.

Serves 6 to 8

Tips

The mirasol is an orange-red chile pepper with a distinctive fruity flavor. Look for it in specialty food shops or Latin American markets. If you can't find it, even in its dried version, substitute a dried ancho pepper or a large fresh jalapeño pepper.

If you're heat-averse, after slitting the pepper, scrape out the seeds.

- Preheat oven to 350°F (180°C)
- 11- by 7-inch (2 L) shallow earthenware or glass baking dish

3 lbs	all-purpose potatoes, peeled and diced	1.5 kg
8 oz	feta cheese, crumbled	250 g
4 oz	mozzarella cheese, diced	125 g
1 tsp	salt	5 mL
¼ cup	extra virgin olive oil, divided	60 mL
½ cup	heavy or whipping (35%) cream	125 mL
1	fresh or dried mirasol chile pepper (see Tips, left)	1

1. In a large bowl, combine potatoes, feta and mozzarella cheeses, salt and 1 tbsp (15 mL) olive oil. Toss well. Transfer to baking dish and add cream, jostling the dish a bit to ensure that potatoes are evenly covered.

2. Slice chile pepper lengthwise and place deep in center of the dish, cut sides up. Fill pepper halves with remaining 3 tbsp (45 mL) olive oil. Transfer to preheated oven and bake until potatoes are tender and golden brown, 1 to 1½ hours. Remove from oven and spoon the hot olive oil from the pepper over the potatoes. Serve immediately.

Potato & Chorizo Hash with Sweet Pepper Sauce

Make this dish for a special weekend brunch or lunch to accompany a soufflé, or just serve it with poached or fried eggs. This is one of those homey, enjoy-anytime dishes that you will make often.

Makes 4 servings

Tip

Cured (often called "dry") chorizo is a flavorful, spicy Spanish-style sausage. If you can't find it, use any spicy cured sausage, such as pepperoni, in its place. Mexican-style chorizo (often called "wet") is different — it is a fresh sausage, not dry-cured, and therefore needs to be cooked.

Sweet Pepper Sauce

2 tbsp	olive oil	30 mL
2	large red, yellow or orange bell peppers, seeded and finely chopped	2
1	clove garlic, crushed	1
1	onion, chopped	1
1 tbsp	sweet paprika	15 mL
1 tsp	crushed red pepper flakes	5 mL
1 cup	chicken broth	250 mL
1 cup	chopped canned tomatoes, with juice	250 mL
	Salt and freshly ground black pepper	

Hash

1½ lbs	new potatoes, scrubbed and cut crosswise into quarters	750 g
1 tsp	salt	5 mL
½ lb	cured chorizo sausage (see Tip, left)	250 g
1 tbsp	olive oil	15 mL
1	clove garlic, finely chopped	1
1	onion, finely chopped	1
½ cup	oil-packed sun-dried tomatoes, drained, cut in half if large	125 mL
2 tbsp	chopped fresh cilantro leaves	30 mL
4	sprigs fresh cilantro	4

1. *Sweet Pepper Sauce:* In a large, heavy skillet, heat oil over medium heat. Cook peppers, garlic and onion, stirring, for about 12 minutes or until just beginning to color. Stir in paprika and red pepper flakes and cook, stirring, for 5 minutes.

2. Stir in chicken broth and tomatoes with juice, season to taste with salt and freshly ground pepper and bring to a boil. Reduce heat and simmer for about 30 minutes or until thickened. Reduce heat to very low, cover and keep warm.

3. *Hash:* Place potatoes in a large saucepan and add boiling water to barely cover. Add salt, cover loosely and bring to a boil over high heat. Reduce heat and cook for 7 minutes or until almost cooked through. Drain well. Set aside.

4. On a cutting board, carefully cut chorizo in half lengthwise. Cut each half crosswise into 1-inch (2.5 cm) pieces. In a heavy skillet, warm oil over medium-high heat. Sauté chorizo for 3 minutes. Stir in garlic, onion and sun-dried tomatoes and cook for 10 minutes.

5. Stir in reserved potatoes and cook for about 10 minutes or until potatoes are cooked through. Stir in cilantro. Remove from heat.

6. Spoon a quarter of the sauce onto each of four individual serving plates. Top each with a quarter of the hash and a sprig of cilantro. Serve immediately.

Jansson's Temptation

A fine old Swedish dish, this was apparently named for a famous Swedish opera singer and food lover. At first glance it might seem designed for anchovy lovers. Actually the original ingredient was sprats, which are little sardine-like fish. In Sweden, sprats have long been known as *ansjovis*, so you can see where the confusion arose. I like this for breakfast or brunch, served alongside scrambled eggs with chives.

Makes 6 servings

Tips

When seasoning, be aware that you may only need to add pepper, as the anchovies may be salty.

Use a mandoline or food processor fitted with a slicing blade to cut potatoes into very thin, uniform slices. Then slice into uniform matchstick strips.

- **Preheat oven to 400°F (200°C)**
- **Mandoline or food processor (see Tips, left)**
- **13- by 9-inch (3 L) baking dish, buttered**
- **Rimmed baking sheet, lined with parchment paper**

2 lbs	large floury potatoes, peeled	1 kg
3	large onions, thinly sliced	3
9 oz	anchovies in olive oil, drained well and finely chopped (about 48 anchovies)	255 g
	Salt and freshly ground black pepper	
2½ cups	heavy or whipping (35%) cream	625 mL
	Whole milk (optional)	

1. Slice potatoes thinly (⅛ inch/3 mm). Then, working with a few slices at a time, stack and cut into matchsticks; transfer to a bowl of cold water as you work. When all the potatoes have been sliced, drain and dry thoroughly on a clean tea towel.

2. Arrange half the potatoes in prepared dish and top evenly with half the onions. Evenly arrange chopped anchovies over onions and season lightly with salt and freshly ground pepper (see Tips, left). Top with remaining onions and finish with a layer of potatoes.

3. Place baking dish on prepared baking sheet. Carefully pour in cream, then add just enough milk to fill dish to about 1 inch (2.5 cm) below top of potato mixture.

4. Cover with lightly buttered foil and bake in preheated oven for 45 minutes. Uncover and bake for another 10 minutes or until top is golden brown and edges are bubbling. Let stand in its pan on a wire rack for 10 minutes before serving.

Variations

Substitute sardines, sprats or even smoked salmon or gravlax (salt-cured unsmoked salmon) for the anchovies.

Islay Crab Cakes

With or without potato? That is the question where crab cakes are concerned, probably because some of those made with mashed potato are, generally speaking, stingy with the crab. Not these, which are inspired by crab cakes I enjoyed in Islay, one of the larger of the many scattered southern Inner Hebrides Islands, off the west coast of Scotland. These islands are renowned for the quality of their fish, seafood and — single malt whisky! Serve these with lemon mayonnaise (see Tips, below) or Basil Aïoli (page 99). This makes a great lunch dish with a salad of mixed greens.

Makes 4 servings

Tips

Use any leftover mash, from dry-mashed to Classic Mash Deluxe (page 50).

Make a quick lemon mayonnaise using 1 cup (250 mL) of store-bought mayonnaise. Whisk in 1 tbsp (15 mL) each finely grated lemon zest and lemon juice and 1 tsp (5 mL) Dijon mustard. This will keep, covered and refrigerated, for up to 1 week.

1½ lbs	crabmeat	750 g
2 cups	mashed potatoes (see Tips, left)	500 mL
1	egg, lightly beaten	1
3	green onions, finely chopped	3
2 tbsp	finely chopped flat-leaf parsley leaves	30 mL
1 tsp	salt	5 mL
1 tsp	freshly ground white pepper	5 mL
¼ tsp	cayenne pepper	1 mL
1 cup	all-purpose flour (approx.)	250 mL
⅓ cup	olive oil (approx.)	75 mL

1. In a large bowl, stir together (or use your hands) crabmeat, mashed potatoes, egg, green onions, parsley, salt, white pepper and cayenne. Cover with plastic wrap and refrigerate for at least 30 minutes or up to 4 hours.
2. Using lightly floured hands, shape mixture into eight cakes. Spread flour on a plate and lightly dredge each cake on both sides.
3. In a large skillet, heat oil over medium-high heat. Cook cakes for 5 to 6 minutes per side or until golden brown (use additional oil if necessary). Serve immediately.

Smoked Salmon Scalloped Spuds

When you are planning a Sunday brunch gathering, put this dish together the night before (see Tips, below). Serve these scalloped potatoes alongside scrambled eggs with chives and pan-seared tomato halves.

Makes 4 to 6 servings

Tips

If you are making this dish ahead of time, assemble it completely, adding the cream and the cheese. Cover and refrigerate overnight.

Even if you aren't assembling it ahead of time, let the dish sit at room temperature for a while before baking to allow the potatoes to absorb the cream and milk.

You can make this preparation with uncooked potatoes too. Just increase the oven time by about 20 minutes and add an extra ½ cup (125 mL) cream or milk.

- Preheat oven to 350°F (180°C)
- 10-cup (2.5 L) baking dish, buttered
- Rimmed baking sheet, lined with parchment paper

8	medium red-skinned potatoes, cooked, peeled and sliced	8
8 oz	smoked salmon, cut into strips	250 g
6	green onions, white parts with a bit of green, finely chopped	6
3	cloves garlic, minced	3
	Salt and freshly ground black pepper	
1 cup	table (18%) cream	250 mL
	Whole milk (optional)	
½ cup	freshly grated Grana Padano or Parmesan cheese	125 mL

1. In prepared baking dish, arrange a third of the potatoes. Evenly top with half of the salmon, a third of the green onions and half of the garlic. Sprinkle with salt and freshly ground pepper. Repeat, finishing with a final layer of potatoes. Place dish on prepared baking sheet and transfer, on baking sheet, to center rack of oven.

2. Carefully pour cream evenly over potato mixture until potatoes are almost covered (add a little milk if necessary). Scatter evenly with cheese and bake in preheated oven for 45 minutes or until all the cream has been absorbed and top is golden brown and crisp.

3. Remove from oven and let stand in its pan on a wire rack for 10 minutes before serving. Just before serving, sprinkle with remaining green onions.

Potato Fritters with Salmon & Dill

I devised these little fritters one day when I found myself with leftover hot-smoked salmon fillets. They are great for lunch served with wedges of lemon and tartar sauce or a piquant chili sauce and a big green salad. They also make a nice hors d'oeuvre.

Makes 4 to 6 servings

Tips

If you have enough, use leftover mashed potatoes, but I think these are at their best when prepared with fresh.

To cook the potatoes for this recipe, follow Step 1, Classic Mash Deluxe (page 50) adding 1 tsp (5 mL) salt to the water.

These fritters can also be made a little smaller and served as hors d'oeuvres.

In a pinch you can use drained canned salmon, but try to keep the pieces fairly intact.

- Preheat oven to 140°F (60°C)
- Rimmed baking sheet, lined with paper towels
- Deep, heavy skillet

2 lbs	floury potatoes, peeled and cooked (see Tips, left)	1 kg
3 tbsp	butter	45 mL
3	eggs, separated	3
1/2 tsp	lemon herb seasoning	2 mL
1/4 cup	finely chopped fresh dill fronds	60 mL
	Salt and freshly ground black pepper	
1 cup	dry bread crumbs	250 mL
1/2 lb	cooked salmon fillet, cut into chunks	250 g
	Vegetable oil	

1. Using a potato masher, mash hot cooked potatoes with butter until smooth. Set aside and let cool to room temperature.
2. One at a time, beat egg yolks into cooled potatoes, mixing well after each addition. Stir in lemon herb seasoning and dill. Season to taste with salt and freshly ground pepper.
3. In another bowl, whisk egg whites together until frothy. Set aside.
4. Scatter bread crumbs on a large plate. With slightly oiled hands, shape potato mixture, about 1/4 cup (60 mL) at a time, into balls, forming a well in the center of each. Place a chunk of salmon in each well, then cup potato mixture around chunk to enclose it. Dip ball into egg whites, roll in bread crumbs to coat and transfer to prepared baking sheet.
5. Add oil to a deep, heavy skillet to a depth of about 2 inches (5 cm). Place over high heat. Heat oil until a cube of bread dropped into the oil floats and turns golden brown. In batches and using a slotted spoon, carefully add potato balls and fry for about 3 minutes or until golden brown. Transfer to baking sheet lined with paper towels and keep warm in preheated oven until serving.

Smoked Haddock with Yukon Golds in Mustard Beurre Blanc

This is a pleasing light lunch or supper dish, just right for a warm summer day when you want something a little richer and more substantial than a simple salad but less demanding than meat. While the amount of butter seems high, remember that beurre blanc is the classic French butter sauce — *butter* being the operative word.

Makes 4 servings

Tips

Use good quality unsalted butter for this recipe.

Classic beurre blanc uses no cream. I have included some here because it helps to keep the mixture from separating. When whisking in the butter, add the next piece just before the last piece has completely melted; this helps to control the temperature of the sauce, which should be warm, not hot.

2 lbs	small waxy or baby Yukon Gold potatoes, scrubbed	1 kg
1 tsp	salt	5 mL
Beurre Blanc		
1½ cups	dry white wine	375 mL
3 tbsp	white wine vinegar	45 mL
2	shallots, minced	2
2 tbsp	heavy or whipping (35%) cream	30 mL
1¾ cups	unsalted butter, chilled and cubed, divided	425 mL
	Freshly ground white pepper	
1 tbsp	grainy mustard	15 mL
1 tsp	Dijon mustard	5 mL
4	pieces smoked haddock (each 7 oz/200 g)	4
2 cups	whole milk (approx.), warmed	500 mL
	Fresh chervil or flat-leaf parsley sprigs	

1. Place potatoes in a large saucepan and add boiling water to barely cover. Add salt, cover loosely and bring to a boil over high heat. Reduce heat and cook for 20 minutes or until potatoes are tender.

2. *Beurre Blanc:* Meanwhile, in a heavy saucepan, combine wine, vinegar and shallots over high heat and boil for about 10 minutes or until reduced by about three-quarters and syrup-like. Reduce heat to very low and whisk in cream until blended. Whisk in chilled butter a few cubes at a time, until all the butter has been incorporated and a sauce has formed (do not let it boil; see Tips, left). Season to taste with a little salt and white pepper and whisk again. Whisk in grainy and Dijon mustards until blended. Cover and keep warm over very low heat.

3. Drain potatoes well. Set aside until cool enough to handle. Peel, slice and keep warm.

4. Place haddock in a shallow saucepan and pour in enough warm milk to cover. Bring to a gentle boil. Reduce heat and simmer for 5 to 7 minutes or until fish is opaque. Carefully drain fish, discarding cooking liquid. Cover and keep warm.

5. Divide potatoes among four warmed individual serving plates. Cover each serving with an eighth of the beurre blanc, then top with a piece of fish and another eighth of the beurre blanc. Garnish each with a sprig of chervil and serve immediately.

Variations

This preparation will also work well with salmon or trout fillets in place of the smoked haddock, if you prefer.

Salmon, Leek & Potato Tourte

A tourte is a sort of tart or pie, but shallower. This version combines smoked salmon, thinly sliced waxy potatoes and vibrant leeks, all housed in flaky phyllo pastry. This makes a lovely spring lunch or supper dish with a bright green salad.

Makes 6 servings

Tips

Working with phyllo is not difficult if you remember a few cardinal rules: let it thaw in the refrigerator overnight; cover it with a damp tea towel as you work with it sheet by sheet; and don't stint on the butter — phyllo pastry has almost no fat, so it needs it. If you don't use the entire package, put the remainder back in the freezer for later use.

Make sure to wash the leeks thoroughly by slitting them open lengthwise and spreading them apart while rinsing clean under cold running water.

- **Preheat oven to 400°F (200°C)**

2 tbsp	butter	30 mL
2	leeks (white and light green parts only), trimmed and thinly sliced (see Tips, left)	2
	Salt and freshly ground black pepper	
4	sheets phyllo pastry	4
½ cup	melted butter (see Tips, left)	125 mL
1 lb	waxy potatoes, steamed or boiled until tender, peeled and thinly sliced	500 g
8 oz	smoked salmon	250 g
2 tbsp	chopped fresh chives	30 mL
2	eggs	2
3 tbsp	heavy or whipping (35%) cream	45 mL
2 tbsp	mascarpone cheese	30 mL

1. In a skillet, heat butter over medium heat. Cook leeks, stirring, for about 10 minutes or until softened. Season to taste with salt and freshly ground pepper. Set aside and let cool completely.

2. Lay one phyllo sheet on a rimmed baking sheet and generously brush with a little of the melted butter. Layer with a second sheet and repeat butter application. Leaving a 1-inch (2.5 cm) border around the edge of the phyllo, evenly arrange a layer of potato slices on top, then a layer of leeks. Top with smoked salmon and sprinkle evenly with chives.

3. In a small bowl, whisk together eggs, cream and mascarpone until blended and smooth. Pour over smoked salmon. Lay a third phyllo sheet over the filling and brush with a little of the melted butter, then add the fourth sheet and brush with butter again. Trim edges of dough to make them even and gently press together to seal. Bake in preheated oven for 20 to 25 minutes or until filling is set and pastry is golden brown. Let stand on a wire rack for 10 minutes before serving.

Haystack Potato Crisps with Poached Egg & Smoked Salmon

This satisfying little dish is certainly wonderful for breakfast, but don't limit it to just that meal — it's great absolutely any time of the day or night. This is a quick meal to make with a cooking partner: one can be in charge of poaching the eggs and the other concentrating on the potato crisps. If another hungry couple invades, just double the recipe. If you're timid about poaching eggs, scrambled or fried eggs will work just fine.

**Makes
2 servings**

Tip
When poaching eggs add a little vinegar to the water. It will help the eggs to hold together. Don't add salt to the water; it has the opposite effect.

2	large floury potatoes, peeled	2
1	shallot, peeled	1
3 tbsp	melted butter	45 mL
2 tbsp	all-purpose flour	30 mL
	Salt and freshly ground black pepper	
3 tbsp	olive oil, divided	45 mL
4 oz	sliced smoked salmon	125 g
2	large eggs, poached (see Tips, left)	2

1. Using the coarse side of a box grater, shred potatoes and shallot onto a clean tea towel. Gather towel around potato mixture and squeeze over the sink to wring out as much moisture as possible. Transfer to a bowl. Toss in butter and flour. Season to taste with salt and freshly ground pepper. Toss until all traces of flour disappear, but don't overmix.

2. In a large skillet, heat 1 tbsp (15 mL) oil over medium-high heat. Using a large spoon, scoop up a quarter of the potato mixture at a time and drop into pan. Repeat until all four dollops are in the pan. Using a metal spatula, flatten each and cook for about 3 minutes per side or until very crisp and deep golden brown.

3. Transfer one potato crisp each to two warmed individual serving plates. Top each with a slice of salmon, another potato crisp and another slice of salmon. Crown each with a poached egg. Add a good grind of pepper and serve immediately.

Grande Luxe Gratin

If this potato gratin were a train, it would be the Orient Express. If it were a hotel, it would be New York's St. Regis. If it were a dress, it would be a ball gown by Valentino, and if it were a single malt Scotch, it would be a 32-year-old Ardbeg. Well, you get the picture — it's big, it's over the top and it's all yours to enjoy, at least once a year.

Makes 4 to 6 servings

Tip

Placing the baking dish on a lined baking sheet will make any spillover easier to clean up.

- **10-cup (2.5 L) oval baking dish**
- **Rimmed baking sheet, lined with parchment paper or foil (see Tip, left)**
- **Preheat oven to 375°F (190°C)**

2	cloves garlic, halved	2
5 tbsp	butter	75 mL
6	large floury potatoes, peeled and thinly sliced	6
	Salt and freshly ground black pepper	
2 cups	shredded Gruyère cheese	500 mL
3	egg yolks, lightly beaten	3
2½ cups	heavy or whipping (35%) cream	625 mL
	Milk (optional)	

1. Rub garlic halves over the bottom and sides of baking dish, then discard cloves. With a little of the butter, lightly grease dish.
2. Arrange a third of the potato slices in the dish, slightly overlapping edges. Dot with some of the butter and sprinkle with salt and freshly ground pepper (do not add cheese). Repeat, using a third of the potatoes to create a second layer. Scatter evenly with a third of the cheese. Repeat with remaining potatoes and scatter evenly with a third of the cheese. Transfer dish to prepared baking sheet.
3. In a bowl, whisk together egg yolks and cream. Pour over potatoes to cover (if necessary, add a little milk). Scatter evenly with remaining cheese. Bake in preheated oven for 75 minutes or until potatoes are cooked through, top is golden brown and edges are bubbling (if browning too quickly, cover loosely with buttered foil). Remove from oven and transfer dish to a wire rack. Let stand for 5 minutes before serving.

Variation

If you want to make your guests swoon, sauté 1 lb (500 g) or so of assorted sliced wild mushrooms in butter with a few crushed garlic cloves, until the mushrooms are beginning to brown. Use as the gratin's center layer.

Sensational Spuds on the Side

Potatoes in supporting roles — that's what this chapter is all about. But far from being relegated to the sidelines, potatoes served as an accompaniment prove just how invaluable and versatile this vegetable can be. Often, the main course wouldn't be the same without them. Think pot roast with a tumble of boiled potatoes tossed with butter and parsley or Pot Roast Crusties (page 227), savory meatloaf with crispy baked potatoes (The Only Baked Potato, page 62), fried chicken with mash (Classic Mash Deluxe, page 50) or for something a little different, Yukon Gold Bay Leaf Mash, page 223), or fried fish (Real English Chips, page 64).

White Purée Avalon

This elegant side dish with the understated moniker was created by Toronto chef Chris McDonald at Avalon, his former restaurant. It was served regularly alongside his fabulous bone-in sirloin. While the original recipe included white turnip, I decided to pump up the potato content a bit more. Either way, this dish is also wonderful with any number of rustic stew-like preparations or really good roast chicken.

Makes 4 to 6 servings

Tips

For this quantity of beans, cook ½ cup (125 mL) dried navy or cannellini (small white kidney) beans, or use the same variety of canned beans, thoroughly rinsed and drained.

Leeks can be gritty. To clean leeks, split them in half lengthwise and run under water to remove all traces of dirt.

- **Food mill or large fine-mesh sieve and wooden pestle**

1	knob celeriac, peeled and cubed	1
1 tsp	salt	5 mL
3	large floury potatoes, peeled and quartered	3
1	head garlic, separated into cloves and peeled	1
1	large leek (white and light green parts only), chopped (see Tips, left)	1
1	onion, quartered	1
1 cup	cooked white beans, drained	250 mL
¼ cup	unsalted butter	60 mL

1. Bring a large pot of water to a boil over high heat. Add celeriac and salt. Cover loosely and cook for 15 minutes. Add potatoes, garlic, leek and onion, and reduce heat to medium. Simmer, loosely covered, until tender, about 30 minutes. Drain and return to pot.
2. Add beans and stir to combine. In batches, push mixture through food mill to purée (do not use a food processor).
3. Return purée to a clean pot and reheat over medium heat, stirring constantly and rapidly with a wooden spoon to prevent sticking. Remove from heat and stir in butter until blended. Serve immediately.

Med Mash

Forget the butter and cream and choose a really good extra virgin olive oil to blend in with your mash. There are many good olive oils on the market in a wide variety of flavors, any of which would work well in this recipe. However, this is one instance when I think a more assertive oil should be used. Olive oils from Sicily, renowned for their strong, almost peppery quality and their flavor of newly crushed olives, would be my preference.

Makes 4 to 6 servings

Tips

There are roughly two potatoes per pound (500 g), depending on their size. Russets are the most common variety of floury potatoes. For more about the types and varieties of potatoes, see A World of Potatoes, pages 25 to 48.

If you are not serving them immediately, cover the surface of the mashed potatoes with a clean tea towel or napkin and replace the saucepan lid. The cloth will absorb any moisture and keep the mash hot.

2 lbs	floury potatoes, peeled and quartered (see Tips, left)	1 kg
1 tsp	salt	5 mL
½ cup	whole milk (approx.)	125 mL
⅓ cup	extra virgin olive oil	75 mL
6	oil-packed sun-dried tomatoes, finely chopped	6
¼ cup	freshly grated Parmesan cheese	60 mL
3 tbsp	chopped fresh basil leaves	45 mL
3 tbsp	chopped flat-leaf parsley leaves	45 mL

1. Place potatoes in a large saucepan and add cold water to barely cover (if you use too much water you will end up with watery mash). Add salt, cover loosely and bring to a boil over high heat. Place lid firmly on saucepan, reduce heat and cook for 20 minutes or until potatoes are tender all the way through when prodded with the tip of a paring knife. Drain, leaving potatoes in the saucepan. Return to very low heat and shake the pot back and forth to remove any trace of moisture (this is an important step — the drier the cooked potato, the lighter and fluffier your mash will be).

2. With saucepan still over heat, add olive oil and, using a potato masher, mash in thoroughly. Bang masher against the rim of the saucepan so any sticking potato mixture falls into the pot. Tilt saucepan slightly and, using a flat whisk, wooden spoon or large fork, briskly stir mixture to incorporate air into the mash, until smooth, creamy and fluffy. (You may decide that it needs a little more olive oil; if so, stir it in now.) Stir in sun-dried tomatoes, cheese, basil and parsley. Serve immediately (see Tips, left).

Variation

Add roasted garlic, to taste, along with the sun-dried tomatoes.

Saffron Mash

While vibrant saffron is a decidedly Spanish spice, I first tasted these ethereal mashed potatoes in a restaurant in London. Since then I've seen them pop up at different bistros and fine dining establishments on this side of the Atlantic. Saffron is expensive but one never needs a lot of it to make something really special, as in this delightful recipe. This is particularly good with grilled fish such as cod, haddock or hake, if you can find it. The color and texture of this mash are glorious.

Makes 4 to 6 servings

Tips

To crush garlic, use the broad side of a chef's knife to crush each clove. Then remove the skin and discard.

Make sure to warm the olive oil and add it gradually to the mashed potato mixture. It may seem like a lot, but it is the quality of the extra virgin olive oil that makes these potatoes what they are.

If you are not serving them immediately, cover the surface of the mashed potatoes with a clean tea towel or napkin and replace the saucepan lid. The cloth will absorb any moisture and keep the mash hot.

½ cup	whole milk	125 mL
2	cloves garlic, crushed (see Tips, left)	2
2	sprigs fresh thyme	2
2 lbs	floury or all-purpose potatoes, peeled and quartered	1 kg
1 tsp	salt	5 mL
2	generous pinches saffron	2
½ to 1 cup	extra virgin olive oil, warmed	125 to 250 mL

1. In a small saucepan, combine milk, garlic and thyme and bring to a boil. Remove from heat, cover and set aside for 10 minutes to infuse flavors. Using a fine-mesh sieve, strain into a bowl and sprinkle with saffron. Set aside.

2. Place potatoes in a large saucepan and add cold water to barely cover. Add salt, cover loosely and bring to a boil over high heat. Reduce heat and cook for 20 minutes or until potatoes are tender all the way through when prodded with the tip of a paring knife. Drain, leaving potatoes in the saucepan. Return to very low heat and shake the pot back and forth to remove any trace of moisture (this is an important step — the drier the cooked potato, the lighter and fluffier your mash will be).

3. With saucepan still over heat, add milk mixture and, using a potato masher, mash in thoroughly. Add the olive oil, ¼ cup (60 mL) at a time, in a thin stream; mash until potato mixture starts to get fluffy and looks glossy and rich (you may not need to use all the oil). Bang masher against the rim of the saucepan so any sticking potato mixture falls into the pot. Tilt saucepan slightly and, using a flat whisk, wooden spoon or large fork, briskly stir potato mixture to incorporate air into the mash, until smooth, creamy and fluffy. (You may decide that it needs a little more oil if you haven't used it all; if so, stir it in now.) Serve immediately.

Yukon Gold Bay Leaf Mash

This recipe was developed by Chef Stephen Treadwell when he was at the Tiara Dining Room of the Queen's Landing Inn in Niagara-on-the-Lake, Ontario. Since 2006 Chef Treadwell has been operating his own, highly successful restaurant, Treadwell Farm to Table Cuisine in Port Dalhousie, which continues his philosophy of showcasing local growers and suppliers of quality foods. In the past the chef paired this simple yet sumptuous side dish with maple roasted salmon and a reduction of Cabernet Sauvignon and mustard seed.

Makes 2 to 4 servings

Tips

Use the very best extra virgin olive oil for this recipe.

Be sure to follow the instructions for properly baking potatoes on page 62.

If you're not using the skins to hold the mash, top them with butter and gobble them up.

3 to 4	bay leaves, crushed	3 to 4
1 cup	extra virgin olive oil	250 mL
5	large Yukon Gold potatoes, baked (see Tips, left) and cooled enough to handle	5
¼ cup	chopped flat-leaf parsley leaves	60 mL
	Salt and freshly ground black pepper	

1. Place bay leaves in a small bowl. In a small sauté pan, warm oil over medium heat. Pour over bay leaves and set aside to infuse for 1 hour.

2. Halve each potato lengthwise and scoop flesh into a bowl. Cover with a clean tea towel to keep warm and set aside.

3. Strain oil through a fine-mesh sieve into a small jug or bowl, discarding bay leaves. Stir in parsley until just blended.

4. Using a fork, gradually stir oil into potato flesh, roughly incorporating it and slightly mashing the flesh. Transfer to a serving dish or divide evenly among the skins. Season to taste with salt and pepper and serve immediately.

Steakhouse Mash

These potatoes really shine when served next to — or beneath — a seared strip loin or rib-eye steak.

Makes 4 to 6 servings

Tips

Be sure not to add too much water when cooking potatoes for mash. Otherwise you'll end up with watery mash.

After you've salted the water for boiling the potatoes, taste it. You should be able to slightly taste the salt. If not, add a little more. Potatoes are nothing without the right amount of salt, and adding it following the cooking process just doesn't work.

If you are not serving them immediately, cover the surface of the mashed potatoes with a clean tea towel or napkin and replace the saucepan lid. The cloth will absorb any moisture and keep the mash hot.

To roast garlic: Cut a thin slice from the top of the head, drizzle with a little olive oil and wrap tightly in foil. Bake in a 350°F (180°C) oven for 20 minutes, until soft. The cloves can then be squeezed out of their thin skins, lightly chopped and added directly to the mash.

2½ lbs	floury potatoes, peeled and quartered	1.25 kg
1 tsp	salt (see Tips, left)	5 mL
6	slices double-smoked bacon, chopped	6
2	large shallots, finely chopped	2
1 cup	very finely chopped trimmed mushrooms (caps and stems)	250 mL
1	head garlic, roasted and separated into cloves (see Tips, left)	1
¼ cup	butter (approx.), softened	60 mL
¼ cup	heavy or whipping (35%) cream	60 mL
½ cup	whole milk (approx.)	125 mL
¼ cup	finely chopped flat-leaf parsley leaves	60 mL

1. Place potatoes in a large saucepan and add cold water to barely cover (see Tips, left). Add salt, cover loosely and bring to a boil over high heat. Reduce heat and cook for 20 minutes or until potatoes are tender.

2. Meanwhile, in a skillet, sauté bacon over medium-high heat until softened and releasing its fat. Stir in shallots and mushrooms and sauté for about 20 minutes or until bacon is cooked through and slightly crisp and shallots and mushrooms are softened and beginning to brown. Squeeze garlic cloves out of their skins, chop coarsely and stir into bacon mixture. Remove from heat, set aside and keep warm.

3. Drain potatoes and return to the saucepan over very low heat, shaking the pot back and forth to remove any trace of moisture.

4. With saucepan still over heat and using a potato masher, mash in butter. Gradually add cream and milk, mashing well after each addition. Bang masher against the rim of the saucepan so any sticking potato mixture falls into the pot. Tilt saucepan slightly and, using a flat whisk, wooden spoon or large fork, briskly stir potato mixture to incorporate a little air into the mash, until mixture is smooth, creamy and fluffy. (You may decide that it needs a little more butter or milk; if so, stir it in now.) Scraping any brown bits from bottom and sides of skillet, add bacon mixture to potato mixture and fold in. Stir in parsley and serve immediately.

Sweet Potato Mash with Pancetta & Parmesan

This is a great side dish that works very well with chicken, turkey, pork or grilled sausages.

Makes 4 to 6 servings

Tip

If you have any leftover mash, shape it into little cakes and fry in butter to serve alongside eggs for breakfast.

3	large sweet potatoes (about 3 lbs/1.5 kg), peeled and cut into 1-inch (2.5 cm) cubes	3
1 tsp	salt	5 mL
3 tbsp	butter, divided	45 mL
1	onion, finely chopped	1
2	cloves garlic, crushed	2
4 to 5 oz	pancetta, cubed	125 to 140 g
1/2 cup	freshly grated Grana Padano or Parmesan cheese	125 mL
1 tbsp	finely chopped flat-leaf parsley leaves	15 mL
1 tsp	finely chopped fresh rosemary leaves	5 mL
	Salt and freshly ground black pepper	

1. Place sweet potatoes in a large saucepan and add cold water to barely cover. Add salt, cover loosely and bring to a boil over high heat. Reduce heat and cook for 15 minutes or until sweet potatoes are tender. Drain well.

2. Meanwhile, in a skillet, melt 2 tbsp (30 mL) butter over low heat. Add onion and cook, stirring, for about 10 minutes or until softened. Stir in garlic and cook, stirring, for 1 to 2 minutes. Transfer to a small bowl, scraping in any bits from bottom of pan. Set aside.

3. Return pan to heat. Increase heat to medium-high and cook pancetta, stirring, for about 5 minutes or until beginning to brown and crisp up. Scrape into onion mixture, including any bits from bottom of pan. Set aside.

4. Return sweet potatoes to a clean saucepan. Using a fork, mash coarsely. Stir in onion and pancetta. Stir in cheese, parsley and rosemary. Season to taste with salt and freshly ground pepper and serve immediately.

Variations

Replace some of the sweet potatoes with carrots, parsnips or turnip — all good mashing mates.

Yorkshire Pudding Potatoes

When I was a girl, my Nottingham-born mum made the world's finest roast beef dinners every Sunday. Roast beef, rich gravy, lovely green beans, roasties, mashed turnip and — the best part as far as I was concerned — Yorkshire puddings so perfect they almost defied description. I wonder what my dear mum would have made of these delightful Yorkshires with their mashed potato filling?

Serves 6 to 8

Tip

Make sure your oven is at the specified temperature. Otherwise your puddings won't achieve maximum puffiness.

- **8 ramekins or custard cups ($\frac{3}{4}$ cup/175 mL)**

2½ lbs	floury or all-purpose potatoes, peeled and quartered	1.25 kg
1 tsp	salt	5 mL
4	eggs	4
½ cup	whole milk	125 mL
½ cup	all-purpose flour	125 mL
1 tsp	salt	5 mL
¼ cup	melted butter	60 mL
¼ cup	dry bread crumbs	60 mL

1. Place potatoes in a large saucepan and add cold water to barely cover. Bring to a boil over high heat. Add salt, return to a boil, reduce heat and cook for 20 minutes or until potatoes are tender. Drain well. Return potatoes to saucepan over very low heat and shake the pot back and forth to remove any trace of moisture. Transfer to a large bowl and mash roughly. Set aside until they are no longer steaming.

2. Preheat oven to 425°F (220°C).

3. In another bowl, whisk together eggs, milk, flour and salt. Add to cooled potatoes and mix well. Brush the ramekins with melted butter and sprinkle with bread crumbs, rolling around to coat. Tap out any excess.

4. Using a rubber spatula, scoop the potato mixture into prepared ramekins, smooth the tops and let rest for a few minutes. Bake in preheated oven until golden and puffed, about 25 minutes. Serve immediately in the ramekins.

Pot Roast Crusties

I call these pot roast potatoes because they go so well with a nice traditional beef pot roast. But they also work very well alongside braised beef, beef steak, roast pork or lamb or a big, shiny ham.

Makes 6 to 8 servings

Tip

Pat scrubbed potatoes dry with a clean tea towel or paper towels; if they still seem damp, let air-dry for about 10 minutes.

- **Preheat oven to 350°F (180°C)**
- **Roasting pan, lined with parchment paper**

2 lbs	small red-skinned potatoes, scrubbed and thoroughly dried (see Tip, left)	1 kg
½ cup	olive oil	125 mL
1 cup	dry bread crumbs	250 mL
2 tbsp	sweet paprika	30 mL
2 tsp	herbes de Provence	10 mL
	Salt and freshly ground black pepper	

1. Halve potatoes lengthwise and transfer to a large bowl. Add oil and toss to coat. Add bread crumbs, paprika and herbes de Provence and toss to coat. Season to taste with salt and freshly ground pepper.

2. Using tongs so as not to disturb the coating, arrange potatoes in a single layer, cut side up, in prepared roasting pan.

3. Roast in preheated oven for about 50 minutes or until cooked through and crusty. Serve immediately.

Chunky Chip Roasties with Fresh Thyme

Use big, beautiful baking (floury or all-purpose) potatoes for this recipe. These also make great pass-around appetizers when you have friends over.

Makes 4 to 6 servings

Tip

Pat scrubbed potatoes dry with a clean tea towel or paper towels; if they still seem damp, let air-dry for about 10 minutes.

- Preheat oven to 425°F (220°C)
- 2 rimmed baking sheets, nonstick or lined with parchment paper

5	large floury or all-purpose potatoes, scrubbed and thoroughly dried (see Tip, left)	5
⅓ cup	olive oil	75 mL
	Salt and freshly ground black pepper	
6	sprigs fresh thyme	6

1. Using a sharp chef's knife, slice each potato in half lengthwise, then slice each half lengthwise into four wedges, creating eight wedges per potato. Transfer to prepared baking sheet(s) and toss with oil to coat. Season to taste with salt and pepper and arrange in a single layer.
2. Roast on center rack(s) in preheated oven, turning once or twice to ensure even browning, for about 20 minutes. Meanwhile, pull thyme leaves from their stems, discarding stems.
3. Carefully pull out oven rack and scatter thyme leaves over potatoes, using tongs to turn potatoes so they are coated on all sides. Slide rack back into oven and roast for 10 to 15 minutes longer or until tender and golden brown. Serve immediately.

Variations

Vary the herbs; rosemary, oregano and marjoram are all good choices. If you use fresh basil or mint, add after you have removed the potatoes from the oven and just before serving — but don't forget to turn the potatoes after they have cooked for 20 minutes.

Try this recipe with sweet potatoes; the cooking time will be slightly less.

Using a chile-infused oil instead of olive oil provides a nice bit of spice.

Oven-Roasted Potatoes & Parsnips with Curry

This easy preparation takes the concept of crusty oven-roasted root vegetables one step further, with the addition of a little fragrant curry seasoning. This is very good with any roasted meat.

Makes
6 servings

Tips

Cut potatoes and parsnips into evenly sized pieces, not too small.

Stirring the vegetables as they cook encourages browning and slight caramelizing on as many sides as possible. Don't crowd the roasting pan, or the vegetables will steam together rather than roast.

- Preheat oven to 400°F (200°C)
- Roasting pan large enough to accommodate vegetables in a single layer

5	large floury or all-purpose potatoes, scrubbed and cut Into chunks (see Tips, left)	5
6	shallots, peeled	6
5	large parsnips, peeled and cut into chunks	5
1	head garlic, separated into cloves and peeled	1
1/3 cup	olive oil	75 mL
2 tbsp	curry powder	30 mL
	Salt and freshly ground black pepper	

1. In a large bowl, toss potatoes, shallots, parsnips, garlic, oil and curry powder to coat. Season to taste with salt and freshly ground pepper. In a large roasting pan, arrange vegetables in a single layer. Roast in preheated oven, stirring occasionally, for 45 to 60 minutes or until cooked through and potatoes and parsnips are crusty and golden brown. (If they are browning too quickly and have not yet cooked through, cover with foil.) Serve immediately.

Variations

Substitute turnips, rutabaga, beets, celeriac, carrots or sweet potatoes for the parsnips.

Exotic Spiced Roasties

I love this dish, which uses small whole new potatoes roasted with flavorful Indian spices. You will have more of the spice mixture than you need for this recipe, but it is a great pantry staple. And once you have tasted these potatoes, you will make them often.

Makes 4 to 6 servings (and about ½ cup/ 125 mL spice mixture)

Tips

The spice combo in this recipe lends an Indian flavor to food. It can be used as a dry rub on boneless chicken or pork chops before grilling or searing.

I prefer to use sea salt rather than refined table salt because it has a much cleaner, crisper taste.

You can also serve these as an appetizer, presented on the end of wooden skewers. Accompany with a cooling dip of plain yogurt combined with chopped fresh mint and cilantro.

- Preheat oven to 400°F (200°C)
- Rimmed baking sheet, lightly brushed with olive oil
- Glass jar with tight-fitting lid

Spice Mixture

1 tbsp	ground cardamom	15 mL
1 tbsp	cayenne pepper	15 mL
1 tbsp	ground coriander	15 mL
1 tbsp	ground cumin	15 mL
1 tbsp	paprika	15 mL
1 tsp	ground cinnamon	5 mL
1 tsp	ground cloves	5 mL
1 tsp	freshly ground black pepper	5 mL
1 tsp	ground nutmeg	5 mL
1 tsp	turmeric	5 mL
1 tsp	salt	5 mL
1 tsp	granulated sugar	5 mL

Potatoes

2 lbs	small waxy new potatoes, lightly scrubbed and thoroughly dried	1 kg
¼ cup	olive oil	60 mL

1. *Spice Mixture:* In a small bowl, combine cardamom, cayenne, coriander, cumin, paprika, cinnamon, cloves, pepper, nutmeg, turmeric, salt and sugar. Mix well. Transfer to a glass jar with a tight-fitting lid and store in a cool, dark place for up to 2 weeks.
2. *Potatoes:* Using a fork, prick each potato a few times and transfer to a large bowl. Add oil and 1 to 2 tbsp (15 to 30 mL) of the spice mixture. Toss to coat.
3. Arrange in a single layer on prepared baking sheet. Roast in preheated oven, turning once or twice, for 45 minutes to 1 hour or until tender. Serve immediately.

Spiced Roast Potatoes with Yogurt & Mint

Spicy-hot roast potatoes licked with cooling yogurt and fresh mint are so nice when you have a platter of cold leftover roast lamb or beef to be eaten up. Indian chefs often add yogurt to potatoes as they roast. In this instance the yogurt is added after the roasting so the potatoes can get nice and crusty.

Makes 4 servings

Tip

I prefer to use sea salt rather than refined table salt because it has a much cleaner, crisper taste and enhanced mineral content.

- **9-inch (2.5 L) square baking dish (preferably one that can go from oven to table)**
- **Preheat oven to 350°F (180°C)**

4	floury potatoes, peeled and cut into uniform chunks	4
1 tsp	salt	5 mL
3 tbsp	vegetable oil	45 mL
2	onions, finely sliced	2
2	chopped fresh red chiles	2
2	cloves garlic, crushed	2
½ tsp	cumin seeds	2 mL
½ tsp	turmeric	2 mL
¼ cup	plain yogurt	60 mL
Pinch	cayenne pepper	Pinch
⅓ cup	fresh mint leaves	75 mL

1. Place potatoes in a large saucepan and add cold water to barely cover. Add salt, cover loosely and bring to a boil over high heat. Reduce heat and parboil for 10 to 15 minutes, until potatoes still offer some resistance when tested with a small blade; they should not be cooked through. Drain well. Return potatoes to saucepan over very low heat and shake the pot back and forth to remove any trace of moisture. Set aside.

2. In a skillet, heat oil over medium heat. Cook onions for about 10 minutes or until softened. Stir in chiles, garlic and cumin seeds and cook, stirring, for 1 minute. Add potatoes and turmeric and toss to coat. Transfer to baking dish, scraping spiced oil and vegetables over potatoes.

3. Roast in preheated oven for 30 to 35 minutes or until potatoes are beginning to crisp. Remove from oven and immediately spoon yogurt over (don't stir). Sprinkle with cayenne and scatter evenly with mint leaves. Serve immediately.

Smoke & Spice Roasted Potatoes

The smokiness from the chipotle peppers infuses these new potatoes and complements the variety of seasonings used in this simple recipe.

**Makes
6 servings**

Tip

During the summer you can barbecue the potatoes to give them additional flavor. If you do, parboil them for 10 minutes or so beforehand.

- **Preheat oven to 375°F (190°C)**

2 tbsp	smoked paprika	30 mL
1½ tsp	chili powder	7 mL
1 tsp	dried thyme	5 mL
1 tsp	dried sage	5 mL
1 tsp	dried basil	5 mL
½ tsp	curry powder	2 mL
½ tsp	salt	2 mL
½ tsp	freshly ground black pepper	2 mL
2	canned chipotle peppers in adobo sauce	2
¼ cup	olive oil	60 mL
1	large clove garlic, minced	1
4 lbs	small new potatoes, scrubbed and cut into ½-inch (1 cm) slices	2 kg
2 tbsp	chopped fresh chives	30 mL

1. In a large bowl, combine paprika, chili powder, thyme, sage, basil, curry powder, salt and freshly ground pepper. Set aside.
2. Using a sharp chef's knife, finely chop chipotle peppers and scrape into seasoning mixture along with their sauce. Stir in oil and garlic until blended.
3. Add potatoes and toss to coat. Evenly spread over a rimmed baking sheet. Roast in preheated oven for about 20 to 30 minutes or until potatoes are cooked through and edges are crisp. Serve immediately.

New Potatoes with Thai Flavors

A friend in England sent me this recipe, which, she says, may not be authentic Thai but works beautifully for potato-heads who love Thai food. So, to test that theory, I tried teaming it with chicken satay with peanut sauce — she's right.

**Makes
4 servings**

Tip

This recipe can easily be doubled.

1½ lbs	new potatoes, scrubbed	750 g
1 tsp	salt	5 mL
1 tbsp	vegetable oil	15 mL
1 to 2	red Thai chiles, seeded and minced	1 to 2
1	stalk lemon grass, trimmed and finely chopped	1
1 tsp	minced gingerroot	15 mL
	Freshly ground black pepper	
¼ cup	chopped fresh cilantro leaves	60 mL

1. Place potatoes in a large saucepan and add boiling water to barely cover. Add salt, cover loosely and bring to a boil over high heat. Reduce heat and cook for 20 minutes or until potatoes are tender. Drain well. Transfer to a serving bowl. Set aside and keep warm.

2. In a small saucepan, heat oil over medium heat. Stir-fry chiles, lemon grass, ginger and salt and freshly ground pepper to taste for about 5 minutes or until vegetables are softened. Add to potatoes and toss. Add cilantro and toss well. Serve immediately.

Lemon Spice Spuds

This preparation is inspired by Greek-style potatoes infused with lemon and olive oil, to which I have added some fragrant Indian ingredients. These are especially nice with lamb kebabs or chops and some haricots verts, those ultra-skinny green beans.

Makes 4 to 6 servings

Tips

Garam masala is an Indian seasoning blend, the phrase translating as "hot spices." This recipe may make a little more than you will need for the potatoes. Store any remaining garam masala in a small jar with a tight-fitting lid; keep in a dark, dry place for up to a month. There are many uses for this mixture in Indian dishes, curries and soups. Try some sprinkled on butternut squash before baking or rubbed into chicken or pork before roasting. If you don't feel like making your own, look for garam masala in specialty food shops or Indian grocery stores.

Garam masala: In a spice grinder, grind 1 piece (about 2 inches/5 cm) cinnamon stick, ⅓ whole nutmeg, 1 tbsp (15 mL) cardamom seeds and 1 tsp (5 mL) each black peppercorns, black cumin (nigella) seeds, whole cloves and any color mustard seeds into a fine powder. Transfer to a small jar with a tight-fitting lid.

- **Preheat oven to 400°F (200°C)**
- **Roasting pan**

2 lbs	floury potatoes, scrubbed and cut into coarse chunks	1 kg
1 tsp	salt	5 mL
2 tbsp	garam masala (see Tips, left)	30 mL
1 tbsp	ground turmeric	15 mL
½ cup	extra virgin olive oil	125 mL
3	cloves garlic, minced	3
1 tbsp	chopped gingerroot	15 mL
	Zest and freshly squeezed juice of 1 large lemon	
	Salt and freshly ground black pepper	

1. Place potatoes in a large saucepan and add cold water to barely cover. Add salt and bring to a boil. Cover loosely, reduce heat and parboil for 5 minutes. Drain well. Transfer to a bowl and set aside until cool enough to handle. Using the tines of a fork, rough up edges of potatoes (to help them absorb flavorings and crisp up). Add garam masala and turmeric and toss to coat.

2. In a large skillet, heat oil over medium heat. Add potatoes to skillet along with garlic, ginger and lemon zest and juice. Season to taste with salt and freshly ground pepper. Toss to coat.

3. Using a rubber spatula, transfer potatoes to a roasting pan, scraping in oil and spice mixture and tossing to coat. Roast in preheated oven, turning occasionally, for about 1 hour or until potatoes are crusty and golden brown.

Pan-Fried Sweet Potatoes with Gremolata

Gremolata is the classic garnish for osso buco, a northern Italian veal shank dish. It is a fragrant mixture of lemon zest, parsley and garlic, sometimes with added bread crumbs. Here it does a nice job of lifting the flavor of sweet potatoes. This is a lovely dish to serve alongside roast chicken or pork.

Makes 4 servings

Tip

For a nice color contrast, add a few handfuls of baby spinach to the sweet potato mixture for the last 5 minutes of cooking time.

4 oz	pancetta, cubed	125 g
1 tbsp	olive oil	15 mL
1	large sweet potato (about 1 lb/500 g), peeled and cut into 1-inch (2.5 cm) chunks	1
¼ cup	butter	60 mL
⅓ cup	bread crumbs	75 mL
1	small bunch flat-leaf parsley, stems trimmed, finely chopped	1
	Finely grated zest of 1 lemon	
	Salt and freshly ground black pepper	

1. In a heavy skillet over medium heat, combine pancetta and oil. Cook, stirring, for 1 to 2 minutes.
2. Toss sweet potato into pancetta. Cook, without stirring, for about 10 minutes or until sweet potato pieces are golden brown on the bottom. Using tongs, turn and cook for 6 to 10 minutes more or until tender and browned on the other side. Remove from heat, cover and set aside.
3. In another skillet, melt butter over medium heat until bubbling. Stir in bread crumbs and cook, stirring, until golden brown and crisp (don't let them burn). Remove from heat and stir in parsley and lemon zest. Season to taste with salt (remember, the bacon may be salty) and freshly ground pepper.
4. Scrape bread crumb mixture over sweet potato mixture and toss to combine. Serve immediately.

Variation

Substitute orange zest — a flavor very compatible with sweet potatoes — for the lemon.

Danish Sugar-Browned Potatoes

And now for something completely different, as the saying goes — a dish of caramelized potatoes. In Denmark this is known as *brunede kartofler*, and it's a tradition for special dinners such as at Christmas and on other feast days. Serve with roast pork and some sautéed red cabbage.

Makes 4 to 6 servings

Tips

As specified, small waxy potatoes are the best choice. Leave them whole so they can roll around nicely in the sugary glaze. Or use larger waxy potatoes and cut them into roundish pieces.

This dish also works well if you leave the skins on the potatoes.

- **Cast-iron or heavy skillet**

2 lbs	small waxy potatoes, scrubbed	1 kg
1 tsp	salt	5 mL
¼ cup	granulated sugar	60 mL
¼ cup	butter	60 mL
2 tbsp	water	30 mL

1. Place potatoes in a large saucepan and add boiling water to barely cover. Add salt, cover loosely and bring to a boil over high heat. Reduce heat and cook for 15 to 20 minutes or until potatoes are just tender. Drain well. Set aside until cool enough to handle. Peel off skins and set potatoes aside.

2. In cast-iron skillet over medium-low heat, scatter sugar to about ¼ inch (0.5 cm) thick. Without stirring, melt until sugar is turning light brown around the edges. Stir in butter and heat until melted and bubbling.

3. Gently toss in potatoes (don't break them up) and cook, shaking to coat with sugar glaze, for about 15 minutes or until evenly coated and heated through. Serve immediately.

Duck Fat Potatoes

I could have come up with a different name for this simple preparation that marries spuds with liquid gold — otherwise known as duck fat — but really, sometimes you just have to call it what it is, and this is glorious. I prepared these potatoes to accompany a Christmas dinner that included crown roast of pork, and everyone agreed that they outshone the meat.

Makes 4 servings

Tips

Chances are you may not have duck fat on hand unless you have been enjoying duck and rendering and saving the fat (a culinary golden rule). However, you can purchase duck fat at specialty food shops or even online these days.

Any variety of potatoes can be used for this with good results. However, if you opt for potatoes with a thicker, rougher skin, such as russet potatoes, you may want to peel them first.

4	large all-purpose potatoes, peeled and cut into large chunks	4
1/3 cup	duck fat, melted (see Tips, left)	75 mL
4	large cloves garlic, crushed	4
	Salt	
2 tbsp	finely chopped fresh rosemary leaves	30 mL

1. In a skillet, combine potatoes, duck fat and garlic. Toss well. Cover and cook over medium to low heat, stirring occasionally, for 25 to 30 minutes or until tender.

2. Drain off any residual fat (you can keep it for another use), season to taste with salt and stir in rosemary. Increase heat to medium and cook, stirring a few times, for another 10 minutes or until crisp. Serve immediately.

Variation

Goose Fat Potatoes: Substitute goose fat for the duck fat.

Fingerling Slices in Duck Fat

Here's another recipe for potatoes in duck fat, this time using fingerling potatoes instead of the floury variety. You might assume that I really love what this particular fat contributes to potatoes — and you would be right.

Makes 4 servings

Tip

If you roast a duck, make sure to save the fat. It will keep for a long time covered and refrigerated or frozen. If you don't have any on hand, you can purchase duck fat at specialty food shops or even online these days.

- **Large cast-iron or heavy skillet**

¼ cup	duck fat (see Tip, left)	60 mL
1½ lbs	fingerling potatoes, sliced lengthwise into thirds	750 g
1	large clove garlic, finely chopped	1
¼ cup	chopped fresh thyme leaves	60 mL
	Salt and freshly ground black pepper	

1. In skillet, melt duck fat over medium-high heat. Toss in potatoes, garlic and thyme. Season to taste with salt and freshly ground pepper. Cook over moderate heat for 25 to 30 minutes or until potatoes are cooked through, golden and crisp.

Sautéed Fingerlings with Asparagus & Mint

This is a lovely dish to make whenever you spy some long, slightly knobby fingerlings. These potatoes have a wonderfully smooth, waxy texture and loads of flavor. They are stylish enough to serve with the season's first asparagus — for best results, choose pencil-thin stalks. This dish is a wonderful accompaniment to a big clove-studded ham, roast leg of lamb or lamb chops.

Makes 4 to 6 servings

Tip

If you're using asparagus with thicker stalks, blanch it in boiling water for a minute or so before adding to the potatoes.

After trimming the asparagus, use a vegetable peeler to pare down the ends to reveal the bright green color. It makes for a pretty contrast.

1½ lbs	fingerling potatoes, scrubbed	750 g
1 tsp	salt	5 mL
1 lb	slender asparagus, trimmed (see Tip, left)	500 g
2 tbsp	butter	30 mL
2 tbsp	olive oil	30 mL
15	fresh mint leaves	15
	Freshly ground black pepper	

1. Place potatoes in a large saucepan and add boiling water to barely cover. Add salt, cover loosely and bring to a boil. Reduce heat and cook for 12 minutes or until potatoes are almost cooked through. Drain well. Set aside until cool enough to handle. Cut lengthwise into slices ½ inch (1 cm) thick (or cut into thirds if potatoes are not too large). Slice asparagus spears on the diagonal into thirds.

2. In a skillet, warm butter and oil over medium heat. Cook potatoes and asparagus, stirring occasionally, for about 10 minutes or until potatoes are golden brown on both sides and asparagus is tender. Remove from heat. Season to taste with salt and freshly ground pepper. Add mint and toss together. Transfer to a serving platter and serve immediately.

Hot Chile Spuds

A few slightly exotic ingredients go a long way in this potato dish designed for heat-seekers. Although it is not entirely authentic, this would make a nice addition to a selection of East Indian dishes.

**Makes
4 servings**

Tips

Use long red chiles or small bird's-eye (Thai) chiles in this recipe.

You can cut back on the heat level by slitting open the chiles and scraping out the seeds and membranes. It's a good idea to wear rubber gloves when handling hot chiles.

2 lbs	small waxy potatoes, scrubbed and halved	1 kg
2 tsp	salt, divided	10 mL
¼ cup	vegetable oil	60 mL
½ tsp	crushed coriander seeds	2 mL
½ tsp	crushed cumin seeds	2 mL
¼ tsp	crushed red pepper flakes	1 mL
1	onion, thinly sliced	1
2	red chile peppers, minced (See Tips, left)	2
3 tbsp	chopped cilantro leaves	45 mL
3 tbsp	chopped basil leaves	45 mL

1. Place potatoes in a large saucepan and add boiling water to barely cover. Add 1 tsp (5 mL) salt, return to a boil, reduce heat and cook for 20 minutes or until potatoes are tender but firm. Drain potatoes and set aside.
2. In a heavy skillet, heat oil over medium heat. Stir in coriander seeds, cumin seeds, red pepper flakes and remaining 1 tsp (5 mL) salt and toast, stirring, for about 1 minute or until fragrant. Stir in onion and cook, stirring, for about 5 minutes or until softened.
3. Stir in potatoes, chiles, cilantro and basil. Reduce heat to low, cover and cook gently, stirring occasionally, for about 10 minutes or until potatoes are fully cooked.

Punjabi Potatoes & Cauliflower

Northern Indian tables often feature potatoes, especially in concert with cauliflower. Here is a typical version called *aloo gobi*, which works well as part of an Indian meal or in partnership with roast chicken or pork.

Makes 4 to 6 servings

Tip

Look for the fragrant spice mixture garam masala at Indian food shops or other specialty food outlets. Or, if you prefer, make your own (see Tips, page 234).

- **Large wok or skillet**

½ cup	vegetable oil	125 mL
3	large floury or all-purpose potatoes, peeled, halved and cut into coarse chunks	3
1 lb	cauliflower, trimmed and broken into florets	500 g
3	onions, finely chopped	3
1	piece gingerroot (about 2 inches/5 cm), peeled and slivered	1
1 tsp	ground coriander	5 mL
1 tsp	salt	5 mL
½ tsp	cayenne pepper	2 mL
½ tsp	turmeric	2 mL
1 tsp	garam masala (see Tip, left)	5 mL
½ tsp	cumin seeds, roasted and ground	2 mL

1. In a wok, heat oil over medium-high heat. Stir-fry potatoes for about 10 minutes or until just beginning to color but not cooked through. Using a slotted spoon, transfer to a plate lined with paper towels. Working in batches if necessary, stir-fry cauliflower for 3 to 4 minutes or until golden brown and tender-crisp. Using a slotted spoon, transfer to a plate lined with paper towels.

2. Pour off half the oil and return wok to heat. Stir-fry onions for about 5 minutes or until fragrant and beginning to color. Add ginger and stir-fry for 1 minute. Add coriander, salt, cayenne and turmeric and stir-fry for 1 minute.

3. Stir in potatoes and cauliflower, mixing well, and add ¼ cup (60 mL) water. Reduce heat to medium, cover and cook, stirring occasionally, for about 5 minutes or until potatoes are tender (add a little more water if mixture is becoming too dry and sticking to the pan).

4. Remove from heat and gently stir in garam masala and cumin. Serve immediately.

O'Brien Home Fries

I don't know who O'Brien was — a potato-loving Irish national, I would assume — but I've always liked his or her home fries, which feature onion and nubs of green bell pepper. The cheese is not traditional but it makes them even better. You can also add a mixture of green and red, yellow or orange bell peppers, if you wish. This is great with hefty sausages, smoked fish or eggs.

Makes 4 to 6 servings

Tip

For best results, refrigerate the cooked potatoes and chill well before dicing.

- **Large cast-iron or heavy skillet**

¼ cup	olive oil	60 mL
1 tbsp	butter	15 mL
1	green bell pepper, chopped	1
1	onion, sliced	1
6	boiled potatoes, cooled and diced (see Tip, left)	6
1 tsp	cayenne pepper	5 mL
	Salt and freshly ground black pepper	
¾ cup	shredded sharp (aged) Cheddar, Asiago or other strong-flavored cheese	175 mL

1. In a large cast-iron skillet, heat oil and butter over medium-high heat. Sauté bell pepper and onion for 10 minutes or until softened. Add potatoes and cayenne and stir to combine. Season with salt and freshly ground pepper to taste. Cook, stirring occasionally, for 15 to 20 minutes or until crisp. Stir in cheese and serve immediately.

The Ultimate Hash Browns

This is a luxurious dish — earthy, rich and bang on with a big rare steak or prime rib.

Makes 6 to 8 servings

Tips

To make them easier to shred, boil the potatoes the night before you plan to serve them (or early the same day), refrigerating them until you are ready to use them.

I've used lower-starch red-skinned potatoes to give the hash browns a bit more texture than usual. If you have potatoes that are other than red-skinned (that is, all-purpose or floury) you can certainly use them.

Use any assortment of mushrooms you like. This dish tastes very good even with good old button mushrooms, but chanterelles and shiitake mushrooms really make it sing.

If you prefer, use a food processor fitted with the shredding disk to shred the potatoes.

- **Large cast-iron or heavy skillet**

3 lbs	red-skinned potatoes, scrubbed	1.5 kg
2 tbsp	olive oil (approx.)	30 mL
¾ lb	wild mushrooms, coarsely chopped	375 g
½ cup	butter	125 mL
1	large onion, finely chopped	1
	Salt and freshly ground black pepper	
1¼ cups	heavy or whipping (35%) cream	300 mL

1. Place potatoes in a large saucepan and add cold water to barely cover. Add 1 tsp (5 mL) salt, cover loosely and bring to a boil over high heat. Reduce heat and cook for about 25 minutes or until potatoes are slightly underdone in the center. Drain well and let cool. Cover with plastic wrap and refrigerate for at least 6 hours or overnight.

2. In a large cast-iron skillet, heat oil over medium-high heat. Cook mushrooms, without stirring, for about 10 minutes, adding a little more oil if necessary. When bottoms begin to crisp, carefully turn and cook, undisturbed, to crisp other side. Remove from heat and set aside.

3. Peel potatoes and discard skins. Using the coarse side of a box grater, shred. Set aside.

4. In a large skillet, heat butter over medium-high heat. Sauté onion for about 10 minutes or until softened and beginning to brown. Add half of the potatoes, season to taste with salt and pepper, then add reserved mushrooms. Cover with the remaining potatoes and season again.

5. Cook, without stirring, for about 6 minutes or until bottom is starting to brown. Using a metal spatula, carefully lift and turn potato mixture in sections. Stir a little, then pour half the cream over the top. Cook, without stirring, for about 5 minutes. Stir a little, then pour remaining cream all over the mixture. Cook, without stirring, for 5 to 7 minutes or until cream has been absorbed and mixture is crusty. Serve immediately.

Skillet Potato Galette

Not a galette in the true sense of the word (see page 252 for the real thing), this dish is sort of a cross between home fries and a gratin. It is an easy preparation that requires minimum effort but produces great comfort food. It's especially nice when served with something simple such as a quiche (perhaps made without cheese), pan-seared seasoned boneless chicken breasts, or even a big mixed salad.

Makes 4 to 6 servings

Tip

I prefer to use sea salt rather than refined table salt because it has a much cleaner, crisper taste.

- **Cast-iron or heavy skillet**

2 tbsp	butter	30 mL
2	cloves garlic, minced	2
2	large onions, cut into ¼-inch (0.5 cm) slices	2
¼ cup	olive oil	60 mL
2 lbs	small red-skinned potatoes, scrubbed and sliced ¼ inch (0.5 cm) thick	1 kg
	Salt and freshly ground black pepper	
1 cup	shredded Jarlsberg or Swiss cheese	250 mL
¼ cup	chopped flat-leaf parsley leaves	60 mL

1. In a cast-iron skillet, melt butter over medium-high heat. Sauté garlic and onions for about 10 minutes or until softened. Add oil and potatoes and season to taste with salt and freshly ground pepper. Cook potatoes, turning once, for about 15 minutes or until tender and golden brown.

2. Meanwhile, in a bowl, combine cheese and parsley. Sprinkle over potatoes and let cook, without stirring, for about 10 minutes or until cheese has melted. Serve immediately.

Potato & Fresh Sage Gratin

For this dish you need waxy potatoes. My favorite ones to use here are lovely long, knobby fingerling potatoes. I have also made this dish with great success using Yukon Golds — the all-purpose champion — and red-skinned potatoes. That's part of the beauty and appeal of potato dishes: no matter which variety you choose, you will always end up with something wonderful to eat.

Makes 4 to 6 servings

Tips

Make sure to use fresh sage leaves, not ground dried sage, because the flavor of fresh is superior. Ground sage will slightly discolor the potatoes and taste too overpowering.

In case the mixture boils over, lining the baking sheet with parchment makes cleanup much easier.

- Preheat oven to 375°F (190°C)
- 10-inch (25 cm) oval, round or square baking dish
- Rimmed baking sheet, lined with parchment paper

2 lbs	fingerling potatoes or other waxy potatoes, scrubbed	1 kg
4	cloves garlic, thinly sliced	4
1¼ cups	heavy or whipping (35%) cream	300 mL
	Salt and freshly ground black pepper	
¼ cup	olive oil, divided	60 mL
20	fresh sage leaves	20
½ cup	freshly grated Grana Padano or Parmesan cheese	125 mL

1. If using fingerlings, halve the potatoes lengthwise (if they are on the large side, slice lengthwise into thirds; if using standard round potatoes, slice thinly). In a large bowl, toss together potatoes, garlic and cream to coat. Season to taste with salt and pepper.
2. Using 2 tbsp (30 mL) oil, grease baking dish. Using a large spoon, arrange half of the potatoes in dish, scatter with half of the sage leaves and arrange the remaining potatoes on top. Pour any cream from bowl evenly over potato mixture. Scatter with remaining sage leaves and drizzle with remaining oil.
3. Loosely cover dish with parchment or buttered foil (it shouldn't touch potato mixture). Bake in preheated oven for 20 minutes. Uncover and bake until crusty and brown, about 20 minutes. Sprinkle evenly with cheese and bake for about 5 minutes or until cheese has melted and is golden brown. Remove from oven and let stand for 10 minutes before serving.

Variation

Add a bit of chopped cooked bacon along with the sage.

Yukon Gold Pavé

Pavé is French for "paving stone." It's usually used to describe layered foods that are cut into attractive squares or rectangles. This is a great dish to make ahead, as it can be prepared early and then finished at the last moment. It does contain a good deal of cream, but this very rich potato gratin is not something you would enjoy every day. It makes a delicious special accompaniment to roast chicken or pan-seared rib-eye.

Makes 6 servings

Tips

Yukon Gold potatoes are a good choice for this recipe but you can use any large floury or all-purpose potatoes.

Use a mandoline or the slicing blade of a food processor to cut potatoes into thin, uniform slices.

Weighting the pavé (with something heavy and ovenproof) is vital to the success of this dish. The best tool for this job is a foil-wrapped brick, if you have one.

- **Preheat oven to 350°F (180°C)**
- **Parchment paper**
- **Two 8-inch (2 L) square nesting baking pans or dishes**

4	large Yukon Gold potatoes, peeled and thinly sliced lengthwise (see Tips, left)	4
3 cups	heavy or whipping (35%) cream	750 mL
3 tbsp	fresh thyme leaves	45 mL
	Butter	
	Salt and freshly ground black pepper	
½ cup	freshly grated Grana Padano or Parmesan cheese	125 mL
2 tbsp	olive oil	30 mL

1. In a large bowl, using your hands, gently toss potatoes with cream and thyme. Set aside for 10 minutes to allow cream to soak into potatoes.
2. Cut two strips of parchment paper, each slightly larger than twice the size of the baking pans (enough to cover the bottom and sides of the pan and fold comfortably over the top of the potatoes). Grease each strip lightly with butter, then place, buttered side up and overlapping, in bottom of one pan, letting edges drape over rim.
3. Arrange four layers of potato slices evenly over bottom of pan. Season to taste with salt and freshly ground pepper. Scatter evenly with half of the cheese. Cover with another four layers of potatoes. Season to taste with salt and freshly ground pepper and sprinkle evenly with remaining cheese. Fold parchment tightly overtop to make a packet. Cover tightly with foil. Place second pan atop the first and set a weight on top.

4. Bake in preheated oven for $1\frac{1}{2}$ hours or until potatoes are tender. Remove from oven. With weight in place, let cool on a wire rack. With weight still in place, refrigerate for at least 4 hours or up to overnight.

5. When ready to serve, remove weight, top pan and foil. Fold back the top sheet of parchment. Place a baking sheet or cutting board on top of the baking pan and invert to turn out the pavé. Remove the parchment paper.

6. With a sharp chef's knife, carefully trim sides to make the pavé as square as possible. Cut into $2\frac{1}{2}$-inch (6 cm) squares.

7. In a large sauté pan, warm oil over medium heat. In batches, if necessary, sear pavé squares, turning once with tongs, for about 5 to 6 minutes or until heated through and golden brown on top and bottom. Serve immediately.

Potato & Celeriac Dauphinoise

Sporting a very French and rather fancy name for a potato gratin, a dauphinoise always features cream, milk and cheese (especially nutty Gruyère). This version, which includes all those things plus celeriac (celery root), may not be completely traditional but it is certainly delish. Serve with pan-seared halibut or rib-eye steaks.

Makes 6 servings

Tips

Although you can cut the celeriac and potatoes with a sharp knife, using a mandoline or a food processor fitted with the slicing blade makes short work of the job and produces lovely thin, uniform slices.

Because they oxidize quickly, while you work, slip the slices of potato and celeriac into a bowl of cold water with a little lemon juice so they don't discolor. Make sure to drain and dry the slices before adding to the baking dish.

- Preheat oven to 350°F (180°C)
- Mandoline or food processor fitted with the slicing blade (see Tips, left)
- 8-inch (2 L) square baking dish

2	large cloves garlic, halved	2
3 tbsp	butter	45 mL
1	onion, sliced	1
1	small knob celeriac (about 1 lb/500 g), peeled and thinly sliced	1
1 lb	large new potatoes, peeled and thinly sliced	500 g
4 oz	Gruyére cheese, shredded	125 g
	Salt and freshly ground black pepper	
1¾ cups	heavy or whipping (35%) cream	425 mL
1 cup	whole milk	250 mL
¼ tsp	ground nutmeg	1 mL

1. Rub garlic halves over bottom and sides of baking dish. Set garlic aside.
2. In a skillet, melt butter over medium heat. Cook onion, stirring, for about 10 minutes or until softened but not beginning to brown.
3. Arrange a single layer of celeriac on bottom of prepared baking dish, sprinkle with a quarter of the onion, then half of the potatoes, then another quarter of the onion. Sprinkle evenly with half of the cheese. Season to taste with salt and freshly ground pepper. Repeat layers of celeriac, onion and potatoes.
4. In a small saucepan, combine cream, milk and reserved garlic over medium heat and cook, stirring occasionally, until warmed through (do not let mixture boil). Remove garlic and pour cream mixture evenly over potato mixture. Sprinkle evenly with remaining cheese and the nutmeg.
5. Loosely cover with parchment paper and bake in preheated oven for 45 minutes. Uncover and cook for about 15 minutes more or until potato mixture is tender and top is golden brown.

Tartiflette

I love the name of this luxurious dish, a French preparation from the Savoy region. Apparently it was conceived as a marketing tool to help sales of France's fantastic Reblochon cheese. I can't imagine anyone needing encouragement to eat this luscious cheese, but I love the combination they came up with: potatoes, bacon and Reblochon — yum. Make a large, lively salad of bitter greens, sweet bell peppers and other crunchy vegetables and serve this sumptuous dish alongside.

Makes 4 to 6 servings

Tips

As with most good-quality cheeses, there really is no substitute for the unique qualities of Reblochon. However, if you can't obtain it, use another soft washed-rind cheese such as Époisses, Oka or raclette.

Whether you trim the rind from the cheese is a matter of taste. Personally, I like it when the melting cheese and the crust from the rind blend with the other ingredients — it adds flavor.

You can buy a piece of bacon from a butcher or deli counter. If you prefer, substitute pancetta, cut into cubes.

- Large cast-iron or heavy ovenproof skillet with lid

2 tbsp	olive oil, divided	30 mL
6 oz	lean smoked bacon, cut into lardons (small cubes)	175 g
2	onions, sliced	2
2 tbsp	butter	30 mL
3 lbs	waxy potatoes, peeled and cut into 1-inch (2.5 cm) cubes	1.5 kg
6 tbsp	heavy or whipping (35%) cream	90 mL
1 lb	Reblochon cheese, rind removed (see Tips, left) and thinly sliced	500 g

1. In a large cast-iron skillet, warm 1 tbsp (15 mL) oil over medium heat. Cook bacon, stirring, for about 5 minutes or until beginning to brown. Using a slotted spoon, transfer to a small bowl.

2. In same skillet, cook onions over medium heat, stirring, for 6 to 7 minutes or until lightly browned. Add the remaining oil and butter, stirring to melt butter. Stir in potatoes and cream, cover and cook, stirring occasionally, for about 20 minutes or until potatoes are tender and browned. Uncover and cook for 5 to 7 minutes longer, until potatoes are crisp.

3. Meanwhile, preheat oven to 375°F (190°C). Add reserved bacon to potatoes and stir to combine. Lay cheese slices on top. Transfer to preheated oven and bake for about 15 minutes or until cheese has melted and top is golden brown and crusty (turn on the broiler if necessary). Serve immediately.

Raeann's One Potato, Two Potatoes Casserole

This is a very good recipe from a very good friend. Remember this when you are asked to bring a potato dish to the next big game party. It's terrific as a sidekick to sticky ribs, chicken wings, chili or stew.

Makes 4 to 6 servings

Tip

Grana Padano is one of Italy's finest cheeses. Think of it as the slightly younger sister of the king, Parmigiano-Reggiano (the original Parmesan). It is also a hard cow's-milk cheese made in northern Italy, but aged less, making it marginally less expensive. Subtler, less nutty and a tad less complex than its older brother, Grana Padano owes its flavor profile to being made in a different region (the cows graze on different grasses) and only from partly skimmed milk, while Parmigiano-Reggiano is made from a combination of whole and skim milk. It should be noted that in Italy Parmigiano-Reggiano is seldom used in cooking — by that I mean grated for serving over pasta or risotto or in other dishes. It is reserved simply for splendid eating enjoyment, on its own with a ripe pear or with prosciutto and a dab or two of well-aged balsamic vinegar.

- Preheat oven to 375°F (190°C)
- 11- by 7-inch (2 L) baking dish, lightly buttered

3	each large floury potatoes and sweet potatoes, peeled and cut into 2-inch (5 cm) chunks	3
3½ tsp	salt, divided	17 mL
2	green onions (white parts and some of the green), trimmed and finely chopped	2
½ cup	butter	125 mL
1 cup	shredded Swiss cheese	250 mL
½ cup	shredded sharp (aged) Cheddar cheese	125 mL
	Freshly ground black pepper	
1¼ cups	whole milk	300 mL
1 cup	fine dry bread crumbs	250 mL
⅓ cup	freshly grated Grana Padano or Parmesan cheese (see Tip, left)	75 mL
3 tbsp	melted butter	45 mL
2 tbsp	chopped flat-leaf parsley leaves	30 mL

1. Place floury potatoes and sweet potatoes in separate large saucepans. To each pot add cold water to barely cover and 1 tsp (5 mL) salt. Cover loosely and bring to a boil over high heat. Reduce heat and cook for 15 to 20 minutes or until potatoes are tender (the sweet potatoes will take a little less time to cook). Drain well. Transfer to a large bowl.

2. Using a fork, slightly break up potatoes. Stir in green onions, butter, Swiss and Cheddar cheeses and 1½ tsp (7 mL) salt. Season to taste with pepper. Gently toss.

3. Transfer to prepared baking dish. Pour milk evenly over mixture. Set aside for about 20 minutes to soak in.

4. Meanwhile, in a bowl, toss together bread crumbs, Grana Padano, melted butter and parsley. Sprinkle evenly over potatoes. Bake in preheated oven for 20 to 25 minutes or until hot and crusty. Serve immediately.

Pommes Boulangerie

The word *boulanger* means baker in French. At a time when not everyone had a home oven, housewives would take dishes to slow-cook in the village baker's big bread ovens. These are so easy to make and go with so many other foods — lamb, chicken, pork, fish — you will make them often. Not only that, they can be made with different varieties of potatoes — floury, large new potatoes or fingerlings.

**Makes
4 servings**

Tip

Don't use a mandoline or the slicing blade of a food processor to slice the potatoes paper thin for this recipe. They need to be a lot thicker. A sharp knife will do.

- **Preheat oven to 350°F (180°C)**
- **11- by 7-inch (2 L) baking dish**

4 cups	chicken broth (approx.)	1 L
2 tbsp	butter, divided	30 mL
1	large onion, thinly sliced	1
2	cloves garlic, finely chopped	2
1 tbsp	chopped fresh thyme leaves	15 mL
1 tbsp	chopped fresh rosemary leaves	15 mL
2 lbs	floury potatoes, peeled and sliced ¼ inch (0.5 mm) thick (see Tip, left)	1 kg
	Salt and freshly ground black pepper	

1. In a saucepan, bring chicken broth to a boil over high heat. Reduce heat to low and simmer. Using half the butter, grease baking dish. Set aside.
2. In a skillet, melt remaining butter over medium heat. Cook onion, stirring, for about 10 minutes or until softened and beginning to color. Stir in garlic, thyme and rosemary and cook, stirring, for 1 to 2 minutes.
3. In prepared baking dish, arrange a third of the potatoes. Season to taste with salt and freshly ground pepper. Top with half of the onion mixture, spreading evenly, and another third of the potatoes. Season to taste with salt and freshly ground pepper. Repeat.
4. Add enough broth to baking dish to barely cover the potatoes (don't add all of it if you don't need it). Bake in preheated oven for 50 to 60 minutes or until potatoes are cooked through and golden brown. Remove from the oven and let stand in pan on a wire rack for 5 minutes before serving.

French Potato Galette

In France the word *galette* has many different meanings. It can refer to a round, flat cake or to a tart, savory or sweet. It is also used to describe a potato dish that consists of ultra-thin slices of potato set in a circular pattern in a heavy skillet, then fried on both sides until the slices meld together and the whole thing resembles one giant potato chip! It makes a wonderful accompaniment to grilled sirloin, or use it as a foundation for pan-seared fillets of salmon or tuna. You can also top it with slices of smoked salmon, drizzled with a bit of crème fraîche or thinned sour cream and sprinkled with chives and capers.

Makes 1 serving

Tips

You have to make these galettes one at a time, so if you plan on making a few, keep them warm in a low oven — though I have to say they really are best just scarfed up as they are made.

I prefer to use sea salt rather than refined table salt because it has a much cleaner, crisper taste.

- **Mandoline or food processor fitted with the slicing blade**
- **Small or medium nonstick skillet or well-seasoned cast-iron pan**

1	large floury potato, peeled	1
1 tbsp	butter, melted	15 mL
1 tbsp	extra virgin olive oil	15 mL
	Salt and freshly ground black pepper	

1. Using a mandoline or food processor fitted with slicing blade, slice potatoes very thinly, about 1/8 inch (3 mm) thick. In a large bowl, combine butter and oil. Add potatoes. Season to taste with salt and freshly ground pepper. Using your hands, toss until potatoes are well coated.

2. In a skillet, working from the center and covering the bottom of the pan, arrange about 12 of the largest potato slices in a spiral, slightly overlapping edges and using smaller slices here and there between the larger ones. Using a metal spatula, gently but firmly press down on galette.

3. Cook over medium-high heat, without disturbing potatoes, for 10 to 12 minutes, until it is crisping slightly around the edges. Using metal spatula, gently lift and loosen edges of potato cake, then shake pan to free bottom (potato slices should adhere in one mass). Flip galette and cook for 6 minutes, until it is golden brown on the underside.

4. Flip once or twice more for a total of 2 minutes or until potato is cooked through, golden brown and very crisp. Season to taste with salt and freshly ground pepper. Serve immediately.

Black Dog Potato Galette with Smoked Cheddar

Since we introduced the customers at our pub to the pleasures of smoked Cheddar in everything from sandwiches and burgers to creamy potato gratins and our version of French onion soup, it has become a permanent fixture in the Black Dog kitchen. It is especially good in this recipe, which features Yukon Gold potatoes.

**Makes
6 servings**

Tips

Use a mandoline or the slicing blade of a food processor to cut thin even, uniform slices.

I prefer to use sea salt rather than refined table salt because it has a much cleaner, crisper taste.

- **Preheat oven to 350°F (180°C)**
- **9-inch (2.5 L) round or square baking dish**

4	large Yukon Gold potatoes, peeled and sliced ⅛ inch (3 mm) thick (see Tips, left)	4
½ cup	butter, melted	125 mL
10 oz	smoked Cheddar cheese, shredded	285 g
	Salt and freshly ground black pepper	

1. In a baking dish, arrange a single layer of potato slices over bottom, slightly overlapping edges. Brush with a quarter of the butter, sprinkle a quarter of the cheese evenly overtop, and sprinkle with salt and pepper. Repeat with remaining butter, cheese and seasonings to make additional layers, ending with a layer of cheese.
2. Cover with buttered foil and bake in preheated oven for 40 to 45 minutes. Uncover and bake for 10 minutes more or until cheese is melted, golden brown and crusty. Remove from oven. Transfer dish to a wire rack and let stand for 10 minutes before serving.

Variation

Try this with other smoked cheeses such as smoked Gouda.

Soufflé Wafer Potatoes

We have the French to thank for these exquisite spuds. Apparently this wonderful dish was created in the 17th century, when Louis XIV's chef tried to salvage some limp *pommes frites* that he had made as part of an elaborate dinner. The King and his entourage arrived late, so the frites got cold and soggy and the chef was horrified. In a mad attempt to revive them, he put the cold potatoes in very hot fat. They puffed up and — *voilà!* — he had created a glorious new way to enjoy potatoes, and probably saved his job in the process. Even though this recipe serves four, I think you should make these for just yourself and someone you love truly, madly, deeply.

**Makes
4 servings**

Tips

The chances of this are slim, but if you happen to have a large quantity of clarified beef fat in your refrigerator, now is the time to use it. Substitute for the oil and enjoy.

The oil should come a little over halfway up the sides of the pot. Do not overfill; leave at least 3 inches (7.5 cm) of headspace at the top.

If you don't have a thermometer, drop a small cube of dry bread into the heated oil; if it floats, the oil is hot enough.

- **Mandoline**
- **Large heavy pot, Dutch oven or deep fryer**
- **Candy/deep-frying thermometer (if not using a deep fryer)**

4	large floury potatoes, peeled	4
	Vegetable oil	
	Salt	

1. Using a mandoline, cut potatoes lengthwise into even slices about $\frac{1}{8}$ inch (3 mm) thick. Trim any square corners from the ends to make long oval shapes. Transfer to a bowl of ice water. Let sliced potatoes stand in cold water for at least 30 minutes or up to 24 hours, sloshing them about a bit to help release the surface starch.

2. Place 4 to 6 inches (10 to 15 cm) oil in a large, heavy pot (see Tips, left). Heat over medium-high heat until thermometer registers 325°F (160°C).

3. Drain potatoes, transfer to a clean tea towel or paper towels and pat dry (they must be completely dry). Carefully add a few slices to the oil and cook for about 4 to 5 minutes, until light brown, using a slotted spoon to move the slices about in the oil as they cook. Using slotted spoon, transfer to paper towels and let cool before the second fry. Repeat with remaining slices.

4. Increase heat until thermometer registers 375°F (190°C). A few at a time, carefully return chips to oil — they should puff up almost immediately — and cook for a second time, stirring constantly, for about 1 minute or until puffed and golden brown. Using slotted spoon, transfer to a baking sheet lined with paper towels and let drain. Repeat with the remaining slices. Season to taste with salt and serve immediately.

Spiced & Baked Sweet Potato Fries

Retain all the flavor and goodness of sweet potatoes by baking them with a little oil and some seasoning. Vary the seasonings to suit your taste, or try steak seasoning or just a bit of chili powder. If you can obtain it, chipotle powder adds a nice smoky heat to the potatoes. Serve with a sour cream or plain yogurt dip to which you have added some fresh chopped chives or green onions.

**Makes
6 servings**

- **Preheat oven to 425°F (220°C)**
- **2 rimmed baking sheets, lined with parchment paper**

6	sweet potatoes, scrubbed if necessary	6
3 tbsp	olive oil	45 mL
2 tbsp	chili powder	30 mL
¼ tsp	cayenne pepper or hot paprika	1 mL
	Salt and freshly ground black pepper	

1. Peel sweet potatoes, if desired. Slice each in half lengthwise, then slice each half lengthwise into four wedges (you'll have eight wedges per potato). In a large bowl or large resealable plastic bag, combine sweet potato wedges, oil, chili powder and cayenne. Season to taste with salt and freshly ground pepper. Toss to coat (or turn and gently squeeze bag).

2. Arrange wedges on prepared baking sheets. Roast in center of preheated oven, tossing once or twice, for 25 minutes.

3. Transfer to top rack of oven and cook for 10 minutes more or until cooked through and crisp. Serve immediately.

Twice-Baked Sweet Potatoes with Apple Crisp Topping

This may sound like a dessert but it is meant to be a unique accompaniment for roast pork or ham. It came to me that sweet potatoes and apples are often featured in Thanksgiving dinners — the sweet potatoes in the form of a casserole, often topped with brown sugar and miniature marshmallows before being baked. And apples appear in the guise of everyone's favorite fall or winter dessert — crunchy apple crisp. It works!

Makes 6 servings

Tips

Choose an apple variety that is not too sweet. Granny Smith, Cortland and Paula Red are all good choices.

Make sure to take time to toast the walnuts for this, stirring in a frying pan over medium heat or in a preheated 350°F (180°C) oven for 6 to 8 minutes. It makes such a difference. Just watch that they don't burn as you are toasting them — when they become fragrant, they're done.

Lining the baking sheet with parchment paper makes cleanup much easier.

- **Rimmed baking sheet, lined with parchment paper (see Tips, left)**
- **Preheat oven to 400°F (200°C)**

6	sweet potatoes, scrubbed	6

Filling

3	apples, peeled, cored and chopped	3
	Finely grated zest of 1 lemon	
4 oz	softened cream cheese	125 g
1 tbsp	butter	15 mL

Topping

½ cup	butter, softened	125 mL
½ cup	packed light brown sugar	125 mL
½ cup	all-purpose flour	125 mL
¼ tsp	ground cinnamon	1 mL
¼ tsp	ground ginger	1 mL
Pinch	ground nutmeg	Pinch
1 cup	walnut halves, toasted and chopped (see Tips, left)	250 mL
6 tbsp	melted butter	90 mL

1. Place sweet potatoes on prepared baking sheet and bake in preheated oven, turning occasionally, for 45 to 60 minutes or until softened.
2. *Filling:* Meanwhile, in a bowl, combine apples, lemon zest, cream cheese and 1 tbsp (15 mL) butter. Using a rubber spatula, blend thoroughly.

3. Reduce oven temperature to 350°F (180°C) and remove sweet potatoes from oven. Set aside until cool enough to handle. Slice open lengthwise along top of each and scoop most of the flesh into the apple mixture (don't scrape the skins clean; leave some of the flesh). Set skins aside. Using a spatula, blend well. Divide mixture evenly among reserved potato skins.

4. *Topping:* In another bowl, combine butter and brown sugar until blended and smooth. Stir in flour, cinnamon, ginger and nutmeg until blended. Stir in walnuts. Evenly spoon over apple mixture and drizzle with melted butter. Bake in oven for about 20 minutes or until topping is crisp.

Variation

Add 6 miniature marshmallows to each portion of filling, or use a few to top the filled sweet potatoes before baking.

Sage Potato Crisps

This is a lovely, simple method of preparing fingerling potatoes — they look so pretty with fresh sage leaves pressed into them. Besides being a nice side dish to accompany roast chicken or other poultry, these make a wonderful accompaniment to glasses of bubbly.

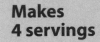

**Makes
4 servings**

Tip

I prefer to use sea salt rather than refined table salt because it has a much cleaner, crisper taste and enhanced mineral content.

- **Preheat oven to 375°F (190°C)**
- **Baking dish, large enough to accommodate 12 fingerling potato halves**

12	fingerling potatoes (about 1 lb/500 g), scrubbed	12
1 tsp	salt	5 mL
24	fresh sage leaves	24
⅓ cup	olive or canola oil	75 mL
	Salt and freshly ground black pepper	

1. Place potatoes in a large saucepan and add boiling water to barely cover. Add salt, cover loosely and bring to a boil over high heat. Reduce heat and cook for 8 to 10 minutes or until potatoes still offer some resistance when pierced with a small knife. Drain well. Set aside until cool enough to handle. Slice in half lengthwise, then press a sage leaf onto cut side of each half.

2. In baking dish, arrange potatoes cut side up and drizzle with oil. Bake in preheated oven for 15 minutes or until cooked through and golden brown. Using tongs, transfer to a plate lined with paper towels. Season to taste with salt and freshly ground pepper. Serve immediately.

Burgermeister Potatoes

This is another old recipe I found among my mum's collection. How could I resist a potato recipe with this great name? Pair these with schnitzel or burgers.

Makes 4 servings

1 lb	floury potatoes, peeled and cut into large chunks	500 g
1 tsp	salt	5 mL
⅓ cup	heavy or whipping (35%) cream	75 mL
5 to 7 tbsp	butter, divided	75 to 105 mL
¼ tsp	ground nutmeg	1 mL
	Salt and freshly ground black pepper	
2	egg yolks, lightly beaten	2
⅓ cup	all-purpose flour	75 mL
¼ cup	chopped flat-leaf parsley leaves	60 mL
2 to 4 tbsp	olive oil, divided	30 to 60 mL
2 to 4 tbsp	butter, divided	30 to 60 mL

1. Place potatoes in a large saucepan and add cold water to barely cover. Add salt, cover loosely and bring to a boil over high heat. Reduce heat and cook for 20 minutes or until potatoes are tender. Drain well.

2. Return potatoes to saucepan over very low heat. Using a potato masher, mash in cream, 3 tbsp (45 mL) butter and the nutmeg. Season to taste with salt and freshly ground pepper. Stir in egg yolks and flour to blend. Stir in parsley. Set aside until cool enough to handle.

3. Using lightly floured hands, shape potato mixture into small patties.

4. In a large frying pan, melt 2 tbsp (30 mL) each of the oil and butter over medium heat. In batches, cook patties, adding more oil and butter as necessary, for 2 to 3 minutes per side or until golden brown. Serve immediately.

Variation

Make the patties bite-sized and use them as a base for hors d'oeuvres, with toppings such as smoked salmon or Brie and cherry tomatoes.

Potato Skin Poutine

As a child I could never understand why anyone would eat a baked potato and leave the skin — the best part! So when potato skins became popular in pubs and diners, I couldn't have been happier. However, more often than not they are a disappointment — soggy or deep-fried and unappealing. The following recipe produces potato skins that are neither of those things. They are baked until crackling on the outside with a fluffy interior, which is scooped out, blended with a bit of bacon and green onion and topped with poutine's bedmates, cheese curds and gravy. Good enough to side with a serious steak any day.

Makes 4 servings

Tips

Pat scrubbed potatoes dry with a clean tea towel or paper towels; if potatoes still seem damp, let them air-dry for about 10 minutes.

You can cheat a little here and use packaged or canned beef gravy if you like, but it doesn't take long to make this from-scratch version.

Boursin is the perfect cream cheese for this filling.

- **Preheat oven to 375°F (190°C)**
- **Baking dish, large enough to accommodate 4 potatoes**

4	large floury potatoes, scrubbed and thoroughly dried (see Tips, left)	4
¼ cup	olive oil	60 mL
	Coarse salt	

Filling

6 oz	softened herb and garlic cream cheese	175 g
½ cup	sour cream	125 mL
¼ cup	milk	60 mL
8	slices bacon, cooked and crumbled	8
4	slender green onions (white parts with a bit of green), trimmed and finely chopped	4

Gravy

2 tbsp	butter	30 mL
2 tbsp	all-purpose flour	30 mL
1½ cups	beef broth	375 mL
1 tbsp	Worcestershire sauce	15 mL
8 oz	white cheese curds	250 g

1. Using the tines of a fork, prick each potato a few times, then rub each with 1 tbsp (15 mL) oil and a little coarse salt. Place potatoes directly on oven rack and bake in preheated oven for 1½ to 2 hours or until flesh is tender and skin is super-crisp.

2. *Filling:* In a bowl, combine cream cheese, sour cream and milk and blend until smooth. Stir in bacon and green onions. Set aside.

3. *Gravy:* In a skillet, melt butter over medium-high heat. Whisk in flour and cook, whisking to prevent lumps, for about 6 minutes or until browned (not too dark). Add broth in a thin stream, whisking to blend. Whisk in Worcestershire sauce. Bring to a gentle boil, reduce heat to very low and simmer, stirring occasionally, until thickened.

4. Reduce oven temperature to 350°F (180°C). Transfer potatoes to a cutting board and set aside until cool enough to handle. Slice in half lengthwise and scoop out most of the flesh, adding to bowl with cheese mixture (leave some flesh on the skins). Set skins aside.

5. Using a spatula, blend potato flesh into cheese mixture. Evenly divide among potato skins. Transfer to a baking dish and bake for 10 minutes or until heated through.

6. Remove potatoes from oven (do not turn oven off). Ladle a generous spoonful of gravy over each and top with a quarter of the cheese curds. Bake for about 10 minutes or until curds have melted. Serve with remaining gravy on the side.

Pommes de Terre Lorette

This delightful recipe is actually two in one. Duchesse potatoes are made first; these are sort of fortified mashed potatoes, blended with egg and butter (great just on their own and especially when piped round the edges of a dish such as coquilles St. Jacques). Then we make a portion of pâte à choux, France's easy-to-make pastry dough, and the two are combined to make what may be the most elegant fried spuds anywhere. Pommes de Terre Lorette may remind you visually of potato puffs, but the real thing has a much finer pedigree.

Makes 4 to 6 servings

Tips

Don't hesitate to make these because you fear pastry making. No other pastry is as easy to make as pâte à choux.

The oil should come a little over halfway up the sides of the pot. Do not overfill; leave at least 3 inches (7.5 cm) of headspace at the top.

If you don't have a thermometer, drop a small cube of dry bread into the oil; if it floats, the oil is hot enough.

- Potato ricer, food mill or sieve
- Large heavy pot, Dutch oven or deep fryer
- Candy/deep-frying thermometer (if not using a deep fryer; see Tips, left)
- Pastry bag (optional)

2 lbs	floury potatoes, peeled and quartered	1 kg
1 tsp	salt	5 mL

Pâte à Choux

1 cup	water	250 mL
¼ cup	butter	60 mL
¼ tsp	salt	1 mL
⅛ tsp	ground nutmeg	0.5 mL
1 cup	all-purpose flour	250 mL
5	eggs	5
4 cups	vegetable oil	1 L

1. Place potatoes in a large saucepan and add cold water to barely cover. Add salt, cover loosely and bring to a boil over high heat. Reduce heat and cook for 30 minutes or until potatoes are quite soft. Drain well. Return potatoes to saucepan over very low heat and shake the pot back and forth to remove any trace of moisture. Transfer to a potato ricer and press into a bowl. Set aside.

2. *Pâte à Choux:* In a heavy saucepan, combine water, butter, salt and nutmeg over high heat and bring to a boil. Reduce heat to medium and, using a wooden spoon, beat in flour all at once, beating for 1 to 2 minutes or until mixture pulls away from sides of pan. Remove from heat. Let cool for 2 to 3 minutes. One at a time, using a wooden spoon or an electric mixer on medium speed, beat in eggs, beating well after each addition to incorporate.

3. Place 4 to 6 inches (10 to 15 cm) oil in a large, heavy pot (see Tips, page 262). Heat over medium-high heat until thermometer registers 375°F (190°C). (If you're using a deep fryer, follow the manufacturer's instructions.) Preheat oven to 140°F (60°C).

4. Stir reserved potatoes into pâte à choux until blended. Using moistened hands, pull off a portion of dough and shape into a short (1 inch/2.5 cm) log or a small egg shape, as desired. Repeat until all dough has been shaped. (Alternatively, transfer dough to a pastry bag and pipe the dough, snipping off appropriate lengths with scissors as it emerges.)

5. Using a slotted spoon, transfer shaped dough to oil in batches and cook, turning occasionally, for 2 to 3 minutes or until golden brown all over. Using slotted spoon, transfer to a baking sheet lined with paper towels as completed. Place in oven to keep warm as you work. Serve hot.

Potato, Parsnip & Onion Patties

Sumptuous mashed potato (leftover or freshly made) paired with the sweet nuttiness of parsnips and onion makes a harmonious trio. This is particularly good as a side dish to baked ham. When made a little smaller, these patties can be used as a vehicle for many good things — a bit of smoked salmon or trout blended with crème fraîche, slices of spicy sausage or a combination of salsa and melting Brie.

Makes 4 to 6 servings

Tips

Japanese panko bread crumbs are now widely available in supermarkets and can be put to good use here. If you use them in place of regular dry bread crumbs, increase the amount to about 1 cup (250 mL).

Dry mash simply means mashing without butter, milk or cream.

2 tbsp	butter	30 mL
1	onion, finely chopped	1
3	floury potatoes, peeled, cooked and dry mashed (see Tips, left)	3
3	large parsnips, peeled, cooked and dry mashed	3
2	eggs, lightly beaten	2
1/4 cup	all-purpose flour (approx.)	60 mL
Pinch	ground nutmeg	Pinch
	Salt and freshly ground black pepper	
1/2 cup	dry bread crumbs (see Tip, left)	125 mL
1/2 cup	vegetable oil (approx.)	125 mL

1. In a small skillet, melt butter over medium-high heat. Sauté onion for about 5 minutes or until softened.

2. In a large bowl, combine mashed potatoes and parsnips. Add onion, scraping in any bits from sides and bottom of pan. Stir in eggs, about half the flour and the nutmeg. Season to taste with salt and freshly ground pepper. Stir well, adding more flour as necessary, until mixture holds together enough to shape into cakes. Using your hands, shape dough into patties about 1/2 inch (1 cm) thick. Place bread crumbs in a small bowl. One at a time, dredge patties in bread crumbs to lightly coat.

3. In a skillet, heat oil over medium heat. In batches, cook patties, turning once, for 3 to 4 minutes per side or until golden and crisp. Transfer to a plate lined with paper towels. Keep warm until ready to serve.

Paper Bag Potatoes

This recipe is an example of cooking *en papillote*, a method whereby food is cooked in a parchment paper pouch. The steam created inside the parcel helps to cook the food, the flavors are sealed in and, when the paper is slit open at the table, wonderfully fragrant aromas are released. This method is a great treatment for small new potatoes, as their delightful flavor is kept intact. Paper Bag Potatoes are a lovely choice to serve with young lamb and the first asparagus or fiddleheads of the season.

Makes 4 to 6 servings

Tips

If you prefer, use a sturdy brown paper bag to prepare these spuds, folding over the end twice to seal the packet. If you find it easier to work with, foil also makes a great package, but make sure to oil it first. You can also make individual packages if you wish.

If the potatoes are mini-sized they may be left whole.

- Preheat oven to 350°F (180°C)
- Rimmed baking sheet
- Parchment paper

3 lbs	small new potatoes (about 12), scrubbed and thickly sliced (see Tips, left)	1.5 kg
6	shallots, quartered	6
3 tbsp	chopped fresh mint leaves	45 mL
3 tbsp	chopped flat-leaf parsley leaves	45 mL
2 tsp	salt	10 mL
1 tsp	freshly ground black pepper	5 mL
¼ cup	butter, diced	60 mL

1. Cut a length of parchment paper about twice as long as the baking sheet, then center paper on sheet. Arrange potatoes on paper, leaving enough of a border to provide a good fold. Evenly scatter with shallots, mint and parsley. Sprinkle with salt and freshly ground pepper and dot with butter. Loosely fold the parchment in thirds, bringing the two short sides together on top, and fold 2 or 3 times to make a seal. Fold up the edges twice to seal as well.

2. Bake in preheated oven for 45 minutes. Carefully transfer package to a large serving platter. Slit open at the table (being careful to avoid the very hot escaping steam) and serve.

Potato Noodles

These rustic noodles have great Old World flavor and style. They are absolutely wonderful with any stew or with sauced preparations, such as meatballs in a sour cream sauce. They are also delicious just tossed with chopped parsley and served with crisp pan-fried meats such as schnitzel.

Makes 4 to 6 servings

Tip
Cook the potatoes the day before you intend to make the noodles.

- **Large cast-iron or heavy skillet**

6	large floury potatoes, scrubbed and halved	6
4 tsp	salt, divided	20 mL
1	egg	1
1	egg yolk	1
2 to 3 cups	all-purpose flour	500 to 750 mL
⅓ cup	butter	75 mL

1. Place potatoes in a large saucepan and add cold water to barely cover. Add 1 tsp (5 mL) salt, cover loosely and bring to a boil over high heat. Reduce heat and cook for 20 minutes or until potatoes are tender. Drain well. Set aside until cool enough to handle. With a paring knife, peel off skins. Return potatoes to saucepan over very low heat and shake the pot back and forth to remove any trace of moisture. Using a potato masher, mash. Set aside to cool. Transfer to a large bowl, cover with plastic wrap and refrigerate until ready to use, for at least 1 hour or overnight.

2. Bring potatoes to room temperature if necessary. Using a wooden spoon, stir in egg, egg yolk and remaining 1 tbsp (15 mL) salt to blend. Stir in flour a little at a time until mixture forms a smooth dough that can be handled and kneaded without sticking (you may not need to use all the flour).

3. On a lightly floured surface, shape dough into a ball and divide in half. Roll out each ball of dough to a thickness of about ½ inch (1 cm). Slice the dough into lengthwise strips 1 inch (2.5 cm) wide and about 1½ inches (4 cm) long. Repeat with remaining dough.

4. In a cast-iron skillet, melt butter. Cook noodles, stirring frequently, for 10 to 12 minutes or until beginning to get golden brown all over. Serve immediately.

Spud & Onion Stuffing

Perfect for a turkey, this stuffing is very easy to make. You can also use this moist, flavorful stuffing with boneless pork loin, a chicken or a whole chicken breast. A friend of mine uses it to fill large portobello mushroom caps before baking. Very easy and very good, this may make more than you need (see Tips, below).

Makes enough stuffing for a 12-lb (5.5 kg) turkey

Tips

If the stuffing mixture looks too dry, add a little more melted butter or a drizzle or two of good olive oil.

The stuffing may be covered and kept in the refrigerator to use the following day. If you are stuffing something smaller than a turkey and have extra, shape any remaining stuffing into balls the size of golf balls and freeze in resealable bags to use another time. Or fry it up in a skillet with a little butter and serve at breakfast or brunch with eggs and bacon or sausage. No need for toast!

5 cups	hot Classic Mash Deluxe (page 50)	1.25 L
2	eggs, lightly beaten	2
½ cup	butter	125 mL
1 cup	chopped onion	250 mL
1 cup	chopped celery	250 mL
6 cups	dry bread cubes	1.5 L
½ cup	chopped fresh chives	125 mL
½ cup	chopped flat-leaf parsley leaves	125 mL
2 tsp	salt	10 mL
2 tsp	freshly ground black pepper	10 mL

1. In a bowl large enough to accommodate the dressing, combine potato and eggs. Mix well.
2. In a skillet, melt butter over medium-high heat. Sauté onion and celery for about 10 minutes or until softened. Let cool slightly. Add to potato mixture. Add bread cubes, chives, parsley, salt and pepper and mix well (for best results, use your hands). Set aside to cool before stuffing turkey.

Sweet Potato, Apple & Sausage Stuffing

This terrific stuffing combines sweet potato with sausage and other traditional stuffing ingredients. It's a perfect recipe for anyone who likes to serve sweet potatoes with turkey but wonders how to fit both in the oven at the same time. Try this stuffing with butterflied pork tenderloin, in chicken or as a filling for portobello mushroom caps.

Makes enough stuffing for a 10- to 12-lb (4.5 to 5.5 kg) turkey

Tips

You'll need two large sweet potatoes for this recipe. You can peel them, cut into chunks and cook in boiling salted water until tender or, for more intense flavor, prick all over with the tines of a fork and roast in a 400°F (200°C) oven for about an hour.

Buy bulk sausage meat or use plain pork sausage — slit down the middle and remove meat from casings, discarding casings.

If the stuffing seems too wet, add about ½ cup (125 mL) more bread cubes. If it seems too dry, add orange juice, a little at a time, until it reaches the desired consistency.

Let the stuffing cool completely before using.

½ cup	butter	125 mL
2	stalks celery, finely chopped	2
1	onion, finely chopped	1
1	large Granny Smith apple, peeled, cored and finely chopped	1
4 cups	hot cooked and mashed sweet potatoes (see Tips, left)	1 L
2 cups	dry bread cubes, about ½ inch (1 cm)	500 mL
3 tbsp	chopped flat-leaf parsley leaves	45 mL
1 tbsp	dried sage	15 mL
1 tbsp	dried thyme	15 mL
	Salt and freshly ground black pepper	
1	egg, lightly beaten	1
8 oz	sausage meat (see Tips, left)	250 g

1. In a large skillet, melt butter over medium heat. Cook celery and onion, stirring, for about 10 minutes or until softened. Remove from heat. Let cool and transfer to a large bowl.

2. Stir apple, sweet potato, bread cubes, parsley, sage and thyme into celery mixture. Season to taste with salt and freshly ground pepper. Add egg and sausage and mix well (for best results, use your hands). Set aside to cool completely before using to stuff poultry or meat (if stuffing vegetables, you don't need to wait until it is cool).

Main Courses with Meat, Poultry, Fish & Seafood

For some, it simply isn't dinner — or supper, brunch or even lunch — without potatoes, and that's not a claim that many (if any) other foods can make. This chapter is devoted to potatoes that really strut their stuff when teamed with beef, lamb, pork, chicken and all manner of fish and seafood. These are potatoes that work hard to make these splendid dishes what they are — wonderful and interchangeable main courses that you will turn to again and again.

Beef & Wild Mushrooms in Stout with Champ

In Belgium and France they would call this rich beef stew cooked in beer a carbonnade. It would probably be accompanied by good crusty bread and butter. My Irish roots demand mashed potatoes with green onions and butter, and that's called champ.

Makes 4 servings

Tips

Any assortment of mushrooms may be used here.

This stew is even better the next day.

- **Large, heavy pot or Dutch oven**

Carbonnade

2 lbs	lean stewing beef, cut into chunks and patted dry	1 kg
	Salt and freshly ground black pepper	
2 tbsp	olive oil	30 mL
1	large onion, chopped	1
3 tbsp	packed brown sugar	45 mL
2 tbsp	all-purpose flour	30 mL
2 cups	hot beef broth	500 mL
1½ cups	stout (dark beer)	375 mL
2 tbsp	red wine vinegar	30 mL
2	bay leaves	2
1 tbsp	butter	15 mL
4	strips bacon, diced	4
4 oz	wild mushrooms, trimmed and sliced	125 g
1	large Spanish onion, chopped	1

Champ

2 lbs	floury potatoes, peeled	1 kg
1 tsp	salt	5 mL
⅔ cup	whole milk	150 mL
4	green onions, finely chopped	4
3 tbsp	butter (approx.)	45 mL
¼ cup	finely chopped flat-leaf parsley leaves	60 mL

1. *Carbonnade:* Season beef to taste with salt and freshly ground pepper. In a large, heavy pot, heat oil over medium-high heat. Add beef and sear all over, turning with tongs. Transfer to a plate and set aside.

2. Add onion and sauté for about 10 minutes or until beginning to soften. Stir in brown sugar and sauté for about 10 minutes or until mixture is beginning to brown. Stir in flour until blended. Stir in beef broth and stout and bring to a boil. Cook, stirring, for about 10 minutes. Stir in vinegar and bay leaves. Season to taste with salt and freshly ground pepper. Reduce heat to medium and return beef and any accumulated juices back to pot. Reduce heat, cover and gently simmer for 1½ to 2 hours or until beef is tender.

3. In a skillet, melt butter over medium heat. Cook bacon, mushrooms and onion, stirring, for about 12 minutes or until bacon is cooked and vegetables are softened. Drain off fat and transfer bacon mixture to beef mixture, stirring to combine. Reduce heat to very low, cover and keep warm.

4. *Champ:* Cut potatoes into uniform chunks. Place potatoes in a large saucepan and add cold water to barely cover. Add salt, cover loosely and bring to a boil over high heat. Reduce heat and cook for 20 minutes or until potatoes are tender.

5. Meanwhile, in a small saucepan over medium heat, warm milk. Stir in green onions and bring just to a gentle boil. Reduce heat and simmer for about 15 minutes or until onions are tender and flavors have infused.

6. Drain potatoes well. Return to saucepan over very low heat and shake the pot back and forth to remove any trace of moisture. Using a potato masher, mash in butter. Mash in milk mixture until smooth.

7. Mound a quarter of the champ on each of four warmed individual shallow soup plates, making a little well in the center. Add a small knob of butter to melt. Spoon a quarter of the carbonnade alongside. Sprinkle with parsley and serve immediately.

Short Ribs of Beef with Soaked Spuds

Short ribs of beef, slowly cooked until the meat is fork-tender, make one of the most satisfying of dishes. These are always on our winter menu at the Black Dog. This dish is chock full of old-fashioned flavors. Potato halves form a bed for the beef, soaking up the lovely rich essence of the meat as it cooks.

Makes 4 servings

Tips

Make sure to wash leeks thoroughly by slitting them open lengthwise and spreading them apart while rinsing clean under cold running water.

Be sure to start preparing this dish at least the night before you intend to serve it.

Ask the butcher to keep the short ribs in pairs and cut them into pieces that are 2 inches (5 cm) long. Before you marinate them, trim as much fat from the ribs as possible; otherwise your sauce will be too fatty.

While red-skinned potatoes are specified because they take on such a nice quality after being soaked with the meat juices, any potatoes can be used, with the exception of very small ones.

- **Large, heavy pot or Dutch oven**

3 lbs	beef short ribs, 2 inches (5 cm) long	1.5 kg
2	large onions, quartered	2
3 cups	dark beer or red wine	750 mL
1 tsp	salt	5 mL
1 tsp	freshly ground black pepper	5 mL
6	sprigs fresh flat-leaf parsley	6
2	sprigs fresh rosemary	2
2	sprigs fresh thyme	2
1	bay leaf	1
1	leek, trimmed and halved (see Tips, left)	1
	Salt and freshly ground black pepper	
2 tbsp	butter	30 mL
2 tbsp	olive oil	30 mL
3 cups	beef broth	750 mL
2 lbs	red-skinned potatoes, scrubbed and halved	1 kg
¼ cup	chopped flat-leaf parsley leaves	60 mL

1. In a large bowl, combine ribs, onions, beer, salt and pepper. Using kitchen string, tie parsley, rosemary, thyme, bay leaf and leek together into a bouquet garni and tuck well down into rib mixture. Mix well (use your hands if necessary). Cover and refrigerate for at least 6 hours or up to overnight, turning once or twice to ensure that the ingredients are submerged in the liquid.

2. When you're ready to cook, preheat oven to 350°F (180°C). Reserving marinade, remove ribs and pat dry with paper towels. Season to taste with additional salt and freshly ground pepper.

3. In a large, heavy pot, heat butter and oil over medium heat. Sear ribs all over, using tongs to turn once or twice, for about 12 minutes or until lightly browned. Transfer to a platter as completed. Drain off all but 2 tbsp (30 mL) fat.

4. Add reserved marinade with bouquet garni to pot, scrape up any brown bits from bottom, and cook for about 10 minutes or until thickened and reduced by half. Stir in beef broth and return to a boil. Tuck ribs down into liquid (they should be almost covered), adding more beef broth if necessary. Cover, transfer to preheated oven and cook for 1 hour. Uncover and, using tongs, turn ribs over in liquid. Cover and cook, stirring occasionally, for another hour.

5. Using tongs, carefully transfer ribs to a platter, then remove and discard bouquet garni. Place potato halves, cut side down, on bottom of pot. Arrange ribs over potatoes and, if necessary, add a little more beef broth. Cover and cook for 1 hour or until meat and potatoes are tender. Remove from oven.

6. Using tongs, transfer ribs and potatoes to a platter and keep warm. Using a fine-mesh sieve, strain cooking liquid into a saucepan, pressing against solids to extract as much flavor as possible and scraping underside of the sieve into pot.

7. If sauce needs thickening, bring to a boil over medium-high heat and simmer for 1 to 2 minutes. If not, let it sit for a few minutes, then skim off some of the fat that rises to the surface. Season to taste with additional salt and freshly ground pepper, if necessary.

8. Divide ribs and potatoes evenly among four warmed wide, shallow individual serving bowls. Pour sauce over all. Sprinkle with parsley and serve immediately.

Char-Grilled Rib-Eye of Beef with Gratin Dauphinoise

Here is the recipe to impress that important person in your life. It is specifically designed for two beef-and-potato-lovers to enjoy — although, having said that, it wouldn't be difficult to increase the quantity. This is nice with a peppery salad of watercress or some steamed green beans. And don't forget the horseradish!

Makes 2 servings

Tips

If you prefer, use an indoor grill or a cast-iron grill pan to cook the steak. Preheat indoor grill or grill pan to high before adding steak. Whether you are barbecuing or indoor grilling, lightly grease the grill with a little olive oil before placing the beef on it.

Use a mandoline or food processor fitted with a slicing blade to cut potatoes into very thin, uniform slices.

A boneless rib-eye makes for easier carving than one that still has the ribs attached.

Start by making the potato gratin — this method is the easiest yet.

- Preheat oven to 375°F (190°C)
- 6-cup (1.5 L) baking dish, lightly buttered
- Preheat barbecue to high (see Tips, left)

2 cups	heavy or whipping (35%) cream	500 mL
3	cloves garlic, crushed	3
¼ tsp	ground nutmeg	1 mL
	Salt and freshly ground black pepper	
3	large all-purpose potatoes, peeled and thinly sliced (see Tips, left)	3
1 tsp	Dijon mustard	5 mL
1 tsp	grainy mustard	5 mL
4	large shallots, finely chopped	4
1 cup	port	250 mL
1 cup	Madeira	250 mL
2 lbs	boneless beef rib-eye, brought to room temperature and patted dry	1 kg
1 cup	beef broth	250 mL
2 tbsp	unsalted butter	30 mL
1 tbsp	Worcestershire sauce	15 mL

1. In a large, heavy saucepan, combine cream, garlic and nutmeg over medium heat. Season to taste with salt and freshly ground pepper. Whisking constantly, bring to a boil. Stir in potatoes to coat. Transfer to prepared dish and bake in preheated oven for about 40 minutes or until potatoes are tender and top is golden brown. Remove from oven, cover with foil and keep warm.

2. Meanwhile, in a small bowl, whisk together Dijon and grainy mustards and set aside. In a small saucepan, combine shallots, port and Madeira and bring to a boil over high heat. Boil rapidly until liquid has evaporated. Remove from heat.

3. Season beef to taste with salt and freshly ground pepper and place on preheated barbecue. Cook, turning, for 15 minutes per side or until medium rare. Remove from grill and immediately slather with mustard mixture, then shallots. Set aside to rest.

4. In a small saucepan, heat beef broth over high heat. Whisk in butter and Worcestershire sauce and bring to a boil. Reduce heat and simmer while you carve the beef.

5. Evenly divide potato gratin between two warmed dinner plates. Slice beef thinly and overlap slices alongside potatoes. Spoon butter sauce around edge and serve immediately.

Braised Oxtails with Potato Gnocchi

The lowly oxtail is a much-neglected cut of beef. However, that may change as the nose-to-tail philosophy of eating is popularized by chefs and social-minded carnivores. No rushing is involved where the cooking of oxtail is concerned — it's slow food at its very best. This is a very hefty main course, just the thing for a cold wintry evening.

Makes 4 to 6 servings

Tips

Ask the butcher to cut the oxtails for you if they don't come precut.

Make sure to wash the leeks thoroughly by slitting them open lengthwise and spreading them apart while rinsing clean under cold running water.

Plan to make this the day before you want to serve it.

- **Large, heavy pot or Dutch oven**

4 lbs	oxtails, trimmed of excess fat and cut into 2-inch (5 cm) pieces	2 kg
	Salt and freshly ground black pepper	
3 tbsp	all-purpose flour	45 mL
½ cup	olive oil	125 mL
1	onion, chopped	1
2	leeks, trimmed and chopped (see Tips, left)	2
2	carrots, peeled and chopped	2
2	cloves garlic, chopped	2
2	plum tomatoes, diced	2
3 cups	dry red wine (approx.)	750 mL
2 cups	water (approx.)	500 mL
3 tbsp	butter, divided	45 mL
1	recipe Potato Gnocchi (page 188)	1
3 tbsp	chopped flat-leaf parsley leaves	45 mL

1. In a large bowl, cover oxtails with cold water. Set aside to soak at room temperature (or refrigerate, if kitchen is very warm) for 2 hours. Drain and rinse under cold running water, then thoroughly pat dry. Sprinkle all over with salt and freshly ground pepper. Place flour in a large resealable plastic bag, add oxtails and shake until lightly coated, shaking off excess flour.

2. In a large, heavy pot, heat oil over medium heat. Add oxtails and cook, turning often, until browned all over, about 15 minutes. Using tongs, transfer oxtails to a bowl and set aside. To the same pot, add onion, leeks, carrots and garlic. Cook, stirring, for about 6 minutes, until softened. Add tomatoes and stir into mixture.

3. Return oxtails to pot, including any accumulated juices. Add wine and water, increase heat to high and boil gently for 3 minutes. Reduce heat, cover loosely and simmer, checking occasionally to ensure the liquid is not evaporating too quickly, for 4 to 5 hours or until oxtails offer no resistance when pierced with the tip of a thin knife. (The cooking liquid should have thickened slightly; if mixture begins to look too dry, add a little more wine or water.)

4. Using a slotted spoon, transfer oxtails to a large platter, reserving cooking liquid. Set aside until cool enough to handle. Pull meat from bones carefully, discarding small bones, cartilage and vegetables. Coarsely chop meat and transfer to a bowl. Cover with plastic wrap and refrigerate.

5. Set a fine-mesh sieve over a large bowl. Strain cooking liquid through sieve and discard solids. Let liquid cool, cover with plastic wrap and refrigerate for at least 4 hours or up to 12 hours.

6. When you're ready to serve, remove and discard solidified fat from surface of cooking liquid (it will be quite easy to remove). In a large saucepan, bring cooking liquid to a gentle boil over medium-high heat. Season to taste with salt and freshly ground pepper. Reduce heat to medium and cook for about 15 minutes or until slightly thickened and sauce-like. Whisk in 1 tbsp (15 mL) butter, then stir in oxtail meat and simmer until heated through.

7. Meanwhile, prepare Potato Gnocchi. Divide cooked gnocchi among four to six warmed individual pasta bowls. Generously top each with braised oxtail and sauce. Sprinkle with parsley and serve immediately.

Malone's Dublin Coddle

Ask any number of Dubliners how to make a traditional coddle and you will receive different impassioned responses. A "feed of coddle" is dear to the hearts of Dubliners, invoking much the same emotions as Irish stew. Traditionally it is a combination of big floury potatoes, onions, bacon and sausages in a heavy pot with lots of freshly ground black pepper. This is set to cook slowly for about an hour, at which point the coddle (*coddle* means to cook slowly) receives a handful of chopped parsley before being served with soda bread and butter. The following recipe is not traditional, as I have included a piece of corned beef brisket, which makes it more North American Irish, I guess. And instead of the potatoes being on the bottom, they are mashed and spooned around the finished coddle. Serve with buttered cabbage, and don't forget the soda bread. Reserve this for St. Patrick's Day celebrations when you plan on feeding a crowd.

Makes 8 to 10 servings

Tips

Corned beef brisket is beef that has been cured in salt brine, usually with additional pickling spices; it is generally available in supermarkets. It is uncooked, unlike the corned or smoked beef you buy at the deli counter, and it requires long, slow cooking, making it ideal for a coddle.

Choose large pork sausages such as English-style breakfast "bangers" for this recipe.

If you wish to serve this in individual dishes, spoon the mashed potatoes into soup plates, then arrange the meat and vegetables on top.

Leftover cooking liquid can be used for making soup or cooking beans.

- **Large, heavy pot or Dutch oven**

2 lbs	corned beef brisket (see Tips, left)	1 kg
1	piece back (Canadian) bacon (about 2 lbs/1 kg)	1
2	bay leaves	2
2	sprigs fresh thyme	2
1 tbsp	whole peppercorns	15 mL
1 lb	pork sausages (see Tips, left)	500 g
4	carrots, peeled and coarsely chopped	4
2 lbs	floury potatoes, peeled	1 kg
4	stalks celery, trimmed and coarsely chopped	4
4	small onions, quartered	4
¼ cup	butter	60 mL
½ cup	half-and-half (10%) cream	125 mL
½ cup	chopped flat-leaf parsley leaves	125 mL
3 tbsp	chopped chives	45 mL

1. Place corned beef and bacon in a large, heavy pot and add cold water just to cover. Add bay leaves, thyme and peppercorns. Cover and bring to a boil over high heat. Cover loosely, reduce heat and simmer, regularly skimming foam from surface, for about 90 minutes or until meat is tender. Add sausages and carrots, pushing into the liquid around the meat, and cook for 10 minutes, adding a little hot water if the level has reduced a great deal (you should be able to submerge the vegetables).

2. Add potatoes, celery and onions and cook for 15 to 20 minutes or until vegetables are tender, again adding hot water if needed. Using a slotted spoon, transfer potatoes to a bowl, cover with a clean tea towel and keep warm. Using slotted spoon, transfer remaining vegetables to the center of a warmed large platter and keep warm. Using tongs, transfer beef and bacon to a cutting board and slice thickly. Arrange over vegetables and keep warm.

3. Using a potato masher, mash butter into potatoes. Mash cream into potatoes, followed by parsley and chives. Using a wooden spoon, briskly stir mashed potatoes until smooth. Spoon potatoes around meat and vegetables on platter. Ladle a little cooking liquid over all, if desired. Serve immediately.

Pastel de Papas

Think of this as a Latin American shepherd's pie. *Pastel* is the lovely word for pie and *papas* is the word for potatoes in Chile, where this beef and potato pie is almost a national way of life. Traditionally the filling includes quartered hard-boiled eggs, but I prefer my boiled eggs at breakfast with toast soldiers, so I have omitted them and instead added a few stuffed green olives to the requisite black ones. Also traditional is the ritual bit of sugar added to the surface of the crust.

Makes 4 to 6 servings

Tip

I prefer to use sea salt rather than refined table salt because it has a much cleaner, crisper taste and enhanced mineral content.

- **8-cup (2 L) round baking or soufflé dish, lightly buttered**
- **Preheat oven to 350°F (180°C)**

Potatoes

3 lbs	floury potatoes, peeled and cut into chunks	1.5 kg
1 tsp	salt	5 mL
2 tbsp	butter	30 mL
½ cup	whole milk	125 mL
1 tsp	ground nutmeg	5 mL
	Freshly ground black pepper	

Filling

2 tbsp	olive oil	30 mL
2	cloves garlic, finely chopped	2
2	onions, finely chopped	2
1½ lbs	lean ground beef	750 g
½ cup	seedless black raisins, soaked in warm water and drained	125 mL
½ cup	pitted black olives	125 mL
½ cup	pimento-stuffed or pitted manzanilla olives	125 mL
1 tbsp	sweet paprika	15 mL
1 tsp	ground cumin	5 mL
	Salt and freshly ground black pepper	
2 tsp	granulated sugar (optional)	10 mL

1. *Potatoes:* Place potatoes in a large saucepan and add cold water to barely cover. Add salt, cover loosely and bring to a boil over high heat. Reduce heat and cook for 20 minutes or until tender.

2. Drain potatoes well. Return to saucepan over very low heat and shake the pot back and forth to remove any trace of moisture. Using a potato masher, mash potatoes. Mash in butter, then milk. Add nutmeg and season to taste with salt and freshly ground pepper. Using a wooden spoon, stir potatoes briskly until they are smooth and hold their shape. Set aside.

3. *Filling:* Meanwhile, in a large skillet, warm oil over medium heat. Cook garlic and onions, stirring, for about 6 minutes or until softened. Add beef and cook, breaking up with a spoon, for about 10 minutes or until no longer pink. Add raisins, black and manzanilla olives, paprika and cumin and stir well. Season to taste with salt and freshly ground pepper. Cover and remove from heat.

4. In prepared baking dish, spread a thick (1 inch/2.5 cm) layer of mashed potatoes on bottom and up sides to within 1/2 inch (1 cm) of the rim. Carefully transfer beef, pan juices and any crispy bits clinging to bottom of skillet into center of dish. Top with remaining mashed potatoes, shaping into a slight dome. Sprinkle evenly with sugar, if using. Bake in preheated oven for about 30 minutes or until pie is hot in the center (check with a small knife blade) and potato is golden brown and crusty on the peaks. Serve in baking dish at the table.

Cottage Pie for Mac

I made this pie for my dear 94-year-old father-in-law, Arnold McIntosh, one Boxing Day. It was wonderful to see how much he enjoyed it (we all agreed it was rather good). Cottage pie is what most people think of as shepherd's pie, and they are similar. But tradition dictates that shepherd's pie is made with ground or leftover lamb, while cottage pie is always beef based.

Makes 6 servings

Tip
Make the mashed potatoes while the beef mixture is simmering.

- **11- by 7-inch (2 L) baking dish**

¼ cup	olive oil, divided	60 mL
2 lbs	lean ground beef	1 kg
	Salt and freshly ground black pepper	
3	onions, finely chopped	3
2	cloves garlic, finely chopped	2
4	sprigs fresh thyme	4
2	plum tomatoes, chopped	2
2 tbsp	tomato paste	30 mL
1⅓ cups	dark beer, such as Guinness	325 mL
5 tbsp	Worcestershire sauce	75 mL
1¼ cups	beef broth	300 mL

Topping

2 lbs	floury potatoes, peeled and quartered	1 kg
1 tsp	salt	5 mL
¼ cup	butter	60 mL
¼ cup + 3 tbsp	shredded sharp (aged) Cheddar cheese	95 mL
1	large egg yolk	1

1. In a large skillet, warm 2 tbsp (30 mL) oil over high heat. Add beef and season to taste with salt and freshly ground pepper. Cook, stirring and breaking up meat, for 15 minutes or until uniformly brown and no hint of pink remains. Set a large sieve or colander over a bowl. Add beef and drain off fat. Set beef aside and discard fat.

2. Return skillet to medium high-heat and add remaining 2 tbsp (30 mL) oil. Sauté onions, garlic and thyme for about 8 minutes or until onions are softened and beginning to color. Stir in beef, tomatoes and tomato paste and cook for about 5 minutes or until well blended. Stir in beer and Worcestershire sauce and bring to a boil. Cook at a lively boil until liquid has been reduced by half. Stir in beef broth and return mixture to a boil. Reduce heat and simmer for 20 to 25 minutes or until thickened. Remove from heat.

3. *Topping:* Meanwhile, place potatoes in a large saucepan and add cold water to barely cover. Add salt, cover loosely and bring to a boil over high heat. Reduce heat and cook for 20 minutes or until tender.

4. Preheat oven to 350°F (180°C). Drain potatoes well. Return to saucepan over very low heat and shake the pot back and forth to remove any trace of moisture. Remove from heat and mash a few times, then mash in butter. Add $1/4$ cup (60 mL) cheese and egg yolk and mash for 1 to 2 minutes, until blended. Using a wooden spoon, stir briskly until smooth.

5. Transfer beef mixture to baking dish. Spoon mashed potato mixture evenly overtop, then, using the back of a fork, rough up the surface a little. Scatter evenly with remaining cheese. Bake in preheated oven for about 30 minutes or until top is golden brown and edges are bubbling. Remove from heat and let stand in pan on a wire rack for 10 minutes before serving.

Variation

Cook some chunked carrots and/or parsnips along with the potatoes and mash them all together for the topping.

Red Flannel Hash

Most everyone assumes that the red in red flannel hash stems from the beets — and so it does. But old stories prevail about the origins of the dish and include a disgruntled wife adding her husband's red flannel long johns to a mess of hash she was preparing at a logging camp. Apparently the dish, complete with shredded red flannel, was very well received. When the loggers wanted the dish again the next day, with no more long johns to dispose of, our wily wife added beets — and what do you know, the loggers liked it just as much. This classic brunch dish is a great way to use up leftover boiled potatoes.

Makes 4 servings

Tip

I prefer to use sea salt rather than refined table salt because it has a much cleaner, crisper taste and enhanced mineral content.

2 tbsp	butter	30 mL
1 tbsp	olive oil	15 mL
2	onions, chopped	2
2 cups	diced corned beef (about 1 lb/500 g)	500 mL
2 cups	diced cooked all-purpose potatoes	500 mL
2 cups	diced cooked beets (not pickled)	500 mL
	Salt and freshly ground black pepper	
¼ cup	chopped flat-leaf parsley leaves	60 mL

1. In a large skillet, heat butter and oil over medium-high heat. Sauté onions for about 10 minutes or until beginning to color. Stir in corned beef, potatoes and beets until thoroughly mixed. Season to taste with salt and freshly ground pepper. Cook, without stirring, for about 15 to 20 minutes, until mixture is beginning to brown and crisp up on the bottom.

2. Slip a spatula under about a third of the mixture and check if the bottom is browning. If so, flip that section over, patting it down before moving on to next third, then repeating this step. Do this a few more times as the mixture cooks and gets crispy and brown. (Do not stir — you want a nice brown crust.) Sprinkle with parsley and serve immediately.

Variation

Set some perfectly poached eggs in the center of this classic brunch dish, or serve scrambled eggs alongside.

Mash & Mince with Guinness

Mince and tatties is a classic Scottish dish that my man-with-Scottish-roots loves. In fact, a few hours before we were married in North Berwick, a little town in Scotland, he enjoyed a big helping of this savory mixture. Certainly this delicious combination of ground beef and onions, cooked slowly and long in a bit of stock and served with mashed spuds, has fed generations of Bravehearts. I've played with the general theme a bit by adding an Irish component (my own roots!) in the form of Guinness, the stout of champions. Serve with green peas and chunky carrots tossed with butter and parsley.

Makes
4 servings

Tip

If the beef mixture becomes too thick as it cooks, stir in a little more Guinness, beef broth or water until it reaches the desired consistency.

Mince

3 tbsp	butter	45 mL
2	large onions, finely chopped	2
2 lbs	lean ground beef	1 kg
1 tsp	dried rosemary	5 mL
1 tsp	dried thyme	5 mL
	Salt and freshly ground black pepper	
1 cup	Guinness or other dark beer	250 mL
1 cup	full-flavored beef broth	250 mL
2 tbsp	tomato paste	30 mL
2 tbsp	Worcestershire sauce	30 mL

Mash

1	recipe Classic Mash Deluxe (page 50)	1

1. *Mince:* In a large skillet, melt butter over medium-high heat. Sauté onions and beef, breaking up meat, for about 10 minutes or until beef is browned. Stir in rosemary and thyme. Season to taste with salt and freshly ground pepper, stirring well.
2. Stir in Guinness, beef broth, tomato paste and Worcestershire sauce and bring to a boil. Reduce heat and simmer, stirring often, for about 40 minutes or until thickened and sauce-like (see Tip, left).
3. Meanwhile, prepare Classic Mash Deluxe.
4. When you're ready to serve, pour a quarter of the mince into the center of each of four warmed individual serving plates, then surround with mash. Serve immediately.

Lamb Shoulder with Potatoes & Tomatoes

This warming dish, a perfect example of the marriage between lamb and potatoes, demonstrates how compatible these ingredients really are. In Greece and Italy they are often combined with great success. Serve this with a green vegetable and crusty bread and butter. This is by no means a sophisticated preparation, but sometimes that's just what you want.

Makes 4 to 6 servings

Tips

Either fresh or canned tomatoes work well here.

Lamb shoulder is a wonderful cut that I don't think gets enough culinary attention. It is full of flavor and generally less expensive than leg or chops. If you can't obtain fresh lamb, look for frozen lamb in your supermarket freezer.

The potatoes will be quite soft when the dish is done, squooshing and breaking down into the liquid, which helps to thicken it.

- Preheat oven to 350°F (180°C)
- Large casserole or baking dish, preferably ceramic or terra cotta

2 lbs	lamb shoulder, trimmed of excess fat and cut into chunks	1 kg
2 lbs	all-purpose potatoes, peeled and quartered	1 kg
4 cups	chopped peeled Roma (plum) tomatoes	1 L
1/3 cup	extra virgin olive oil, divided	75 mL
	Finely grated zest of 1 lemon	
3	sprigs fresh rosemary	3
2	cloves garlic, chopped	2
1	large onion, thinly sliced	1
1/4 cup	chopped flat-leaf parsley leaves	60 mL
2 tsp	dried oregano	10 mL
	Salt and freshly ground black pepper	
1 cup	dry white wine	250 mL
1 cup	chicken broth	250 mL

1. In baking dish, combine lamb and potatoes. In a large bowl, toss together tomatoes, 1/4 cup (60 mL) oil, lemon zest, rosemary, garlic, onion, parsley and oregano. Season to taste with salt and freshly ground pepper. Pour over lamb mixture and stir gently. Pour in wine and broth and, using your hands, give everything a good mix. Drizzle with remaining oil.
2. Cover and bake in preheated oven for 2 1/2 hours or until lamb and potatoes are quite tender. Serve in warmed individual shallow serving bowls.

Nigel's Lancashire Hot Pot

Seldom do meat and potatoes come together as easily and harmoniously as in this traditional lamb and potato preparation from the north of England. Named for the straight-sided pottery baking dish in which it is cooked, Lancashire hot pot has many regional variations on the original theme. I think the original — like this version from my good friend Nigel — is the best. Tradition dictates it be served with pickled red cabbage or pickled beets, and don't forget the pint of ale.

Makes 4 servings

Tips

If you can't easily obtain neck of lamb, use shoulder or boneless stewing lamb. This recipe doesn't brown the meat beforehand (making it even easier to put together) but rather follows a more old-fashioned method where the only cooking that the meat receives is in the oven, resulting in a more flavorful dish.

If you don't have a covered casserole or individual dishes with lids, cover tightly with foil.

Lamb broth cubes are available. If you can't obtain them, use chicken or vegetable broth.

- Preheat oven to 350°F (180°C)
- Deep casserole or baking dish or 4 deep individual-serving ovenproof dishes, with cover(s)

2 lbs	neck of lamb, cubed (see Tips, left)	1 kg
3 tsp	salt, divided	10 mL
1 tsp	ground white pepper, divided	5 mL
1 tbsp	all-purpose flour	15 mL
¼ cup	butter (approx.), melted, divided	60 mL
1	large onion, coarsely chopped	1
2 lbs	all-purpose or floury potatoes, peeled and thinly sliced	1 kg
1½ cups	lamb, chicken or vegetable broth	375 mL

1. Place lamb in a large bowl. Season with 1 tsp (5 mL) salt and a good pinch of white pepper. Scatter the flour over the meat and toss together to coat the meat. Transfer to baking dish and set aside.

2. In a skillet, combine 1 tbsp (15 mL) melted butter, 1 tsp (5 mL) salt and the onion. Sauté over medium-high heat for 5 minutes, until onions are softened but not browned. Add to lamb along with any pan juices, distributing evenly.

3. Place potatoes in a bowl. Add remaining melted butter. Season with 1 tsp (5 mL) salt and another pinch of white pepper and toss together to coat well. Arrange sliced potatoes in layers, overlapping the slices, on top of the onions and lamb. Gradually pour broth over mixture, allowing it to seep down into the dish.

4. Cover with the lid and bake in preheated oven for 30 minutes. Reduce oven temperature to 250°F (120°C) and continue to bake for 2½ hours. Remove from oven and remove the lid. Increase oven temperature to 350°F (180°C) and bake for another 20 to 30 minutes or until golden brown. Let stand for 15 minutes before serving.

Sloan's Lamb Stew with Spuds & Stout

This is my version of an Irish classic and, since my dad came from the north of Ireland, I don't add carrots to it. In some parts of Ireland it just isn't Irish stew without carrots, so if you feel that way, by all means include them. Like most stews and braises, this one is even better the next day — if there are any leftovers. Serve with plenty of good white bread and butter.

Makes 4 servings

Tips

I don't mind bones in my stew because I think the extra flavor more than makes up for their peskiness. All meat is better cooked on the bone, I think, but if you prefer, substitute boneless stewing lamb.

Check the stew as it cooks to make sure it's not drying out. If necessary, add a little more beef broth or water.

- **Large, heavy pot or Dutch oven**

3 lbs	bone-in shoulder lamb chops, trimmed of excess fat (see Tips, left)	1.5 kg
	All-purpose flour	
3 tbsp	bacon drippings or butter	45 mL
4	onions, quartered	4
2 cups	beef broth	500 mL
1 cup	Murphy's Irish Stout or other dark beer	250 mL
	Salt and freshly ground black pepper	
10 to 12	small all-purpose potatoes, peeled or unpeeled	10 to 12
1 tbsp	butter	15 mL
3 tbsp	chopped flat-leaf parsley leaves	45 mL

1. Pat chops dry with paper towels. Lightly dust with flour, shaking off excess. In a large, heavy pot, melt bacon drippings over medium heat. In batches, sear chops on both sides for about 10 minutes in total or until browned. Return chops to pot and add onions, broth and stout, lifting chops so liquid flows under and over them. Season to taste with salt and freshly ground pepper.

2. Arrange potatoes over chops, pressing down to slightly submerge in liquid. Bring to a boil over high heat. Reduce heat, cover and simmer for about 2 hours or until potatoes are cooked through and chops are quite tender.

3. Using a slotted spoon, place a quarter of the meat and vegetables in each of four warmed individual shallow serving bowls. Quickly swirl butter into cooking juices in pot, then ladle over each serving. Sprinkle with parsley and serve immediately.

Sautéed Fingerlings with Asparagus & Mint (page 239)

Beef & Wild Mushrooms in Stout with Champ (page 270)

Souvlaki with Lemon Potatoes (page 294)

Green Chile Chicken Curry with New Potatoes (page 303)

The Nacho Wedge (page 336)

Sweet Potato Pancakes with Maple Butter (page 400)

Carolina Sweet Potato Pie (page 410)

Dark Chocolate & Orange Potato Cheesecake (page 422)

Lamb with Sweet Potato & Chiles

With its Middle Eastern ingredients, this is not your average lamb stew, although it is just as easy to pull together. Serve this fragrant dish with brown basmati rice, couscous or bulgur.

Makes 4 to 6 servings

Tips

Poblano peppers are mild green chiles. If you can't find them fresh, substitute 2 red bell peppers.

Roasting peppers can be done easily in a very hot oven (500°F/260°C). If roasting in the oven, rub peppers with a little olive or vegetable oil, place on a baking sheet lined with parchment paper or foil and roast until blackened almost all over, using tongs to turn once or twice. Transfer to a bowl and cover with plastic wrap. Let the peppers steam beneath the plastic wrap for 30 minutes or so before peeling and removing seeds and membranes.

- Large steamer
- Large, heavy pot or Dutch oven

1½ lbs	sweet potatoes, unpeeled and sliced crosswise 1½ inches (4 cm) thick	750 g
3 tbsp	olive oil	45 mL
2	cloves garlic, crushed	2
1 lb	lean boneless leg of lamb, cut into 1-inch (2.5 cm) chunks and patted dry	500 g
1 tbsp	all-purpose flour	15 mL
2 tsp	turmeric	10 mL
½ tsp	ground cumin	2 mL
½ tsp	salt	2 mL
½ tsp	cayenne pepper	2 mL
2 tbsp	freshly squeezed lemon juice	30 mL
2 cups	chicken broth	500 mL
3	poblano chiles, roasted, peeled, seeded and cut into strips (see Tips, left)	3
½ cup	pomegranate juice	125 mL

1. In a large steamer, steam sweet potatoes for about 25 minutes or until tender. Using tongs, remove from steamer and set aside until cool enough to handle. Using a paring knife, peel off skins, cut pieces in half and set aside.

2. In a large, heavy pot, heat oil over medium-high heat. Sauté garlic for about 1 minute, without letting it brown. Add lamb, in batches if necessary, and sear all over for 6 or 7 minutes or until browned. Add flour, turmeric, cumin, salt and cayenne and cook, turning lamb, for about 4 minutes or until coated with spices. Stir in lemon juice and scrape up any brown bits from bottom of pan. Add chicken broth and bring to a boil. Reduce heat and simmer, uncovered, for about 1 hour or until lamb is tender (test with the tip of a knife).

3. Stir in sweet potatoes, chiles and pomegranate juice and simmer for 5 minutes. Serve over your favorite grain. If you like, top the lamb with a little Greek yogurt.

Honest-to-Goodness Shepherd's Pie

As mentioned in my Cottage Pie for Mac recipe (page 282), what many think of as shepherd's pie is actually cottage pie, because the latter is made with beef. Well, here is the genuine article — shepherd's pie made with not just any old lamb, but the wonderful meat from lamb shanks, braised slowly until the meat is falling off the bone, then combined with vegetables and topped with creamy mash to bake in the oven until golden brown. Enough to make any Scottish shepherd very happy!

Makes 4 servings

Tips

For a more robust result, substitute Big Cheese Mash (page 54) for the topping.

Frozen lamb shanks are fine for this recipe. Look for them in large supermarkets. If they seem small, increase the number to equal the weight needed for this dish.

- **Preheat oven to 350°F (180°C)**
- **Large, heavy ovenproof pot or Dutch oven**
- **10-cup (2.5 L) baking dish**

4	lamb shanks (about 4 lbs/2 kg)	4
	Salt and freshly ground black pepper	
¼ cup	olive oil	60 mL
2	large onions, quartered	2
2	large carrots, peeled, trimmed and sliced into thirds	2
2	stalks celery, trimmed and sliced into thirds	2
4	cloves garlic, chopped	4
2	sprigs fresh thyme	2
1	bay leaf	1
4 to 5 cups	chicken broth (approx.)	1 to 1.25 L
1 cup	finely chopped flat-leaf parsley leaves	250 mL

Topping

2 lbs	floury potatoes, peeled and quartered	1 kg
1 tsp	salt	5 mL
¼ cup	butter	60 mL
¼ cup	table (18%) cream	60 mL
1	large egg yolk	1

1. Pat lamb dry and season to taste with salt and freshly ground pepper. In a large, heavy pot, warm oil over medium-high heat. Sear lamb (two shanks at a time if necessary), using tongs to turn occasionally, for about 10 minutes or until browned all over.

2. Remove from heat and add onions, carrots, celery, garlic, thyme and bay leaf, nestling vegetables in and around shanks. Add enough chicken broth to cover meat and vegetables. Cover and braise in preheated oven for $2\frac{1}{2}$ to 3 hours or until the meat is falling off the bones.

3. Using tongs, transfer lamb and vegetables to a platter. Remove and discard thyme and bay leaf. Return pot with braising liquid to stovetop over high heat and boil, stirring occasionally, until reduced by about two-thirds. Season to taste with salt and freshly ground pepper if necessary; if the broth is lacking in flavor, add a chicken or beef bouillon cube and stir until dissolved.

4. Pull meat from bones, shredding it into pieces (not too small) and discarding any fat, gristle and bone. Cut vegetables into small pieces. In a bowl, stir together meat, vegetables, reduced braising liquid and parsley, then transfer to baking dish.

5. *Topping:* Meanwhile, toward the end of the braising time for the lamb, place potatoes in a large saucepan and add cold water to barely cover. Add salt, cover loosely and bring to a boil over high heat. Reduce heat and cook for 20 minutes or until potatoes are tender. Drain well. Return potatoes to saucepan over very low heat and shake the pot back and forth to remove any trace of moisture. Remove from heat. Using a potato masher, mash potatoes a few times, then mash in butter. Mash in cream and egg yolk. Using a wooden spoon, briskly stir mashed potatoes until smooth. Cover with a clean tea towel, replace the lid, and keep warm until lamb is cooked.

6. Evenly spoon mashed potatoes over lamb mixture and, using a fork, rough up the surface. Bake in preheated oven for 25 to 30 minutes or until mixture is heated through and topping is golden brown. Let stand in pan on a wire rack for 10 minutes before serving.

Variation

Replace half the potatoes with an equal amount of mashed rutabaga.

Grilled Lamb Tenderloins & Double Scalloped Potatoes with Chèvre

As the name would suggest, lamb loins are very tender, so a brief cooking time is recommended. The tenderloins would be equally good served with small new potatoes tossed with butter and mint or oven-roasted until golden and crisp. Serve with steamed asparagus, green beans or fiddleheads, if available.

Makes 4 servings

Tips

Look for frozen boneless lamb loins in the freezer section of most large supermarkets. They are always good value and very easy to prepare.

Plan to make this in advance so the lamb can marinate for at least a couple of hours.

If you don't have access to a barbecue, you can cook the lamb under a preheated broiler, turning once, in a preheated grill pan or on an indoor grill, according to the manufacturer's instructions.

Use a mandoline or food processor fitted with a slicing blade to cut potatoes into thin, uniform slices.

- Barbecue (see Tips, left)
- Mandoline or food processor fitted with slicing blade
- 9-inch (23 cm) square baking dish, buttered

1½ to 2 lbs	boneless lamb loin	750 g to 1 kg
¼ cup	chopped fresh rosemary	60 mL
¼ cup	extra virgin olive oil	60 mL
	Salt and freshly ground black pepper	

Scalloped Potatoes

3 cups	heavy or whipping (35%) cream	750 mL
¾ cup	soft goat cheese	175 mL
4	large Yukon Gold potatoes, peeled and very thinly sliced (see Tips, left)	4
2	sweet potatoes, peeled and very thinly sliced	2
	Salt and freshly ground black pepper	

1. In a bowl, combine lamb, rosemary and oil. Season to taste with salt and freshly ground pepper. Toss until lamb is well coated. Cover and refrigerate for at least 4 hours or up to 12 hours. Let stand at room temperature for about 30 minutes before grilling.

2. *Scalloped Potatoes:* Preheat oven to 350°F (180°C). In a small saucepan, heat cream and cheese over medium heat, whisking until cheese is melted and mixture is smooth and creamy. Set aside to cool to room temperature.

3. In a large mixing bowl, combine Yukon Gold and sweet potato slices. Sprinkle generously with salt and freshly ground pepper. Pour cooled cream mixture over potatoes. Using your hands, toss until potatoes are well coated.

4. In prepared baking dish, start layering the slices of potato, overlapping them as you work. Cover with any remaining cream mixture, pouring it evenly over potatoes.

5. Bake in preheated oven for about 1 hour or until potatoes offer no resistance to a small knife blade inserted in the center and are golden brown on the surface and bubbling around the edges. (Check once or twice during baking, and if top is browning too quickly, cover loosely with foil.) Remove from oven, uncover if necessary, and let stand in pan on a wire rack for 10 minutes before serving.

6. When you're ready to cook the lamb, preheat barbecue to high. Using paper towels, pat lamb dry. Season to taste with additional salt and freshly ground pepper. Grill for 3 to 4 minutes per side for medium rare.

7. Slice lamb. Divide scalloped potatoes among four warmed individual serving plates. Top with slices of lamb.

Souvlaki with Lemon Potatoes

Fans of restaurant-style Greek souvlaki and lemony spuds will go for this easy dish in a big way. Make it on the barbecue on a hot summer day and serve with a classic Greek salad, featuring ripe tomatoes, black olives, red onion, feta cheese and cucumber tossed in a herb vinaigrette.

Makes 6 servings

Tips

Marinade: In a small bowl, whisk together 4 cloves minced garlic, the finely grated zest of 1 lemon, $\frac{1}{2}$ cup (125 mL) freshly squeezed lemon juice, 3 tbsp (45 mL) olive oil, $1\frac{1}{2}$ tsp (7 mL) dried oregano and 2 tsp (10 mL) sweet paprika. Season to taste with salt and freshly ground black pepper.

Usually meat and potatoes are cooked on separate skewers when grilling, because of their different cooking times. But in this case the potatoes receive a little precooking so they can be teamed with the pork on the same skewer.

Use wooden skewers (presoaked) to ensure that the meat and potatoes stay in place while cooking.

- **6 soaked wooden skewers, at least 6 inches (15 cm) long (see Tips, page 99)**

$1\frac{1}{2}$ lbs	boneless pork, cut into chunks	750 g
$1\frac{1}{2}$ lbs	small red-skinned potatoes, scrubbed	750 g
1 tsp	salt	5 mL
	Fresh lemon wedges	

1. Place pork in a large resealable plastic bag. Add marinade (see Tips, left). Seal and massage marinade into pork. Set aside.

2. Place potatoes in a large saucepan and add boiling water to barely cover. Add salt, cover loosely and bring to a boil over high heat. Reduce heat and parboil for 10 minutes or until potatoes are just tender. Drain well and rinse under cold running water until cooled (make sure potatoes are well cooled before proceeding). Using the tines of a fork, pierce each potato a few times, then transfer to bag with pork. Seal bag and turn and massage to coat pork and potatoes with marinade. Refrigerate for at least 2 hours or preferably longer, for up to 12 hours. Remove from refrigerator 30 minutes before cooking.

3. Lightly oil grill and preheat to high. Set a colander over a bowl and pour pork mixture into colander, collecting marinade in bowl. Evenly divide pork and potatoes among six skewers. In a small saucepan, bring marinade to a boil. Reduce heat and simmer for about 10 minutes.

4. Reduce grill heat to medium and grill skewers, turning to brown all over and basting with marinade, for 15 minutes or until potatoes are tender and pork is just barely pink in the center. Remove from grill and serve immediately with fresh lemon wedges.

French Potato Galette with Bacon

There are no eggs, cream or milk in this gratin-like preparation of potatoes, bacon and Gruyère cheese. Serve this with a lovely green salad and a robust red wine.

Makes 6 servings

Tips

Use a mandoline or food processor fitted with a slicing blade to cut potatoes into very thin, uniform slices.

If you have purchased really good old-fashioned bacon, it may well have a rind. If so, use kitchen shears to neatly trim it away before using.

- **Mandoline or food processor, fitted with slicing blade (optional)**
- **10-cup (2.5 L) oval or round baking dish, lightly greased**

2½ lbs	Yukon Gold potatoes, peeled	1.25 kg
8 oz	double-smoked bacon, thinly sliced	250 g
¾ lb	shredded Gruyère cheese	375 g
	Freshly ground black pepper	

1. Soak potatoes in a bowl of cold water for about 15 minutes. Drain well and pat dry with paper towels. Slice as thinly as possible (see Tips, left), transfer slices to a bowl of fresh cold water and soak for 5 minutes. Drain and pat dry with paper towels.

2. Preheat oven to 425°F (220°C). Working from the center, arrange bacon like bicycle spokes over bottom and sides of prepared dish, allowing a little more than half the length of each slice to hang over the rim. Cover bacon with a third of the potato slices and sprinkle with a third of the cheese. Repeat twice. Fold overhanging bacon back over potato mixture (mixture will be exposed in the center).

3. Bake in preheated oven for about 1 hour or until bacon is cooked and potatoes are tender and golden. Remove from oven and let stand in pan on a wire rack for 15 minutes before serving. Season with freshly ground pepper and serve.

Pork Chops with Dijon Cream & Pommes Fondant

Pommes fondant is the classic name for big, thick ovals or circles of potato fried in butter until golden brown. They benefit from being made about an hour ahead of when you want to serve them, so they can slowly absorb the butter. Serve with sautéed rapini or a crisp green salad that contains some bitter greens, which will provide a nice counterpoint to the buttery richness of the potatoes.

Makes 6 servings

Tip
Choose medium-sized potatoes to make it easier to cut them into the desired shape. If you start with large potatoes it will be difficult. If you have an oval cookie or biscuit cutter, after trimming the ends and slicing a bit off the sides, place the potato on a cutting board and push the cutter firmly down onto it to cut through and create the oval shape.

- **2-inch (5 cm) cookie cutter**
- **Heavy frying pan large enough to accommodate potatoes in a single layer without crowding**

Pommes Fondant

6	Yukon Gold potatoes, peeled	6
6 tbsp	unsalted butter (approx.), diced	90 mL
	Salt and freshly ground black pepper	
¼ cup	water (approx.)	60 mL

Pork Chops

6	boneless pork loin chops, 1¼ inches (3 cm) thick	6
¼ cup	olive oil	60 mL

Sauce

⅔ cup	brandy	150 mL
1½ cups	chicken or beef broth	375 mL
2 to 3 tbsp	cold butter	30 to 45 mL
⅓ cup	heavy or whipping (35%) cream	75 mL
3 tbsp	Dijon mustard	45 mL
½ cup	chopped flat-leaf parsley leaves	125 mL

1. *Pommes Fondant:* Square off each potato by slicing a bit from each end. Now slice a bit from each side (save trimmings for another use) so that the potatoes have a flattish base on which to stand. If you like, use a paring knife to trim the edges further to achieve an oval shape, or as close to it as you can manage.

2. Place butter in a heavy frying pan large enough to hold potatoes in one layer without crowding. Arrange potatoes over butter and place over medium heat. Season to taste with salt and freshly ground pepper. As the butter melts, add water. Reduce heat to low and cook, turning potatoes two to three times, for 25 to 30 minutes or until cooked through and golden brown all over (if pan dries out, add a little more butter and/or water). Set aside and keep warm.

3. *Pork Chops:* Pat chops dry with paper towels. Thoroughly rub all over with oil. Generously sprinkle with salt and freshly ground pepper. Heat a heavy frying pan over high heat until hot. Sear chops, turning once, for about 1 minute per side. Reduce heat to medium and cook for about 4 minutes per side (until just a hint of pink remains) or to your taste. Transfer to a warmed platter and keep warm.

4. *Sauce:* Splash brandy into the hot frying pan, scraping up any brown bits from bottom. Cook for 1 minute or until alcohol has evaporated, then add broth. Cook on high heat until liquid has been reduced by one-third. Reduce heat to medium. Stir in butter, 1 tbsp (15 mL) at a time, until blended. Whisk in cream and mustard and cook, stirring, until blended and thickened into sauce. Season to taste with salt and freshly ground pepper. Pour over steaks. Sprinkle with parsley and serve immediately, with Pommes Fondant on the side.

Variations

Beef steaks, lamb chops or even boneless chicken breasts can be used here. The smooth mustard sauce goes very well with many meats.

Netherlands Hotchpotch

In the U.K. hotchpotch, a stew-like preparation, is usually based on lamb or mutton with carrots, onions, potatoes and sometimes barley. In Holland *hotchpotch* refers to a number of dishes that all have potatoes as their base; kale, endive, carrots, cabbage and even apples are all likely candidates for this dish. And then there is this version, which includes Holland's other famous export — Gouda — to make it even better. This is a good accompaniment to smoked sausage. (This one's for you, Joel!)

**Makes
4 servings**

Tips

It is important to keep your mashed potatoes hot while working, because that will help to semi-melt the cheese. Keep the pot over low heat while mashing.

It may seem unusual to blend uncooked endives with the hot potato mixture, but the contrast in textures is very appealing.

2½ lbs	floury potatoes, peeled and cut into chunks	1.25 kg
1 tsp	salt	5 mL
¼ cup	butter	60 mL
⅔ cup	whole milk	150 mL
1 tbsp	Dijon mustard	15 mL
Pinch	ground nutmeg	Pinch
1 lb	Belgian endive, trimmed and cut into strips (see Tips, left)	500 g
12 oz	Gouda cheese, diced	375 g
8 oz	back (Canadian) bacon, cooked and cut into strips	250 g
1 tbsp	white wine vinegar	15 mL

1. Place potatoes in a large saucepan and add cold water to barely cover. Add salt, cover loosely and bring to a boil over high heat. Reduce heat and cook for 20 minutes or until potatoes are tender. Drain well. Return potatoes to saucepan over very low heat and shake the pot back and forth to remove any trace of moisture. Over heat and using a potato masher, mash in butter. Then mash in milk until nice and fluffy. Mash in mustard and nutmeg.
2. Stir in endive, cheese, bacon and vinegar. Divide evenly among four warmed individual serving plates and serve immediately.

Italian Cottage Pie

This is a nice variation on the theme of potato-topped pies. The Italian components are creamy mascarpone cheese in the mash, along with a little grated Grana Padano or Parmesan cheese, and Italian-style pork sausages in the filling.

Makes 4 to 6 servings

Tips

Choose either hot or mild pork (or turkey) sausages, as you prefer.

Potato Topping: Using 2 lbs (500 g) floury potatoes, peeled and quartered, follow instructions for boiling potatoes in Step 1, Classic Mash Deluxe (page 50), being sure to add 1 tsp (5 mL) salt to the cooking water. After the moisture has been removed from the potatoes remove the saucepan from the heat. Using a potato masher, mash a few times, then mash in 3 tbsp (45 mL) butter. Mash in 8 oz (250 g) mascarpone cheese and 1 cup (250 mL) whole milk. Using a wooden spoon, briskly stir mashed potatoes until smooth. Set aside.

- Preheat oven to 400°F (200°C)
- 11- by 7-inch (2 L) baking dish

2 tbsp	olive oil	30 mL
2 lbs	hot or mild Italian sausage, casings removed	1 kg
1	onion, finely chopped	1
1	stalk celery, finely chopped	1
1	large carrot, peeled and finely chopped	1
2	cloves garlic, finely chopped	2
1	can (28 oz/796 mL) diced tomatoes with juice	1
1 tbsp	dried oregano	15 mL
1 tbsp	dried basil	15 mL
1 tsp	dried red pepper flakes	5 mL
	Salt and freshly ground black pepper	
	Potato Topping (see Tips, left)	
3 tbsp	dry bread crumbs	45 mL
3 tbsp	freshly grated Grana Padano or Parmesan cheese	45 mL

1. In a large skillet, heat oil over medium-high heat. Sauté sausage for about 15 minutes or until no longer pink. Using a slotted spoon, transfer to a bowl and set aside. Add onion, celery, carrot and garlic to pan and sauté for about 10 minutes or until vegetables have softened and are beginning to color. Return meat to pan, mixing well. Stir in tomatoes with juice, oregano, basil and pepper flakes. Season to taste with salt and freshly ground pepper and bring to a boil. Cover loosely, reduce heat and simmer for 15 minutes, until slightly thickened. Set aside.

2. Using a slotted spoon, transfer sausage mixture to baking dish. Spoon Potato Topping over meat mixture. Using the back of a fork, rough up the surface a little. Scatter evenly with bread crumbs and Grana Padano. Bake in preheated oven for 15 minutes. Reduce oven temperature to 350°F (180°C) and bake for 45 minutes or until top is golden brown and edges are bubbling. Let stand in pan on a wire rack for 10 minutes before serving.

Pork, Apple & Potato Crumble

The harmonious combination of pork and apple reaches new heights in this hearty preparation, which adds chunks of potato to make it complete.

**Makes
4 servings**

Tips

Other than shoulder or butt, almost any boneless pork may be used here, such as pork loin or chops.

Try to use an apple variety that won't break down completely when cooked, such as Cortland, Spartan or Granny Smith.

Hard cider is a fermented (alcoholic) beverage. If you prefer, you can substitute sweet cider.

- **Preheat oven to 350°F (180°C)**
- **8-cup (2 L) baking dish**

1½ lbs	boneless pork (see Tips, left), cut into 1-inch (2.5 cm) chunks	750 g
½ cup	all-purpose flour	125 mL
1 tsp	sweet paprika	5 mL
	Salt and freshly ground black pepper	
2 tbsp	olive oil	30 mL
1 lb	all-purpose potatoes, peeled and sliced	500 g
3	apples, peeled, cored and cut into ½-inch (1 cm) chunks	3
1	large onion, thinly sliced	1
2 cups	hard cider (see Tips, left)	500 mL
2 tsp	herbes de Provence, divided	10 mL
¾ cup	soft whole wheat bread crumbs	175 mL
½ cup	shredded sharp (aged) Cheddar cheese	125 mL

1. In a large plastic bag, combine pork, flour and paprika. Season to taste with salt and freshly ground pepper. Toss together, massaging the meat to coat. Shake off excess flour. In a large skillet, heat oil over medium-high heat. Sear pork, turning, for about 6 minutes or until just beginning to color.

2. Arrange potato slices in a baking dish. Scrape pork and any accumulated juices over potatoes. Arrange apples and onion on top.

3. In skillet that pork was seared in, warm cider over medium heat, scraping up any brown bits from bottom of pan. Season to taste with salt and freshly ground pepper. Stir in 1 tsp (5 mL) herbes de Provence. Pour over pork and vegetables in baking dish. Cover with a lid or foil and bake in preheated oven for 45 minutes.

4. Meanwhile, in a small bowl, combine bread crumbs, cheese and the remaining herbes de Provence. Remove baking dish from oven, uncover and sprinkle evenly with bread crumb mixture. Return to oven and bake uncovered for 20 to 25 minutes or until golden brown. Let stand on wire rack for 15 minutes before serving.

Sausage, Apple, Potato & Fennel Puff Tart

Cooking more potatoes than you need for one meal means that something good can come together quickly the next day. This is very much the case with this delicious, quick-to-make savory tart that is as nice when served as an appetizer for company as it is for your family for dinner. Add a sprightly green salad, which can include the rest of the fennel bulb, very thinly sliced.

Makes 4 to 6 servings

Tips

Any sausage can be used here, but one that has a little fennel in its makeup is especially good.

Frozen puff pastry is one of the home cook's best friends; just make sure to take it from the freezer in time for it to thaw. For best results, choose puff pastry that has been made with butter.

This is an open-faced tart. If you prefer, roll out additional puff pastry for a lid and increase baking time slightly.

● **Preheat oven to 375°F (190°C)**

3	shallots, thinly sliced	3
2	cloves garlic, very thinly sliced	2
¼ cup	sour cream	60 mL
¼ cup	extra virgin olive oil, divided	60 mL
	Salt and freshly ground black pepper	
4	slices double-smoked bacon, diced	4
2	apples, peeled, cored and sliced	2
12 oz	frozen puff pastry, thawed	375 g
	All-purpose flour	
1 lb	fresh pork sausage, casings removed, crumbled	500 g
5	white- or red-skinned waxy potatoes, cooked and thinly sliced crosswise	5
¼	small fennel bulb, thinly sliced	¼

1. In a small bowl, stir together shallots, garlic, sour cream and 1 tbsp (15 mL) oil. Season to taste with salt and freshly ground pepper. Set aside.

2. In a skillet, heat 1 tablespoon (15 mL) oil over medium heat. Cook bacon, stirring, for 1 minute. Add apples and cook, stirring, for about 12 minutes or until apples are just beginning to color. Remove from heat and set aside.

3. On a lightly floured surface, roll out puff pastry ½ inch (1 cm) thick into a circle or square as desired. Transfer to a baking sheet or pizza pan. Spread evenly with 2 tbsp (30 mL) of the shallot mixture. Evenly arrange bacon, apples, sausage, potato slices and fennel on top. Dot with remaining shallot mixture and drizzle with remaining oil. Season to taste with salt and freshly ground pepper.

4. Bake in preheated oven for 20 to 25 minutes, until bottom of pastry is golden brown and sausage is no longer pink. Let stand for 10 minutes before serving.

Soccer Player Spuds

My husband, who played the game for many years, is an avid soccer fan. It was he who first told me about a famous Brazilian player and this dish, which he used to enjoy at his favorite restaurant in São Paulo. Whether he enjoyed it before or, more likely, following a game, I don't know. I do know that this makes a good choice for the "morning after." It may seem a bit bizarre to combine potatoes and rice in one dish, but somehow it works. Serve with a fresh spicy salsa.

**Makes
4 servings**

Tip
While skinny shoestring potatoes are traditional in this dish, you could also use diced cooked potatoes, which is great if you have leftovers.

3 tbsp	olive oil	45 mL
4	slices double-smoked bacon, diced	4
1	large onion, finely chopped	1
4	eggs, lightly beaten	4
3	green onions (white part with a bit of green), finely chopped	3
2 cups	cooked rice	500 mL
1 cup	finely chopped flat-leaf parsley leaves	250 mL
4 cups	frozen shoestring potatoes, prepared according to package instructions	1 L

1. In a large skillet, heat oil over medium heat. Cook bacon, stirring, for about 5 minutes or until softened but not cooked through. Add onion and cook for 2 minutes or until just beginning to soften. Add eggs; after a few seconds, draw a spatula back and forth through them until partially cooked.
2. Stir in green onions, rice and parsley. Toss in potatoes and cook for 1 to 2 minutes or until heated through. Serve immediately.

Green Chile Chicken Curry with New Potatoes

For all of you who, like me, still crave potatoes while enjoying a fragrant chicken curry, this one's for you. Just because there are potatoes in the mix doesn't mean you can't still serve this with good basmati rice.

Makes 4 servings

Tip

If you can't obtain small new potatoes, larger ones will work fine if you cut them into smaller chunks. Just make sure they are waxy and thin-skinned.

- **Mini food processor or large mortar and pestle**
- **Wok or skillet**

2	fresh long green chiles, seeded and chopped	2
1 cup	fresh cilantro leaves	250 mL
1 tbsp	chopped gingerroot	15 mL
1 tbsp	Asian fish sauce	15 mL
2 tsp	ground cumin	10 mL
1	red onion, chopped	1
2 tbsp	vegetable oil	30 mL
1 lb	boneless, skinless chicken (thighs or breasts), cut into small chunks	500 g
8 oz	small waxy new potatoes, scrubbed and halved	250 g
1½ cups	coconut milk	375 mL
1 cup	chicken broth	250 mL
3 or 4	strips lime zest	3 or 4
	Freshly squeezed juice of 1 small lime	
	Fresh cilantro sprigs	

1. In a mini food processor (or use a large mortar and pestle), pulse chiles, cilantro, ginger, fish sauce, cumin, onion and oil, scraping down sides, until blended and smooth. Transfer to a wok over medium heat and cook, stirring, for about 5 minutes or until fragrant. Add chicken and stir-fry for 2 to 3 minutes or until slightly cooked.

2. Stir in potatoes, coconut milk, chicken broth and lime zest and juice and bring to a boil. Reduce heat and simmer for about 25 minutes or until chicken and potatoes are tender and cooked through and mixture has thickened. Using tongs, remove lime zest and discard. Garnish with cilantro sprigs and serve immediately.

Potato Dumplings with Chicken & Tarragon Cream

Chicken served with sumptuous potato dumplings packs a lot of comfort into one simple dish. This version gussies things up a bit by using chicken breasts with a little cream and fresh tarragon.

Makes 4 to 6 servings

Tips

You can prepare the mashed potatoes ahead of time, but no later than the same day. Try to keep them warm or reheat gently in the microwave before using in this recipe.

If you have extra dumplings, place in another greased baking dish, add a little chicken broth and bake alongside the main dish.

Dumplings: Peel, boil and dry-mash 6 floury potatoes. In a large bowl, using a wooden spoon, beat mashed potatoes with 2 large eggs, ½ cup (125 mL) all-purpose flour and 1½ tsp (7 mL) salt until fairly fluffy. Using lightly floured hands, shape mixture into 1-inch (2.5 cm) round dumplings.

These dumplings also work well with a beef or lamb stew and you can make them a little smaller and float them atop a sturdy vegetable soup. They should cook through in 15 to 20 minutes.

- Preheat oven to 375°F (190°C)
- 4-cup (1 L) baking dish

1½ cups	chicken broth	375 mL
1 cup	dry white wine	250 mL
6	black peppercorns	6
3	sprigs fresh flat-leaf parsley	3
1	onion, chopped	1
1	stalk celery, chopped	1
4	large chicken breasts	4
1¼ cups	table (18%) cream	300 mL
2 tbsp	chopped fresh tarragon leaves	30 mL
	Salt and freshly ground black pepper	
2 tbsp	chopped flat-leaf parsley leaves	30 mL

1. In a large skillet, combine broth, wine, peppercorns, parsley, onion and celery over medium-high heat. Add chicken and bring to a gentle boil over high heat. Reduce heat, cover loosely and simmer for 20 minutes, until no hint of pink remains. Using tongs, transfer to a cutting board and set aside until cool enough to handle. Remove skin and bones and pull apart meat into coarse chunks. Transfer to a baking dish.

2. Strain cooking liquid through a fine-mesh sieve into a clean skillet. Discard solids. Place skillet over high heat, bring to a boil, reduce heat and boil gently for about 10 minutes or until thickened. Stir in cream and tarragon. Season to taste with salt and pepper. Pour over chicken.

3. Arrange dumplings (see Tips, left) over chicken, pushing down into liquid to partially submerge. Bake in preheated oven, uncovered, for 25 to 30 minutes or until dumplings have puffed up slightly and are cooked through. Sprinkle with parsley and serve.

Poached Monkfish with Potato Risotto & Crispy Bacon

Lovely snowy white monkfish is often wrapped in prosciutto. In this recipe a few strips of crispy bacon are used as a garnish and the vibrant color and flavor of smoked pork provide a nice contrast to the fish.

**Makes
4 servings**

Tips

The "risotto" is obviously a bit of a play on words, because what we have here is diced potatoes cooked in a little vegetable broth until tender.

Although you can substitute frozen peas, you'll achieve the best results if you make this using garden-fresh, just-shelled peas.

2 tbsp	olive oil	30 mL
2	shallots, finely chopped	2
1	clove garlic, crushed	1
2 lbs	waxy new potatoes, scrubbed and finely diced	1 kg
5 cups	chicken or vegetable broth, divided	1.25 L
¾ cup	heavy or whipping (35%) cream	175 mL
	Salt and freshly ground pepper	
8	slices double-smoked bacon	8
4	monkfish fillets, each about 7 oz (210 g)	4
1½ cups	fresh green peas, cooked	375 mL

1. In a large saucepan, heat oil over medium-high heat. Sauté shallots and garlic for about 5 minutes, not letting garlic brown. Add potatoes and sauté until opaque. Add 3 cups (750 mL) chicken broth a little at a time, stirring frequently after each addition until almost all the liquid has been absorbed, for a total of about 15 minutes, until potatoes are tender. Stir in cream and season to taste with salt and freshly ground pepper. Reduce heat to low and keep warm.

2. In a skillet, sauté bacon over medium-high heat until crisp. Using tongs, transfer to a plate lined with paper towels, roll up and keep warm.

3. In a large skillet, heat remaining broth over medium heat (do not boil). Add monkfish and gently poach for about 4 minutes or until fish is no longer translucent. One or 2 minutes before fish has finished poaching, stir peas into potato mixture and heat through for 1 or 2 minutes. Using tongs or a metal spatula, transfer fish to a cutting board and carefully slice each fillet into thirds.

4. Evenly divide potato mixture among four warmed individual pasta bowls. Top each with three slices of monkfish, then garnish with two slices of bacon. Serve immediately.

County Cork Fish Pie with Champ

I was inspired to create this memorable dish when I first enjoyed it in Ireland. It didn't hurt that the fish and seafood had been caught mere hours before I enjoyed it.

Makes 6 to 8 servings

Tips

You can use a combination of types of fish in this recipe, to accommodate availability. But if you are particularly fond of just one type, that's fine too. In addition to cod, haddock, hake, salmon or pollock fillets or any mixture thereof, work very well.

Start cooking the potatoes for the champ at the same time as you begin to cook the filling.

If you prefer, bake this pie in 6 to 8 single-serving ovenproof dishes.

- **10-cup (2.5 L) ovenproof serving dish (see Tips, left)**

Filling

2	small onions, quartered	2
1	small carrot, peeled and sliced	1
1	small bay leaf	1
1	sprig fresh thyme	1
3	black peppercorns	3
3¼ cups	whole milk, divided	800 mL
4	eggs	4
½ cup	butter, divided	125 mL
1 cup	sliced mushrooms	250 mL
	Salt and freshly ground black pepper	
2½ lbs	cod fillets (see Tips, left)	1.25 kg
2 tbsp	all-purpose flour	30 mL
6 oz	medium shrimp, peeled, deveined, cooked and halved lengthwise	175 g
¼ cup	table (18%) cream	60 mL
2 tbsp	chopped flat-leaf parsley leaves	30 mL

Champ

3 lbs	floury potatoes, quartered	1.5 kg
1 tsp	salt	5 mL
1¼ cups	whole milk	300 mL
6 to 8	green onions (white part with a bit of green), finely chopped	6 to 8
¼ cup	butter	60 mL
3 tbsp	melted butter (for drizzling)	45 mL

1. *Filling:* In a saucepan, combine onions, carrot, bay leaf, thyme, peppercorns and 2 cups (500 mL) milk and bring to a boil over high heat. Reduce heat and simmer for 3 to 4 minutes. Remove from heat and let stand for 15 minutes. Set a fine-mesh sieve over a small bowl and strain. Set liquid aside and discard solids.

2. Place eggs in a small saucepan and add water to cover. Bring to a boil, then remove from heat and let stand for 10 to 12 minutes. Drain, rinse under cold running water, peel and chop coarsely. Set aside.

3. In a small skillet, melt ¼ cup (60 mL) butter over medium heat. Cook mushrooms, stirring, for about 6 minutes or until softened. Season to taste with salt and freshly ground pepper. Set aside.

4. In a large, wide saucepan or skillet, in batches if necessary, arrange fish in a single layer. Cover with milk mixture. Season generously with salt and pepper and bring to a boil. Reduce heat and simmer for 4 minutes or until fish is just cooked and no longer translucent. Using a slotted spoon, carefully transfer to a large plate. If necessary, without breaking up fish, remove and discard any bones and skin. Set a fine-mesh sieve over a measuring cup and strain cooking liquid. Set liquid aside and discard solids.

5. In a large saucepan, melt remaining ¼ cup (60 mL) butter over low heat. Whisk in flour and cook for half a minute, then whisk in cooking liquid. Cook, whisking, until smooth and thick. Remove from heat and gently stir in shrimp, cream, parsley, reserved eggs, mushrooms (with any accumulated liquid in pan) and fish. Season to taste with salt and freshly ground pepper. Spoon into a serving dish (or individual serving dishes) and set aside.

6. *Champ:* Place potatoes in a large saucepan and add cold water to barely cover. Add salt, cover loosely and bring to a boil over high heat. Reduce heat and cook for 20 minutes or until potatoes are tender. Drain potatoes well. Return to saucepan over very low heat and shake the pot back and forth to remove any trace of moisture. Remove from heat, cover with a clean tea towel and let stand for about 10 minutes or until cool enough to handle.

7. Preheat oven to 350°F (180°C). In a small saucepan, warm milk over medium heat. Add green onions, increase heat to high, and bring to a boil. Reduce heat and simmer for 2 minutes. Remove from heat and let stand for 5 minutes.

8. When potatoes are cool enough to handle, peel off skins with a paring knife. Return potatoes to pot and mash, using a potato masher. Mash in butter and then milk mixture. Using a wooden spoon, stir briskly to incorporate a little air into the mash. Season to taste with salt and freshly ground pepper.

9. Spoon mashed potatoes over fish mixture, drizzle with melted butter and bake in preheated oven for about 30 minutes or until top is beginning to color and edges are bubbling (if you wish, broil to brown the top). Remove from heat. Let stand in pan on a wire rack for 10 minutes before serving in warmed individual soup plates.

Salmon & Potato Cakes with Lemon Butter

Fish cakes are often composed of cod or haddock, but I love the flavor that good salmon lends to this simple preparation. In Scotland I enjoyed salmon fish cakes like these ones, dipped in a little finely ground oatmeal before frying, which gave them a lovely crunchy finish. Serve with fresh watercress tossed in vinaigrette and a wedge of lemon.

Makes 4 servings

Tip

If you cannot obtain fresh chervil, use additional parsley, although you will miss the slightly anise-like flavor that chervil provides. If you are using extra parsley, try adding some chopped fresh tarragon for a nice bit of flavor.

1 lb	cooked salmon fillet, cooled and skinned	500 g
1½ cups	mashed potato	375 mL
3 tbsp	chopped flat-leaf parsley leaves	45 mL
3 tbsp	chopped fresh chervil leaves (see Tip, left)	45 mL
1 tbsp	ketchup	15 mL
1 tsp	Worcestershire sauce	5 mL
1 tsp	dry mustard	5 mL
2 to 3 tbsp	all-purpose flour	30 to 45 mL
3 tbsp	olive oil	45 mL
6 tbsp	butter, divided	90 mL
½ cup	heavy or whipping (35%) cream	125 mL
3 tbsp	freshly squeezed lemon juice	45 mL
1	thin green onion (white part with a bit of green), finely chopped	1
	Salt and freshly ground black pepper	

1. Place salmon in a bowl and use your fingers to gently break it up. Transfer half to another bowl and set aside. Using a fork, blend mashed potato, parsley, chervil, ketchup, Worcestershire sauce and mustard into one portion of the salmon. Add remaining salmon and mix gently so as not to break it up too much. Using lightly floured hands, shape salmon mixture into four fat, substantial (not flat and thin) cakes. Transfer to a plate, cover with plastic wrap and refrigerate for at least 30 minutes or until well chilled.

2. Place flour in a shallow dish. Dip fish cakes in flour, shaking off excess. In a large skillet, heat oil and 3 tbsp (45 mL) butter over medium heat until butter begins to foam. Add fish cakes and cook, turning once, for 3 to 4 minutes per side or until golden brown (see Variation, page 309).

3. Meanwhile, in a small saucepan, combine cream and remaining 3 tbsp (45 mL) butter over low heat. Reduce heat to very low. Stir in lemon juice and green onion. Simmer over very low heat (don't let it boil) until heated through. Season sauce to taste with salt and freshly ground pepper.

4. Pour a little sauce onto each of four individual serving plates. Lay fish cake over sauce on each plate and drizzle with more sauce. Serve immediately.

Variation

If you prefer, after flouring, you can bake the fish cakes in an ovenproof skillet. Preheat oven to 400°F (200°C). Heat oil and butter, add cakes, sear over medium heat on both sides for a minute in total and then transfer to preheated oven. Bake for about 12 minutes or until cakes are heated through.

Crisp Potato-Wrapped Halibut

Like brown paper packages tied up with string, these lovely little golden brown potato parcels hold a special prize inside: moist, snow-white halibut with all its natural flavors intact, thanks to being encased in paper-thin slices of potato. This may be a little tricky for the novice cook, but even a less than perfect attempt will be delicious.

Makes 4 servings

Tips

You really do need a mandoline for this recipe to achieve the ultra-thin slices of potato. If they are sliced too thickly, they won't be wrappable.

If you prefer, very lightly steam the potato slices beforehand to make them a little more pliable — just don't cook them through.

Clarified butter (also known as drawn butter) is easy to make. Since you will lose about a quarter of your original butter amount during the process, you'll need ¾ cup (175 mL) butter to make the amount required for this recipe. Place butter in a small saucepan and melt over low heat until milk solids accumulate on the bottom of the pan and the pure butterfat has risen to the top. Carefully pour off clear butterfat and discard remaining water and milk solids. Clarified butter will keep, tightly covered, in the refrigerator for about one month. (By the way, this is also known as ghee in Indian cooking.)

- Mandoline

3 to 4	large floury or all-purpose potatoes, peeled and halved lengthwise	3 to 4
3 tbsp	olive oil, divided	45 mL
	Salt and freshly ground black pepper	
4	halibut fillets (each about 5 oz/150 g), skinned and lightly seasoned with salt and freshly ground black pepper	4
½ cup	clarified butter, divided (see Tips, left)	125 mL
2	large leeks (white and light green parts only), trimmed and finely chopped (see Tips, page 311)	2
½ tsp	curry powder	2 mL
¼ cup	dry white wine	60 mL
1 cup	heavy or whipping (35%) cream	250 mL

1. Using a mandoline and slicing lengthwise, cut potatoes into slices that are thin enough to fold without snapping but not so thin that they are completely translucent (see Tips, left). On a piece of plastic wrap, lay out 5 or 6 slices in a row, slightly overlapping the long edges. Then make another, identical row, overlapping the short ends of the slices in the first row so that the slices form a rectangle. Lightly brush with a little of the oil. Season to taste with salt and freshly ground pepper.

2. Center a seasoned fish fillet on the rectangle. Then, using the plastic wrap to help, fold over the potato slices to enclose the fish, pressing down to adhere them to the fish. Wrap parcel up tightly in the plastic. Transfer to a baking sheet. Repeat with the remaining potato slices and fish. Refrigerate for 1 hour to chill and set.

3. In a skillet, heat about 2 tbsp (30 mL) clarified butter over medium heat. Add leeks, season to taste with salt and freshly ground pepper and cook gently, stirring, for 5 to 7 minutes or until softened. Just before the leeks have softened completely, stir in curry powder and wine and cook for 2 minutes. Season to taste with salt and freshly ground pepper. Stir in cream and simmer for 5 minutes or until reduced and thickened into sauce. Remove from heat and keep warm.

4. Preheat oven to 140°F (60°C). Heat a large, preferably nonstick skillet over medium-high heat. Add 3 to 4 tbsp (45 to 60 mL) clarified butter. Working with two parcels at a time, remove plastic wrap and place in pan, seam side down. Cook for about 4 minutes or until bottoms are golden brown. Using a metal spatula, carefully turn over and cook for 2 to 3 minutes or until golden and crisp. Transfer to a platter lined with paper towels and keep warm in preheated oven. Repeat with remaining butter and parcels.

5. Spoon a mound of the leek mixture onto each of four individual serving plates. Top each with a fish parcel, seam side down, and serve immediately.

Variations

Use cod, haddock or sea bass in place of the halibut.

Pan-Seared Sea Bass with Baked Porcini Potatoes, Spinach & Lemon Oil

This is a lovely dish to present to any fish-and-potato-lover. In addition to sea bass, the recipe showcases thick slices of large waxy potatoes with pungent porcini mushrooms and wilted spinach in a lemon vinaigrette. It's a great dish to serve to company.

**Makes
4 servings**

Tip

If you really don't care for fish with the skin on, you can remove it, but the skin is especially nice when allowed to get very crisp in a hot pan. If you do decide to remove it, serve the fish with the other side facing up.

- **Preheat oven to 400°F (200°C)**
- **Ovenproof skillet**

3½ oz	dried porcini mushrooms	105 g
2 lbs	large waxy potatoes, scrubbed	1 kg
7 tbsp	extra virgin olive oil, divided	105 mL
4 oz	butter	125 g
	Salt and freshly ground black pepper	
1 tbsp	fresh thyme leaves	15 mL
4	skin-on sea bass fillets, each about 7 oz (210 g) and ¾ inch (2 cm) thick	4
1 tbsp	freshly squeezed lemon juice	15 mL
1 lb	spinach	500 g

1. In a bowl, combine mushrooms and 2⅔ cups (650 mL) boiling water. Set aside to soak for 15 minutes. Place a fine-mesh sieve over a bowl and strain mushrooms. Set aside soaking liquid. Pat mushrooms dry with paper towels and set aside.

2. Cut potatoes crosswise into thirds. In an ovenproof skillet, heat 1 tbsp (15 mL) oil and the butter over medium-high heat until butter is foaming. Add mushrooms and sauté for 1 to 2 minutes. Add reserved mushroom soaking liquid and bring to a boil. Add potatoes (you need just 2 thick pieces per portion; if you have extra, place in cold water, cover and refrigerate for another use). Season to taste with salt and freshly ground pepper. Add thyme. Cover and bake in preheated oven for 15 minutes. Using tongs, turn potatoes over, cover and bake for 15 minutes longer or until softened. Remove from oven and keep warm (leave the oven on).

3. Season fish to taste with salt and freshly ground pepper. Wipe the skillet clean and heat 2 tbsp (30 mL) oil over medium-high heat until hot and shimmering. Using tongs, carefully place fish, skin side down, in pan and cook for 1 minute. Transfer pan to oven and bake for 12 to 15 minutes or until fish has turned from opaque to snow-white. Remove from oven and keep warm.

4. In a bowl, whisk lemon juice with 3 tbsp (45 mL) oil. Set aside.

5. In a saucepan, warm remaining 1 tbsp (15 mL) oil over medium-high heat. Quickly wilt spinach, using tongs to toss it around slightly (it will take only a minute). Remove from heat and season to taste with salt and freshly ground pepper. Keep warm.

6. Place two pieces of potato on each of four warmed individual serving plates. Top with mushroom mixture, spinach and then a fillet, skin side up (see Tip, page 312). Drizzle lemon oil around edge of each plate. Serve immediately.

Variations

Substitute halibut or even tuna for the sea bass. If using tuna, reduce the cooking time.

Cod with Shrimp Butter & Parsley Mash

Fish and mashed potatoes is one of my favorite food combinations; there's something about the two together that really satisfies. However, because color balance is as important as a variety of textures on a plate, and since the fish in question is lovely creamy white cod, I have added a bit of color — in the form of a little mustard and parsley for the mash and tiny pink shrimp with fresh herbs for the fish. As my mum was fond of saying, we also eat with our eyes.

**Makes
4 servings**

Tip

This recipe relies on a substantial quantity of butter to make the sauce, which at its heart is the classic French butter sauce *beurre blanc*. However, this is not something you make every day, and it's the absolutely perfect sauce for fish.

- **Large ovenproof skillet**

4	cod fillets (each 6 to 7 oz/175 to 200 g)	4
	Salt and freshly ground black pepper	
	Zest of ½ lemon	
2 tbsp	fresh thyme leaves	30 mL
4	large floury potatoes, peeled and cut into chunks	4
1 tsp	salt	5 mL
3 tbsp	butter	45 mL
¼ cup	table (18%) cream	60 mL
½ tsp	Dijon mustard	2 mL
½ tsp	dry mustard	2 mL
3 tbsp	finely chopped flat-leaf parsley leaves	45 mL

Sauce

2	shallots, finely chopped	2
1½ cups	dry white wine	375 mL
3 tbsp	white wine vinegar	45 mL
2 tbsp	heavy or whipping (35%) cream	30 mL
1½ cups	unsalted butter, chilled and cubed	375 mL
	Salt and freshly ground white pepper	
8 oz	cooked salad shrimp	250 g
3 tbsp	finely chopped chives	45 mL
3 tbsp	finely chopped dill fronds	45 mL
¼ cup	olive oil	60 mL

1. Lightly season fish with salt and freshly ground pepper. Rub all over with lemon zest and thyme, pressing to adhere. Transfer to a plate, cover with plastic wrap and refrigerate for at least 1 hour or up to 4 hours.

2. Place potatoes in a large saucepan and add cold water to barely cover. Add salt, cover loosely and bring to a boil over high heat. Reduce heat and cook for 20 minutes or until potatoes are tender. Drain well. Return potatoes to saucepan over very low heat and shake the pot back and forth to remove any trace of moisture. Remove from heat. Using a potato masher, mash in 3 tbsp (45 mL) butter. Mash in cream, Dijon mustard, dry mustard and parsley. Using a wooden spoon, briskly stir mashed potatoes until smooth. Cover with a clean tea towel, replace the lid and keep warm.

3. *Sauce:* Preheat oven to 425°F (220°C). In a heavy-bottomed saucepan, combine shallots, wine and vinegar over high heat. Boil for about 10 minutes or until reduced by three-quarters and syrup-like. Reduce heat to very low and whisk in cream until blended. Add butter a few cubes at a time, whisking to incorporate before adding next batch (do not boil). Season sauce to taste with salt and freshly ground white pepper and whisk again. Add shrimp, chives and dill and stir until shrimp are coated. Cover and remove from heat. Keep warm.

4. In a large, ovenproof skillet, heat oil over medium-high heat until hot and shimmering. Place fish, skin side down, in pan and cook for 1 to 2 minutes. Then transfer to preheated oven and bake for 7 to 8 minutes (a little longer if the fillets are thick) or until firm to the touch.

5. Evenly divide mashed potatoes among four warmed individual serving plates. Top each with a fillet and carefully spoon sauce over the fish. Serve immediately.

Variations

Substitute salmon or seared scallops for the cod. To sear scallops, pat them dry with paper towels, as any moisture on the surface will keep them from browning nicely, and season with salt and pepper. Heat a nonstick skillet over medium-high heat for 1 to 2 minutes Add a little oil and butter and heat until quite hot. Add scallops (don't crowd the pan) and sear, undisturbed, until one side is browned and crisp, 2 to 4 minutes. Using tongs, turn and sear until the second side is well browned and the scallops are almost firm to the touch, 2 to 4 minutes.

Smoked Haddock & Grainy Mustard Mash

I first enjoyed this combination in Scotland and then again in North Yorkshire, where smoked haddock is king. This is wonderful as a brunch or supper dish, served alongside poached eggs on buttered thick-cut toast.

**Makes
4 servings**

Tip

When making this dish, it is worth searching out naturally smoked haddock, which gets its coloring from the smoke, not added dye. Dyed smoked haddock is always more pronounced in color — quite yellow. Look for products that state this on the label; a good fishmonger should offer this product.

2 lbs	floury potatoes, peeled and quartered	1 kg
1 tsp	salt	5 mL
¼ cup	butter	60 mL
¼ cup	table (18%) cream	60 mL
¼ tsp	ground nutmeg	1 mL
2 lbs	smoked haddock fillets (see Tip, left)	1 kg
	Whole milk	
1½ cups	heavy or whipping (35%) cream	375 mL
2 tsp	grainy mustard	10 mL
1 tsp	Dijon mustard	5 mL
Pinch	salt	Pinch
¼ cup	finely chopped chives	60 mL

1. Place potatoes in a large saucepan and add cold water to barely cover. Add salt, cover loosely and bring to a boil over high heat. Reduce heat and cook for 20 minutes or until potatoes are tender. Drain well. Return potatoes to saucepan over very low heat and shake the pot back and forth to remove any trace of moisture. Remove from heat. Using a potato masher, mash a few times, then mash in butter. Mash in table cream and nutmeg. Using a wooden spoon, briskly stir mashed potatoes until smooth. Cover with a clean tea towel, replace the lid and keep fairly warm.
2. Place haddock fillets in a shallow saucepan or skillet over medium high-heat. Add enough cold water to come just below the top of the fish, then add enough milk to cover. Simmer, uncovered, for 8 minutes.
3. Meanwhile, in a small, heavy saucepan, bring heavy cream to a gentle boil over medium heat. Whisk in grainy and Dijon mustards and a pinch of salt. Keep warm.
4. Using a slotted spoon, carefully remove fillets from poaching liquid. Peel off skin and divide into four portions. Spoon a quarter of the mashed potatoes onto each of four warmed individual serving plates. Top each with a portion of haddock, then pour mustard sauce over fish. Sprinkle with chives and serve immediately.

Lobster Tails with Creamy Horseradish Mash

Reserve this easy-to-prepare dish for a special occasion, perhaps a birthday or the anniversary of someone whose idea of heaven is lobster and potatoes. Serve with your favorite green vegetable.

Makes 4 servings

Tip

Frozen lobster tails are widely available, easy to work with and quick to cook. For best results thaw overnight in the refrigerator; this creates the best texture in the cooked lobster.

2 lbs	floury potatoes, peeled and cut into chunks	1 kg
1 tsp	salt	5 mL
½ cup	whole milk	125 mL
¾ cup	butter, divided	185 mL
¼ cup	half-and-half (10%) cream	60 mL
½ cup + ⅓ cup	freshly grated horseradish	200 mL
4	frozen lobster tails (each about 4 oz/125 g), thawed (see Tip, left) and removed from shells	4
2 tbsp	chopped fresh chives	30 mL

1. Place potatoes in a large saucepan and add cold water to barely cover. Add salt, cover loosely and bring to a boil over high heat. Reduce heat and cook for 20 minutes or until potatoes are tender. Drain well. Return potatoes to saucepan over very low heat and shake the pot back and forth to remove any trace of moisture. Add milk and ¼ cup (60 mL) butter, increase heat to high and bring to a boil. Remove from heat, add ½ cup (125 mL) horseradish and, using a potato masher, mash until potatoes are smooth. Using a wooden spoon, briskly stir mashed potatoes until light and fluffy. Cover with a clean tea towel, replace lid and keep warm.

2. In a skillet, melt remaining ½ cup (125 mL) butter over medium heat. Add remaining ⅓ cup (75 mL) horseradish, lobster tails and chives. Cook, turning lobster tails once or twice, for 5 to 6 minutes or until no longer translucent.

3. Evenly divide mashed potato mixture among four warmed individual serving plates. Top each with a lobster tail. Spoon butter mixture over potatoes and lobster and serve immediately.

Crispy Potato Nests with Scallops & Shrimp

The trick to this impressive little dish is readiness. A willing sidekick won't hurt either. Read the recipe through and make sure you have everything at hand in the form required (of course, this is a good rule of thumb for recipes in general). These golden potato nests also make a pretty edible container for curried chicken salad, barbecued pork and peppers, stir-fries, scrambled eggs with bits of mushroom and bacon, or old-fashioned creamed salmon.

Makes 6 servings

Tips

Choose medium potatoes for this recipe, about 6 oz (175 g) each. If you use larger potatoes, you will need just four.

Use the coarse side of a box grater to shred the potatoes.

The oil should come a little over halfway up the sides of the pot. Do not overfill; leave at least 3 inches (7.5 cm) of headspace at the top.

If you don't have a thermometer, drop a small cube of dry bread into the oil; if it floats, the oil is hot enough.

- Preheat oven to 140°F (60°C)
- Large heavy pot, Dutch oven or deep fryer
- 2 strainer baskets (1 large and 1 smaller), lightly oiled
- Candy/deep-frying thermometer (if not using a deep fryer)
- Rimmed baking sheet, lined with paper towels
- Wok (optional)

1 lb	large shrimp, shelled, deveined and halved	500 g
2 tbsp	freshly squeezed lemon juice	30 mL
1 lb	large scallops, halved	500 g
2 tbsp	milk	30 mL
6	all-purpose or floury potatoes, peeled (see Tips, left)	6
½ cup	cornstarch	125 mL
1 tsp	salt	5 mL
	Vegetable oil	
1 tsp	sesame oil	5 mL
8 oz	snow peas	250 g
3	green onions, trimmed and sliced diagonally	3
2 tbsp	hoisin sauce	30 mL

1. In a bowl, combine shrimp and lemon juice. In another bowl, combine scallops and milk. Set aside.
2. Coarsely shred potatoes into a bowl of cold water (see Tips, left). Drain in a colander under cold running water until water runs clear. Transfer to a large, clean tea towel, gather towel around potatoes and squeeze over the sink to wring out as much moisture as possible (use a second tea towel if necessary). In a bowl, toss potatoes with cornstarch and salt until potatoes have absorbed all the cornstarch.

Tips

You will need two long-handled wire strainers, one slightly smaller than the other. When I first devised this recipe, I used a couple of wire-mesh strainers I found in a shop specializing in Asian kitchenware. You may also find an actual bird's-nest fryer, a device that consists of two small frying baskets with long handles.

The nests may be made 3 hours in advance and can be reheated for a few minutes in a 350°F (180°C) oven.

3. Place 4 to 6 inches (10 to 15 cm) oil in a large, heavy pot (see Tips, page 318). Heat over medium-high heat until thermometer registers 350°F (180°C). (If you're using a deep fryer, follow the manufacturer's instructions.) Place one-sixth of the potatoes in the large strainer basket. Press the small strainer basket down on top of them, forming the potatoes into a nest shape. Holding the handles of both baskets firmly together, carefully lower potatoes into oil and cook for about 2 to 3 minutes or until nest is crisp and golden brown. Holding the handles of both baskets firmly together, carefully lift them out. Remove small basket, invert large basket and tap nest onto a baking sheet lined with paper towels. Transfer to preheated oven to keep warm. Repeat with the remaining potatoes to make 6 to 8 nests.

4. Drain shrimp and scallops, discarding soaking liquids. In a wok or sauté pan, combine 3 tbsp (45 mL) vegetable oil and sesame oil over high heat. Stir-fry shrimp and scallops for 2 minutes. Add snow peas, green onions and hoisin sauce and stir-fry for about 1 minute or until shrimp and scallops are just cooked and no longer translucent.

5. Transfer nests to a large warmed serving platter. Evenly divide seafood mixture among nests and serve immediately.

Oyster Pie with Top Mash

Now here's a dish for Christmas Eve or maybe New Year's Eve. Choose this fabulous pie when you're feeling flush with moolah, when you've just received a long-awaited raise, when you've finally lost that last five pounds . . . or when none of the above apply but you want to feel as though they do. If it's possible for something to be at once elegant and comforting, this dish — which brings Ireland to mind — is it.

Makes 4 to 6 servings

Tips

Cut oysters on a grooved cutting board to collect all the residual liquor.

Oysters for this dish should be firm and slightly salty, such as bluepoints from the Atlantic or Quilcene oysters from Puget Sound.

Buy fresh oysters from a reputable supplier and explain how you will be using them. Good suppliers know their stuff and will recommend the best oysters for the job, and they'll be happy to shuck them for you. Ask the fishmonger to include the liquor from the oysters.

If you prefer, you can use a piping bag to pipe pointed peaks of mashed potatoes over the oysters.

- **Preheat oven to 400°F (200°C)**
- **8-cup (2 L) baking dish or casserole**
- **Piping bag, optional (see Tips, left)**

Topping

2 lbs	floury potatoes, peeled and quartered	1 kg
1 tsp	salt	5 mL
1/3 cup	butter	75 mL
1/2 cup	whole milk	125 mL
1/2 cup	table (18%) cream	125 mL
1/2 cup	finely chopped fresh chives	125 mL

Filling

24	oysters, shucked and cut in half, liquor reserved (see Tips, left)	24
	Chicken broth	
4	slices double-smoked bacon, diced	4
1	onion, chopped	1
1	carrot, peeled and grated	1
1	small red bell pepper, seeded and finely chopped	1
1 cup	frozen corn kernels, thawed and drained	250 mL
1 cup	frozen peas, thawed and drained	250 mL
6 tbsp	butter	90 mL
6 tbsp	all-purpose flour	90 mL
1 cup	heavy or whipping (35%) cream	250 mL
	Salt and freshly ground black pepper	

1. *Topping:* Place potatoes in a large saucepan and add cold water to barely cover. Add salt, cover loosely and bring to a boil over high heat. Reduce heat and cook for 20 minutes or until potatoes are tender. Drain well. Return potatoes to saucepan over very low heat and shake the pot back and forth to remove any trace of moisture. Mash in butter. Gradually mash in milk and table cream. Using a wooden spoon, beat mashed potatoes vigorously to incorporate a little air into the mixture, until smooth and creamy. Fold in chives. Cover with a clean tea towel, replace pan lid and keep warm.

2. *Filling:* Pour reserved oyster liquor into a measuring cup and add enough chicken broth to make 2 cups (500 mL). Set aside.

3. In a large skillet over medium-high heat, sauté bacon for about 5 minutes or until almost cooked through. Drain off half the fat. Add onion to skillet and sauté for about 5 minutes or until softened. Add carrot and sauté for about 5 minutes. Add red pepper, corn and peas and sauté for about 3 minutes or until pepper is tender-crisp.

4. Add butter and let melt, then stir in flour, using a flat whisk to incorporate flour into butter. Cook, stirring, for 3 minutes. Gradually add oyster liquor mixture, whisking to prevent lumps, and cook, stirring, for 3 minutes. Gradually add heavy cream, stirring constantly until blended. Reduce heat to low. Season to taste with salt and freshly ground pepper and gently simmer for about 5 minutes or until thickened and smooth (if the mixture thickens too much, add $1/4$ cup/60 mL milk and whisk it into the mixture).

5. Remove pan from heat and gently stir in oysters and any collected liquor. Pour into baking dish. Using a wide metal spatula, dab mashed potatoes on top, forming peaks (see Tips, page 320). Bake in preheated oven for about 20 minutes or until filling is bubbling around edges and potatoes are golden brown with crisp peaks. Let stand in pan on a wire rack for 5 minutes before serving.

Steamed Clams with Chorizo & Potatoes

If your week has been particularly hectic, choose to make this for Friday-night dinner. It takes no time to make, requires little effort and is loaded with flavor. This just cries out for crusty bread as an accompaniment.

Makes 4 servings

Tips

Choose any kind of potato. Each variety lends its own qualities to the clams and chorizo.

Mexican-style chorizo needs to be cooked, as it is a fresh sausage, not dry-cured and ready to eat. If you cannot obtain it, you can substitute fresh hot Italian sausage or spicy lamb sausage.

- **Large stockpot**

3 tbsp	olive oil	45 mL
2	large potatoes, peeled and cut into ½-inch (1 cm) cubes	2
1	red bell pepper, seeded and diced	1
1	onion, chopped	1
	Salt and freshly ground black pepper	
24	littleneck clams	24
2 lbs	fresh chorizo sausages (see Tips, left), cut into ¼-inch (0.5 cm) slices	1 kg
3	cloves garlic, chopped	3
2 cups	cherry or grape tomatoes, halved	500 mL
2 cups	chicken broth	500 mL
1 cup	dry white wine	250 mL
¾ cup	freshly squeezed lemon juice	175 mL
½ cup	chopped fresh basil leaves	125 mL
½ cup	chopped flat-leaf parsley leaves	125 mL
2 tbsp	granulated sugar	30 mL

1. In a large stockpot, heat oil over medium-high heat. Sauté potatoes, red pepper and onion for 10 to 15 minutes or until potatoes are almost cooked through and beginning to color. Season to taste with salt and freshly ground pepper.

2. Stir in clams, chorizo, garlic, tomatoes, chicken broth, wine, lemon juice, basil, parsley and sugar and bring to a boil. Reduce heat, cover and simmer for 8 to 10 minutes or until clams have opened. Using tongs, remove and discard any clams that have not opened.

3. Using a slotted spoon, evenly divide clams and chorizo among four warmed individual soup or pasta bowls. Ladle vegetables and broth overtop and serve immediately.

Variation

Substitute mussels for the clams.

Vegetarian Mains to Satisfy

Whether you are a die-hard lover of meat and potatoes, a strict vegetarian or one of the growing number of "flexitarians," you will find lots of culinary inspiration in this chapter. Potatoes and sweet potatoes have long formed the culinary backbone of many cultures, as illustrated by this collection of recipes that borrows a little from all of them. Although there is a bit of a detour into light suppers, these recipes focus on vegetarian dishes that anchor the main meal of the day.

Buttered Bubble & Squeak

Named for the sounds that emanate from the pan as it cooks, this is the English name for an Irish dish known as colcannon. It is a tradition on All Hallows Eve (Halloween), the ancient Celtic New Year's Eve. Often little charms would be added to this dish for children to discover. Some maintain that true bubble and squeak contains meat while colcannon does not. Either way, it makes a lovely comforting dish, and it's rather perfect alongside a platter of roasted or grilled vegetables or, if you're not eating vegetarian, good-quality sausages.

Makes 4 to 6 servings

Tips

Use regular white cabbage or leafy green Savoy.

In my opinion, this dish should be made with leftover mashed potato and cabbage (or, even more traditionally, kale). Somehow it's not as good when the central ingredients are made freshly. You can use any mashed potatoes you prefer, from Classic Mash Deluxe (page 50) to dry-mashed to those that have been flavored with garlic.

3 tbsp	butter (approx.)	45 mL
3 tbsp	olive oil	45 mL
4	green onions (white part with a bit of green), finely chopped	4
2 cups	cooked cabbage or kale (see Tips, left)	500 mL
3 cups	leftover mashed potatoes	750 mL
	Salt and freshly ground black pepper	
	Butter for melting	

1. In a large, heavy skillet, heat butter and oil over medium-high heat. Sauté onions for about 8 minutes or until just softened. Toss in cabbage. Using a fork, stir in potatoes, breaking them up coarsely. Season to taste with salt and freshly ground pepper and cook, stirring, until potatoes are heated through.
2. Transfer to a warmed serving dish. Make a well in the center and add a big knob of butter to melt. Serve immediately.

Variation

One Sunday morning my husband shaped some leftover colcannon into little patties and fried them with a little double-smoked bacon. Leftover leftovers never tasted so good.

Fennel, Potato & White Bean Stew

This fragrant, earthy dish combines many flavorful vegetables with a little Indian spice. It is a great dish for cold-weather months. Serve this with a rice pilaf or squares of firm polenta and perhaps some Grana Padano or another hard aged cheese.

Makes 4 to 6 servings

Tip

Instead of soaking the dried beans overnight (an option, if you prefer), I have used a hot soaking method, which makes it possible to prepare and enjoy this dish on the same day.

- **Large soup pot**

8 oz	dried white beans, such as navy or cannellini	250 g
1 lb	red-skinned waxy potatoes, scrubbed and halved	500 g
1 tsp	salt	5 mL
¼ cup	extra virgin olive oil	60 mL
2	fennel bulbs, trimmed (fronds reserved), cored and thinly sliced	2
2	carrots, peeled and finely chopped	2
1	large white onion, finely chopped	1
4	cloves garlic, crushed	4
1 tbsp	curry powder	15 mL
4 cups	vegetable or light chicken broth	1 L
4	fresh or canned plum tomatoes, peeled and chopped	4

1. Place beans in a large bowl and add enough boiling water to cover. Let stand for 10 minutes and drain. Repeat the process once more.
2. Meanwhile, place potatoes in a large saucepan and add boiling water to barely cover. Add salt, cover loosely and bring to a boil over high heat. Reduce heat and cook for 20 minutes or until potatoes are tender. Drain well. Set aside until cool enough to handle. Slice thickly and set aside.
3. In a large pot, warm oil over medium heat. Cook fennel, carrots and onion, stirring, for 5 minutes. Stir in garlic and curry powder and cook, stirring, for about 5 minutes or until fragrant. Stir in beans and vegetable broth and bring to a boil. Reduce heat and simmer for about 1 hour or until beans are tender (do not overcook).
4. Increase heat to medium, stir in potatoes and tomatoes and simmer until potatoes are heated through.
5. Meanwhile, finely chop fennel fronds. Evenly divide stew among 4 to 6 warmed individual serving bowls. Garnish with fennel fronds and serve immediately.

Potato & Porcini Croustade

Far from being a poor substitute for fresh porcini, fine-quality dried porcini are wonderfully flavorful. This rustic free-form tart relies on frozen puff pastry, which makes it quite easy to put together.

Makes 4 to 6 servings

Tips

Use as wide an assortment of mushrooms as possible, combining regular mushrooms with chanterelle, oyster or cremini mushrooms for this rustic, satisfying tart.

To rehydrate mushrooms: Place dried porcini in a small bowl and add warm water to cover. Set aside to soak for 1 hour. Place a fine-mesh sieve over a bowl and add porcini, collecting soaking liquid in bowl. Set soaking liquid aside.

When rehydrated, a small portion of dried porcini goes a long way toward making a larger quantity of common mushrooms much more interesting.

If you like, add a few pieces of good blue cheese to the exposed potatoes in the croustade, 15 minutes before the end of baking.

- Preheat oven to 400°F (200°C)
- Nonstick baking sheet or regular baking sheet lined with parchment paper or Silpat

2 oz	dried porcini mushrooms, rehydrated (see Tips, left)	60 g
3	large floury potatoes, peeled	3
8 oz	assorted fresh mushrooms, trimmed and sliced	250 g
4	shallots, finely sliced	4
3	cloves garlic, finely chopped	3
2 tbsp	chopped flat-leaf parsley leaves	30 mL
1 tsp	chopped fresh rosemary leaves	5 mL
1 tsp	chopped fresh thyme leaves	5 mL
	Salt and freshly ground black pepper	
8 oz	frozen puff pastry, thawed	250 g
1½ cups	table (18%) cream	375 mL

1. Chop rehydrated porcini finely and transfer to a large bowl. Cut potatoes into ¼-inch (0.5 cm) slices and add to porcini along with fresh mushrooms. Add shallots, garlic, parsley, rosemary and thyme. Season to taste with salt and pepper. Toss.

2. On a lightly floured surface, roll pastry into a rectangle about ¼ inch (0.5 cm) thick. Transfer to prepared baking sheet. Pile potato mixture in the center of the pastry, leaving a 3-inch (8 cm) border. Fold edges up and over mixture, overlapping as necessary around edges and leaving center of potato mixture exposed.

3. In a bowl, combine ½ cup (125 mL) of the reserved mushroom-soaking liquid and cream. Pour into center of potatoes. Bake in preheated oven for 20 minutes. Reduce oven temperature to 375°F (190°C) and bake for 40 minutes or until crust is golden brown. Remove from oven. Let stand on a wire rack for about 15 minutes before serving.

Indian-Spiced Potatoes & Spinach

This is a full-flavored, robust vegetarian dish that will win favor with everyone, even the most committed carnivores. Serve with basmati rice, Indian flatbreads and chutney.

Makes 4 to 6 servings

Tips

Look for black mustard seeds in Indian food shops or specialty food stores.

The quantity of green chiles used in this recipe may prove a bit too powerful for some, so feel free to reduce the number. If you're worried about the heat, you can also remove the membranes and seeds before chopping (wear rubber gloves when handling chiles).

1 lb	all-purpose potatoes, peeled and cut into 1-inch (2.5 cm) chunks	500 g
1 tsp	salt	5 mL
2 tbsp	vegetable oil	30 mL
1 tsp	black mustard seeds	5 mL
1 tsp	cumin seeds	5 mL
3	fresh green chiles, finely chopped (see Tips, left)	3
1	large onion, sliced	1
2 tbsp	chopped gingerroot	30 mL
1 tbsp	turmeric	15 mL
1 tbsp	curry powder	15 mL
1	large tomato, chopped	1
1 lb	baby spinach leaves	500 g
1 cup	canned coconut milk	125 mL
2 tbsp	freshly squeezed lemon juice	30 mL
¼ cup	chopped fresh cilantro leaves	60 mL

1. Place potatoes in a large saucepan and add cold water to barely cover. Add salt, cover loosely and bring to a boil over high heat. Reduce heat and cook for 20 minutes or until potatoes are tender. Drain well and set aside.

2. In a large skillet, heat oil over medium-high heat until shimmering. Add mustard seeds and cook carefully (stand back — they will sputter and pop), stirring, until seeds have stopped popping. Add cumin seeds and stir-fry for a few seconds. Add chiles and onion and stir-fry for about 10 minutes or until onion is beginning to color. Add ginger and stir-fry for about 1 minute. Add turmeric and curry powder and stir-fry for 1 to 2 minutes.

3. Add potatoes and toss to coat. Add tomato and stir-fry for about 2 minutes or until it is releasing its juices. Stir in spinach; it will wilt somewhat as it cooks — add a lid for a minute to speed up the process. Stir in coconut milk and lemon juice until blended. Reduce heat and simmer for about 5 minutes or until mixture is slightly thickened and everything is heated through. Just before serving, stir in cilantro.

Samosa-Spiced Potato Pitas

All the usual fragrant spices that go into making our favorite Indian snack — samosas — are here, along with the prerequisite potatoes and peas. But this time, instead of being housed in pastry and deep-fried or baked, the filling is used to stuff pita pockets.

Makes 6 servings

Tip

Garam masala is an Indian spice mixture. It is available in specialty stores and East Indian food shops. If you can't obtain it easily, substitute an equal quantity of curry powder or make your own (see Tips, page 234).

1 lb	mini red or white potatoes, scrubbed and cut into ½-inch (1 cm) pieces	500 g
1 tsp	salt	5 mL
1	small red onion, finely chopped	1
1	large clove garlic, finely chopped	1
1 cup	sweet green peas, thawed if frozen	250 mL
⅓ cup	plain yogurt	75 mL
3 tbsp	chili sauce or salsa	45 mL
1 tbsp	olive oil	15 mL
1 tsp	ground cumin	5 mL
1 tsp	ground coriander	5 mL
¼ tsp	cayenne pepper	1 mL
1 tsp	garam masala (see Tip, left)	5 mL
	Salt and freshly ground black pepper	
3	6-inch (15 cm) pita breads, halved crosswise and warmed	3

1. Place potatoes in a saucepan and add boiling water to barely cover. Add salt, cover loosely and return to a boil over high heat. Reduce heat and cook for 20 minutes or until potatoes are tender. Drain well. Return potatoes to saucepan and, using a wooden spoon, stir in onion, garlic, peas, yogurt, chili sauce, oil, cumin, coriander, cayenne and garam masala. Season to taste with salt and freshly ground pepper.

2. Return pan to stovetop over medium heat and simmer gently, stirring occasionally, for 3 to 4 minutes to let flavors soak into potatoes. Remove from heat. Using wooden spoon, partially crush potatoes, leaving some pieces intact.

3. Fill each pita half with one-sixth of the potato mixture. Serve hot or warm.

Variation

Use a traditional Indian bread such as naan and roll it around the filling.

Sweet Potato & Chickpea Curry

This is very nice served with some brown basmati rice.

Makes 6 to 8 servings

Tips

If you're heat-averse, remove the seeds and membranes of the chile peppers before chopping.

You can use drained, rinsed canned chickpeas for this curry, but the texture of dried chickpeas that you have soaked and cooked is preferable. If using dried chickpeas, you will need about 7 oz (200 g). Soak them overnight in cold water to cover by a couple of inches, drain and cook the next day in about three times their volume of fresh water (don't add salt). Depending on the age of your chickpeas, they will need 45 minutes to 1 1/2 hours to get relatively tender (in my experience they never get really tender, but that is as it should be).

Greek-style yogurt is available in well-stocked supermarkets. You can use regular yogurt in this recipe, but your sauce will not be as lustrous and thick.

1/4 cup	olive or vegetable oil	60 mL
4	cloves garlic, minced or crushed in a garlic press	4
2	onions, finely chopped	2
1 or 2	fresh Thai or Scotch bonnet chiles, finely chopped (see Tips, left)	1 or 2
1 tsp	ground ginger	5 mL
1 tsp	ground turmeric	5 mL
1 tsp	ground cumin	5 mL
1 tsp	ground coriander	5 mL
1 tsp	ground cinnamon	5 mL
1/2 tsp	ground nutmeg	2 mL
2 lbs	sweet potatoes, peeled and cut into 1/2-inch (1 cm) chunks	1 kg
2 1/2 cups	vegetable or chicken broth	625 mL
2 cups	coconut milk	500 mL
2 tbsp	freshly squeezed lime juice	30 mL
4 cups	cooked chickpeas (see Tips, left)	1 L
6 oz	small mushrooms, trimmed and quartered	175 g
1 cup	plain Greek-style (pressed) yogurt (see Tips, left)	250 mL
2 tbsp	chopped fresh cilantro leaves	30 mL
2 tbsp	chopped fresh mint leaves	30 mL

1. In a large skillet, heat oil over medium-high heat. Sauté garlic, onions and chiles for about 10 minutes or until softened. Stir in ginger, turmeric, cumin, coriander, cinnamon and nutmeg and sauté gently for 5 minutes.

2. Stir in sweet potatoes to coat with spice mixture. Increase heat to high, stir in vegetable broth, coconut milk and lime juice and bring to a boil. Reduce heat, cover loosely and simmer for 20 to 25 minutes or until potatoes are tender.

3. Stir in chickpeas and mushrooms and simmer for 10 minutes or until chickpeas are heated through and mushrooms are tender. Turn off heat and stir in yogurt just until blended (do not allow to boil), then remove from heat. Just before serving, quickly stir in cilantro and mint. Serve immediately.

World's Best Vegetable Burger

We've all had them in a restaurant or from the grocer's freezer: vegetable-based burgers that made you regret your choice. Many are bean based, and while there is nothing theoretically wrong with beans, often the combinations lack appeal. Enter the potato (in two forms) to save the day! To serve these as burgers, melt a slice of sharp (aged) Cheddar, Havarti or pepper Jack cheese on top of each patty and serve with a full-flavored chili sauce or salsa. Or simply serve as vegetable patties with a lively salad.

Makes 4 to 6 servings

Tips

If you don't want to bother roasting an eggplant just for this recipe, pick up some roasted or grilled eggplant from a deli counter. If it is especially oily, drain on paper towels. You can also substitute an equal quantity of roasted red bell peppers.

To drain moisture from zucchini, grate the zucchini onto a clean tea towel. Gather up the towel and twist it over the sink to help remove as much liquid as possible.

If you're not using leftover red-skinned potatoes, undercook the potatoes slightly for this recipe, as they will receive additional cooking time in the form of the burger. For the mash, use dry-mashed potatoes, garlic mash or even leftover Classic Mash Deluxe (page 50).

While whole wheat bread crumbs are a little more nutritious, for convenience you can use any dry bread crumbs.

¼ cup	olive oil, divided	60 mL
2	cloves garlic, minced	2
1	large onion, finely chopped	1
1	large carrot, peeled and finely diced	1
½ tsp	ground ginger	2 mL
1 tsp	ground cumin	5 mL
1 cup each	chopped roasted or grilled eggplant, skin on, and cooked unpeeled red-skinned potatoes (see Tips, left)	250 mL
1	small zucchini, coarsely grated and squeezed to remove moisture (see Tips, left)	1
3 tbsp	chopped flat-leaf parsley leaves	45 mL
1	egg, lightly beaten	1
1 cup	mashed potato, warmed (see Tips, left)	250 mL
2 tbsp	all-purpose flour	30 mL
	Salt and freshly ground black pepper	
1½ cups	dry whole wheat bread crumbs (see Tips, left)	375 mL

1. In a large skillet, heat 2 tbsp (30 mL) oil over medium-high heat. Sauté garlic and onion for about 12 minutes or until softened and beginning to color. Add carrot, ginger and cumin and sauté until carrot is almost softened, 10 minutes. Add eggplant, potatoes, zucchini and parsley and sauté for 3 minutes. Remove from heat. Set aside to cool.

2. Transfer mixture to a large bowl and add egg, mashed potato and flour. Using your hands, blend thoroughly. Season to taste with salt and freshly ground pepper and mix again (if mixture seems too loose, add a little more flour). Shape into 6 patties.

3. Scatter bread crumbs on a plate. Dip both sides of patties in crumbs, shaking off excess. Transfer to another plate.

4. In a large skillet, heat remaining 2 tbsp (30 mL) oil over medium heat. Fry patties for 6 or 7 minutes in total or until golden brown. Serve immediately.

Potato & Late Summer Vegetable Paella

When is a paella not a paella? Well, I guess in this recipe, where diced red-skinned new potatoes stand in for the traditional rice. I have given it this name because the first time I made it I used a wide, shallow paella pan, but a skillet will work just as well.

Makes 6 servings

Tip

If you want to, it isn't hard to add a few seafood and meat components to the paella. Sauté peeled, deveined shrimp, boneless chicken or chunks of lean pork in Step 1 before sautéing the onion mixture. Remove and set aside while you make the dish, then add when the peppers have almost finished cooking. You can also add some steamed mussels or clams, along with their cooking liquid, after the paella is cooked. Or serve it as is alongside roast chicken or grilled fish or as a bed for grilled skewered lamb or pork. It's also good over cooked grains or pasta.

• **Paella pan, wok or large skillet**

¼ cup	olive oil	60 mL
2	red onions, halved and thinly sliced	2
2	cloves garlic, minced	2
1 tbsp	chopped fresh thyme	15 mL
1 tbsp	chopped fresh marjoram leaves	15 mL
1 tbsp	chopped fresh oregano leaves	15 mL
	Salt and freshly ground black pepper	
4	red-skinned waxy potatoes, peeled and cut into 1-inch (2.5 cm) chunks	4
2	white turnips, peeled and cut into 1-inch (2.5 cm) chunks	2
4	large ripe tomatoes, peeled and chopped (see Tips, page 362)	4
2	zucchini, trimmed and cut into small chunks	2
1	yellow bell pepper, seeded and cut into 1-inch (2.5 cm) chunks	1
1	red bell pepper, seeded and cut into 1-inch (2.5 cm) chunks	1
2 tbsp	chopped flat-leaf parsley leaves	30 mL

1. In paella pan, heat oil over medium-high heat. Sauté onions, garlic, thyme, marjoram and oregano for about 10 minutes or until onions are softened. Season to taste with salt and freshly ground pepper. Stir in potatoes and turnips and sauté for 10 minutes. Stir in tomatoes and zucchini. Reduce heat, cover loosely and simmer for about 20 minutes or until potatoes are tender.

2. Stir in yellow and red peppers and cook, stirring, for about 6 minutes or until peppers are tender-crisp. Season to taste with salt and freshly ground pepper. Sprinkle with parsley and serve immediately.

Stilton, Onion & Potato Bake

Sometimes all you want for dinner is comfort, and this is it. It's quite rich and filling, so all you need is a nice green salad, properly dressed with a lemony vinaigrette.

Tips

Make sure to allow enough time for the onions to really soften and cook in the butter, at least 20 minutes.

Stilton is the best blue cheese for this recipe, but other blue cheeses may be substituted.

- Preheat oven to 400°F (200°C)
- 11- by 7-inch (2 L) baking dish, bottom and sides well buttered

3 lbs	floury potatoes, peeled and halved	1.5 kg
1 tsp	salt	5 mL
4	onions, halved	4
⅓ cup	butter, divided	75 mL
⅔ cup	whole milk	150 mL
	Freshly ground black pepper	
7 oz	Stilton cheese, crumbled (see Tips, left)	210 g
3 tbsp	freshly grated Grana Padano or Parmesan cheese	45 mL

1. Place potatoes in a large saucepan and add cold water to barely cover. Add salt, cover loosely and bring to a boil over high heat. Reduce heat and cook for 20 minutes or until potatoes are tender. Drain well. Return to saucepan over very low heat and shake the pot back and forth to remove any trace of moisture.

2. Meanwhile, slice each onion half into 4 or 5 segments. In a heavy skillet, melt half the butter over medium-low heat. Cook onions, stirring occasionally, for about 20 minutes or until softened, reducing heat to low if browning too quickly.

3. Add remaining butter to potatoes in pot and, using a potato masher, mash thoroughly. Mash in milk. Using a wooden spoon, stir potatoes briskly, incorporating a little air into the mash.

4. Spoon half the potatoes into prepared baking dish, smoothing surface. Layer cooked onions evenly overtop. Season to taste with freshly ground pepper. Sprinkle Stilton evenly overtop. Spoon in the remaining mashed potatoes, smoothing lightly with the back of a large spoon or spatula. Sprinkle evenly with Grana Padano.

5. Bake in preheated oven for 30 minutes or until top is golden and edges are bubbling. Remove from oven and let stand on a wire rack for 5 minutes before serving.

Potato & Tomato Cheese Bake

This is a lovely main course when served with greens such as a broccoli salad or rapini sautéed with garlic and tossed with a little lemon juice.

Makes 4 to 6 servings

Tips

You can vary the cheese here, using another sheep's milk cheese such as Spain's famous Manchego, Grana Padano or fontina if you like, but try to include a smoked cheese such as smoked Cheddar or Gouda for extra flavor.

While it isn't really necessary, if you prefer, peel the tomatoes. With a sharp paring knife, cut a small X in the base of the tomato, then plunge into a large pot of boiling water for 2 minutes. Remove with a slotted spoon. Working from the base, peel off the skin.

Don't substitute dried oregano in this recipe, as the fresh herb really makes all the difference.

- **Preheat oven to 400°F (200°C)**
- **11-by 7-inch (2 L) baking dish, lightly greased**

1 cup	grated Pecorino Romano cheese, divided	250 mL
¼ cup	extra virgin olive oil, divided	60 mL
6	large Yukon Gold potatoes, scrubbed and cut crosswise into thin slices	6
3	cloves garlic, minced	3
2	onions, thinly sliced	2
1 lb	ripe firm Roma (plum) tomatoes, seeded and diced (see Tips, left)	500 g
4 tsp	chopped fresh oregano leaves	20 mL
1 tsp	salt	5 mL
½ tsp	freshly ground black pepper	2 mL
8 oz	smoked mozzarella cheese, thinly sliced	250 g

1. In a large bowl, using your hands, thoroughly mix ½ cup (125 mL) Pecorino Romano, 2 tbsp (30 mL) oil, potatoes, garlic, onions, tomatoes, oregano, salt and freshly ground pepper. Transfer to prepared baking dish. Drizzle with remaining 2 tbsp (30 mL) oil and sprinkle with remaining ½ cup (125 mL) Pecorino Romano. Cover with lightly buttered foil (do not let it touch the cheese) and bake in preheated oven for 45 minutes.

2. Uncover and evenly arrange mozzarella slices over potato mixture. Broil for 5 minutes or until cheese is bubbling and browned. Let stand for 10 minutes on a wire rack before serving.

Potato & Pumpkin Dumplings with Wild Mushroom Cream

These savory little dumplings are quite versatile, as they can be teamed with a number of sauces — a bright-tasting tomato sauce with fresh herbs, a simple butter and cheese treatment, or this rich, sumptuous sauce based on crème fraîche and chanterelles, those lovely trumpet-shaped mushrooms with such wonderful flavor.

Makes 6 servings

Tips

Any mushroom may be used in this recipe, but for added flavor try to include a few unconventional ones such as chanterelle, oyster or shiitake mushrooms.

Crème fraîche is available in well-stocked supermarkets or specialty shops. Or you can make your own (page 132).

Dumplings

1 lb	all-purpose or floury potatoes, peeled and cut into 2-inch (5 cm) chunks	500 g
2 tsp	salt, divided	10 mL
1 cup	canned pumpkin purée	250 mL
1/8 tsp	ground nutmeg	0.5 mL
1	egg yolk	1
1¾ cups	all-purpose flour	425 mL

Sauce

2 tbsp	olive oil	30 mL
2 tbsp	butter	30 mL
1	shallot, finely chopped	1
6 oz	fresh chanterelles (see Tips, left), sliced	175 g
⅔ cup	crème fraîche (see Tips, left)	150 mL
¼ cup	chopped flat-leaf parsley leaves	60 mL
1 tbsp	chopped fresh sage leaves	15 mL
	White pepper	

1. *Dumplings:* Place potatoes in a large saucepan and add cold water to barely cover. Add 1 tsp (5 mL) salt, cover loosely, and bring to a boil over high heat. Reduce heat and cook for 20 minutes or until potatoes are tender. Drain well. Return potatoes to saucepan over very low heat and shake the pot back and forth to remove any trace of moisture. (This step is important, because if they are wet the potatoes will absorb too much flour, which in turn will produce heavier dumplings.)

2. Transfer potatoes to a large bowl. Using a potato masher, mash until smooth. Mash in pumpkin purée, remaining 1 tsp (5 mL) salt, nutmeg and egg yolk until well blended. Gradually add the flour ½ cup (125 mL) at a time, kneading gently until a soft dough forms (you may not need all the flour). Knead several times until dough is firm and pliable. Using your hands, shape into a ball. Transfer to a lightly floured surface and divide into two portions.

3. Gently knead each half until a smooth, soft dough forms. Divide each half into 6 pieces and, using your palms, roll each into a long sausage about ¾ inch (2 cm) in diameter. Working with one roll at a time, cut into pieces about 1 inch (2.5 cm) long and transfer to a clean tea towel lightly dusted with flour as they are cut (do not let them touch). Cover with another clean tea towel. (At this point dumplings and towels can be covered with plastic wrap and refrigerated until ready to cook the same day.) Set aside.

4. Bring a large pot of salted water to a boil.

5. *Sauce:* Meanwhile, in a skillet, heat oil and butter over medium-high heat. Sauté shallot for 1 or 2 minutes. Add mushrooms and sauté for 10 to 12 minutes or until softened and beginning to color. Stir in crème fraîche and simmer, stirring, for about 5 minutes or until blended and melted into mushrooms. Add 1 or 2 tbsp (15 to 30 mL) water to thin sauce and simmer for about 1 minute. Stir in parsley and sage and season to taste with salt and white pepper. Reduce heat to very low and keep warm.

6. In batches, using a slotted spoon, transfer dumplings to boiling water. After 3 to 4 minutes they will bob to the surface. Using slotted spoon, transfer to a bowl and keep warm as you cook the remaining dumplings.

7. Spoon a portion of dumplings into each of six warmed individual pasta bowls. Cover each with mushroom sauce and serve immediately.

The Nacho Wedge

I'm here to tell you to forget corn chips when making nachos. Use much healthier crisp, oven-roasted potato wedges and top with all the usual nacho suspects — chiles, beans, cheese, olives, green onions, diced tomato. This is a great dish to serve at your next big televised game day. Add salsa, guacamole and perhaps even a dollop of sour cream, just to round things off.

Makes 6 to 8 servings

Tips

If you have a favorite spice blend that you use for chicken or ribs, use it to season the potatoes before roasting.

For this quantity of beans, it's probably easiest to use canned black beans, unless you have cooked dried ones from scratch and have some leftover.

Plan on serving these spuds directly from the baking tray, but let everyone know how hot it is.

● **Preheat oven to 400°F (200°C)**

6	large floury potatoes, scrubbed	6
1/4 cup	olive oil	60 mL
2 tsp	sweet paprika	10 mL
1/2 tsp	garlic salt	2 mL
1/2 tsp	dried oregano	2 mL
1/4 tsp	cayenne pepper	1 mL
	Freshly ground black pepper	
2 cups	shredded Monterey Jack cheese	500 mL
1/2 cup	cooked black beans, drained and rinsed	125 mL
3	tomatoes, diced	3
3	green onions, chopped	3
1/2 cup	sliced black olives	125 mL
1	jalapeño pepper, thinly sliced, or 1/4 cup (60 mL) canned sliced jalapeño peppers	1

1. Halve potatoes lengthwise, then cut into thick wedges of uniform thickness. Transfer to a bowl. Add oil, paprika, garlic salt, oregano, cayenne and freshly ground pepper to taste and toss until potatoes are well coated.

2. Transfer potatoes to baking sheets, lining them up nicely (do not let them touch). Bake in preheated oven, turning once or twice, for about 30 minutes or until golden brown and cooked through.

3. Top potatoes with half the cheese, then beans, tomatoes, green onions, olives and remaining cheese. Return to oven and bake for about 5 minutes or until cheese has melted (broil if necessary). Serve immediately (see Tips, left).

Sweet Potato Soufflé with Gruyère

Perfectly delicious and not at all difficult to make, this savory soufflé uses a small amount of mashed sweet potato. It makes a great dinner accompanied by a mixed bean salad. If you choose to side it with that, add some crunch to the beans in the form of sliced celery, cucumber or sweet peppers.

Makes 6 servings

Tips

Serve sweet potatoes the day or so before you plan on making the soufflé, and make a little extra to purée.

Egg whites will take less time to become stiff if they are at room temperature. If you forget to take the eggs from the fridge beforehand, place the eggs (in their shells) in a bowl of warm tap water for no more than 2 minutes before using. Move them around a couple of times in the water during that time.

Vary the Gruyère flavor by replacing some of it with an equal quantity of your favorite blue cheese, or substitute with Cambozola, a harmonious combination of Gorgonzola and Camembert.

- Preheat oven to 375°F (190°C)
- Electric mixer
- Soufflé dish, lightly buttered

3 tbsp	butter, softened	45 mL
1	shallot, finely chopped	1
1	clove garlic, finely chopped	1
1½ tbsp	all-purpose flour	22 mL
	Salt and freshly ground black pepper	
½ tsp	herbes de Provence	2 mL
½ cup	whole milk (approx.)	125 mL
1 cup	sweet potato purée (see Tips, left)	250 mL
6 oz	Gruyère cheese, shredded	175 g
4	eggs, separated	4

1. In a large saucepan, melt butter over medium heat. Cook shallot and garlic, stirring, for about 5 minutes or until softened (do not brown). Whisk in flour and cook for about 30 seconds. Season to taste with salt and freshly ground pepper. Whisk in herbes de Provence. Whisk in milk and cook, whisking to prevent lumps, for about 4 minutes or until thickened (if it looks as if it needs more milk, add a little and whisk again). Stir in sweet potato purée and cook for about 1 minute or until blended. Remove from heat and stir in cheese until melted.

2. Place egg yolks in a bowl. Whisk in a small spoonful of the sweet potato mixture until incorporated, then whisk this tempered mixture back into the sweet potato mixture until blended. Set aside.

3. Using a mixer at high speed, beat egg whites until stiff peaks form. Using a rubber spatula, stir one-third of the egg whites into the sweet potato mixture, then gently fold in the remaining egg whites, being careful not to break them up too much. Gently transfer to prepared soufflé dish. Bake in preheated oven for 30 to 35 minutes, until soufflé is puffed and golden brown. Serve immediately.

Potato & Gruyère Custard Tart

This is a bit of a "wow!" dish, even though it consists of simple, everyday ingredients. Somehow when they all come together, housed within golden pastry, the whole is quite impressive. Inspired by tarts composed of similar ingredients that abound in country bakeries in France, this version is lovely when teamed with a simple salad of sharp, peppery greens dressed in a mustard vinaigrette. How French is that?

**Makes
6 servings**

Tip

If you have a pastry recipe of your own that you rely on, use it here instead of the one provided.

- **10-inch (25 cm) pie plate or flan pan**
- **Mandoline or food processor fitted with slicing blade (optional)**

Pastry

2 cups	all-purpose flour	500 mL
¼ tsp	salt	1 mL
¾ cup	unsalted butter, chilled and cut into cubes	175 g
⅓ cup	ice water (approx.)	75 mL

Filling

2	large floury potatoes, peeled	2
1 tsp	salt	5 mL
2 tbsp	butter, divided	30 mL
	Salt and freshly ground black pepper	
1	extra-large egg	1
½ cup	heavy or whipping (35%) cream	125 mL
4 oz	Gruyère cheese, shredded	125 g

1. *Pastry:* In a bowl, combine flour and salt. Using a pastry blender or two knives, cut in butter until mixture is crumbly. Add ice water, a few spoonfuls at a time, and stir to form a dough, adding a little more water as necessary until dough holds together (you may not need all the water). Shape into a ball, wrap in plastic wrap and refrigerate for about 1 hour.
2. On a lightly floured surface, roll out dough and cut to fit pie plate. Line plate with pastry, trimming off excess around rim. Place on a baking sheet and set aside. Preheat oven to 375°F (190°C).

3. *Filling:* Fill a saucepan with cold water. Using a mandoline or sharp chef's knife, cut potatoes into very thin, uniform slices and transfer to cold water. When finished slicing, drain saucepan and refill with enough fresh cold water to barely cover potatoes. Add salt, cover loosely and bring to a boil over high heat. Reduce heat and parboil potatoes for about 5 minutes or until slightly cooked. Drain well, transfer to a clean tea towel and pat dry.

4. Arrange potatoes in a single layer over pastry, overlapping slices. Dot with butter and sprinkle with salt and freshly ground pepper. Repeat twice more. Cover with foil and bake in preheated oven for 45 minutes or until potatoes are tender.

5. Meanwhile, in a bowl, whisk together egg and cream. Evenly pour egg mixture over potatoes and scatter evenly with cheese. Carefully return to oven and bake for 20 minutes or until mixture has set and cheese is beginning to turn golden brown. Remove from oven and let stand on a wire rack for 10 minutes before serving.

New Year's Eve Gratin

A sumptuous potato and fennel gratin, this dish is so rich and filling that all it needs is a salad on the side. That said, this was a feature at one of our New Year's Eve dinners at the Black Dog. We served small portions with roasted sirloin of beef.

Makes 6 to 8 servings

Tip

Slicing the fennel and potatoes on a mandoline will produce the fine, thin slices needed for this recipe.

- **Preheat oven to 350°F (180°C)**
- **Mandoline (optional)**
- **11- by 7-inch (2 L) baking dish, lightly buttered**

2	small fennel bulbs, trimmed, halved lengthwise and cored	2
2 tbsp	extra virgin olive oil	30 mL
2 tbsp	butter	30 mL
1	large onion, thinly sliced	1
4	large floury potatoes, peeled and thinly sliced	4
2 cups	heavy or whipping (35%) cream	500 mL
8 oz	shredded Gruyère cheese	250 g
	Salt and freshly ground black pepper	
2 tbsp	chopped fresh tarragon leaves	30 mL
2 tbsp	chopped flat-leaf parsley leaves	30 mL
¼ cup	freshly grated Grana Padano or Parmesan cheese	60 mL

1. Thinly slice fennel crosswise (see Tip, left). In a large skillet, heat oil and butter over medium heat. Cook fennel and onion for about 10 minutes or until softened. Set aside to cool.
2. In a large bowl, thoroughly combine potatoes, cream and cheese. Season to taste with salt and freshly ground pepper. Add fennel mixture, scraping in any bits from bottom of pan. Stir in tarragon and parsley. Transfer to prepared baking dish.
3. Sprinkle evenly with Grana Padano and cover with parchment paper. Bake in preheated oven for 1 hour. Uncover and bake for 20 minutes or until potato mixture is cooked through and top is golden brown.

Potato, Olive & Feta Cake

This is a lovely deep-dish sort of potato cake layered with fresh herbs, olives and tangy feta cheese, topped with a crisp bread-crumb crust. Panko are Japanese bread crumbs that become exceptionally crispy when cooked.

Makes 4 to 6 servings

Tips

Panko bread crumbs are available in most large supermarkets, but if you can't obtain them, regular dry bread crumbs will do.

You can vary the herbs as you wish but if you want to echo the Grecian influence, try to include some fresh oregano and mint in the mix.

Use your favorite olives.

If the feta cheese is quite wet, drain well on paper towels before crumbling.

If you prefer, use a mandoline to produce thin, even slices of potato.

- Preheat oven to 375°F (190°C)
- 9-inch (23 cm) glass pie plate, lightly greased

2 lbs	floury potatoes, scrubbed	1 kg
1⁄3 cup	extra virgin olive oil, divided	75 mL
1	large red onion, finely chopped	1
	Salt and freshly ground black pepper	
4 tbsp	finely chopped fresh herbs such as flat-leaf parsley, oregano, mint, chives, thyme or tarragon, divided (see Tips, left)	60 mL
1⁄3 cup	finely chopped black or green olives, or a mixture, divided	75 mL
8 oz	feta cheese, crumbled, divided	250 g
3 tbsp	finely chopped pine nuts	45 mL
1⁄2 cup	panko or other dry bread crumbs	125 mL

1. Slice potatoes very thinly lengthwise, transferring to a bowl of cold water. Drain and rinse under cold running water until water runs clear. Thoroughly pat dry and set aside.
2. In a skillet, heat 2 tbsp (30 mL) oil over medium heat. Cook onion, stirring, for about 15 minutes or until softened, being careful not to let it brown. Remove from heat and set aside.
3. In prepared pie plate, arrange a third of the potatoes in a single layer over the bottom, slightly overlapping slices as necessary. Sprinkle with salt and freshly ground pepper. Evenly scatter with half the onion, half the herbs, half the olives and a third of the feta. Repeat once more. Finish with a layer of potato. Drizzle with 1 tbsp (15 mL) oil and set aside.
4. In a bowl, stir together remaining feta, pine nuts, panko and 2 tbsp (30 mL) oil. Scatter evenly over potatoes, pressing down with palms to adhere. Drizzle with remaining oil. Bake in preheated oven for 40 minutes.
5. Pull out oven rack and, using a spatula, gently press down on cake to compact it. Return to oven, increase temperature to 450°F (230°C) and bake for 15 minutes or until potatoes are cooked through and top is browned. Let stand on a wire rack for 10 minutes before serving. Cut into wedges and serve hot or warm.

Two-Potato Tian with Tomato & Sweet Pepper

A tian generally comprises a number of layered ingredients, usually vegetables. It is served either hot or cold. This recipe, a little simpler, features both regular and sweet potatoes layered with a blend of cheeses and a vibrant tomato sauce. It's perfect to make ahead and serve for a special lunch or dinner, preceded by a bowl of homemade minestrone (in the winter) or chilled cucumber soup (in the summer) and good crusty bread.

Makes 4 servings

Tip

Vary the cheeses, using combinations that appeal to you. Try mozzarella, Monterey Jack or Asiago in place of the Cheddar and fontina, or any combinations thereof that suit your taste.

- **11- by 7-inch (2 L) baking dish, oiled**

3 tbsp	olive oil, divided	45 mL
1	large onion, chopped	1
3	cloves garlic, finely chopped	3
1 tsp	red pepper flakes	5 mL
1 tsp	dried oregano	5 mL
1½ tsp	salt, divided	7 mL
	Freshly ground black pepper	
1	small red, yellow or orange bell pepper, seeded and chopped	1
2½ cups	fresh or canned Roma (plum) tomatoes, chopped	625 mL
2 cups	vegetable or chicken broth	500 mL
3 tbsp	tomato paste	45 mL
2	large floury potatoes, scrubbed	2
2	large sweet potatoes, peeled	2
1 tsp	dried basil	5 mL
½ tsp	freshly ground black pepper	2 mL
1½ cups	shredded sharp (aged) Cheddar cheese	375 mL
1 cup	shredded fontina cheese	250 mL
½ cup	freshly grated Grana Padano or Parmesan cheese	125 mL

1. In a large skillet or saucepan, heat 2 tbsp (30 mL) oil over medium-high heat. Sauté onion, garlic, pepper flakes, oregano, ½ tsp (2 mL) salt and freshly ground pepper for about 6 minutes or until softened. Add bell pepper and sauté for 5 minutes. Stir in tomatoes and any accumulated juice and cook for 10 minutes. Stir in vegetable broth and tomato paste and bring to a boil, stirring well. Reduce heat and simmer for 30 minutes or until thickened. Taste and adjust seasoning with additional salt and freshly ground pepper, if necessary. Set aside.

2. Cut potatoes and sweet potatoes into slices ¼ inch (0.5 cm) thick and transfer to a large bowl. Toss in basil, remaining 1 tbsp (15 mL) oil, remaining 1 tsp (5 mL) salt and freshly ground pepper to coat. Set aside.

3. In a small bowl, combine Cheddar and fontina cheeses. Spread ¼ cup (60 mL) of the tomato sauce over bottom of prepared baking dish. Arrange a third of the potato mixture over sauce, spoon on about 1 cup (250 mL) more sauce and then ½ cup (125 mL) of the cheese mixture. Repeat once more, layering potatoes, sauce and cheese mixture. Sprinkle evenly with Grana Padano. Cover with parchment paper, then foil. Bake in preheated oven for about 45 minutes. Uncover and bake for 15 minutes or until top is golden brown. Let stand on a wire rack for 10 minutes before serving.

Roasted Vegetable Torte with Crispy Potato Roof

The secret to making this beautiful vegetarian main course is good organization. While it may seem like a long, involved process, it isn't really. The assembly will go very smoothly if you just make sure to give yourself enough time for each of the steps. Then it is just a case of layering the prepared vegetables and setting on the crown of potatoes and cheese.

Makes 6 servings

Tips

Once you have mastered this version, which uses a springform pan to make one big torte, you can experiment with making individual ones in separate molds. A friend of mine uses recycled tuna cans (top lid discarded) to form sweet little mini tortes.

During the hot-weather months you could easily grill the vegetables instead of roasting them.

- Preheat oven to 400°F (200°C)
- 2 or 3 large baking sheets, preferably nonstick
- 8-inch (2 L) springform pan

²⁄₃ cup	extra virgin olive oil, divided	150 mL
2	green zucchini, trimmed and cut lengthwise into ¼-inch (0.5 cm) slices	2
2	yellow zucchini, trimmed and cut lengthwise into ¼-inch (0.5 cm) slices	2
2	onions, sliced	2
2	cloves garlic, minced	2
	Salt and freshly ground black pepper	
2	large eggplants, trimmed and cut crosswise into ¼-inch (0.5 cm) slices	2
2	portobello mushrooms, stemmed and sliced	2
1	large red bell pepper, halved and seeded	1
1	large yellow or orange bell pepper, halved and seeded	1
3	firm ripe plum tomatoes, sliced	3
12	fresh basil leaves, stacked and sliced thinly	12
1 cup	freshly grated Grana Padano or Parmesan cheese	250 mL
3	large floury potatoes, scrubbed and thinly sliced, placed in cold water	3

1. In a large skillet, heat 2 tbsp (30 mL) oil over medium-high heat. Sauté zucchini, onions and garlic for 10 minutes. Season to taste with salt and freshly ground pepper. Set aside.

2. In a large bowl, combine eggplant, mushrooms and red and yellow peppers, then drizzle with $1/4$ cup (60 mL) oil and toss. Sprinkle with salt and freshly ground pepper. Arrange in a single layer on 1 or 2 baking sheets, as necessary. Bake in preheated oven, turning once or twice, for 25 to 30 minutes or until softened but not browned. Remove from oven and set aside.

3. In a springform pan, arrange a single layer of eggplant, slightly overlapping slices. Evenly layer with half the zucchini mixture, half the remaining eggplant mixture, then half the tomatoes. Scatter evenly with about half the basil and sprinkle with half the cheese. Repeat this layering process once more reserving the rest of the cheese for the potatoes.

4. Drain potatoes and pat dry with paper towels. Transfer to a bowl and drizzle generously with $1/4$ cup (60 mL) oil. Season to taste with salt and freshly ground pepper and toss. Arrange potatoes over the layered torte, slightly overlapping slices and pressing to adhere. Sprinkle with remaining cheese. Place on a rimmed baking sheet covered with parchment paper. Bake in preheated oven for 30 to 40 minutes or until potatoes are cooked through and top is golden brown. Remove from oven and turn off oven.

5. Cover torte with parchment paper, then cover with foil, tucking it under the bottom of the pan and all around the sides. Place a weight, such as a foil-wrapped brick or a panini weight, on top of torte. Carefully return to oven and leave to firm up in the residual heat for about 1 hour.

6. Remove from oven and let stand at room temperature for about 30 minutes before removing sides of pan. Using a sharp chef's knife, slice into wedges and serve at room temperature.

Roasted Eggplant & Potato Tarts

Everyone loves these sweet little tarts. Besides being a great centerpiece for a light meal, they are also a nice change (or addition) to standard picnic fare. Serve these free-form tarts warm or at room temperature with cold chicken and a tomato and avocado salad.

Makes 6 tarts

Tip

Good-quality frozen puff pastry is widely available in supermarkets. Look for a brand that is butter based for best results.

- Preheat oven to 400°F (200°C)
- 4¾-inch (12 cm) cookie cutter
- Baking sheet, lined with parchment paper

10 oz	frozen puff pastry, thawed	300 g
2	eggplants, about 1 lb (500 g) each, thinly sliced crosswise	2
¼ cup	extra virgin olive oil, divided	60 mL
3	waxy potatoes, peeled and thinly sliced	3
2	onions, thinly sliced	2
2 tbsp	chopped fresh thyme leaves	30 mL
3	cloves garlic, thinly sliced	3
	Salt and freshly ground black pepper	

1. On a lightly floured surface, roll out pastry to ¼ inch (0.5 cm) thickness. Using a lightly floured cutter, cut out 6 circles and transfer to prepared baking sheet. Set aside.

2. Lightly brush eggplant slices all over with a little of the oil. In a sauté pan over medium heat, cook eggplant in batches, stirring, for 4 minutes, until golden brown. Using tongs, transfer to a baking sheet as completed and set aside.

3. Add a little more oil to pan and cook potatoes, turning once, for 2 minutes per side or until golden. Using tongs, transfer to baking sheet with eggplants.

4. Adding a little more oil to pan if necessary, cook onions and thyme, stirring, for about 10 minutes or until onions are softened. Remove from heat and let cool.

5. Spoon a sixth of the onion mixture onto center of each pastry circle and top with eggplant, potato and garlic slices. Season to taste with salt and freshly ground pepper. Drizzle with remaining oil. Bake in preheated oven for 20 to 25 minutes or until pastry is golden.

Potato & Asparagus Tart

Soft, cheese-influenced mashed potatoes, crispy golden phyllo pastry and bright green asparagus come together easily to make a delicious spring lunch or dinner dish.

Makes 4 servings

Tips

Snap off the woody ends of the asparagus and use a vegetable peeler to peel the lower portion of the stalk.

Working with phyllo is not difficult if you remember a few cardinal rules: let it thaw in the refrigerator overnight, have a damp tea towel on hand to keep it covered as you work with it sheet by sheet, and don't stint on the butter — phyllo pastry has almost no fat, so it needs it. If you don't use the entire package, put the remainder back in the freezer for another use.

If you use oil-packed sun-dried tomatoes make sure to drain and pat them dry really well; otherwise the oil clinging to them will color the mashed potato mixture. You can also use halved fresh cherry or grape tomatoes.

- Preheat oven to 375°F (190°C)
- 11- by 7-inch (2 L) glass baking dish, buttered

1 lb	floury or all-purpose potatoes, peeled and quartered	500 g
1 tsp	salt	5 mL
1 lb	fresh asparagus, trimmed	500 g
4 oz	sharp (aged) Cheddar cheese, shredded	125 g
4 oz	herb and garlic cream cheese or soft goat's milk cheese, crumbled	125 g
3	large eggs	3
1 cup	heavy or whipping (35%) cream	250 mL
3 tbsp	dry-packed sun-dried tomatoes, chopped	45 mL
5	sheets phyllo pastry	5
½ cup	melted butter	125 mL

1. Place potatoes in a large saucepan and add cold water to barely cover. Add salt, cover loosely and bring to a boil over high heat. Reduce heat and cook for 20 minutes or until potatoes are tender. Using a slotted spoon, transfer to a large bowl (reserve cooking water in pot). Set aside.

2. Add asparagus to hot cooking water, increase heat to high, return to a boil and blanch for 2 minutes. Using tongs, transfer to a colander and drain well. Set aside.

3. Using a potato masher, mash potatoes until smooth. Mash in Cheddar and cream cheese. Set aside.

4. In a small bowl, whisk together eggs and cream. Stir into mashed potato mixture along with tomatoes. Set aside.

5. Place one sheet of phyllo in prepared baking dish, draping ends over rim, and brush with a little melted butter. Cover with another sheet and brush with melted butter. Repeat until all five sheets are layered in the dish, saving a little melted butter to drizzle over tart. Tuck under draped ends around edges of dish to form a rim.

6. Using a rubber spatula, evenly spread mashed potato mixture over phyllo. Arrange asparagus on top. Drizzle with remaining butter. Bake in preheated oven for about 25 minutes or until filling is puffed and pastry is crisp and golden. Let stand on a wire rack for 10 minutes.

Omelette Savoyarde

As with so many classic dishes, there are myriad versions of this, and perhaps only one or two that bear any resemblance to the original. I have seen recipes for this French omelet that include bacon and ham and onions and those that do not, and others that omit what I consider the central ingredient — potatoes. The original version serves the omelet set on a slice of cooked ham, which I think handles everything nicely. Serve with a simple green salad.

Makes
2 servings

Tip

Any cooked potatoes may be used in this recipe.

- **Preheat broiler**
- **9-inch (23 cm) ovenproof skillet**

6 tbsp	butter	90 mL
2	boiled potatoes, sliced crosswise ¼ inch (0.5 cm) thick	2
8	eggs, lightly beaten with 1 tbsp (15 mL) cold water	8
	Salt and freshly ground black pepper	
3 oz	Gruyère cheese, thinly sliced	90 g

1. In an ovenproof skillet, melt butter over medium-high heat. Sauté potatoes until lightly browned.

2. Season beaten eggs to taste with salt and freshly ground pepper. Pour over potatoes, reduce heat to medium and cook, tipping and rotating pan occasionally to help omelet set, for 1 to 2 minutes. Using a metal or rubber spatula, carefully draw edges toward center to let liquid egg slip underneath.

3. Lay cheese slices on top and place under preheated broiler for about 1 to 2 minutes to set the top of the omelet and melt cheese.

Cheddar & Potato Pie

This recipe came about when I had planned to make a conventional pie at a friend's cottage and realized the kitchen wasn't equipped with a pie dish. So I just formed the pie on a baking sheet. Baking it on a sheet gives it a quirky appearance. Once assembled, it should be a little taller, with straighter sides, than a regular pie because the ingredients are slightly mounded. Serve with an onion and tomato chutney.

Makes
4 servings

Tips

The quality of the Cheddar you use is most important, because the pie consists of little more than cheese and potatoes. Try to obtain a good sharp (aged) Cheddar for this recipe, at least six years old or more.

Use your favorite pastry recipe or make a double batch of the crust for Potato & Gruyère Custard Tart (page 338). You will need enough for a double-crust pie, or two 10-inch (25 cm) circles.

The small pastry circle should be about 9 to 10 inches (23 to 25 cm) in diameter.

● **Preheat oven to 400°F (200°C)**

3	large all-purpose or floury potatoes, peeled and cut into ¼-inch (0.5 cm) slices	3
¼ cup	butter	60 mL
1 tbsp	olive oil	15 mL
2	large onions, chopped	2
¼ cup	chopped chives	60 mL
3 tbsp	chopped flat-leaf parsley leaves	45 mL
	Freshly ground black pepper	
8 oz	sharp (aged) Cheddar cheese, shredded	250 g
	Pastry for a 10-inch (25 cm) double-crust pie (see Tips, left)	
1	large egg yolk, beaten with 1 tbsp (15 mL) water	1

1. Place potatoes in a large saucepan and add cold water to barely cover. Add 1 tsp (5 mL) salt, cover loosely and bring to a boil over high heat. Reduce heat and cook for 3 to 4 minutes or until potatoes are just tender. Drain well. Transfer to a large bowl and set aside to cool.

2. In a skillet, heat butter and oil over medium-high heat. Sauté onions, chives and parsley for about 10 minutes or until onions are softened (do not let brown). Add to cooled potatoes. Add cheese and mix well.

3. On a lightly floured surface, roll out pastry to form two circles, one a bit larger than the other (see Tips, left).

4. Place smaller pastry circle on a baking sheet. Center potato mixture on top, leaving a 1½-inch (4 cm) border.

5. Brush beaten egg around edges of pastry. Cover potato mixture with larger pastry circle and, using your fingers, press edges together to seal. Trim edges if necessary, then crimp, using a fork. Brush remaining beaten egg over pastry. Using the tip of a sharp knife, cut 3 or 4 vents in the top. Bake in preheated oven for 40 to 50 minutes or until pastry is golden brown.

Hot Pepper & Potato Hash with Oven Eggs

Some people love eggs for dinner. I'm one who does but my husband does not, so I have to content myself with enjoying this for breakfast, brunch or lunch. However, it also makes a superb dinner.

Makes 4 servings

Tips

If you're shopping in an Italian market, look for passata and use it instead of regular crushed tomatoes.

This makes quite a bit of tomato sauce, but it will last for about a week refrigerated. It makes a great gift for any heat-seekers you may know. The sauce is excellent on vegetable burgers or spread on toasted baguette slices and topped with melted Brie.

Serve up this hash with lots of hot buttered toast.

- **Preheat oven to 375°F (190°C)**
- **Large ovenproof skillet**

Hot Pepper Sauce

3 tbsp	olive oil	45 mL
2 lbs	green bell peppers, seeded and cut into 1-inch (2.5 cm) squares	1 kg
8 to 10	jalapeño peppers, stems trimmed, cut crosswise ¼ inch (0.5 cm) thick	8 to 10
2 tsp	salt	10 mL
2 cups	crushed tomatoes (see Tips, left)	500 mL

Hash

2	large floury potatoes, peeled and diced	2
1 tsp	salt	5 mL
¼ cup	extra virgin olive oil	60 mL
1	red onion, finely chopped	1
	Freshly ground black pepper	
2 tsp	butter, divided	10 mL
4	extra-large eggs	4
¼ cup	freshly grated Grana Padano cheese (see Variation, page 351)	60 mL
3 tbsp	chopped flat-leaf parsley leaves	45 mL

1. *Hot Pepper Sauce:* In a large, deep saucepan, heat oil over medium-high heat. Sauté green peppers, jalapeño peppers and salt, coating peppers thoroughly with oil. Reduce heat and simmer, stirring occasionally, for about 20 minutes or until peppers are softened but not beginning to brown.

2. Stir crushed tomatoes into pepper mixture and simmer, stirring often, for about 30 minutes or until peppers are completely tender (if the mixture is getting too thick, add a little water). Remove from heat and set aside to cool. Transfer 1½ cups (375 mL) to a small bowl and set aside. (Transfer remaining sauce to a jar with a tight-fitting lid and refrigerate for another use for up to 5 days.)

3. *Hash:* Place potatoes in a large saucepan and add cold water to barely cover. Add salt, cover loosely and bring to a boil over high heat. Reduce heat and cook for 4 minutes or until potatoes are just tender. Drain well.

4. In a large ovenproof skillet, combine oil and potatoes over high heat and cook, stirring to coat potatoes with oil. Reduce heat to medium and cook, tossing potatoes, for about 12 minutes or until golden brown and crisp. Stir in onion and cook, stirring, for about 3 minutes or until slightly softened. Turn off heat.

5. In a colander, drain potato mixture to remove excess oil. Return mixture to skillet. Gently stir in reserved hot pepper sauce, then level mixture in pan and make four small wells. Add about ½ tsp (2 mL) butter to each well, then crack an egg into it and sprinkle with cheese and parsley.

6. Transfer skillet to preheated oven and bake for about 6 minutes, until whites are set (longer for a firmer yolk). Divide evenly among four warmed dinner plates.

Variation

Substitute another aged cheese such as Cheddar or Asiago for the Grana Padano.

Sautéed Mushrooms & Potatoes with Garlic, Parsley & Poached Egg

This makes a lovely light main course. Choose the assortment of mushrooms you wish or even just good old white button mushrooms. Serve over thick-cut toast.

Makes 4 servings

Tips

Remove each poached egg from the simmering water with a slotted spoon. Pat the bottom of the spoon on paper towels to absorb any water before transferring to plate.

If you prefer you can gently fry the eggs instead of poaching them. Just make sure they are softly fried so you still have some lovely liquid yolk to blend with the mushrooms.

- **Large cast-iron or heavy skillet**

8 oz	waxy potatoes, scrubbed	250 g
1 tsp	salt	5 mL
¼ cup	butter	60 mL
3 tbsp	extra virgin olive oil	45 mL
1 lb	assorted mushrooms, trimmed and sliced ¼ inch (0.5 cm) thick	500 g
6	cloves garlic, finely chopped	6
	Freshly ground black pepper	
1 tbsp	freshly squeezed lemon juice	15 mL
1 cup	finely chopped flat-leaf parsley leaves	250 mL
1 tsp	vinegar	5 mL
4	large eggs	4

1. Place potatoes in a large saucepan and add boiling water to barely cover. Add salt, cover loosely and bring to a boil over high heat. Reduce heat and cook for 15 minutes or until potatoes are just tender. Drain well and let cool enough to handle. Cut each potato in half (if large, cut into chunks).

2. In a skillet, heat butter and oil over medium-high heat. Sauté mushrooms and potatoes for about 15 minutes or until golden brown. Toss in garlic, season to taste with salt and freshly ground pepper and sauté for about 1 minute. Remove from heat. Stir in lemon juice and parsley. Reduce heat to very low and cover to keep warm.

3. Pour enough water into a large, shallow saucepan to come 3 inches (8 cm) up the sides. Bring to a boil over high heat. Add vinegar and reduce heat to a simmer. Break each egg into a little dish or cup and gently slip, one at a time (or all together if you are a confident egg poacher), into simmering water. Cook for 5 minutes for a soft yolk and cooked white, or as desired.

4. Evenly divide mushroom mixture among four warmed individual serving plates and top each with a poached egg (see Tips, left). Serve immediately.

Potato & Sweet Red Pepper Tortilla

Both regular and sweet potatoes are used in this variation of Spain's famous tortilla. It's nice served warm or at room temperature. A big green salad, perhaps with chunks of avocado and halved cherry tomatoes, dressed in a sprightly vinaigrette, is a logical accompaniment.

Makes 4 servings

Tip

I prefer to use sea salt rather than refined table salt because it has a much cleaner, crisper taste and enhanced mineral content.

- **Preheat oven to 350°F (180°C)**
- **Rimmed baking sheet, lightly greased**
- **9-inch (2.5 L) square baking dish, lightly greased**

1	large Yukon Gold potato, peeled and diced, about 1 cup (250 mL)	1
1	large sweet potato, peeled and diced, about 1 cup (250 mL)	1
2 tbsp	olive oil, divided	30 mL
1	small red bell pepper, seeded and diced	1
1	onion, diced	1
	Salt and freshly ground black pepper	
4	eggs	4
¼ cup	table (18%) cream	60 mL

1. On prepared baking sheet, toss together potato, sweet potato and 2 tsp (10 mL) oil. Bake in preheated oven for 15 minutes or until tender. Remove from oven and let cool.
2. In a medium skillet, heat remaining oil over high heat. Sauté red pepper and onion for 5 to 6 minutes or until softened. Remove from heat and set aside to cool.
3. In a bowl, combine roasted potatoes and red pepper mixture. Season to taste with salt and freshly ground pepper.
4. In a large bowl, whisk together eggs and cream. Toss into bowl with potato mixture. Transfer to prepared baking dish and bake in preheated oven for 25 minutes or until set. Let cool slightly for 15 minutes or so before serving.

Variations

Tortilla can be served like this as a main course or, because it is also very nice at room temperature, cut into little cubes and served as tapas, the way they do in Spain. It makes a wonderful little bite with glasses of dry sherry. It can also be chilled, sandwiched between slices of crusty bread and taken on a picnic.

Frittata with New Potatoes & Mint

Fresh mint and new potatoes were always cooked together in my childhood home, so that's why I thought to combine them in this classic Italian open-faced omelet. I like to serve this with halves of beefsteak tomatoes, oven-roasted (or grilled), then drizzled with extra virgin olive oil and splashed with balsamic vinegar.

Makes 4 to 6 servings

Tip

I prefer to use sea salt rather than refined table salt because it has a much cleaner, crisper taste and enhanced mineral content.

- **Large cast-iron or ovenproof skillet**

8 oz	waxy new potatoes, scrubbed	250 g
1½ tsp	salt, divided	7 mL
3 tbsp	olive oil, divided	45 mL
1	onion, chopped	1
1 cup	whole fresh mint leaves	250 mL
¼ cup	chopped flat-leaf parsley leaves	60 mL
8	eggs	8
3 tbsp	fresh bread crumbs	45 mL
3 tbsp	freshly grated Grana Padano or Parmesan cheese	45 mL
2 tsp	all-purpose flour	10 mL
2 tsp	table (18%) cream	10 mL
¼ tsp	freshly ground black pepper	1 mL

1. Place potatoes in a saucepan and add boiling water to barely cover. Add 1 tsp (5 mL) salt, cover loosely and bring to a boil over high heat. Reduce heat and cook for 5 to 7 minutes (you do not want them to be completely tender). Drain well. When cool enough to handle, coarsely chop.

2. In a large ovenproof skillet, warm 2 tbsp (30 mL) oil over medium heat. Cook onion, stirring, for about 5 minutes or until softened. Remove from heat and stir in mint and parsley. Transfer to a small bowl. Set aside to cool.

3. In a bowl, whisk together eggs, bread crumbs, cheese, flour, cream, remaining salt and pepper. Stir in potatoes and reserved onion mixture. Preheat broiler to high.

4. Wipe skillet clean. Over medium heat, swirl remaining oil to coat. Add egg mixture and cook, running a narrow metal spatula around edges to lift up cooked egg and allow uncooked egg to run underneath, until frittata is set and bottom is cooked and golden brown. Transfer skillet to oven and place 6 inches (15 cm) beneath preheated broiler. Broil for about 1 to 2 minutes or until top is set and golden brown. Cut into wedges and serve immediately or let cool to room temperature.

Sweet Potato & Sage Frittata

Quite simple and fragrant with the chunks of roasted sweet potato and an accent of fresh sage, this makes a nice brunch or lunch dish for two. Serve with pan-seared tomato halves and buttered thick-cut toast.

Makes 2 servings

Tips

This dish also pairs perfectly with a bright tomato chutney or salsa.

- **Preheat oven to 400°F (200°C)**
- **8-inch (2 L) baking dish**

1	large sweet potato, peeled and diced	1
1	shallot, minced	1
1	clove garlic, minced	1
2 tbsp	olive oil	30 mL
	Salt and freshly ground black pepper	
4	eggs, lightly beaten	4
1 cup	table (18%) cream	250 mL
1/2 cup	freshly grated Grana Padano or Parmesan cheese	125 mL
1/4 cup	coarsely chopped fresh sage leaves	60 mL

1. In a baking dish, toss together sweet potato, shallot, garlic and oil. Season to taste with salt and freshly ground pepper. Bake in preheated oven for 25 minutes or until sweet potato is softened.
2. Meanwhile, in a bowl, whisk together eggs, cream and cheese.
3. Pull out oven rack and gently stir egg mixture into sweet potato. Sprinkle evenly with sage. Return to oven and bake for 15 to 20 minutes or until golden and somewhat firm. Serve warm or cool.

Variation

Allow frittata to cool to room temperature, slice thinly and toss the frittata strips with a fresh-tasting vinaigrette over mixed salad greens. This works with many frittatas.

Sweet Potato Risotto

A variation on the usual risotto, using butternut squash, this version results in a colorful, flavorful dish. It's perfect for fall dinners alongside sautéed rapini or a broccoli salad. If you are not a strict vegetarian, this is also a lovely choice with pan-seared or oven-roasted salmon or halibut.

Makes 4 to 6 servings

Tips

You will need both cooked and raw sweet potato for this. To speed things up, make extra cooked sweet potato the day before; you will need one large potato (1 lb/500 g) baked. Then choose a smaller one (about 10 oz/300 g) for the uncooked component. Place the diced raw sweet potato in cold water if chopping ahead of time; drain well and pat dry before using.

Plump and snowy white, Arborio rice is revered for its special properties. Because of its high starch content, it is the short-grained, semi-round rice recommended for risotto, the classic dish of the northern Italian kitchen. Its size enables it to absorb lots of cooking liquid while developing an ultra-creamy quality yet always retaining its true, firm heart — what the Italians call *all'onda*, or waviness.

- **Dutch oven**

6 cups	vegetable or chicken broth	1.5 L
2 tbsp	butter	30 mL
¼ cup	extra virgin olive oil	60 mL
2	cloves garlic, minced	2
1	onion, finely chopped	1
1	stalk celery, finely chopped	1
2 cups	Arborio rice (see Tips, left)	500 mL
½ cup	dry white wine	125 mL
1	small sweet potato (about 10 oz/300 g), peeled and finely diced	1
½ cup	heavy or whipping (35%) cream	125 mL
1	large sweet potato (about 1 lb/500 g), baked and mashed	1
1 cup	freshly grated Grana Padano or Parmesan cheese	250 mL
1 tbsp	finely chopped flat-leaf parsley leaves	15 mL

1. In a large saucepan, bring broth to a boil over high heat. Reduce heat to maintain a steady, slightly bubbling simmer throughout the rest of the cooking.

2. In a Dutch oven, heat butter and oil over medium-high heat. Sauté garlic, onion and celery for 4 minutes, being careful not to let garlic brown. Stir in rice and cook, stirring, for 1 minute. Pour in wine and cook, stirring, for about 1 minute or until wine is absorbed.

3. Using a ladle, add hot broth, about $1/2$ cup (125 mL) at a time, and simmer, stirring and scraping bottom and sides of pan and letting rice absorb each addition before adding the next (if you find the broth evaporates too quickly, slightly reduce the heat). Repeat this procedure, ladling in hot broth and stirring and scraping pan, for 15 to 20 minutes, at which point rice will still be fairly firm. (At this stage, if you have used most or all of the broth, continue with hot water.)

4. Add diced raw sweet potato and another ladle of broth (or hot water), stirring until liquid has been absorbed. Stir in cream and continue to simmer, adding liquid as needed, for 5 to 10 minutes or until rice is tender but still has a firm heart, sweet potato is cooked through and mixture is creamy.

5. Stir in mashed sweet potato, cover and remove from heat. Let stand for 10 minutes. Just before serving, stir in cheese and parsley. Serve immediately.

Big Baked Sweet Potatoes with Black Bean Chili

I am not a nutritionist but I think I can state with assurance that this sweet potato and black bean combination makes for a good source of protein, and it's especially good with warm cornbread alongside. If you don't feel like turning on the oven and baking the potatoes, steam chunks of sweet potato and add them to the finished chili, then serve everything over quinoa, bulgur or brown rice for even more nutrients.

Makes 4 to 8 servings

Tips

If the sweet potatoes you choose for this recipe are really big (1 pound/500 g or just under), there is a good chance that one will be sufficient for two diners — unless you are truly famished.

If you are familiar with Scotch bonnet peppers (close relatives of habanero peppers) you will know they are not to be trifled with. Removing the membrane and seeds will make them less fiery but you should still be wary of their heat. Don't touch your face during or after chopping, and use thin rubber gloves. The peppers can be omitted if you like.

- **Preheat oven to 400°F (200°C)**
- **Rimmed baking sheet, lined with parchment paper**
- **Large, heavy pot or Dutch oven**

| 4 | large sweet potatoes, scrubbed (see Tips, left) | 4 |

Chili

¼ cup	olive oil	60 mL
4	cloves garlic, minced	4
2	stalks celery, chopped	2
1	large red onion, chopped	1
1	large carrot, peeled and chopped	1
1	large red bell pepper, seeded and chopped	1
1	Scotch bonnet pepper, seeded and finely chopped (see Tips, left)	1
2 tsp	cocoa powder	10 mL
2 tsp	salt	10 mL
1 tsp	chili powder	5 mL
1 tsp	ground cumin	5 mL
1 tsp	ground cinnamon	5 mL
½ tsp	freshly ground black pepper	2 mL
6 cups	cooked black beans (see Tips, page 359)	1.5 L
1	can (28 oz/796 mL diced tomatoes) with juice	1
	Salt and freshly ground black pepper	
	Zest and freshly squeezed juice of 1 lime	
1 cup	sour cream	250 mL
½ cup	chopped fresh cilantro leaves	125 mL

Tip

For this quantity of beans, soak and cook 3 cups (750 mL) dried black beans or use 3 cans (each 14 to 19 oz/398 to 540 mL) cooked black beans, drained and rinsed. You can choose to omit some of the black beans and replace with any other bean you like.

1. Using the tines of a fork, prick each sweet potato a few times. Transfer to prepared baking sheet and bake in preheated oven for 45 to 60 minutes, depending on size, until tender and cooked through.

2. *Chili:* Meanwhile, in a large, heavy pot, heat oil over medium-high heat. Sauté garlic, celery, onion, carrot, red pepper and chile pepper for about 15 minutes or until softened and beginning to color. Stir in cocoa, salt, chili powder, cumin, cinnamon and pepper and cook for 1 minute (if mixture looks dry, stir in a splash of water).

3. Stir in beans and tomatoes with juice, scraping up any brown bits from bottom of pan, and bring to a boil. Reduce heat and simmer for about 20 minutes or until mixture has thickened slightly. Taste and adjust seasoning with salt and freshly ground black pepper. Stir in lime juice.

4. Using a sharp knife, cut each sweet potato in half and plate either a half or a whole one per serving. Top with a portion of chili. Dollop each with sour cream and sprinkle with cilantro. Serve immediately.

Curried Sweet Potato Ravioli with Brown Butter & Toasted Cashews

With their pungency and spicy heat, fragrant curry seasonings effectively balance the natural sweetness of sweet potatoes. This is an especially nice combination of textures because of the softness of the pasta and sweet potato filling and the buttery crunch of the cashews.

Makes 4 to 6 servings

Tip

Toasting the cashews in a dry skillet gives them a lovely crunch; just take care not to burn them, as they take very little time to toast. Add cashews to a skillet placed over medium-high heat, allow to heat for a minute or two, then toss them around a bit. When they are fragrant and beginning to brown slightly, remove from heat. You can also oven-toast the cashews on a baking sheet in a 400°F (200°C) oven, but watch them carefully so they don't burn.

- Preheat oven to 375°F (190°C)
- Rimmed baking sheet, lined with parchment paper

2 lbs	sweet potatoes	1 kg
3 tbsp	butter	45 mL
1 tbsp	olive oil	15 mL
2	shallots, minced	2
2 tsp	curry powder	10 mL
1/4 tsp	ground ginger	1 mL
Pinch	cayenne pepper	Pinch
1/2 cup	dry white wine	125 mL
1/2 cup	heavy or whipping (35%) cream	125 mL
2 tbsp	finely chopped flat-leaf parsley leaves	30 mL
	Salt and freshly ground black pepper	
1 tbsp	all-purpose flour	15 mL
40	wonton wrappers	40
3/4 cup	butter	175 mL
1/2 cup	unsalted cashews, toasted (see Tip, left) and chopped	125 mL
1/4 tsp	freshly ground black pepper	1 mL

1. Place sweet potatoes on prepared baking sheet and bake in preheated oven for about 1 hour or until tender. Remove from oven and set aside until cool enough to handle. Slice open, scoop out flesh and transfer to a bowl (discard skins). Using a potato masher, mash; you should have about 2 cups (500 mL).

2. In a large skillet, melt butter and oil over medium heat. Cook shallots, curry powder, ginger and cayenne, stirring gently, for about 5 minutes or until shallots are softened and spices are fragrant.

3. Stir in wine and bring to a boil. Reduce heat and simmer for about 10 minutes or until liquid is reduced by half. Stir in sweet potato and cream and gently cook for 1 or 2 minutes. Remove from heat. Stir in parsley and season to taste with salt and freshly ground pepper. Set aside to cool.

4. On a lightly floured work surface, line up 8 wonton wrappers. Have a small bowl of cold water and prepared baking sheet at hand. Center 1 tbsp (15 mL) sweet potato mixture on each of 4 wrappers. Brush 4 additional wrappers around the edges with a little water, then place each over a filled wrapper and firmly press edges together to seal ravioli. Transfer to prepared baking sheet (do not let ravioli touch). Repeat with the remaining wrappers and sweet potato mixture. Cover with a damp clean tea towel and set aside.

5. Bring a large pot of salted water to a boil over high heat.

6. Meanwhile, in a skillet, melt butter over medium-high heat and cook for about 3 minutes or until beginning to brown. Stir in cashews and remove from heat. Add pepper. Set aside and keep warm.

7. In batches, using a slotted spoon, add ravioli to boiling water and cook for 2 to 3 minutes or until they bob to the surface. Using slotted spoon, transfer to a warmed serving platter and keep warm. Rewarm butter sauce if necessary and pour over ravioli. Serve immediately.

Variations

If you have leftover filling, combine it with a little broth or milk and cream and enjoy it as a soup.

You can also serve the ravioli with a ladleful of rich chicken broth poured over it.

If you prefer, make these ravioli using your own or store-bought fresh pasta dough.

Potato Lasagna with Roasted Tomato & Garlic Sauce

Using thin slices of potato in place of the usual pasta makes this a lasagna with a difference. Somehow it is a little lighter than the conventional version. If you plan on serving this to company, it works very well because both the lasagna and the sauce can be made a day ahead of when you plan to serve it.

Makes 4 servings

- Preheat oven to 375°F (190°C)
- Small roasting pan
- Food processor or blender
- 8-inch (2 L) square baking dish, buttered

Tips

The older the balsamic vinegar, the better the flavor of this simple sauce.

To peel tomatoes, bring a large pot of water to a boil over high heat. Using the tip of a sharp knife, cut a small, shallow X in the base of each tomato. Using tongs, place in boiling water for just 30 seconds, then transfer to a plate. Let cool enough to handle, then peel off skins.

To roast peppers: Using your hands, coat the peppers with a couple of teaspoons (10 mL) olive oil. Place under preheated broiler and broil, turning occasionally, for 10 minutes or until peppers are completely blackened. Transfer to a small bowl, cover with plastic wrap and set aside to steam for about 5 minutes. Peel off the skin and seed the peppers. Don't rinse.

Sauce

3	large ripe tomatoes, peeled (see Tips, left)	3
3	cloves garlic	3
½ cup	extra virgin olive oil	125 mL
¼ cup	balsamic vinegar	60 mL
2	sprigs fresh thyme	2
	Salt and freshly ground black pepper	

Lasagna

2	large floury potatoes, peeled and sliced lengthwise ¼ inch (0.5 cm) thick	2
	Salt and freshly ground black pepper	
½ cup	freshly grated Grana Padano or Parmesan cheese (approx.)	125 mL
4	roasted red bell peppers, seeded and sliced into wide strips (see Tips, left)	4
2	yellow zucchini, trimmed and sliced lengthwise into ¼-inch (0.5 cm) strips	2
4	roasted yellow bell peppers, seeded and sliced into wide strips	4
2	green zucchini, trimmed and sliced lengthwise into ¼-inch (0.5 cm) strips	2
6 oz	mozzarella cheese, thinly sliced	175 g

1. *Sauce:* Cut tomatoes into wedges. In a small roasting pan, lightly toss tomatoes, garlic, oil, vinegar and thyme. Bake in preheated oven for 20 to 25 minutes or until tomatoes are softened. Using tongs, transfer tomatoes and garlic to a bowl. Season to taste with salt and freshly ground pepper. Set a sieve over the bowl and add cooking liquid, pressing down on any solids remaining in sieve and collecting liquid in bowl. Transfer tomato mixture and liquids to a food processor fitted with metal blade and process until puréed and smooth. Set aside.

2. *Lasagna:* Reduce oven temperature to 350°F (180°C). In prepared baking dish, arrange a third of the potatoes over the bottom, slightly overlapping slices. Sprinkle with salt and freshly ground pepper and a quarter of the Grana Padano. Add half the red peppers, half the yellow zucchini, half the yellow peppers and half the green zucchini. Season with salt and freshly ground pepper and sprinkle with a quarter of the Grana Padano. Repeat both potato and vegetable layers, including the Grana Padano. Top with the remaining potatoes and slices of mozzarella.

3. Bake in preheated oven, uncovered, for 1 hour or until potato mixture is bubbling and cheese is golden brown (if cheese is browning too quickly, cover loosely with parchment paper or buttered foil). Remove from oven and let stand on a wire rack for 15 minutes before serving.

4. Meanwhile, in a saucepan, gently reheat sauce. Using a sharp knife, cut lasagna into four neat squares. Ladle a quarter of the sauce onto each of four warmed individual pasta or shallow soup bowls. Top each with a square of lasagna. Sprinkle with additional grated Grana Padano or Parmesan, if desired.

Spaghetti alla Genovese

Pesto with good pasta is a favored dish inside and outside Italy. But if you enjoy this combination in Genoa, in northwest Italy, it will often include waxy new potatoes and lovely ultra-skinny green beans.

Makes 4 to 6 servings

Tip

Toasting the nuts in a dry skillet gives them a nice crispness; just take care not to burn them, as they take very little time to toast. Add the nuts to a skillet placed over medium heat, and cook, stirring, for 6 to 8 minutes or until fragrant. You can also oven-toast nuts on a baking sheet in a 400°F (200°C) oven, but watch them carefully so they don't burn.

• **Food processor or blender**

Pesto

2 or 3	cloves garlic, halved	2 or 3
1 cup	packed basil leaves, rinsed and dried	250 mL
¼ cup	pine nuts or fresh walnuts, lightly toasted (see Tip, left)	60 mL
¼ cup	grated Pecorino Romano cheese	60 mL
¼ cup	freshly grated Grana Padano or Parmesan cheese (approx.)	60 mL
Large pinch	coarse salt	Large pinch
½ cup	extra virgin olive oil	125 mL

Spaghetti

1 tsp	salt	5 mL
2 lbs	small waxy new potatoes, scrubbed and halved	1 kg
8 oz	skinny green beans, trimmed	250 g
1 lb	spaghetti or linguine	500 g

1. *Pesto:* In a food processor fitted with metal blade, pulse garlic, basil, pine nuts, Pecorino Romano, Grana Padano and salt until puréed and smooth. With motor running, add olive oil down the feed tube and blend until creamy and smooth. Set aside.

2. *Spaghetti:* Bring a large pot of water to a boil over high heat. Add salt and potatoes. Cover loosely and return to a boil. Reduce heat and cook for 12 minutes or until potatoes are just tender (do not overcook). Meanwhile, fill a large bowl with cold water and add a handful of ice cubes. Using a slotted spoon, transfer potatoes to ice water to stop the cooking process, reserving cooking water in pot. When cooled slightly, using a slotted spoon, transfer potatoes to a cutting board. Peel, then slice into strips about the same thickness as the beans. Set aside.

3. Return saucepan to stovetop over high heat and bring reserved cooking water to a boil. Add green beans and cook for 3 or 4 minutes, until barely cooked. Add a few more ice cubes to the cold water and, using a small sieve, transfer beans to ice water, reserving cooking water in pot. Let beans cool for 1 to 2 minutes, then drain. Set aside.

4. If necessary, bring cooking water back to a boil. Add pasta and cook for about 8 minutes or until tender but firm. Drain, reserving about $1/4$ cup (60 mL) cooking water.

5. In a large warmed serving bowl, toss pasta, potatoes and green beans. Stir 3 to 4 tbsp (45 to 60 mL) cooking water into the pesto to thin it slightly. Toss pesto with pasta mixture to coat. Sprinkle with additional Grana Padano and serve immediately.

Penne with Potatoes & Arugula

Pasta may not be the first food you think of to team with potatoes — or vice versa — but there is something intrinsically good about these two comfort foods together in one dish. Here, one complements the other, and each is flavorfully supported by peppery arugula and a hit of red onion.

Makes 4 servings

Tips

This recipe is easily doubled.

If you're preparing this in the summer months and are reluctant to turn on the oven, grill or pan-fry the potato slices until crisp.

- **Preheat oven to 400°F (200°C)**

1 lb	waxy new potatoes, scrubbed and sliced	500 g
½ cup	extra virgin olive oil, divided	125 mL
	Salt and freshly ground black pepper	
1 lb	orecchiette (little ear-shaped pasta)	500 g
1	small red onion, very thinly sliced	1
4	cloves garlic, finely chopped	4
1 tbsp	finely chopped fresh lemon thyme (or other lemon herb) leaves	15 mL
2	bunches fresh arugula (about 8 oz/250 g)	2
	Zest and freshly squeezed juice of 1 small lemon	
1 cup	freshly grated Grana Padano or Parmesan cheese	250 mL

1. In a large bowl, toss potatoes and 2 tbsp (30 mL) oil. Season to taste with salt and freshly ground pepper. Transfer to a rimmed baking sheet and bake in preheated oven for about 15 minutes, stirring once or twice, until crisp and golden brown. Remove from oven and set aside.
2. In a large pot of boiling salted water, cook pasta for about 7 minutes or until tender but still firm (do not overcook).
3. Meanwhile, in a large skillet, heat 2 tbsp (30 mL) oil. Sauté onion for about 4 minutes or until softened. Add potatoes, garlic and lemon thyme and cook, tossing, for about 1 minute. Remove from heat.
4. Scoop out ¼ cup (60 mL) pasta cooking water and set aside. Working quickly, drain pasta (do not rinse). Add pasta, reserved cooking water, remaining oil, arugula, and lemon zest and juice to potatoes and toss to combine. Divide evenly among four warmed individual pasta bowls. Sprinkle with cheese.

Potato Taleggio Pasta

A very good choice for a cold, wintry night, this is a true one-dish supper.

Makes 4 to 6 servings

Tips

Use regular or whole wheat fettucine. Be careful not to overcook the pasta, as it will cook a little more in the oven.

Taleggio is one of those inimitable Italian cheeses for which there is really no substitute. However, if you can't find it, use fontina.

- Preheat oven to 450°F (230°C)
- 12-cup (3 L) baking dish, lightly buttered

	Large pot of boiling water	
3	large Yukon Gold potatoes, peeled and cut into small chunks	3
1 tsp	salt	5 mL
1 lb	fettucine (see Tips, left)	500 g
8 oz	cored Savoy cabbage (about ½ head), halved and cut into strips	250 g
3 tbsp	butter	45 mL
12	sage leaves, torn into pieces	12
6	cloves garlic, thinly sliced	6
	Freshly ground black pepper	
1 cup	freshly grated Grana Padano or Parmesan cheese, divided	250 mL
10 oz	taleggio cheese, diced	300 g

1. Place potatoes in a large pasta pot and add cold water just to cover. Add salt, cover loosely and bring to a boil over high heat. Reduce heat and simmer for 3 minutes or until potatoes are softened but not cooked through. Add pasta and cabbage and sufficient boiling water to cook the pasta. Increase heat to high and cook for 7 minutes (pasta should not be completely cooked). Scoop out about 1 cup (250 mL) cooking water into a measuring cup and set aside. Drain. Return pasta and vegetables to pot and set aside.

2. In a skillet over medium heat, melt butter. Stir in sage and garlic and season to taste with salt and freshly ground pepper. Cook for 3 minutes, stirring, or until garlic is tender but not browned. Pour over pasta mixture along with all but 1 heaping tbsp (20 mL) of the Grana Padano. Toss gently.

3. Transfer a third of the pasta mixture to prepared dish and top with a third of the taleggio. Repeat twice. Sprinkle with reserved Grana Padano. Pour about ¼ cup (60 mL) reserved cooking liquid overtop, enough to moisten slightly. Bake in top half of preheated oven for 7 minutes or until cheese has melted. Let stand for 10 minutes on a wire rack before serving.

Baked Potato Herb Gnocchi with Fresh Tomato Relish

Baking the potatoes instead of boiling or steaming them results in little dumplings with real potato flavor that are also a bit lighter than the norm.

Makes 4 to 6 servings

Tip

To peel tomatoes, bring a large pot of water to a boil over high heat. Using the tip of a sharp knife, cut a small, shallow X in the base of each tomato. Using tongs, place in boiling water for just 30 seconds, then transfer to a plate. Let cool enough to handle, then peel off skins.

- **Preheat oven to 375°F (190°C)**

Tomato Relish

8	large ripe Roma (plum) tomatoes, peeled, seeded and diced (see Tip, left)	8
4	green onions, trimmed and finely chopped	4
1	red onion, minced	1
3 tbsp	freshly squeezed lime juice	45 mL
¼ cup	chopped fresh cilantro leaves	60 mL
2 tbsp	chile pepper–infused oil	30 mL
	Salt and freshly ground black pepper	

Gnocchi

4	large floury potatoes, scrubbed	4
2 cups	all-purpose flour	500 mL
2 tsp	salt	10 mL
2 tbsp	chopped fresh basil leaves	30 mL
2 tbsp	chopped flat-leaf parsley leaves	30 mL
1	large egg yolk, lightly beaten	1
3 tbsp	butter, divided	45 mL
6 to 8 tbsp	olive oil, divided	90 to 120 mL
	Freshly grated Grana Padano cheese, optional	

1. *Tomato Relish:* In a bowl, combine tomatoes, green onions, red onion, lime juice, cilantro and oil. Season to taste with salt and freshly ground pepper. Toss, cover and set aside.

2. *Gnocchi:* Place potatoes directly on rack in preheated oven and bake for about 1 hour or until cooked through (if they are really large, bake for an extra 15 minutes). Transfer to a cutting board and set aside until cool enough to handle. Slice potatoes in half lengthwise and scoop out flesh into a large bowl (discard or keep the skins and reheat for a snack). Let cool completely. Using a wooden spoon, stir in flour and salt until blended. Stir in basil and parsley. Stir in egg yolk and mix until mixture forms a smooth, firm dough.

3. Divide dough into thirds and, using your palms, roll each portion into a long sausage about ³⁄₄ inch (2 cm) in diameter. Working with one roll at a time, cut into pieces about 1 inch (2.5 cm) long and transfer gnocchi to a clean tea towel, lightly dusted with flour, as cut (do not allow gnocchi to touch). Cover with another clean tea towel. (At this point, gnocchi and towels can be covered with plastic wrap and refrigerated until ready to cook the same day.)

4. Bring a large pot of salted water to a boil.

5. Using a long-handled strainer or slotted spoon, add gnocchi to the boiling water in batches (about eight at a time, depending upon their size) and cook until they rise to the surface, about 3 minutes. Cook for 1 minute longer, then, using slotted spoon, transfer to a warm, lightly buttered serving dish. Repeat until all gnocchi have been cooked.

6. Preheat oven to 140°F (60°C). In a large skillet, melt 2 tbsp (30 mL) butter over medium-high heat and add 3 tbsp (45 mL) oil. In batches, gently sauté gnocchi, stirring occasionally, until edges are beginning to brown slightly, transferring to oven to keep warm. Add more butter and oil as needed.

7. Evenly divide gnocchi among four to six warmed individual pasta bowls. Sprinkle with Grana Padano to taste and serve with tomato relish on the side.

Gnocchi-roni & Cheese

Here is a recipe for sturdy little potato gnocchi that receive their final cooking in the oven, bathed in a rich cheese sauce. They get a lovely splotchy brown top, like really good mac and cheese. Everybody goes for this in a big way. Serve with a tomato, arugula and avocado salad and good crusty bread.

Serves 4 to 6

Tips

The amount of flour is approximate; add it gradually because you may not need to use it all, or you may use a bit more. Stop adding flour when the dough has lost most of its stickiness and is soft and smooth. The less flour, the lighter the gnocchi will be.

For the same reason, the potatoes are not peeled before boiling. That way they absorb less water, so they absorb less flour and the resulting dough is less heavy.

1½ lbs	floury potatoes, scrubbed and halved (about 2 large)	750 g
1 tsp	salt	5 mL
2	egg yolks, lightly beaten	2
2 cups	all-purpose flour (approx.), divided	500 mL
2 tbsp	butter	30 mL
½ tsp	dry mustard	2 mL
¼ tsp	sweet paprika	1 mL
	Salt and freshly ground black pepper	
1 cup	whole milk, warmed	250 mL
1¼ cups	shredded sharp (aged) Cheddar cheese, divided	300 mL

1. Place potatoes in a large saucepan and add cold water to barely cover. Add salt, cover loosely and bring to a boil over high heat. Reduce heat and cook for 20 minutes or until potatoes are tender. Drain well. Return potatoes to saucepan over very low heat and shake the pot back and forth to remove any trace of moisture. (This step is important, because if they are wet the potatoes will absorb too much flour, which in turn will produce heavier gnocchi.) When potatoes are cool enough to handle, peel, transfer to a bowl and mash roughly. Set aside to cool slightly. Add egg yolks and mash well.

2. Transfer potatoes to a work surface lightly dusted with flour. Gradually add flour, ½ cup (125 mL) at a time, kneading gently until a soft dough forms (you may not need all the flour; see Tips, left). Knead several times until dough is firm and pliable.

3. Divide dough into thirds and, using your palms, roll each portion into a long sausage about ¾ inch (2 cm) in diameter. Working with one roll at a time, cut into pieces about 1 inch (2.5 cm) long. Using the tines of a fork, lightly flatten each piece (the indentations help the sauce to cling). Transfer imprinted gnocchi to a clean tea towel, lightly dusted with flour, as completed (do not allow them to touch). Cover with another clean tea towel. (At this point gnocchi and towels can be covered with plastic wrap and stored in the refrigerator until ready to cook the same day.)

4. Wipe clean the saucepan used to cook the potatoes. Fill with enough water to cook the gnocchi and bring to a boil over high heat. Using a long-handled strainer or slotted spoon, add gnocchi to boiling water in batches (about eight at a time) and cook until they rise to the surface, about 2 minutes. Cook for 1 minute longer, then, using slotted spoon, transfer to a lightly buttered baking dish. Repeat until all gnocchi have been cooked. Set to one side and cover with a lid to keep warm while you prepare the sauce.

5. Discard the gnocchi cooking water and wipe saucepan clean. Add butter and melt over medium heat. Whisk in remaining 2 tbsp (30 mL) flour, mustard, paprika and salt and pepper to taste and whisk together for about 1 minute. Remove from heat and gradually whisk in milk; return to heat and, whisking constantly, bring to a gentle boil. Reduce heat and cook, whisking, until thickened, about 3 minutes. Add 1 cup (250 mL) cheese; stir until melted and sauce is smooth.

6. Preheat broiler to high. Pour sauce over gnocchi, toss to coat and sprinkle with remaining cheese. Place under broiler, watching carefully, just until cheese bubbles and begins to brown in places. Serve immediately.

Hash Brown Pizza with Red Onion Confit

For convenience, pick up a ball of premade pizza dough at the supermarket to make this fantastic recipe, which features crispy hash brown potatoes with crumbled goat's-milk cheese and a delightful onion confit. It's a "wow!" presentation with delicious flavor combinations.

Makes 2 servings

Tips

It's easy and convenient to pick up premade pizza dough, which makes a lovely fresh crust. If you have a favorite recipe, make your own, or use the one on page 374.

The red onion confit is wonderful as an accompaniment to many cheeses and is especially good with omelets or scrambled eggs.

- Small roasting pan or baking dish
- 12-inch (30 cm) pizza pan, lightly oiled, or pizza stone

Confit

2 tbsp	butter	30 mL
2 tbsp	extra virgin olive oil	30 mL
½ cup	granulated sugar	125 mL
1½ lbs	red onions, thinly sliced	750 g
¾ cup	dry red wine	175 mL
⅓ cup + 1 tbsp	red wine vinegar	90 mL

Pizza

3	small red-skinned new potatoes, scrubbed	3
1 tsp	salt	5 mL
6	cloves garlic	6
2 tbsp	extra virgin olive oil (approx.)	30 mL
1 tbsp	chopped fresh rosemary leaves	15 mL
1 tbsp	all-purpose flour	15 mL
	Pizza dough for 12-inch (30 cm) crust (see Tips, left)	
5 oz	soft goat's-milk cheese, crumbled	150 g

1. *Confit:* In a large saucepan, heat butter and oil over low heat. Stir in sugar until completely dissolved. Stir in onions to coat, cover loosely and cook, stirring occasionally, for 30 minutes.

2. Increase heat to high, uncover, stir in wine and vinegar and bring to a boil. Reduce heat and gently simmer for 30 minutes.

3. Increase heat to medium and cook, stirring, for 5 to 8 minutes or until mixture has thickened to a jam-like consistency. Remove from heat and let cool. Transfer 1 cup (250 mL) to a small bowl and set aside. Transfer remaining confit to a jar with a tight-fitting lid and refrigerate for another use for up to 1 month (see Tips, page 372).

4. *Pizza:* Preheat oven to 400°F (200°C). Place potatoes in a large saucepan and add boiling water to barely cover. Add salt, cover loosely and bring to a boil over high heat. Reduce heat and cook for 8 minutes or until potatoes are just tender. Drain well. Set aside until cool enough to handle.

5. Slice potatoes thinly and place in a roasting pan. Toss in garlic, oil and rosemary. Bake in preheated oven, stirring occasionally, for 25 to 30 minutes or until golden brown. Remove from oven and set aside.

6. Increase oven temperature to 500°F (260°C). On a lightly floured surface, roll out dough into a 12-inch (30 cm) circle. Transfer dough to pan and spread evenly with reserved confit, leaving a 1½-inch (4 cm) dough border around edge. Scatter evenly with potatoes. Top with cheese and drizzle with a little oil. Bake in preheated oven for 15 to 20 minutes or until crust is golden brown. Let stand on a wire rack for about 5 minutes before serving.

Potato-Crusted Margherita Pizza

As un-classically Italian as this preparation may sound, it is actually a traditional recipe style from Apulia, in southern Italy. I first had this at a little sidewalk bakery café in the city of Lecce. Serve with an arugula salad dressed with lemon and fresh herb vinaigrette.

Makes one 12-inch (30 cm) pizza

Tips

These are the simplest of pizza toppings — small fresh tomatoes, mozzarella and fresh basil. You can certainly add your favorite toppings, but make sure they don't contribute to a soggy crust; simpler is best.

If you use a pizza stone, make sure it gets preheated in the oven.

If you can obtain fresh mozzarella, so much the better. Make sure to drain and pat it dry before using.

- Preheat oven to 450°F (230°C)
- 12-inch (30 cm) pizza pan, lightly greased, or pizza stone

1	large floury potato, peeled and quartered	1
½ tsp	salt, divided	2 mL
¼ cup	extra virgin olive oil (approx.), divided	60 mL
¾ cup	all-purpose flour (approx.)	175 mL
1 tsp	dried basil	5 mL
15	cherry or grape tomatoes, halved, or 6 firm Roma (plum) tomatoes, sliced	15
	Freshly ground black pepper	
4 oz	Pecorino Romano cheese, grated	125 g
8	fresh basil leaves, stacked and sliced	8
4 oz	mozzarella cheese, cut into ¼-inch (0.5 cm) cubes	125 g

1. Follow Step 1, Classic Mash Deluxe (page 50), adding only ¼ tsp (1 mL) salt to cooking water.
2. Transfer cooked potato to a bowl. Using a potato masher, mash potato with 1 tbsp (15 mL) oil. Knead in remaining ¼ tsp (1 mL) salt and flour, adding flour a little at a time until mixture forms a soft dough (if dough is still sticky, add a little more flour, or, if needed, add a little warm water to help dough come together). Shape into a disk. On a lightly floured surface, roll out dough into a 12-inch (30 cm) round.
3. Transfer dough to prepared pizza pan. Drizzle with 1 tbsp (15 mL) oil and scatter evenly with dried basil. Top with tomatoes, cut side down. Season to taste with salt and freshly ground pepper. Bake in preheated oven for 15 minutes or until edges are golden.
4. Scatter Pecorino Romano over tomatoes, then fresh basil, then mozzarella. Drizzle with remaining oil, return to oven and bake for 10 minutes or until cheese has melted and top is beginning to color. Serve immediately.

Breads, Biscuits, Scones, Griddle Cakes & More

Crusty, moist breads, some with potato in the dough and others topped with potato, flaky scones and biscuits, light-as-air pancakes, muffins, flatbreads and turnovers — all of these and more benefit from the positive influence of the potato. In this chapter you'll find baked goods for breakfast, lunch and dinner, for late-night snacking and cocktail fare and any time at all. Potatoes — both regular and sweet — lend their particular magic to so many good things from the oven and the griddle.

Irish Potato Soda Bread

My mum used to make dozens of loaves of Irish soda bread on the days leading up to St. Patrick's Day. This is her basic recipe, made even more Irish to my mind with the addition of mashed potatoes. Think of it as the natural evolution of a classic. This bread is best enjoyed served warm with butter. By the way, the cross cut into the top of soda breads is not a religious symbol. The ancient Celts revered round shapes, as they were thought to represent the sun. So they shaped their breads into rounds and then used the cross to divide the circle into four sections, representing the four seasons of the Celtic year.

Makes 2 loaves

Tips

Dry-mashed potatoes are mashed without butter, milk or cream.

Make this bread when you have a few leftover boiled potatoes or the equivalent amount of mashed potatoes. You can also boil extra potatoes and refrigerate them for up to 2 days so you have them on hand to make this bread.

Don't make the X too deep or the loaves will open up too much when baking.

These loaves freeze well but because they are quite dense, they take a while to thaw out.

- **Preheat oven to 375°F (190°C)**

3 cups	all-purpose flour (approx.)	750 mL
1 cup	whole wheat flour	250 mL
1 tbsp	baking soda	15 mL
1 tsp	baking powder	5 mL
1 tsp	salt	5 mL
¼ cup	butter, diced	60 mL
4	floury potatoes, boiled and dry mashed	4
1	egg	1
1¾ cups	buttermilk	425 mL

1. In a large bowl, whisk together all-purpose and whole wheat flours, baking soda, baking powder and salt. Using a pastry blender or two forks, cut in butter until mixture is crumbly. Blend in mashed potatoes.

2. In another bowl, whisk together egg and buttermilk. Make a well in the center of flour mixture and add buttermilk mixture all at once, stirring until blended. Turn out onto a lightly floured surface and knead dough, adding a little more flour if necessary to prevent sticking, for 3 to 4 minutes or until smooth.

3. Divide dough in half and shape each portion into a round, flat loaf. Using a sharp knife, cut a shallow X in the top of each loaf. Transfer to a baking sheet and bake in preheated oven for 35 to 45 minutes, until crusty and golden brown and loaves sound hollow when tapped on the bottom.

Variation

Although it's not traditional, sometimes it's nice to add some freshly chopped thyme and parsley to the dry ingredients.

Spiced Sweet Potato Tea Loaf

I love buttered slices of this fragrant quick bread with cups of good strong tea. It is not overly sweet and, like most tea loaves, is easy to put together. It's wonderful with cream cheese too.

Makes 1 loaf

Tips

The mashed sweet potato provides moisture, color and flavor in this bread.

Toasting the nuts in a dry skillet gives them a nice crispness; just take care not to burn them, as they take very little time to toast. Add the nuts to a skillet placed over medium heat and cook, stirring, for 6 to 8 minutes or until fragrant. You can also oven-toast nuts on a baking sheet in a 400°F (200°C) oven just for a few minutes, but watch them carefully so they don't burn.

- Preheat oven to 350°F (180°C)
- 9- by 5-inch (2 L) loaf pan, greased and lined with parchment paper

1 cup	raisins	250 mL
1/3 cup	boiling water	75 mL
2	large eggs	2
1/2 cup	canola or sunflower oil	125 mL
1 cup	dry-mashed sweet potatoes	250 mL
1 1/2 cups	all-purpose flour	375 mL
1/2 cup	whole wheat flour	125 mL
1/2 cup	granulated sugar	125 mL
1 tsp	baking soda	5 mL
1 tsp	ground cinnamon	5 mL
1/2 tsp	ground nutmeg	2 mL
1/2 tsp	ground ginger	2 mL
Pinch	ground allspice	Pinch
1/2 tsp	salt	2 mL
1/2 cup	toasted chopped pecans (see Tips, left)	125 mL

1. Place raisins in a bowl and add boiling water. Set aside to soak until cool.
2. In a bowl, whisk together eggs, oil and 1/4 cup (60 mL) water. Stir in sweet potatoes until blended.
3. In a large bowl, whisk together flours, sugar, baking soda, cinnamon, nutmeg, ginger, allspice and salt. Add sweet potato mixture, pecans, and reserved raisins and soaking liquid, stirring until no traces of flour remain (don't over-mix). Using a rubber spatula, scrape into prepared loaf pan, smoothing the top. Bake in preheated oven for 1 to 1 1/4 hours or until a tester inserted in center comes out clean. Let cool in pan on a wire rack for 30 minutes before turning out and serving.

Mennonite Country Potato Doughnuts

When my daughters were small, we used to make a yearly trek to a Mennonite Relief Sale and Fair. What a feast! Arriving in the early morning meant that we started with the homemade sausage and pancake breakfast. Later on, after walking around to see the sights and take in the auction of beautiful handmade quilts, we would settle down to enjoy a paper plate loaded with outstanding barbecued chicken, creamy coleslaw and, for dessert, fresh strawberry pie with cream. One year, just in case we got hungry on the way home, we nabbed a bag of potato doughnuts — rich, moist and unforgettable — which is what inspired this recipe.

Makes about 3½ dozen doughnuts

Tips

Dry-mashed potatoes are mashed without butter, milk or cream.

If you prefer, you can omit cutting out the center hole and leave the dough as one large circle.

The oil should come a little over halfway up the sides of the pot. Do not overfill; leave at least 3 inches (7.5 cm) of headspace at the top.

If you don't have a thermometer, drop a small square of dry bread into the oil; if it floats, the oil is hot enough.

- **Large heavy pot, Dutch oven or deep fryer**
- **Candy/deep-frying thermometer (if not using a deep fryer)**
- **1 large (about 3 inches/7.5 cm) and 1 small (about 1 inch/2.5 cm) cookie cutter**
- **Baking sheet, lined with paper towels**

1 cup	warm dry-mashed potatoes (see Tips, left)	250 mL
2	eggs	2
1 cup	buttermilk (approx.)	250 mL
⅔ cup	granulated sugar	150 mL
2 tbsp	melted butter	30 mL
1 tbsp	vanilla extract	15 mL
4 cups	all-purpose flour (approx.)	1 L
2 tsp	baking powder	10 mL
1 tsp	baking soda	5 mL
1 tsp	salt	5 mL
1 tsp	ground cinnamon	5 mL
¼ tsp	ground nutmeg	1 mL
6 cups	vegetable oil	1.5 L
	Confectioner's (icing) sugar, optional	

1. Place potatoes in a large bowl. Using a wooden spoon, beat in eggs one at a time, beating well after each addition. Stir in buttermilk, sugar, melted butter and vanilla.

Tips

If you plan on making doughnuts fairly often, you might want to invest in a proper doughnut cutter. They come in different sizes and are available from kitchen and housewares shops or online.

Some doughnut makers swear by using two wooden chopsticks to turn the doughnuts as they are frying and also for transferring them out of the fat to drain.

2. In another bowl, sift together flour, baking powder, baking soda, salt, cinnamon and nutmeg. Gradually add to potato mixture, stirring well after each addition, until mixture forms a dough (you may need to add a little more flour or buttermilk, depending on how the dough comes together). Divide dough in half. Cover each portion with plastic wrap and refrigerate for 1 hour.

3. On a lightly floured surface, roll out one portion of dough to about ¾ inch (2 cm) thick. Using floured large cookie cutter, cut doughnuts with a straight-up-and-down motion (don't twist cutter). Leave dough in place and, using floured small cutter, cut a hole in center of each (see Tips, left). Using a metal spatula, transfer doughnuts to a baking sheet and set aside. (Scraps of dough can be kneaded again briefly, rerolled and cut.) Repeat with second portion of dough.

4. Place 4 to 6 inches (10 to 15 cm) oil in a large, heavy pot (see Tips, 378). Heat over medium-high heat until thermometer registers 375°F (190°C). (If you're using a deep fryer, follow the manufacturer's instructions.)

5. Using a wide metal spatula (see Tips, left) transfer doughnuts to oil, three at a time, and deep-fry for 2 to 3 minutes or until bottoms are golden brown, then turn and deep-fry for 2 to 3 minutes more or until other side is golden brown. Using a wire-mesh strainer, transfer to a baking sheet lined with paper towels. Sprinkle with confectioner's sugar (if using). Repeat until all doughnuts have been cooked.

Classic Potato Focaccia

This is the focaccia you are likely to come across in the south of Italy. It is moist and fragrant and studded with bits of ripe tomato. It is absolutely delicious with a chunk of Parmigiano-Reggiano and a glass of wine.

Makes 2 focaccia

Tips

Because the potatoes are cooked whole and unpeeled, they take a little longer to become tender. But it also means they will not absorb as much water, which is important for the finished product.

You can use a stand mixer fitted with a dough hook for Step 2 if you wish.

When making any sort of yeast bread, remember to keep things warm (the opposite is true when making any sort of pastry, when things should be chilled). To warm your work bowl (or the bowl of your stand mixer, if using), pour very hot tap water or boiling water into the bowl and let stand for 10 minutes or so before draining and using.

- **Two 9-inch (2.5 L) round or square baking pans, lightly oiled**

2	large all-purpose potatoes	2
1 tbsp	salt, divided	15 mL
1 tsp	granulated sugar	5 mL
2¼ tsp	active dry yeast	11 mL
4 to 5 cups	all-purpose flour	1 to 1.25 L
¼ cup	olive oil, divided	60 mL
1	large ripe tomato, cut into chunks	1
½ tsp	dried basil	2 mL
	Freshly ground black pepper	

1. Place potatoes in a saucepan and add cold water to barely cover. Add 1 tsp (5 mL) salt, cover loosely and bring to a boil over high heat. Reduce heat and cook for 20 to 30 minutes or until potatoes are soft and cooked through. Drain well, reserving cooking water. Set cooking water aside until lukewarm. Set potatoes aside until just cool enough to handle. Peel and dry-mash immediately.

2. In a warmed large bowl (see Tips, left), combine 1½ cups (375 mL) of the reserved cooking water and sugar. Sprinkle with yeast and let stand for 10 minutes or until frothy. Using a wooden spoon, stir in mashed potatoes, about 4 cups (1 L) flour, remaining 2 tsp (10 mL) salt and 1 tbsp (15 mL) oil. Add remaining flour a little at a time, stirring until mixture forms a dough. On a lightly floured surface, knead dough for about 10 minutes or until smooth and no longer sticky (add a little more flour if necessary to achieve a smooth dough).

3. Wipe bowl clean and coat surface with a little oil. Add dough and turn to coat with oil. Cover with plastic wrap and a clean tea towel. Let rise in a warm place for 1 to 2 hours or until doubled in volume and indentations remain when dough is poked with two fingers.

4. Preheat oven to 400°F (200°C). With lightly floured hands, divide dough in half. Place each half in a prepared pan, turning to coat with oil. Push and press dough into an even layer. Set aside for about 10 minutes or until dough is slightly puffed.

5. Arrange tomato chunks evenly over dough, pressing lightly to adhere them. Sprinkle with basil. Sprinkle to taste with salt and freshly ground pepper and drizzle with remaining oil. Set aside to rise in a warm place for 20 minutes. Transfer to preheated oven and bake for about 35 minutes, until golden brown and loaves sound hollow when tapped on the bottom.

Variation

If you prefer, omit the dried basil and after the focaccia is baked, scatter freshly chopped basil over the surface.

Potato-Topped Focaccia

The definitive rustic leavened bread, focaccia can be treated to an endless number of toppings, but I think this version, with thin slices of unpeeled waxy potatoes and fresh rosemary, is really one of the best. Serve warm or at room temperature — both are equally good.

Makes two 10-inch (25 cm) square breads

Tips

When making any sort of yeast bread, remember to keep things warm (the opposite is true when making any sort of pastry, when things should be chilled). To warm your work bowl (or the bowl of your stand mixer, if using) pour very hot tap water or boiling water into the bowl and let stand for 10 minutes or so before draining and using.

Use a mandoline or a food processor fitted with slicing blade to cut potatoes into uniformly thin slices.

Focaccia

1½ cups	lukewarm water, divided	375 mL
3 tsp	granulated sugar, divided	15 mL
2¼ tsp	active dry yeast	11 mL
2 tsp	salt	10 mL
5 to 6 cups	all-purpose flour (approx.)	1.25 to 1.5 L
	Olive oil	

Topping

1 lb	red-skinned waxy potatoes, unpeeled	500 g
3	sprigs fresh rosemary	3
4	cloves garlic, minced or crushed in a garlic press	4
1 cup	freshly grated Grana Padano or Parmesan cheese	250 mL
¼ cup	extra virgin olive oil (approx.)	60 mL
	Salt and freshly ground black pepper	

1. *Focaccia:* Fill a measuring cup with hot tap water and set aside for 1 minute, then drain. In warmed cup, combine ½ cup (125 mL) lukewarm water and 1 tsp (5 mL) sugar, stirring until sugar has dissolved. Sprinkle with yeast and set aside for 10 minutes or until frothy.

2. In a warmed large bowl (see Tips, left), combine yeast mixture, salt, remaining 2 tsp (10 mL) sugar and remaining 1 cup (250 mL) lukewarm water. Using a wooden spoon, stir in flour 1 cup (250 mL) at a time, until mixture forms a soft dough (you may not need all the flour).

3. On a lightly floured surface, knead dough, adding a little more flour to keep it from sticking, if necessary, for 5 minutes or until smooth and elastic. Wipe bowl clean and coat with a little oil. Add dough to prepared bowl, turning to coat with oil. Cover with plastic wrap and a clean tea towel. Set aside to rise in a warm place for 2 hours or until doubled in size and indentations remain when dough is poked with two fingers. Punch down dough, cover with plastic wrap and tea towel and let rise in a warm place for about 1 hour.

4. *Topping:* Slice potatoes very thinly (see Tips, page 382) and transfer to a large bowl. Strip leaves from rosemary sprigs, chop coarsely and add to potatoes. Add garlic, cheese and oil to the potato mixture. Season to taste with salt and freshly ground pepper and toss to combine thoroughly. Set aside.

5. Preheat oven to 400°F (200°C). On a lightly floured surface, divide dough in half. Pulling and stretching, work one half into a 10-inch (25 cm) rectangle about 1 inch (2.5 cm) thick (it doesn't have to be perfect), then transfer to a baking sheet and cover with a clean tea towel. Repeat with second half.

6. Uncover dough. Arrange potato mixture evenly overtop. Drizzle with a little more oil if desired. Bake on center rack in preheated oven for about 30 minutes or until potatoes are cooked through and crust is golden and crisp.

Variations

You can vary this recipe by piling the finished bread with mounds of silky prosciutto or fresh arugula drizzled with extra virgin olive oil.

Jewish Potato Bread

I think of this wonderful bread, with its moist interior and lovely crusty top, as a sort of Jewish focaccia, although you will find that it is heavier than the Italian bread. It is rather like a cross between a big latke, or potato pancake, and a savory kugel, which is a potato or noodle dish. You can put this together in no time; it is so easy and fuss-free that you'll want to make it often. This bread is absolutely delicious served warm.

Makes 1 loaf (6 to 8 servings)

Tip

Shred potatoes using the coarse side of a box grater or in a food processor fitted with shredding disk.

- **13- by 9-inch (3 L) baking dish, lightly greased**

¼ cup	warm water	60 mL
⅛ tsp	granulated sugar	0.5 mL
2¼ tsp	active dry yeast	11 mL
2½ lbs	floury potatoes, peeled	1.25 kg
2½ cups	all-purpose flour	625 mL
1 tbsp	salt	15 mL
2 tbsp	olive oil, divided	30 mL
2	onions, thinly sliced and sautéed until lightly browned	2

1. Fill a bowl with hot water and set aside for 1 minute, then drain. In warmed bowl, stir together warm water and sugar until sugar has dissolved. Sprinkle with yeast and set aside for 10 minutes or until frothy.

2. Meanwhile, shred potatoes (see Tip, left). In another bowl, sift together flour and salt. Stir flour mixture into yeast mixture until blended. Stir in potatoes until blended. Lightly grease a bowl with about 1 tsp (5 mL) oil, gather dough into a ball and transfer to bowl. Turn to coat with oil. Cover with a clean tea towel and set aside in a warm place to rise for 1 hour, or until puffed and doubled in size and holes remain when dough is poked with two fingers.

3. Preheat oven to 375°F (190°C). In prepared baking dish, arrange onions over bottom. Evenly spread potato dough over onions and, using a spatula, smooth and slightly flatten.

4. Bake in preheated oven for 20 minutes. Pull out oven rack with dish and lightly brush remaining oil over bread. Return to oven and bake for another 5 to 10 minutes or until top is golden and crusty.

Russian Potato Bread

Hearty and rustic, this rather dense bread is just made to go with soups, braises and stews. It is somewhat flatter than an average loaf and quite crusty. It is also very good sliced thinly and served with cheese.

Makes 1 loaf

- **Baking sheet, lightly greased**

3	potatoes, peeled and diced	3
1 tbsp	salt, divided	15 mL
2 tbsp	butter	30 mL
2½ cups	all-purpose flour	625 mL
1 cup	whole wheat flour	250 mL
½ cup	rye flour	125 mL
2¼ tsp	active dry yeast	11 mL
1 tsp	caraway seeds	5 mL

1. Place potatoes in a large saucepan and add cold water to barely cover. Add 1 tsp (5 mL) salt, cover loosely and bring to a boil over high heat. Reduce heat and cook for 20 minutes or until potatoes are tender. Drain well, reserving ⅔ cup (150 mL) of the cooking water. Return potatoes to saucepan over very low heat and shake the pot back and forth to remove any trace of moisture. Using a large fork, mash potatoes with butter. Set aside.

2. In a bowl, whisk together all-purpose, whole wheat and rye flours, yeast, 2 tsp (10 mL) salt and caraway seeds. Using a wooden spoon, stir in reserved cooking water and mashed potato mixture until mixture forms a soft dough.

3. On a lightly floured surface, knead for 10 to 15 minutes or until dough is smooth and elastic and no longer sticky, adding a little more all-purpose flour if necessary. Grease a bowl lightly with oil and add dough. Turn to coat. Cover with plastic wrap and a clean tea towel and set aside to rise in a warm place for about 1 hour, or until doubled in size and holes remain when dough is poked with two fingers. On a lightly floured surface, punch down dough, then shape into a rough oval. Transfer to prepared baking sheet, cover with clean tea towel and let rise in a warm place for 30 minutes. Preheat oven to 400°F (200°C).

4. Using a sharp chef's knife, cut four shallow diagonal slashes into top of loaf in a crisscross pattern. Bake in preheated oven for 30 minutes or until crust is golden brown and loaf sounds hollow when tapped on bottom.

Cheddar & Onion Potato Braid

This is a splendid moist potato bread made even better by two cheeses and caramelized onions. If you've never braided a yeast bread before, give it a go. It's fun, and even if it isn't perfect, it will still bake up nicely and taste delicious. This bread makes wonderful toast too.

Makes 1 loaf

Tips

When baking, for best results always bring eggs to room temperature before combining. If you forget to take the eggs from the fridge beforehand, place them (in their shells) in a bowl of warm tap water for no more than 2 minutes before using. Move them around a couple of times in the water during that time.

A dough scraper is a very useful tool to have on hand when making bread. It will help in manipulating large balls of dough and is also the perfect tool for dividing dough.

● **Baking sheet, greased**

1 cup	dry-mashed potatoes	250 mL
⅔ cup	whole milk	150 mL
¼ cup	butter	60 mL
3½ to 4 cups	all-purpose flour, divided	875 mL to 1 L
2 tbsp	granulated sugar	30 mL
2¼ tsp	active dry yeast	11 mL
1½ tsp	salt	7 mL
2	large eggs (see Tip, left)	2
½ cup	freshly grated Grana Padano or Parmesan cheese	125 mL
1½ cups	shredded sharp (aged) Cheddar cheese, divided	375 mL
2 tbsp	olive oil	30 mL
1	large onion, thinly sliced	1
1	egg yolk, beaten with 1 tbsp (15 mL) cold water	1

1. In a large saucepan, stir together mashed potatoes, milk and butter over medium heat, stirring until butter melts and mixture is blended. Remove from heat and, if necessary, set aside to cool until lukewarm.

2. In a large bowl, stir together 2 cups (500 mL) flour, sugar, yeast and salt until blended. Using a wooden spoon, gradually stir in mashed potato mixture. Stir in eggs one at a time, mixing well after each addition. Stir in Grana Padano. Add flour 1 cup (250 mL) at a time, stirring until mixture forms a soft dough (you may not need all the flour).

3. On a lightly floured surface, using floured hands, knead dough for about 10 minutes or until smooth and elastic and no longer sticky (knead in a little more flour if necessary). Lightly oil a bowl, add dough and turn to coat. Cover with plastic wrap and a clean tea towel and let rise in a warm place for about 1½ hours, or until doubled in size or holes remain when dough is poked with two fingers.

4. Punch down dough and turn out onto a lightly floured surface. Knead in ¾ cup (175 mL) Cheddar. Divide dough into thirds. Using your palms, roll each third into a 14-inch (35 cm) rope and place ropes on prepared baking sheet, side by side. Pinch ropes together at one end, then braid into a loaf, tucking ends under and pinching together. Cover with clean tea towel and let rise in a warm place for about 1 hour or until doubled in size.

5. Meanwhile, in a skillet, heat oil over medium-high heat. Sauté onion for about 15 minutes or until golden brown. Set aside and let cool. Preheat oven to 375°F (190°C).

6. Uncover loaf and brush with egg yolk mixture. Scatter loaf evenly with onions, then with remaining Cheddar, gently pressing to adhere. Bake in preheated oven for 25 minutes. Reduce oven temperature to 350°F (180°C) and bake for 5 to 10 minutes or until loaf sounds hollow when tapped on bottom. Remove from baking sheet and let cool on a wire rack.

Potato Fougasse

The French flatbread with open slits on its surface is known as fougasse, and it's a speciality of Provence. It is quite similar to Italy's focaccia and, like focaccia, fougasse takes its name from the Latin word for "hearth" — *focus*. There are endless possibilities for toppings, such as fresh herbs, various kinds of cheese, tapenade, roasted garlic or peppers. But I think this one, which features the little olives known as niçoise, from Provence, is especially Gallic.

Makes 2 breads, each about 9 by 14 inches (23 by 36 cm)

Tips

When making any sort of yeast bread, remember to keep things warm (the opposite is true when making any sort of pastry, when things should be chilled). To warm your work bowl (or the bowl of your stand mixer, if using) pour very hot tap water or boiling water in the bowl and let stand for 10 minutes or so before draining and using.

If you prefer, bake one loaf and freeze the dough for the second fougasse. Defrost and let rise in a warm place for about 1 hour before rolling out and baking.

2	large all-purpose potatoes	2
1 tbsp	salt, divided	15 mL
2 tbsp	granulated sugar	30 mL
2¼ tsp	active dry yeast	11 mL
4 to 5 cups	all-purpose flour	1 to 1.25 L
¼ cup	olive oil, divided	60 mL
½ cup	pitted niçoise or other black olives	125 mL
1 tbsp	herbes de Provence	15 mL

1. Place potatoes in a large saucepan and add cold water to barely cover. Add 1 tsp (5 mL) salt, cover loosely and bring to a boil over high heat. Reduce heat and cook for 25 to 30 minutes or until potatoes are tender. Drain well, reserving cooking water. Set aside until cool enough to handle. Peel off skins and immediately dry-mash. Set aside. Let cooking water cool to lukewarm.

2. In a warmed large bowl, combine 1½ cups (375 mL) reserved cooking water and sugar. Sprinkle with yeast and let stand for 10 minutes or until frothy. Stir in mashed potatoes, 4 cups (1 L) flour, 2 tsp (10 mL) salt and 1 tbsp (15 mL) oil, stirring until mixture forms a dough.

3. On a lightly floured surface, knead dough for about 10 minutes or until smooth and no longer sticky (add a little more flour if necessary). Knead in olives, using your fingers to poke them into the dough.

4. Wipe bowl clean and lightly coat with about 1 tsp (5 mL) olive oil. Add dough and turn to coat with oil. Cover with plastic wrap and a clean tea towel and set aside to rise in a warm place for 1 to 2 hours, or until doubled in volume and holes remain when dough is poked with two fingers.

5. Preheat oven to 425°F (220°C). With lightly floured hands, transfer dough to a lightly floured surface. Divide dough in half and gently roll out one half into an oval about 9 by 14 inches (23 by 36 cm). Transfer to prepared baking sheet and, using scissors, make eight to ten 4-inch (10 cm) slits in the center of the dough; open them wide with your fingers. Brush with remaining oil and sprinkle evenly with herbes de Provence. Repeat procedure with second half of dough. Set aside to rise in a warm place for 30 minutes. Bake in preheated oven for about 35 minutes or until golden brown and bread sounds hollow when tapped on bottom.

Potato & Almond Coffee Cake

Here is the cake to make when you have some leftover mashed potato. This is a flourless cake, and while it may sink a little in the center after cooling, the bonus is that it stays moist long after other cakes become dry. This is very good to enjoy with your 11 a.m. coffee.

Makes about 12 servings

Tips

You can use skinned almonds or those that still have their lovely papery brown skin. I prefer the latter because, once ground, they add tiny flecks of brown to the cake, which I like, and I think the texture is nicer. Plus a little added fiber is always good.

If you don't have leftover mashed potatoes, you can quickly microwave a big baking potato until soft, mash it and then proceed with the recipe.

- **Preheat oven to 350°F (180°C)**
- **Blender or mini food processor**
- **9-inch (2.5 L) springform pan, lightly buttered, bottom lined with buttered parchment paper**

1 cup	whole almonds (see Tips, left)	250 mL
1 cup	golden raisins	250 mL
2 tsp	baking powder	10 mL
3	eggs, at room temperature, separated	3
¾ cup	granulated sugar, divided	175 mL
¼ cup	butter, softened	60 mL
2 tbsp	brandy	30 mL
1 cup	cold dry-mashed potatoes (see Tips, left)	250 mL
	Confectioner's (icing) sugar	

1. In a blender, grind almonds to a powder. In a small bowl, combine almond powder with raisins and baking powder. Set aside.

2. In a bowl, beat egg whites until soft peaks form. Beat in half the sugar until stiff, glossy peaks form.

3. In a large bowl, beat remaining sugar and butter until light and creamy. Beat in egg yolks, one at a time, beating well after each addition. Beat in brandy. Using a spatula, gently fold in potatoes, then almond mixture and finally the egg whites. Carefully transfer to prepared pan, gently smoothing batter. Bake in preheated oven for 30 to 40 minutes or until a cake tester inserted in center comes out clean. Remove from oven. Let cool in pan on a wire rack for 15 minutes, then remove sides of pan.

4. Transfer to a serving plate and dust with confectioner's sugar. Serve warm or at room temperature.

Irish Potato & Apple Griddle Cake

Here is a very old and comforting recipe with much tradition behind it. In the Celtic year, October 31 is a very significant date. It is All Saints' Day, which is essentially New Year's Eve because — according to the Celtic calendar — the year starts on November 1, and so begins the ancient Celtic festival Samhain. A number of sacred foods are included in the celebration, among them apples and potatoes. Serve this hot, possibly with a wee bit of thick cream and cups of hot, strong tea.

Makes 4 to 6 servings

Tip

Choose apples that maintain their shape after cooking, such as Granny Smith, Braeburn or Golden Delicious.

• **Cast-iron griddle or skillet**

¼ cup	butter, chilled and cubed	60 mL
1 cup	all-purpose flour (approx.)	250 mL
½ tsp	baking powder	2 mL
½ tsp	salt	2 mL
3 cups	dry-mashed potatoes	750 mL
2	large apples, peeled and cored	2
1 tbsp	granulated sugar	15 mL
1 tsp	ground cinnamon	5 mL
⅛ tsp	ground cloves	0.5 mL
2 tbsp	butter, divided	30 mL

1. In a bowl, using a pastry blender or two knives, cut butter into flour until mixture is crumbly. Add baking powder and salt and mix thoroughly with pastry blender. Add mashed potatoes and, using your hands, blend until mixture forms a dough.

2. On a lightly floured surface, lightly knead dough for about 5 minutes (add a little more flour if dough is sticky). Divide into halves and shape each half into a ball. Roll out each ball into a circle about ½ inch (1 cm) thick, then cover with a clean tea towel and set aside.

3. Working over a bowl, thinly slice apples. Toss in sugar, cinnamon and cloves to coat. Arrange apples evenly in a single layer on one dough circle, leaving a 1-inch (2.5 cm) border. Dot with 1 tbsp (15 mL) butter. Brush the dough border lightly with cold water. Cover with other dough circle, pinching around edges to seal.

4. On a cast-iron griddle, heat remaining butter over medium heat, swirling pan to coat. Using a wide spatula (or by hand) carefully transfer filled dough to griddle. Reduce heat to low and cook for 15 to 20 minutes, turning once halfway through, until apples are tender and crust is speckled golden brown. Serve immediately.

Pratie Oaten Biscuits

Pratie is the Irish word for potatoes, and pratie oaten are traditional little breakfast griddle breads served with eggs, black pudding, sausage and the like. But I have discovered that, if you roll them thinner and bake them, they make wonderful accompaniments to cheese, especially full-flavored cheeses such as aged Cheddar and creamy blue. They are also good spread with lemon curd or homemade jam.

**Makes
4 servings**

Tip

Any plain oatmeal can be used in this recipe. However, old-fashioned rolled oats will give the best texture.

- **Preheat oven to 350°F (180°C)**
- **3-inch (7.5 cm) cookie cutter, round or square**
- **Baking sheet, lined with parchment paper**

2 cups	dry-mashed potatoes	500 mL
1/2 cup	all-purpose flour (approx.), divided	125 mL
1 cup	oatmeal, divided (see Tips, left)	250 mL
1/2 tsp	salt	2 mL
1/2 cup	butter (approx.), melted	125 mL

1. In a bowl, combine mashed potatoes, flour, all but 1 tbsp (15 mL) of the oatmeal and salt. Using your hands, blend until mixture forms a soft dough. Blend in melted butter (if the dough seems too sticky, add a little more flour; if it seems too dry, add a little more melted butter).

2. On a dry surface scattered with remaining 1 tbsp (15 mL) oatmeal, roll out dough as thinly as possible — no thicker than 1/4 inch (0.5 cm). Using lightly floured cookie cutter, cut rounds or squares of dough and transfer to prepared baking sheet. Bake in preheated oven, checking to ensure they are not browning too quickly (if they are, place a piece of parchment paper or foil loosely over the top), for about 20 minutes or until crisp and lightly browned.

3. Remove from oven. Let cool in pan on a wire rack for 15 minutes. Using a metal spatula, transfer biscuits to rack and let cool completely before serving.

All-American Potato Pancakes

These easy-to-make griddle cakes use shredded cooked potato, so they have a different texture and are a little lighter than those made from raw potatoes (see Potato Pancakes with Cinnamon Apples & Yogurt Cheese, page 396). They are great for lunch or a late-night snack served with applesauce or apple butter and a drizzle of maple syrup. They are also easily transformed into savory pancakes (see Tip, below).

Serves 2 to 4

Tip
You can easily transform these into savory pancakes by reducing the sugar to 1 tbsp (15 mL) and adding a little finely chopped onion and parsley to the mixture along with the potatoes.

- **Preheat oven to 140°F (60°C)**
- **Nonstick griddle or skillet**

1 cup	all-purpose flour	250 mL
½ tsp	salt	2 mL
¼ tsp	baking powder	1 mL
3 tbsp	granulated sugar	45 mL
1 cup	whole milk	250 mL
4	eggs	4
3 tbsp	melted butter	45 mL
2½ cups	shredded boiled floury or all-purpose potatoes	625 mL

1. In a large bowl, combine flour, salt, baking powder and sugar. Mix well. Add milk and beat well. Add eggs one at a time, beating well after each addition. Continue to beat until batter is smooth. Beat in melted butter. Add potatoes and mix well.

2. Heat griddle over medium-high heat. Ladle about ¼ cup (60 mL) batter onto hot griddle (do two at a time if you have room) and cook until bubbles form on top and pancake is beginning to dry around the edges, about 1 minute. Flip and cook until golden brown on the bottom, about 1 minute. Transfer to a platter and keep warm in preheated oven while you make the remaining pancakes. Serve hot.

Sweet Potato Coins

Perfect little hors d'oeuvres, these one- or two-bite savories topped with onion confit and Brie are made to be teamed with a glass of bubbly.

Makes about 30

Tips

Caramelized Onion Confit: Heat 2 tbsp (30 mL) each butter and extra virgin olive oil over low heat. Stir in ½ cup (125 mL) granulated sugar until dissolved. Add 1½ lbs (750 g) red onions, thinly sliced, stirring to coat. Cover loosely and cook, stirring occasionally, for 30 minutes. Increase heat to medium, stir in ¾ cup (175 mL) dry red wine and just over ⅓ cup (90 mL) red wine vinegar and bring to a boil. Reduce heat and simmer, uncovered, for 30 minutes. Increase heat to medium and cook, stirring, for about 7 minutes, until mixture becomes thick and jam-like. Remove from heat and let cool.

The red onion confit is wonderful as an accompaniment to many other cheeses, too (try it coupled with Cheddar in a grilled cheese sandwich), on burgers, with sausages or as a hot dog topping. It's especially good with omelets and scrambled eggs. Transfer excess confit to a jar with a tight-fitting lid and refrigerate for up to 1 month.

- **2-inch (5 cm) round cookie cutter**
- **Nonstick skillet**
- **Baking sheet, lined with paper towels**

1 cup	dry-mashed cooked sweet potatoes	250 mL
1 cup	all-purpose flour	250 mL
½ tsp	dried sage	2 mL
3 tbsp	olive oil, divided	45 mL
8 oz	Brie, cut into 2-inch (5 cm) squares	250 g
1 cup	Caramelized Onion Confit (see Tips, left)	250 mL

1. In a bowl, using a wooden spoon, stir together sweet potatoes, flour, sage and 1 tbsp (15 mL) oil until mixture forms a soft dough. On a lightly floured surface, roll dough to ¼ inch (0.5 cm) thick. Using cookie cutter, cut out "coins," rerolling scraps.

2. In a nonstick skillet, warm remaining oil over medium heat, swirling pan to coat. In batches, cook coins, turning once, for about 2 minutes per side or until golden brown. Transfer to prepared baking sheet to absorb any residual oil.

3. Arrange coins on a serving platter and top each with a piece of Brie and a spoonful of confit.

Potato Griddle Scones

Wait until you taste these lovely little scones. It's difficult to say when and how you will enjoy them best — at breakfast, lunch or dinner, as a snack, an appetizer or a party piece, dolled up with smoked salmon or many other toppings. Make a batch licked with butter to enjoy in front of the fire with your significant other.

Makes 2 to 4 servings

Tip

You can omit the cheese in these scones if you wish — they will still be delicious. Or, if you prefer, vary the cheese, substituting Pecorino Romano or smoked Cheddar.

- **Preheat oven to 140°F (60°C)**
- **Cast-iron skillet**

2	large floury potatoes, peeled and cut into chunks	2
1½ tsp	salt, divided	7 mL
1 cup	all-purpose flour	250 mL
1½ tsp	baking powder	7 mL
1 tsp	dry mustard	5 mL
1	egg, beaten	1
⅔ cup	whole milk	150 mL
½ cup	shredded sharp (aged) Cheddar cheese	125 mL
1 tbsp	chopped flat-leaf parsley leaves	15 mL
	Salt and freshly ground black pepper	
3 tbsp	olive or vegetable oil (approx.)	45 mL
	Butter	

1. Place potatoes in a large saucepan and add cold water to barely cover. Add 1 tsp (5 mL) salt, cover loosely and bring to a boil over high heat. Reduce heat and cook for 20 minutes or until potatoes are tender. Drain well. Return potatoes to saucepan over very low heat and shake the pot back and forth to remove any trace of moisture. Using a potato masher, mash potatoes. Transfer to a bowl.

2. In another bowl, whisk together flour, baking powder, dry mustard and remaining ½ tsp (2 mL) salt. Add to mashed potatoes along with egg, milk, cheese and parsley. Using a wooden spoon, stir together until blended. Season to taste with salt and freshly ground pepper. Set aside.

3. Preheat oven to 140°F (60°C). Brush a cast-iron skillet with a little of the oil. Working in batches, scoop up ¼ cup (60 mL) batter and drop onto skillet; using a metal spatula, give each a pat to flatten slightly. Cook for 1 to 2 minutes or until golden brown on the bottom. Turn over and cook for 1 to 2 minutes. Transfer to a baking sheet and keep warm until all of the scones are cooked. Serve warm with butter.

Potato Pancakes with Cinnamon Apples & Yogurt Cheese

Make a series of individual pancakes with this recipe or one giant pancake, as I sometimes like to do, cutting it into wedges to serve. You can make this dish with floury, all-purpose and even waxy potatoes (with the latter you have to try a little harder to keep the shreds together) and it is unfailingly great every time. Be careful with the amount of flour — using too much will make the pancakes leaden. If you make this dish for breakfast, serve it with back (Canadian) bacon or farmer's sausage, or omit the apple topping and serve it with poached or fried eggs on top.

Makes 4 servings

Tips

If you don't work fairly quickly when shredding the potatoes, they may discolor. Transferring them to a bowl of cold water as you work will prevent this, but you will have to work extra diligently to extract the water.

Tossing the apples in lemon juice immediately after they have been sliced prevents browning.

Yogurt cheese is also known as Greek-style yogurt. You can buy it in well-stocked supermarkets or you can make your own. Set a sieve lined with a paper coffee filter over a deep bowl. Spoon 2 cups (500 mL) plain whole milk yogurt into sieve, cover with plastic wrap, refrigerate and let drain for at least 4 hours or up to 12 hours. Transfer to an airtight container and refrigerate until ready to use, discarding liquid.

Topping

1 tbsp	butter	15 mL
1 tbsp	olive oil	15 mL
3	apples (Cortland, Crispin or Spartan), peeled, cored, sliced and tossed with 2 tbsp (30 mL) lemon juice	3
½ tsp	ground cinnamon	2 mL
½ tsp	ground nutmeg	2 mL
Pinch	ground allspice	Pinch
1 tbsp	packed brown sugar	15 mL

Pancakes

1 lb	floury potatoes, peeled	500 g
1	small onion	1
3	eggs, lightly beaten	3
2 to 3 tbsp	all-purpose flour	30 to 45 mL
	Salt and freshly ground black pepper	
3 tbsp	butter (approx.), divided	45 mL
3 tbsp	olive oil (approx.), divided	45 mL
1 cup	yogurt cheese (approx.; see Tips, left)	250 mL

1. *Topping:* In a skillet, heat butter and oil over medium heat. Add apples, cinnamon, nutmeg and allspice and cook, stirring, for 10 minutes. Stir in brown sugar and cook for 15 minutes or until apples are glazed (do not overcook; you do not want the apples to become totally soft). Remove from heat and keep warm.

2. *Pancakes:* Meanwhile, coarsely shred potatoes (use a food processor fitted with shredding blade or a box grater). Using a slotted spoon, transfer to a clean tea towel, leaving liquid behind. Gather towel around potatoes and, holding over the sink, squeeze to wring out as much moisture as possible. Over a small bowl, shred onion. Set aside.

3. In a bowl, beat eggs. Lightly stir together potatoes, onion and 2 tbsp (30 mL) flour (if mixture looks too wet, add a little more flour). Season to taste with salt and freshly ground pepper.

4. Preheat oven to 140°F (60°C). In a large, heavy skillet, heat 1 tbsp (15 mL) butter and 1 tbsp (15 mL) oil over medium-high heat until hot. In batches, drop potato mixture by spoonfuls into pan and, using a metal spatula, gently flatten to about $1/4$ inch (0.5 cm) thick. Cook for about 3 minutes per side or until browned. As completed, transfer to preheated oven to keep warm. Repeat until all the batter has been cooked, adding more butter and oil as necessary and ensuring it is hot before adding next batch.

5. Divide pancakes among four warmed individual serving plates. Top each evenly with apple mixture and a quarter of the yogurt cheese.

Variation

In season, substitute fresh peaches for the apples. Blanch in boiling water and peel before using in recipes.

Aloo Paratha

In northern India these savory flatbreads are often used in place of cutlery to scoop up vegetable and meat dishes, or they are simply enjoyed as a quick snack, rolled up and dipped into cumin-flavored yogurt. Stuffed paratha, as in this recipe, are also popular. Serve with Greek-style yogurt (see Tips, page 396) scented with a bit of toasted cumin or with a chutney based on cilantro and mint (page 152).

Makes 10 parathas

Tips

When rolling out the stuffed breads, don't worry if they are not perfectly round or if some of the potato filling seeps out. You'll find that the potato filling and the dough more or less become as one.

This is a great recipe to make with children (although you may want to reduce the quantity of hot chile pepper) because it is fun and easy and a great introduction to flatbread making.

Filling

1 lb	floury potatoes, washed and halved	500 g
1¼ tsp	salt, divided	6 mL
⅓ cup	finely chopped cilantro leaves	75 mL
½ tsp	minced fresh chile pepper	2 mL
1 tsp	ground cumin	5 mL
1 tbsp	minced gingerroot	15 mL

Bread

3½ cups	whole wheat flour	875 mL
½ tsp	salt	2 mL
⅔ cup	canola or sunflower oil, divided	150 mL
½ tsp	salt	2 mL

1. *Filling:* Place potatoes in a large saucepan and add cold water to barely cover. Add 1 tsp (5 mL) salt, cover loosely and bring to a boil over high heat. Reduce heat and cook for 20 minutes or until potatoes are tender. Drain well. Set aside until cool enough to handle. Peel potatoes and dry-mash. Transfer to a bowl. Stir in cilantro, chile, cumin, ginger and remaining ¼ tsp (1 mL) salt until blended.

2. Using floured hands, divide and shape potato mixture into 10 balls. Set aside.

3. *Bread:* In a large bowl, combine flour, salt, 1 tbsp (15 mL) oil and 1½ cups (375 mL) water. On a lightly floured surface, using lightly floured hands, knead until mixture forms a soft, smooth dough. Divide and shape dough into 10 balls. Transfer to a baking sheet, cover with a clean tea towel and let rest in a warm place for 10 minutes.

4. One at a time, using your hands, slightly flatten dough balls. Place in your palm to form a cup and place a ball of potato filling inside cup. Wrap dough over filling and, using your hands, roll it back into a ball, sealing filling inside the dough. Repeat with remaining dough balls and filling.

5. On a lightly floured surface, using a rolling pin, gently roll out each dough ball into a 6-inch (15 cm) circle. Transfer parathas to a baking sheet, stacking between pieces of parchment paper. Preheat oven to 140°F (60°C).

6. In a cast-iron skillet, warm 1 tbsp (15 mL) oil over medium-high heat, swirling pan to coat. One at a time, cook parathas for 2 minutes per side, turning several times and adding a little more oil if necessary. Transfer to a baking sheet and place in preheated oven to keep warm until ready to serve.

Sweet Potato Pancakes with Maple Butter

Sweet potatoes are a natural for pancakes. They lend lightness and a lovely element of sweetness to the batter and are outstanding with the usual accoutrements of smoky bacon or sausages, not to mention maple syrup or butter.

Makes 4 to 6 servings

Tips

One large sweet potato should be sufficient for this recipe.

You should be able to find maple butter wherever quality maple syrup is produced. It has the consistency of thick honey and is just the thing for these pancakes. If you can't find it, use apple butter or homemade applesauce sweetened with pure maple syrup.

- Preheat oven to 140°F (60°C)
- Cast-iron skillet

1 cup	all-purpose flour	250 mL
1 tbsp	packed light brown sugar	15 mL
1 tsp	baking powder	5 mL
½ tsp	baking soda	2 mL
½ tsp	ground cinnamon	2 mL
½ tsp	ground nutmeg	2 mL
¼ tsp	salt	1 mL
1	large egg, beaten	1
¾ cup	cooled dry-mashed sweet potatoes	175 mL
¾ cup	whole milk	175 mL
½ cup	plain yogurt	125 mL
2 tbsp	butter, melted	30 mL
	Vegetable oil	
	Maple butter (see Tips, left)	

1. In a bowl, stir together flour, sugar, baking powder, baking soda, cinnamon, nutmeg and salt until blended. In another bowl, stir together egg, sweet potatoes, milk, yogurt and melted butter until blended. Using a rubber spatula, gently fold egg mixture into sweet potato mixture (do not overmix).

2. Heat a cast-iron skillet over high heat until hot. Add a little of the oil, swirling pan to coat. Working in batches, add about ¼ cup (60 mL) batter per pancake to pan and cook until little bubbles appear on top. Flip and cook other side until browned. Transfer to a plate and keep warm in preheated oven as you make the rest of the pancakes. Serve immediately with maple butter.

Buttermilk Biscuits with Sweet Potato

Try these the next time you sit down to a Southern-style meal of fried chicken or ribs. These biscuits go into a very hot oven for just a few minutes, so watch them carefully. Serve them hot with plenty of butter. Old-fashioned apple butter or cream cheese blended with a bit of orange zest is a nice accompaniment.

Makes about 12 biscuits

Tip

You need just a little cooked sweet potato for this recipe. Leftover mash is fine, or just microwave and mash a small sweet potato.

- **Preheat oven to 400°F (200°C)**
- **2¹⁄₂-inch (6 cm) cookie cutter**
- **Baking sheet, lightly greased**

3¹⁄₂ cups	all-purpose flour (approx.)	825 mL
2 tsp	baking powder	10 mL
2 tsp	baking soda	10 mL
1 tsp	granulated sugar	5 mL
¹⁄₄ tsp	salt	1 mL
¹⁄₂ cup + ¹⁄₄ cup	butter, chilled and cubed	175 mL
1 cup	dry-mashed sweet potatoes	250 mL
1¹⁄₄ cups	buttermilk (approx.)	300 mL
	Melted butter	

1. In a large bowl, sift together flour, baking powder, baking soda, sugar and salt. Using a pastry blender or two knives, cut in butter until mixture is crumbly.

2. In another bowl, whisk together sweet potatoes and buttermilk until blended. Stir into flour mixture until just incorporated (do not overmix). If mixture seems too dry, add a little more buttermilk. On a lightly floured surface, knead until no longer sticky (add a little more flour if necessary, but try to add as little as possible). Sprinkle a little more flour onto work surface, then roll out dough to ³⁄₄ inch (2 cm) thick. Using lightly floured cutter, cut out biscuits. Using a metal spatula, transfer to prepared baking sheet and lightly brush tops with melted butter. Bake in preheated oven for about 15 minutes or until golden brown. Serve immediately.

Forfar Bridies

A bridie is a savory pastry turnover — usually containing beef or lamb, less often chicken (as in this version) — beloved by the Scottish. Apparently bridies originated many years ago with a woman named Maggie Bridie, who was a sort of traveling baker. Traditionally bridies don't contain potato. So, just to fly in the face of that oversight, these not only contain potato in the filling but the pastry itself is potato based. I don't think Maggie would disapprove, because they're delicious. Serve warm with your favorite chutney or a good strong mustard.

Makes 8 bridies

Tips

Boil the potatoes together, whole and unpeeled so they will absorb the minimum amount of water, removing the small one first when it is tender. The large potato is for the dough, the small one for the filling.

Make sure to wash the leeks thoroughly by slitting them open lengthwise and spreading them apart while rinsing clean under cold running water.

If you have leftover cooked chicken or turkey, by all means use it here. You will need about 12 oz (375 g).

• **Baking sheet, lightly buttered**

Dough

2½ cups	all-purpose flour	625 mL
½ tsp	baking soda	2 mL
1 tsp	salt	5 mL
1 cup	butter, chilled and cubed, divided	250 mL
1	large floury potato, boiled until tender, peeled and shredded (see Tips, left)	1
	Ice water	

Filling

¼ cup	butter	60 mL
2	leeks (white and light green parts only), trimmed and finely chopped (see Tips, left)	2
2	boneless, skinless chicken breasts, cooked and coarsely chopped	2
1	medium floury potato, boiled until tender, peeled and diced (see Tips, left)	1
3 tbsp	cranberry jelly, optional	45 mL
2 tbsp	chopped flat-leaf parsley leaves	30 mL
	Salt and freshly ground black pepper	
1	egg, beaten with 1 tbsp (15 mL) milk	1

1. *Dough:* In a bowl, whisk together flour, baking soda and salt. Using a pastry blender or two knives, cut in butter until mixture is crumbly. Add shredded potato and cut in, using pastry blender, until incorporated and mixture is beginning to form dough. Add ice water about 2 tbsp (30 mL) at a time and, using a fork, stir until mixture forms a soft dough. Divide in half and shape into two disks. Wrap in plastic wrap and refrigerate for about 1 hour or until well chilled.

2. *Filling:* Preheat oven to 400°F (200°C). In a skillet, heat butter over medium-high heat. Sauté leeks for about 10 minutes or until softened. Add chicken, diced potato, cranberry jelly (if using) and parsley. Season to taste with salt and freshly ground pepper. Gently cook for 10 minutes. Remove from heat and set aside to cool.

3. On a lightly floured surface, roll out one portion of dough to 1 inch (2.5 cm) thick. Using a bowl with a 6-inch (15 cm) diameter, cut out four circles. Center a generous spoonful of filling on each circle, dip your finger into egg mixture and run it around the edge of the circle, then fold circle in half and pinch edges together. Using a fork, crimp the edges to seal. Repeat with second portion of dough. Brush tops with remaining egg mixture. Transfer to prepared baking sheet. Bake in preheated oven for 15 minutes, then lower oven temperature to 375°F (190°C) and bake for about 20 minutes or until golden brown. Remove from oven and let stand on the baking sheet for 10 minutes before serving. May be served hot, warm or cold.

Sweet Potato Spice Muffins with Cream Cheese Heart

These are a nice addition to the usual collection of muffin recipes — moist and not too sweet, with a lovely creamy surprise in the center.

Makes 12 muffins

Tips

If you have cooking spray, use it to lightly spray the paper baking cups.

Use cream cheese that comes in a block, not the spreadable kind. The latter has less volume because air is whipped into it to make it easier to spread. For this recipe you need a more solid cream cheese.

To toast walnuts: Place in a dry skillet over medium heat and toast, stirring, for 6 to 8 minutes or until fragrant and just starting to darken (don't let them burn).

- **Preheat oven to 350°F (180°C)**
- **12-cup muffin pan, lined with paper baking cups**

1½ cups	all-purpose flour	375 mL
½ cup	packed brown sugar	125 mL
1½ tsp	baking powder	7 mL
1 tsp	baking soda	5 mL
½ tsp	ground cinnamon	2 mL
½ tsp	ground ginger	2 mL
¼ tsp	ground nutmeg	1 mL
Pinch	ground allspice or cloves	Pinch
½ tsp	salt	2 mL
2	eggs	2
1 cup	dry-mashed sweet potatoes	250 mL
⅔ cup	canola or sunflower oil	150 mL
4 oz	cream cheese (see Tips, left)	125 g
½ cup	toasted chopped walnuts (see Tips, left)	125 mL

1. In a large bowl, whisk together flour, brown sugar, baking powder, baking soda, cinnamon, ginger, nutmeg, allspice and salt. Set aside.

2. In another bowl, stir together eggs, mashed sweet potatoes and oil. Stir into flour mixture until just combined.

3. Divide cream cheese into 12 equal squares. Evenly divide batter among 12 prepared muffin cups, filling each three-quarters full. Center one portion of cream cheese in each, lightly pressing into place. Sprinkle evenly with walnuts. Bake in preheated oven for 18 to 25 minutes or until a cake tester inserted in center comes out without crumbs. (It may be moist from the cheese.) Let cool in pan on a wire rack for 5 minutes, then transfer to rack and let cool for about 15 minutes before serving warm.

A.M. Potato Cheese Muffins

These delightful muffins are my daughter Jenna's invention. While great for breakfast, they will also be welcome at brunch, with soup at lunchtime or at dinner alongside chili or stew.

Makes 12 muffins

Tip

For easier clean-up, line your muffin pan with paper baking cups. If you bake muffins or cupcakes often, invest in a silicone muffin pan liner.

- **Preheat oven to 400°F (200°C)**
- **12-cup muffin pan, greased**

2 cups	all-purpose flour	500 mL
3 tsp	baking powder	15 mL
½ tsp	salt	2 mL
1 tsp	sweet paprika	5 mL
3	large eggs	3
2 cups	dry-mashed potatoes	500 mL
1 cup	buttermilk	250 mL
⅓ cup	butter, melted	75 mL
2 cups	shredded sharp (aged) Cheddar cheese	500 mL

1. In a small bowl, whisk together flour, baking powder, salt and paprika. Set aside.
2. In a large bowl, beat eggs. Using a wooden spoon, stir in potatoes until blended. Stir in buttermilk, melted butter and cheese until blended. Stir in flour mixture until just combined (do not overmix). Divide batter evenly among prepared muffin cups. Bake in preheated oven for 25 minutes or until tops are browned and a tester inserted in center comes out clean. Serve immediately.

Variation

Add about ½ cup (125 mL) chopped ham or crisp bacon bits along with the cheese.

Potato, Ricotta & Anchovy Pizza

Granted there are still those who eschew anchovies in any form, but I suspect they have not enjoyed them fresh and lightly marinated. In Spain they serve marinated anchovies as delectable tapas called *boquerones*, and they are absolutely delicious, not the salty little culprits you may be used to. I have also enjoyed these white anchovies in Sicily, where they are treated to a delicate marinade. This recipe is intended to make two generous individual pizzas.

Makes two 12-inch (30 cm) thin-crust pizzas

- Two 12-inch (30 cm) pizza pans, lightly oiled, or pizza stone
- Mandoline or food processor fitted with slicing blade

Tips

Use boiling or hot tap water to warm the bowl for 15 minutes before draining and using.

Use a mandoline or food processor fitted with slicing blade to cut the potato into uniform paper-thin slices.

If fresh anchovies are not readily available, buy good-quality canned anchovies that are salt-packed or packed in good olive oil. If salt-packed, rinse and pat dry. If packed in olive oil there is no need to rinse or pat dry.

If you use a baking stone, follow the manufacturer's instructions for preheating in a hot oven.

Crust

2½ to 3 cups	all-purpose flour, divided	625 to 750 mL
2¼ tsp	active dry yeast	11 mL
1 tsp	salt	5 mL
1 cup	warm water	250 mL
2 tbsp	olive oil	30 mL

Topping

6 oz	ricotta cheese (drained, if necessary)	175 g
1 cup	freshly grated Grana Padano or Parmesan cheese	250 mL
2	large floury potatoes, cut into paper-thin slices (12 slices per pizza; see Tips, left)	2
4	marinated white anchovies, each cut into thirds	4
	Extra virgin olive oil	
	Cornmeal	

1. *Crust:* In a warmed large bowl (see Tips, left), whisk together 2 cups (500 mL) flour, yeast and salt. Stir in water and oil. Using a wooden spoon, stir in additional flour until mixture forms a soft dough.

2. On a lightly floured surface, knead dough for about 8 minutes or until soft and smooth and no longer sticky (add a little more flour if necessary). Lightly coat a bowl with oil and add dough, turning to coat with oil. Cover with plastic wrap and a clean tea towel and let rise in a warm place for about 1 hour or until doubled in size.

3. Preheat oven to 450°F (230°C). Divide dough in half (one half for each pizza) and, on a lightly floured surface, roll out to fit prepared pan. Transfer to pan and brush with a little oil. Using your fingers, press a few indentations into dough.

4. *Topping:* Leaving a $1/2$-inch (1 cm) dough border around edge, arrange half the ricotta evenly overtop, then half the Grana Padano. Evenly top with half of the potatoes (don't overload; if you have too many potatoes, just toss with a bit of oil and oven-fry alongside pizza) and half the anchovies. Drizzle with a little oil. Repeat for second pizza. Bake in preheated oven for 12 to 15 minutes or until potatoes are cooked through and crust is golden brown. Serve with a little additional extra virgin olive oil drizzled over.

Variations

Substitute fresh sardines or whitebait for the anchovies.

Vary the dough by using half white and half whole wheat or multigrain flour.

Sweet Potato Chews
for Danny Boy

Danny Boy is our big, beautiful black Labrador retriever. He is, obviously, the mascot and icon of our pub, the Black Dog. True to his breed (and not unlike his owners!), there isn't much in the way of food that doesn't interest him (I think my mum was right when she said pets reflect their owners). He loves these chewy treats and so do I, because they are a breeze to make and are all natural and good for him. The longer you bake them, the crispier and chewier they become.

Makes 8 to 10 dog treats

Tip

You can double or triple the recipe. Just make sure to cool completely before storage.

- **Preheat oven to 250°F (120°C)**

1	large sweet potato, scrubbed	1
2 tbsp	olive oil	30 mL
1 tsp	garlic powder	5 mL

1. Slice sweet potato in half lengthwise, then cut into strips about $1/3$ inch (0.75 cm) wide and transfer to a bowl. Toss in oil and garlic powder to coat.

2. Arrange evenly on a baking sheet. Bake in preheated oven, tossing occasionally, for 3 hours. Let cool completely. Store in a jar with a tight-fitting lid. Serve one or two a day to a good dog!

Desserts & Confections

Surprised to find potatoes in a dessert chapter? Well, guess what — potatoes have a long history on the sweet tray, good old white and yellow potatoes as well as the sweet potato. As mentioned on page 28, sweet potatoes are of two types: one has a rather paler hue and the other is moist and full-fleshed, with a deep orange color. The latter is my choice for the following recipes that call for sweet potatoes. I've also included a handful of recipes using white potatoes in a sweet capacity. If you have any doubts as to the use of standard white potatoes in this regard, meet the greatest chocolate cake ever (page 412).

Carolina Sweet Potato Pie

I once knew a family of Carolinians who moved from the South to New York City many years ago. No doubt because of their Southern roots, these folks always called sweet potatoes "Carolinas." This is the pie they made every Thanksgiving, which I think is the best sweet potato pie I have ever tasted. Serve it with unsweetened whipped cream.

Makes one 1-crust pie

Tip
If time is not a factor, cook the sweet potatoes whole, in their skins, for maximum flavor.

- **9-inch (23 cm) pie plate**
- **Handheld blender or electric mixer**

Pastry

2 cups	all-purpose flour	500 mL
¼ tsp	salt	1 mL
½ cup	lard or vegetable shortening, chilled and cut into small pieces	125 mL
5 tbsp	butter, chilled and cut into small pieces	75 mL
¼ cup	ice water	60 mL
1	large egg, lightly beaten	1

Filling

2 lbs	sweet potatoes, peeled and cut into large chunks	1 kg
1 cup	packed dark brown sugar	250 mL
3 tbsp	granulated sugar	45 mL
¼ lb	butter, softened	125 g
1 tsp	ground cinnamon	5 mL
½ tsp	salt	2 mL
¼ tsp	ground ginger	1 mL
¼ tsp	ground nutmeg	1 mL
3	large eggs, separated	3
	Finely grated zest of 1 small orange	
½ cup	freshly squeezed orange juice	125 mL
½ cup	table (18%) cream	125 mL

1. *Pastry:* In a bowl, combine flour and salt. Using a pastry blender or a large fork, cut in lard and butter until mixture is crumbly. In a small bowl, whisk together ice water and egg, then stir a little more than half into flour mixture until blended into a dough (add more egg mixture if dough still looks too crumbly and does not hold together when pressed between your fingers). Divide dough in half and gently flatten each portion into a disk. Wrap separately in plastic wrap and refrigerate one disk for about 2 hours. (Freeze second disk for another use. Uncooked pastry can be frozen for up to 3 months if properly wrapped and sealed.)

2. When you're ready to cook, preheat oven to 425°F (220°C). On a lightly floured surface, roll out dough to fit pie plate. Transfer to pie plate, trimming the edges. Set aside.

3. *Filling:* Place sweet potatoes in a large saucepan and add cold water to barely cover. Cover loosely and bring to a boil over high heat. Reduce heat and cook for 15 to 20 minutes or until potatoes are just tender. Drain well. Transfer to a large bowl and let cool for 1 to 2 minutes. Using a potato masher, mash. Add brown sugar, granulated sugar, butter, cinnamon, salt, ginger and nutmeg and mash until blended. In a separate bowl, thoroughly whisk egg yolks. Using a wooden spoon, beat into mashed sweet potatoes along with orange zest, orange juice and cream until blended.

4. In another bowl, using a handheld blender, beat egg whites until stiff peaks form. Using a rubber spatula, gently fold into sweet potato mixture (do not overmix). Scrape into pie shell, gently smoothing top. Bake in preheated oven for 12 minutes. Reduce oven temperature to 350°F (180°C) and bake for about 35 minutes or until filling is puffed, crust is golden and a tester inserted in center comes out clean. Remove from oven and let cool completely on a wire rack before serving.

Bittersweet Chocolate Potato Cake with Chocolate Orange Icing

It's amazing what a little potato can do to improve the average chocolate cake. Not that this fabulous example could possibly be considered average. This cake has a wonderful deep, dark chocolate flavor and an unfailingly moist texture — courtesy of the mashed potato in it — all of which make it the perfect special-day cake. My mum always added freshly squeezed orange juice to her dark chocolate icing, so I do too. Serve this cake with unsweetened whipped cream.

Makes 8 to 10 servings

Tips

Dutch-process cocoa powder is the professional baker's preferred choice. It has been treated with a small amount of an alkaline solution, which helps to reduce cocoa's natural acidity. This process also darkens the cocoa's color, making it richer, with a smoother, more balanced flavor. It is also called "alkalized cocoa powder" and is generally of high quality, especially if imported from Holland. If you can't obtain it, use the best-quality unsweetened cocoa.

If you don't have a potato ricer, use a sieve (not a fine-mesh one or it will take forever), pressing the mashed potatoes through with a wooden spoon.

Be sure to allow your cakes to cool thoroughly before icing. Otherwise the icing will tend to melt.

- Preheat oven to 375°F (190°C)
- Electric mixer
- Ricer or sieve (see Tips, left)
- Two 8-inch (2 L) square cake pans, lightly buttered and floured

Cake

½ cup	Dutch-process cocoa powder (see Tips, left)	125 mL
2 tbsp	boiling water	30 mL
4 oz	unsweetened chocolate (4 squares), chopped	125 g
¾ cup	whole milk	175 mL
1 cup	butter	250 mL
2 cups	granulated sugar	500 mL
4	large eggs, separated	4
2 tsp	vanilla extract	10 mL
1 cup	dry-mashed potatoes	250 mL
2 cups	all-purpose flour	500 mL
1 tsp	baking powder	5 mL
1 tsp	baking soda	5 mL
1 tsp	salt	5 mL

Icing

5 oz	unsweetened chocolate (5 squares), chopped	150 g
1 cup	unsalted butter	250 mL
3½ cups	sifted confectioner's (icing) sugar	875 mL
⅓ cup	freshly squeezed orange juice	75 mL
Pinch	salt	Pinch

1. *Cake:* Place cocoa powder in a small bowl, then whisk in boiling water to form a paste. Set aside. In a saucepan, combine chocolate and milk over medium heat and warm gently, stirring, until chocolate has melted and blended with milk. Remove from heat and whisk in reserved cocoa paste until blended and smooth. Set aside.

2. Using an electric mixer at medium speed, beat butter and sugar until smooth and creamy. With mixer running, add egg yolks one at a time, beating well after each addition. Beat in vanilla. Gradually beat in reserved chocolate mixture.

3. Place mashed potatoes in a ricer. Press into chocolate mixture, scraping bits clinging to underside into mixture. Stir until blended.

4. In another bowl, whisk together flour, baking powder, baking soda and salt. Slowly beat into chocolate mixture until blended (do not overmix). Set batter aside.

5. In another bowl, using an electric mixer, beat egg whites until stiff peaks form. Using a rubber spatula, gently fold into batter. Divide batter evenly between prepared pans. Place on center rack in preheated oven and bake for 45 to 50 minutes or until a tester inserted in center comes out clean.

6. Remove from oven and let cool in pans on a wire rack for 30 minutes. Turn out cakes and let cool on rack.

7. *Icing:* Place chocolate in a small heatproof bowl set over a saucepan of very hot water. Using a wooden spoon, stir until chocolate has melted. Remove from heat and let cool.

8. In a bowl, using an electric mixer at medium speed, beat butter until light and fluffy. Gradually beat in confectioner's sugar. Using a rubber spatula, scrape in melted chocolate. Beat in orange juice and salt until icing is smooth and creamy.

9. Transfer one cooled cake layer to a cake stand or platter. Spread some of the icing overtop, smoothing to the edges. Top with second cake layer, then ice top and sides of whole cake.

Sweet Potato Pound Cake with Sweet Potato Ice Cream

A double hit of sweet potato sweets, this is a beautifully colored, flavorful cake with a great texture, thanks to the toasted pecans. The sweet potato ice cream does require an ice-cream maker; if you don't have one, just make the cake, buy some good-quality vanilla or rum and raisin ice cream to serve alongside, and ask for an ice-cream maker for your birthday.

Makes 8 servings

- Ice-cream maker
- 9- by 5-inch (2 L) loaf pan, lightly buttered

Tips

You will need a total of 2 cups (500 mL) mashed sweet potatoes to make both preparations, or 2 to 3 sweet potatoes, depending on their size. Dry-mashed sweet potatoes are mashed without butter, milk or cream.

Toasting the nuts in a dry skillet gives them a nice crispness; just take care not to burn them, as they take very little time to toast. Add the nuts to a skillet placed over medium-high heat, allow to heat for a minute or two, then toss them around a bit. When they are fragrant and beginning to brown slightly, remove from heat. You can also oven-toast nuts on a baking sheet in a 400°F (200°C) oven for just a few minutes, but watch them carefully so they don't burn.

Use a spice grinder or mini food processor to grind the pecans along with 1 tbsp (15 mL) of the sugar.

Ice Cream

6	large egg yolks	6
½ cup	packed dark brown sugar	125 mL
½ cup	granulated sugar	125 mL
¼ tsp	salt	1 mL
2 cups	heavy or whipping (35%) cream	500 mL
2 cups	whole milk	500 mL
1½ cups	dry-mashed sweet potatoes	375 mL
1 tsp	ground cinnamon	5 mL
½ tsp	ground ginger	2 mL
½ tsp	ground nutmeg	2 mL

Cake

2 cups	all-purpose flour	500 mL
2½ tsp	baking powder	12 mL
½ tsp	ground cinnamon	2 mL
½ tsp	ground nutmeg	2 mL
½ tsp	salt	2 mL
1 cup	butter, softened	250 mL
1 cup	granulated sugar	250 mL
½ cup	packed light brown sugar	125 mL
½ cup	ground lightly toasted pecans (see Tips, left)	125 mL
1 tsp	vanilla extract	5 mL
4	large eggs	4
½ cup	dry-mashed sweet potatoes	125 mL
½ cup	heavy or whipping (35%) cream	125 mL

1. *Ice Cream:* In a large bowl, whisk together egg yolks, brown sugar, granulated sugar and salt until smooth. Set aside. In a heavy saucepan, combine cream and milk over medium heat and bring to a boil, stirring. Remove from heat. Transfer a large spoonful of the milk mixture to egg yolk mixture, whisk together, then add remaining milk mixture, whisking to blend. Let cool for 15 minutes, stirring now and then. Cover and refrigerate ice-cream mixture for about 2 hours or until cold.

2. Strain cold ice-cream mixture through a fine-mesh sieve into a bowl. Stir in sweet potatoes, cinnamon, ginger and nutmeg until thoroughly blended. Transfer to ice-cream maker, process, and freeze according to manufacturer's instructions.

3. *Cake:* Preheat oven to 350°F (180°C). Into a large bowl, sift together flour, baking powder, cinnamon, nutmeg and salt. Set aside.

4. In a large bowl, using an electric mixer at medium speed, beat butter until light. Beat in granulated sugar and brown sugar until light and fluffy. Stir in pecans and vanilla. Add eggs one at a time, beating lightly before adding and beating well after each addition, scraping down sides of bowl. Using a wooden spoon, stir in mashed sweet potatoes.

5. Beginning and ending with flour mixture, beat flour mixture into butter mixture in three additions, alternating with cream in two additions. Pour into prepared pan and transfer to center rack of preheated oven. Bake for 1 hour and 15 minutes or until top springs back when lightly touched and a tester inserted in center comes out clean. Transfer to a wire rack and let cool for 30 minutes before turning out. Slice and serve barely warm, topped with ice cream.

Sweet Potato Cake with Sugared Bourbon Glaze

Here is a lovely little cake with a stylish glaze that makes the perfect accompaniment to coffee or tea. It is also very nice as the conclusion to a Southern-style meal.

Makes 8 to 10 servings

Tip

If you don't have buttermilk on hand, substitute regular milk to which you have added 1½ tsp (7 mL) of distilled white vinegar. Let stand for 5 minutes before using.

- Preheat oven to 350°F (180°C)
- Electric mixer
- Tube or bundt pan, lightly buttered and floured

Cake

2	small sweet potatoes, peeled and cut into ¾-inch (2 cm) slices	2
2 tsp	salt, divided	10 mL
½ cup	buttermilk	125 mL
1 tsp	vanilla extract	5 mL
2 cups	all-purpose flour	500 mL
2 tsp	baking powder	10 mL
½ tsp	baking soda	2 mL
1 tsp	ground cinnamon	5 mL
½ tsp	ground nutmeg	2 mL
⅓ cup	butter	75 mL
½ cup	granulated sugar	125 mL
2	eggs	2

Glaze

½ cup	packed brown sugar	125 mL
¼ cup	butter	60 mL
3 tbsp	heavy or whipping (35%) cream	45 mL
¼ cup	bourbon	60 mL

1. *Cake:* Place sweet potatoes in a large saucepan and add cold water to barely cover. Add 1 tsp (5 mL) salt, cover loosely and bring to a boil over high heat. Reduce heat and cook for 15 to 20 minutes or until potatoes are just tender. Drain well. Return potatoes to saucepan over very low heat and shake the pot back and forth to remove any trace of moisture. Transfer to a small bowl and let air-dry for about 15 minutes. Using a potato masher, roughly mash potatoes. Mash in buttermilk and vanilla until blended. Set aside.

2. Into a bowl, sift flour, baking powder, baking soda, remaining 1 tsp (5 mL) salt, cinnamon and nutmeg. Set aside.

3. In a large bowl, using an electric mixer at medium speed, beat butter and sugar for about 2 minutes or until fluffy. Beat in eggs one at a time, beating well after each addition. Beginning and ending with flour mixture, beat flour mixture into butter mixture in three additions, alternating with sweet potato mixture in two additions. Pour into prepared pan and bake in preheated oven for 45 to 50 minutes or until a tester inserted in center comes out clean. Remove from oven and set aside to cool in pan on a wire rack for 10 minutes. Place a large plate over cake and invert pan. Place another large plate over cake and invert again so it is right side up. Set aside.

4. *Glaze:* In a small, heavy saucepan, combine brown sugar, butter and cream. Bring to a boil, stirring, over medium heat and cook, stirring, until sugar has dissolved. Boil, stirring often, for about 3 minutes or until mixture has thickened. Remove from heat and stir in bourbon.

5. While cake is still warm, use a skewer to poke holes all over. Spoon half the warm glaze over cake, then let cake cool for 10 minutes. Pour remaining glaze over cake, letting it dribble down sides. Set aside to cool completely before serving.

Variations

You can add about ¹/₂ cup (125 mL) each of raisins and chopped nuts if you wish.

Substitute the rich Cream Cheese Icing (page 418) for the glaze.

Sweet Potato Cinnamon Cake with Pineapple & Coconut & Cream Cheese Icing

I have lost track of the number of traditional carrot cakes I have made for the Black Dog. During the hyper-busy summer season, we make at least one a day. While creating and testing desserts for this book, I decided to make my tried-and-true recipe, substituting sweet potato in place of the carrots. *Voilà* — a star was born.

Makes 10 to 12 servings

Tip

Toasting the nuts in a dry skillet gives them a nice crispness; just take care not to burn them, as they take very little time to toast. Add the nuts to a skillet placed over medium heat, and cook, stirring, for 6 to 8 minutes or until fragrant. You can also oven-toast nuts on a baking sheet in a 400°F (200°C) oven for just a few minutes, but watch them carefully so they don't burn.

- Preheat oven to 350°F (180°C)
- Electric mixer
- Two 9-inch (1.5 L) round cake pans or one 13-by 9-inch (3 L) cake pan, sprayed with nonstick cooking spray and lined with parchment paper also sprayed with nonstick cooking spray

Cake

2 cups	all-purpose flour	500 mL
2 tsp	baking soda	10 mL
1 tsp	salt	5 mL
2 tsp	ground cinnamon	10 mL
½ tsp	ground ginger	2 mL
½ tsp	ground nutmeg	2 mL
¼ tsp	ground allspice	1 mL
2 cups	granulated sugar	500 mL
1¼ cups	canola oil	300 mL
4	large eggs	4
2 cups	shredded peeled sweet potatoes	500 mL
1 cup	canned crushed pineapple, well drained	250 mL
1 cup	sweetened shredded coconut	250 mL
1 cup	chopped toasted walnuts (see Tips, left)	250 mL

Cream Cheese Icing

10 oz	plain cream cheese (not light or whipped), softened	300 g
5 tbsp	butter	75 mL
2½ cups	sifted confectioner's (icing) sugar	625 mL
1 tsp	vanilla extract	5 mL

1. *Cake:* In a bowl, whisk together flour, baking soda, salt, cinnamon, ginger, nutmeg and allspice until blended. Set aside.

2. In a large bowl, beat sugar and oil until blended. Beat in eggs one at a time, beating well after each addition. Stir flour mixture into sugar mixture until blended and no traces of flour are visible. Stir in sweet potatoes, pineapple, coconut and walnuts. Evenly divide batter between prepared pans. Bake in preheated oven for 45 minutes or until a tester inserted in center comes out clean. Let cool in pans on a wire rack for at least 15 minutes before turning out onto rack. Let cool completely.

3. *Icing:* Meanwhile, in a large bowl, using an electric mixer at medium speed, beat cream cheese and butter until light and fluffy. Beat in confectioner's sugar about 1 cup (250 mL) at a time, beating well after each addition. Beat in vanilla. Cover with plastic wrap and refrigerate for about 30 minutes or until just firm enough to spread. Transfer one cake layer to a cake stand or platter. Spread some of the icing overtop, smoothing to the edges. Top with second cake layer, then ice top and sides of whole cake.

Grand Sweet Potato Cheesecake with Pecan Praline Crust & Caramel Cream

This is a serious cheesecake, one that you should plan to make when you have enough people on hand to do it justice. It is big and rich and a little goes a long way. It's perfect for Thanksgiving or Christmas or as the conclusion to any special dinner. Yes, this is a lot of cream cheese, but that's precisely what a real cheesecake calls for. Besides, you don't make a cake like this every day.

Makes 10 to 20 servings

- **Preheat oven to 400°F (200°C)**
- **10-inch (3 L) springform pan**
- **Electric mixer**

Tips

Be sure to use cream cheese that is in block form, not a light or whipped version.

Because the cake should be well chilled before serving, for best results make it a day ahead of time.

Toasting the nuts in a dry skillet gives them a nice crispness; just take care not to burn them, as they take very little time to toast. Add the nuts to a skillet placed over medium heat, and cook, stirring, for 6 to 8 minutes until fragrant. You can also oven-toast nuts on a baking sheet in a 400°F (200°C) oven for just a few minutes, but watch them carefully so they don't burn.

Pecan Praline Crust

1½ cups	finely ground toasted pecans (see Tips, left)	375 mL
1 cup	crisp oatmeal or gingersnap cookie crumbs	250 mL
6 tbsp	butter, softened	90 mL
2 tbsp	packed dark brown sugar	30 mL

Filling

4	large eggs, lightly beaten	4
3	egg yolks, lightly beaten	3
2½ lbs	plain cream cheese (see Tips, left), at room temperature	1.25 kg
1 cup	granulated sugar	250 mL
3 tbsp	all-purpose flour	45 mL
2 tsp	ground cinnamon	10 mL
1 tsp	ground ginger	5 mL
1 tsp	ground nutmeg	5 mL
2 cups	dry-mashed sweet potatoes	500 mL
1 cup	heavy or whipping (35%) cream	250 mL
1 tbsp	vanilla extract	15 mL

Caramel Cream

30	caramel candies	30
3 tbsp	whole milk	45 mL

Tips

When making cheesecake, avoid opening the oven door, as drafts can cause the cheesecake to crack. Also, don't over-bake; cheesecake is done when the edges are slightly puffed and the center still appears a bit soft and moist. It will firm up on cooling. Run a thin-bladed knife around the outside edges of the cheesecake to loosen it from the pan after removing from the oven, to prevent cracking as it cools and contracts.

To make this cake completely over-the-top, dollop each serving with whipped cream.

1. *Pecan Praline Crust:* In a bowl, mix pecans, cookie crumbs, butter and brown sugar until thoroughly blended. Press over bottom and a third of the way up the sides of springform pan. Bake in preheated oven for 6 minutes or until just beginning to brown (watch carefully and don't let it get dark brown, as the nuts will have an acrid taste). Remove from oven and let cool completely on a wire rack. Reduce oven temperature to 350°F (180°C).

2. *Filling:* In a bowl, using an electric mixer at medium speed, beat eggs and egg yolks, cream cheese and sugar until creamy. Beat in flour, cinnamon, ginger and nutmeg until blended. Beat in sweet potatoes, cream and vanilla until blended. Pour into crust and place on center rack in preheated oven. Place a shallow pan of water on the rack below (the moisture will help prevent surface cracks in the baked filling). Bake for $1\frac{3}{4}$ to 2 hours or until set around edges but still a bit wobbly in the center (see Tips, left).

3. Remove from oven. Run a small, thin-bladed knife around edge to loosen cheesecake from pan and remove the sides of the pan. Turn off oven and return cheesecake to oven, leaving door slightly ajar. Let stand in oven for at least 2 hours, then cover loosely with plastic wrap and refrigerate for 2 hours.

4. *Caramel Cream:* In a saucepan over low heat, combine caramel candies and milk and cook, stirring often, until caramels have melted and mixture is blended.

5. Before serving, fill a measuring cup with boiling water. Dip a sharp knife into the water, wipe it dry, then slice cheesecake; wipe blade clean, dip it, dry it and slice again. Plate each wedge, then spoon the caramel sauce over.

Dark Chocolate & Orange Potato Cheesecake

Rich, dark and chocolaty, this splendid cheesecake boasts bittersweet chocolate in the filling and a base of chocolate cookie crumbs. If you wanted to echo the orange element in the filling, serve with a scoop of orange gelato.

Makes 10 to 12 servings

Tip

Use cream cheese that comes in a block, not the spreadable kind, because the latter has less volume owing to the air that is whipped into it to make it easily spreadable. For this recipe you need a more solid cream cheese.

- **Preheat oven to 350°F (180°C)**
- **9-inch (2.5 L) springform pan**
- **Electric mixer**
- **Roasting pan**

Chocolate Crust

3 cups	chocolate cookie crumbs	750 mL
½ tsp	ground cinnamon	2 mL
⅔ cup	butter, melted	150 mL

Filling

2	packages cream cheese, each 8 oz (250 g) (see Tip, left)	2
1 cup	granulated sugar	250 mL
1½ cups	cooled dry-mashed potatoes	375 mL
3	eggs	3
10 oz	bittersweet chocolate, chopped, melted and cooled	300 g
1 tbsp	orange zest, finely chopped	15 mL
2 tbsp	freshly squeezed orange juice	30 mL

1. *Chocolate Crust:* In a bowl, stir together cookie crumbs, cinnamon and melted butter until crumbs are completely moistened. Press over bottom and halfway up the sides of springform pan. Center pan on a large sheet of foil, then gather foil and wrap around base and sides. Transfer to preheated oven and bake for 10 minutes. Remove from oven and let cool completely on a wire rack, leaving foil intact. Reduce oven temperature to 325°F (160°C).

2. *Filling:* In a large bowl, using an electric mixer at medium speed, beat cream cheese and sugar until blended. Beat in mashed potatoes until smooth. Add eggs one at a time, beating well after each addition. Stir in melted chocolate, orange zest and orange juice until incorporated. Using a rubber spatula, scrape into chocolate crust.

3. Place springform pan in roasting pan. Pull out center oven rack and set roasting pan on rack. Pour enough very hot water into roasting pan to come halfway up sides of springform pan. Return rack to preheated oven and bake for 50 minutes or until filling is set around edges but still a bit wobbly in center. Turn off oven and let cheesecake cool in oven for 1 hour. Remove from oven. Transfer from roasting pan to a wire rack and let cool completely.

4. Cover cheesecake and refrigerate for 4 hours. Remove pan sides. Before serving, fill a measuring cup with boiling water. Dip a sharp knife into the water, wipe it dry, then slice cheesecake; wipe blade clean, dip it, dry it and slice again.

Spice & Maple Sweet Potato Cookies

Like all good cookies, these have an old-fashioned quality, with the maple syrup providing a special sweetness. Add 1 cup (250 mL) or so raisins or chopped nuts for variety and, if you are so inclined, a drizzle of vanilla icing to make them even prettier.

Makes 18 to 24 cookies

Tip

Store in an airtight container for up to three days.

- **Preheat oven to 375°F (190°C)**
- **Electric mixer**
- **2 baking sheets, lightly greased or lined with parchment paper**

2 cups	all-purpose flour	500 mL
2 tsp	baking powder	10 mL
½ tsp	baking soda	2 mL
1 tsp	allspice	5 mL
1 tsp	ground cinnamon	5 mL
¼ tsp	salt	1 mL
½ cup	pure maple syrup	125 mL
¼ cup	packed brown sugar	60 mL
½ cup	butter, at room temperature	125 mL
1	large sweet potato, peeled, cooked and dry-mashed	1
1	large egg, beaten	1
1 tsp	vanilla extract	5 mL

1. In a bowl, whisk together flour, baking powder, baking soda, allspice, cinnamon and salt. Set aside.

2. In a bowl, using an electric mixer, beat maple syrup, brown sugar and butter until light and fluffy. Beat in mashed sweet potato, egg and vanilla until blended. Stir in flour mixture in three additions (do not overmix).

3. Drop batter, 1 tbsp (15 mL) at a time, 1 inch (2.5 cm) apart on prepared baking sheets. Bake in preheated oven for 8 to 10 minutes or until golden brown. Let cool in pans on a wire rack for 3 minutes, then, using a metal spatula, transfer to rack. Let cool completely.

Sweet Potato Dessert Soufflé

This light-as-air soufflé is just as nice at the beginning of a meal as it is at the end, being sort of a cross between a savory and a sweet concoction. If you want to maximize the savory side, omit the sugar, cinnamon and nutmeg and add a little full-flavored grated cheese.

Makes 4 to 6 servings

- Preheat oven to 400°F (200°C)
- Handheld blender or electric mixer
- 6-cup (1.5 L) soufflé dish, lightly buttered

3	large sweet potatoes, scrubbed	3
1 tsp	salt (approx.)	5 mL
4	extra-large eggs, separated	4
¼ cup	granulated sugar, divided	60 mL
3 tbsp	butter, divided	45 mL
¾ cup	heavy or whipping (35%) cream	175 mL
¼ tsp	ground cinnamon	1 mL
¼ tsp	ground nutmeg	1 mL

1. Place sweet potatoes in a large saucepan and add cold water to barely cover. Add 1 tsp (5 mL) salt, cover loosely and bring to a boil over high heat. Reduce heat and cook for 15 to 20 minutes or until potatoes are thoroughly cooked. Drain well. Set aside until cool enough to handle. Peel off skins and transfer to a large bowl. Using a potato masher, mash sweet potatoes with egg yolks, 1 tbsp (15 mL) sugar, 2 tbsp (30 mL) butter, cream, cinnamon, nutmeg and a pinch of salt until blended.

2. In another bowl, beat egg whites until stiff peaks form. Using a rubber spatula, gently fold into sweet potato mixture, being careful not to overmix. Carefully pour into prepared soufflé dish, dot with remaining butter and sprinkle with remaining sugar. Bake in preheated oven for about 30 minutes or until puffed and golden brown. Serve immediately.

Yukon Gold Potato Puffs with Sugar & Cinnamon

These golden fritters bring mini doughnuts to mind, especially when dusted with a little confectioner's sugar or cinnamon while still warm. You might also choose to serve them with a little maple syrup or on a glass plate with a base of raspberry coulis and a scoop of good vanilla ice cream — yum.

Makes 4 to 6 servings

Tips

The oil should come a little over halfway up the sides of the pot. Do not overfill; leave at least 3 inches (7.5 cm) of headspace at the top.

If you don't have a candy/deep-frying thermometer, drop a small cube of dry bread into the oil; if it floats, the oil is hot enough.

- **½-inch (1 cm) round cookie cutter**
- **Large, heavy pot, Dutch oven or deep fryer**
- **Candy/deep-frying thermometer (if not using a deep fryer)**
- **Baking sheet, lined with paper towels**

1 lb	Yukon Gold or other all-purpose potatoes, peeled and quartered	500 g
1 tsp	salt	5 mL
½ cup	all-purpose flour	125 mL
	Canola or sunflower oil	
	Confectioner's (icing) sugar	
	Ground cinnamon	

1. Place potatoes in a large saucepan and add cold water to barely cover. Add salt, cover loosely and bring to a boil over high heat. Reduce heat and cook for 15 to 20 minutes or until potatoes are just tender. Drain well. Return potatoes to saucepan over very low heat and shake the pot back and forth to remove any trace of moisture. Using a potato masher, roughly mash and transfer to a large bowl.

2. Add flour to potatoes and mix well, working the mixture to form a soft dough. Using a wooden spoon, stir until mixture forms dough. On a lightly floured surface, using a lightly floured rolling pin, roll out a 12-inch (30 cm) circle. Using a lightly floured cookie cutter and rerolling scraps, cut out about 24 rounds.

3. Place 4 to 6 inches (10 to 15 cm) oil in a large, heavy pot (see Tips, left). Heat over medium-high heat until thermometer registers 325°F (160°C). (If you're using a deep fryer, follow the manufacturer's instructions.) Using a slotted spoon, carefully add potato rounds, three at a time, and cook for about 1 minute or until puffed up and golden brown. Transfer to prepared baking sheet and sprinkle at once with sugar and cinnamon. Serve immediately.

Sweet Potato Cream Cheese Custards

These individual little custards are light and delicious. Garnish with lightly sweetened whipped cream, toasted pecans and curls of dark chocolate.

**Makes
6 servings**

Tip

If you like, you can pour the mixture into a crust made from cookie crumbs, like those used in cheesecakes (see pages 420 and 422), and make one large custard pie. If so, increase baking time to 35 minutes.

- **Preheat oven to 350°F (180°F)**
- **Six 6-oz (175 mL) custard cups, lightly buttered**
- **Roasting pan**
- **Electric mixer or stand mixer**

8 oz	plain cream cheese (not light or whipped), softened	250 g
¼ cup	heavy or whipping (35%) cream	60 mL
1 cup	dry-mashed sweet potatoes	250 mL
½ cup	packed light brown sugar	125 mL
¼ cup	granulated sugar	60 mL
1 tbsp	all-purpose flour	15 mL
½ tsp	ground cinnamon	2 mL
½ tsp	ground ginger	2 mL
¼ tsp	ground allspice	1 mL
3	large eggs	3

1. Place prepared custard cups in a roasting pan (do not let them touch). Set aside.

2. In a large bowl, using an electric mixer at medium speed, beat cream cheese and cream until blended. Beat in sweet potatoes, brown sugar and granulated sugar until blended. Beat in flour, cinnamon, ginger and allspice. Add eggs one at a time, beating well after each addition. Put the kettle on to boil.

3. Evenly divide cream cheese mixture among prepared custard cups. Just before kettle comes to a full boil, remove from heat. Transfer pan with custard cups to center rack in oven. Carefully pour enough hot water from kettle into pan to come halfway up sides of custard cups. Slide rack and pan into oven and bake for 25 to 30 minutes or until edges of custards are firm and centers are still a bit wobbly.

4. Remove from oven and transfer custard cups to a wire rack. Let cool for about 30 minutes. Cover loosely and refrigerate for about 1 hour or until chilled.

Sweet Potato Dumplings with Blackberries & Cream

On the Richter scale of desserts, this one buries the needle. It is very Southern, very old-fashioned and one of the best uses for sweet potatoes ever. Don't restrict yourself to blackberries for this dish. Any ripe fruit in season — berries, peaches, pears, plums, cherries — can be slow-cooked alongside. However, blackberries and blueberries provide the most dramatic color contrast. Plan a light main course if you're going to have these for dessert, and make sure to serve with unsweetened softly whipped cream.

Makes 6 to 8 servings

Tips

Adjust the quantity of sugar according to the sweetness of the fruit.

You don't require a great deal of sweet potato for this recipe, so choose a small one.

Fruit Sauce

4 cups	blackberries (or a combination of berries)	1 L
2 cups	water	500 mL
¾ cup	granulated sugar (approx.; see Tips, left)	175 mL
1 tbsp	freshly squeezed lemon juice (approx.; see Variation)	15 mL

Dumplings

1¼ cups	all-purpose flour	300 mL
2 tsp	baking powder	10 mL
1 tsp	granulated sugar	5 mL
½ tsp	salt	2 mL
1 cup	whole milk	250 mL
½ cup	dry-mashed sweet potatoes	125 mL
2 tbsp	butter, melted	30 mL

1. *Fruit Sauce:* In a large, heavy saucepan, stir together blackberries, water and sugar over high heat and bring to a rapid boil. Reduce heat and simmer, stirring occasionally, for about 5 minutes or until berries have softened and released their juices (do not overcook). Stir in about half the lemon juice, then taste the fruit; if it is too sweet, add a little more lemon juice (see Variation, page 429). Remove saucepan from heat and set aside.

2. *Dumplings:* In a large bowl, whisk together flour, baking powder, sugar and salt. In another bowl, stir together milk and sweet potatoes until smooth. Using a wooden spoon, quickly beat in melted butter, then add to flour mixture all at once, lightly stirring together (do not overmix).

3. Return saucepan containing fruit sauce to stovetop over low heat and bring to a simmer. Drop dumpling batter, 1 tbsp (15 mL) at a time, into pan, using spoon to shape batter into dumplings and gently pushing dumplings into fruit sauce to partially immerse. Cover and cook for 10 minutes (larger dumplings will take a little longer).

4. Spoon sauce into shallow individual serving bowls. Top with dumplings and spoon more sauce overtop.

Variations

Instead of the lemon juice, use other flavorings such as liqueurs or port, depending on the fruit. For instance, if you use raspberries, team with Chambord, a raspberry liqueur. An apricot-based sauce is lovely with amaretto, and a ruby port would be nice with plums or cherries.

Sweet Potato Croissant Pudding with Cranberries & Walnuts

This is a great dessert for a fall or winter evening. Serve it with warmed maple syrup or whipped cream — or both.

Makes 8 to 10 servings

Tips

The croissants in this recipe are not the delicate little beauties you would buy at a good bakery but rather what I think of as supermarket croissants, larger and a little more substantial.

For convenience, you can put this together the day before you plan on serving it — it will only get better. Pop it into the oven when you sit down to dinner and it will be ready when you are.

Toasting the nuts in a dry skillet gives them a nice crispness; just take care not to burn them, as they take very little time to toast. Add the nuts to a skillet placed over medium heat, and cook, stirring, for 6 to 8 minutes until fragrant. You can also oven-toast nuts on a baking sheet in a 400°F (200°C) oven for just a few minutes, but watch them carefully so they don't burn.

- Preheat oven to 350°F (180°C)
- 11- by 7-inch (2 L) baking dish, buttered

6 cups	torn day-old croissants	1.5 L
½ cup	coarsely chopped toasted walnuts (see Tips, left)	125 mL
1 cup	dried cranberries or raisins	250 mL
¼ cup	melted butter	60 mL
1 tsp	ground cinnamon	5 mL
1 tsp	ground ginger	5 mL
¼ tsp	ground nutmeg	1 mL
1 cup	packed light brown sugar	250 mL
3	large eggs	3
2½ cups	half-and-half (10%) cream	625 mL
2 tsp	pure maple syrup	10 mL
2 cups	dry-mashed sweet potatoes	500 mL

1. In a large bowl, using your hands, toss together croissants, walnuts, cranberries, melted butter, cinnamon, ginger and nutmeg. Transfer to prepared baking dish.
2. In another bowl, whisk eggs. Whisk in cream and maple syrup until blended. Stir in sweet potatoes until blended. Pour over croissant mixture and, using your hands, toss together to completely soak croissants. Arrange in an even layer and let stand for 10 minutes.
3. Bake in preheated oven for 50 minutes or until all the liquid has been absorbed and croissant mixture is puffed up. Let stand on a wire rack for 10 minutes before serving.

Irish Potato Pudding

This is another of those old recipes from my mum's collection, the origins of which are lost in time. It is a lovely old-fashioned, comforting preparation that must have come about when an Irish housewife was determined to make a dessert with the ingredients she had on hand — potatoes, butter, eggs and magical Irish whiskey. Serve with thick pouring cream and fresh berries.

Makes 4 to 6 servings

Tip

Don't omit the Irish whiskey. It adds an unmistakable flavor to the pudding.

- **Preheat oven to 350°F (180°C)**
- **Electric mixer**
- **9-inch (2.5 L) baking dish, lightly buttered**

3	large floury potatoes, scrubbed	3
1 tsp	salt	5 mL
1 cup	heavy or whipping (35%) cream	250 mL
4	eggs, separated	4
1 cup	granulated sugar	250 mL
½ cup	Irish whiskey	125 mL
¼ cup	ground almonds	60 mL
1 tbsp	orange extract	15 mL

1. Place potatoes in a large saucepan and add cold water to barely cover. Add salt, cover loosely and bring to a boil over high heat. Reduce heat and cook for 15 to 20 minutes or until potatoes are just tender. Drain well. Set aside until cool enough to handle. Peel off skins and transfer potatoes to a bowl. Using a potato masher, mash potatoes. Mash in cream until smooth. Using a wooden spoon, briskly stir potatoes to incorporate a bit of air into the mash. Add egg yolks, beating well after each addition. Stir in sugar, whiskey, almonds and orange extract until blended. Set aside.

2. In a bowl, using an electric mixer at high speed, beat egg whites until stiff peaks form. Using a rubber spatula, carefully fold into potato mixture (do not overmix). Scrape batter into prepared baking dish. Bake in preheated oven for 40 to 45 minutes or until firm. Let cool on a wire rack for 15 minutes. Serve warm.

Hutchinson's Carrot & Potato Pudding with Proper Custard

I grew up with carrot pudding — which my mum maintained was a little lighter than traditional plum pudding — being served at every Christmas dinner. It was prepared weeks beforehand, and when she made it, my mum would always invite me into the kitchen to give it a good-luck stir. She furthered the tradition by including a solitary coin in the mix — a sixpence — more good luck for the person who came across it in their serving. While it cooked, the magnificent fragrance filled the kitchen with promises of good things to come. When it was presented weeks later on Christmas Day, it would be brought to the table crowned with a sprig of holly and set aflame with brandy. A little more brandy would be added to the requisite jug of creamy custard served alongside. Make sure to serve with what the English call proper custard (also known as crème anglaise), not the packaged article.

Makes 6 to 8 servings

- **6-inch (4-cup/1 L) pudding basin, generously buttered**
- **Large steamer**
- **Electric mixer**

Tips

To reheat the pudding for serving, cover the pudding basin with parchment as described in Step 2 and steam for 1 to 2 hours.

My mum always added a tablespoon or two (15 to 30 mL) of brandy to the finished custard.

You can serve the pudding straightaway, but it is even better if allowed to mature for a couple of weeks (or, even better, months), wrapped well and stored in a cool place.

Pudding

3	eggs	3
1 cup	packed brown sugar	250 mL
	Zest and freshly squeezed juice of 1 lemon	
	Zest and freshly squeezed juice of 1 orange	
1 cup	shredded carrot	250 mL
1 cup	shredded peeled potato	250 mL
1 cup	suet or butter, finely diced	250 mL
1 cup	raisins	250 mL
1 cup	currants	250 mL
1 cup	candied citron peel	250 mL
1 cup	slivered almonds	250 mL
1 cup	fresh bread crumbs	250 mL
1 cup	all-purpose flour	250 mL
1 tsp	salt	5 mL
1 tsp	ground nutmeg	5 mL
½ tsp	ground ginger	2 mL
½ tsp	ground allspice	2 mL

Tips

If you don't have a steamer, choose a large saucepan with a lid and place a trivet in the bottom of it. Make sure that the water comes halfway up the sides of the pudding basin and check frequently to make sure it doesn't boil dry while steaming. Whether you use a proper steamer or a saucepan, it's a good idea to set a timer to go off every 30 minutes or so to remind you to check the water level. Adding a tablespoon (15 mL) of vinegar or a piece of lemon to the steaming water will eliminate those white lines on the saucepan that come from minerals in the water.

If you can't obtain fruit sugar (also known as caster sugar) you can easily make it at home if you have a food processor. Just place regular granulated sugar in the food processer and pulse a few times until it becomes finer — but not a powder.

Proper Custard (makes about 2½ cups/625 mL)

6	extra-large egg yolks	6
½ cup	fruit (superfine) sugar	125 mL
1½ tsp	vanilla extract	7 mL
1 cup	whole milk	250 mL
1 cup	table (18%) cream	250 mL

1. *Pudding:* In a large bowl, whisk eggs. Whisk in brown sugar. Using a wooden spoon, stir in lemon zest and juice, orange zest and juice, carrot, potato, suet, raisins, currants, citron peel and almonds until well incorporated. Stir in bread crumbs. Set aside.

2. In another bowl, sift together flour, salt, nutmeg, ginger and allspice. Whisk together, then stir into egg mixture until no trace of flour is visible. Using a rubber spatula, scrape mixture into prepared pudding basin, smoothing top. Fold a square of parchment paper (large enough to cover top and hang over sides of basin by 2 inches/5 cm) in half and then fold creased edge over to make a 2-inch (5 cm) pleat in the center (to allow for expansion as pudding cooks). Center paper over pudding and, using kitchen string, tie around sides to secure. Trim off excess paper below string.

3. Pour enough boiling water into a large steamer pot to come a little more than halfway up the sides. Transfer pudding basin to steamer and place over water in steamer pot. Cover and steam over high heat, replenishing boiling water often, for 3½ to 4 hours, until pudding is firm and slightly raised in the center.

4. Remove pudding from steamer. Remove parchment paper. If not serving immediately, let it cool completely in the basin, wrap with foil (keeping it in basin), and refrigerate or store in a cool place for up to 2 months (see Tips, page 432). If serving immediately, let stand in basin for about 30 minutes or until just warm, run a small palette knife around edges and turn out onto a serving platter.

5. *Proper Custard:* In a heatproof bowl, using an electric mixer, beat egg yolks, sugar and vanilla until light and fluffy. Set aside.

6. In a saucepan, heat cream and milk over medium-high heat, stirring, and bring to a very gentle boil until edges are rippling. Remove from heat and very slowly pour into egg mixture, whisking egg mixture constantly. Return to saucepan over low heat and cook, stirring, for 3 to 4 minutes or until thick enough to coat the back of a serving spoon. Pour into a jug and serve on the side with pudding.

Potato Marzipan

Here is a handy little preparation that will enable you to make something that is very like authentic (and sometimes pricy) marzipan. Ordinarily I am not a fan of "instant" potatoes; preferring the real thing is pretty much my credo for everything. However, in this recipe, once they are combined with the other ingredients, they produce a mixture that is very pliable and easy to work with. Kids love to model this edible dough into sweet little fruits, vegetables, animals or a myriad other shapes. Once made, the shapes can be painted with food coloring and embellished with other cookie-decorating ingredients. Serve these marzipan treats as part of a sweets offering after dinner or use them as edible decorations for cakes.

Makes about 2 lbs (1 kg)

Tip
If you prefer, substitute an equal quantity of dry-mashed potato for the instant.

- **Food processor**

2 cups	blanched almonds	500 mL
¼ cup	prepared instant mashed potatoes (see Tip, left)	60 mL
4 cups	confectioner's (icing) sugar (approx.)	1 L
1	egg white, lightly beaten	1
¼ tsp	almond extract	1 mL
	Cornstarch	
	Food coloring, optional	
	Melted chocolate, optional	

1. In a food processor fitted with metal blade, process almonds to a fine powder. Transfer to a large bowl. Stir in mashed potatoes and confectioner's sugar until blended.
2. In another bowl, whisk together egg white and almond extract. Gradually beat egg white mixture into potato mixture, adding just enough to make a pliable dough. Shape dough into a ball, cover with plastic wrap and refrigerate for 30 minutes.
3. Lightly dust your hands with cornstarch before working with dough. Break off a little and experiment, making little shapes, then paint with diluted food coloring or dip into melted chocolate. Transfer decorated shapes to a wire rack and let dry completely. Transfer to an airtight container, layered between waxed paper, and store at room temperature. Use within a few days.

Potato Fudge

A little mashed potato goes a long way toward making the texture of this delicious confection satiny smooth. Makes a nice gift for potato-lovers with a sweet tooth.

Makes 24 pieces

Tips

Lining the pan with parchment paper or waxed paper prevents the fudge from sticking. Use a large single sheet and place it in the pan so the edges overhang the rim by 1 inch (2.5 cm). The overhanging edges of the paper provide "handles" so that removing the cooled fudge from the pan is easy and neat.

Toasting the nuts in a dry skillet gives them a nice crispness; just take care not to burn them, as they take very little time to toast. Add the nuts to a skillet placed over medium heat, stirring for 6 to 8 minutes or until fragrant. You can also oven-toast nuts on a baking sheet in a 400°F (200°C) oven for just a few minutes, but watch them carefully so they don't burn.

- Electric mixer
- 8-inch (2 L) square glass baking dish, lined with parchment or waxed paper (see Tips, left)

1 cup	white chocolate chips	250 mL
1	can (14 oz/398 mL) sweetened condensed milk	1
¼ cup	butter	60 mL
¾ cup	dry-mashed potatoes	175 mL
1 tsp	vanilla extract	5 mL
¾ tsp	ground cinnamon	4 mL
⅛ tsp	salt	0.5 mL
8 cups	sifted confectioner's (icing) sugar	2 L
1½ cups	pecans, toasted (see Tips, left) and chopped	375 mL

1. In a heatproof glass or ceramic bowl set over a saucepan of simmering water, heat white chocolate, condensed milk and butter, stirring, until mixture is melted and smooth. Remove from heat and set aside for about 15 minutes or until it has cooled slightly.

2. In a bowl, using an electric mixer at medium speed, beat chocolate mixture, mashed potatoes, vanilla, cinnamon, salt and 4 cups (1 L) confectioner's sugar for 1 to 2 minutes. Scrape down sides of bowl and beat for 2 minutes. Reduce speed to low and beat in the remaining confectioner's sugar, adding ½ cup (125 mL) at a time until incorporated and mixture is very thick and sticky. Stir in pecans and mix just to combine. Using a rubber spatula, scrape mixture into prepared pan, smoothing top.

3. Cover with plastic wrap and refrigerate for about 2 hours or until mixture has hardened into fudge. Remove from refrigerator and, holding parchment paper edges, lift entire block of fudge out of pan and transfer to a cutting board. Using a sharp knife, cut into 24 small squares. Store in an airtight container at room temperature for up to 2 weeks or in the refrigerator for up to 3 weeks.

Variation

Add about ¼ cup (60 mL) dried cranberries or cherries along with the pecans for a nice color contrast.

Chocolate-Covered Potato Chips

Well, really, what *can't* you do with potatoes? These make a terrific gift for anyone who has a thing for both potato chips and chocolate.

Makes 6 servings (about 8 cups/2 L)

Tips

To cut thin uniform slices, use a mandoline or the slicing blade of a food processor. The slices should be about $\frac{1}{16}$ inch (1.5 mm) thick.

Use either milk or dark chocolate or, if you prefer, blend the two.

The oil should come a little over halfway up the sides of the pot. Do not overfill; leave at least 3 inches (7.5 cm) of headspace at the top.

If you don't have a candy/deep-frying thermometer, drop a small cube of dry bread into the oil; if it floats, the oil is hot enough.

- **Mandoline or food processor fitted with slicing blade, optional**
- **Large heavy pot, Dutch oven or deep fryer**
- **Candy/deep-frying thermometer (if not using a deep fryer)**
- **Rimmed baking sheet, lined with paper towels**
- **Double boiler**

4 cups	ice water	1 L
1 tbsp	salt	15 mL
6	large floury potatoes, peeled	6
	Vegetable oil	
1 lb	good quality milk or dark chocolate, chopped, divided	500 g

1. Pour ice water into a large bowl. Stir in the salt to dissolve. Slice potatoes very thinly (see Tips, left), transferring to bowl as you work.
2. Place 4 to 6 inches (10 to 15 cm) oil in a large, heavy pot (see Tips, left). Heat over medium-high heat until thermometer registers 375°F (190°C). (If you're using a deep fryer, follow the manufacturer's instructions.)
3. Meanwhile, drain and rinse potatoes under cold running water until water runs clear. Transfer to a clean tea towel and dry thoroughly.
4. In three batches, using a slotted spoon, carefully add potatoes to oil and cook, jostling with spoon to encourage even cooking, for about 1 minute or until lightly browned and crisp. Using slotted spoon, transfer to prepared baking sheet. Set aside.
5. In the top of a double boiler over simmering water, using a wooden spoon to stir occasionally, melt and heat 12 oz (375 g) chocolate until candy thermometer inserted in center registers 110°F (43°C). Immediately remove from heat and add remaining chocolate, stirring until thermometer registers 90°F (32°C).
6. Using tongs, dip each potato chip into melted chocolate (you can dip the entire chip or just half), transferring to prepared baking sheet as you work. Let cool until chocolate sets.

Library and Archives Canada Cataloguing in Publication

Sloan-McIntosh, Kathleen
    300 best potato recipes : a complete cook's guide / Kathleen Sloan-McIntosh.

Includes index.
ISBN 978-0-7788-0278-5

    1. Cooking (Potatoes). I. Title. II. Title: Three hundred best potato recipes.

TX803.P8S673 2011   641.6'521   C2011-903209-0

Index

T